American College of Physicians

MKSAP® 15

Medical Knowledge Self-Assessment Program®

Nephrology

Nephrology

Contributors

Phyllis August, MD, MPH, Book Editor[2]
Ralph A. Baer Professor of Medical Research
Professor of Medicine and Public Health
Professor of Medicine in Obstetrics and Gynecology
Division of Nephrology and Hypertension
Weill Medical College of Cornell University
New York, New York

Virginia U. Collier, MD, FACP, Associate Editor[2]
Hugh R. Sharp, Jr. Chair of Medicine
Christiana Care Health System
Newark, Delaware
Professor of Medicine
Jefferson Medical College of Thomas Jefferson University
Philadelphia, Pennsylvania

Arlene Chapman, MD[2]
Professor of Medicine
Department of Medicine, Renal Division
Emory University School of Medicine
Atlanta, Georgia

Gerald A. Hladik, MD[1]
Associate Professor of Medicine
Division of Nephrology and Hypertension
University of North Carolina Kidney Center
The University of North Carolina at Chapel Hill
Chapel Hill, North Carolina

Michelle A. Josephson, MD, FACP[2]
Professor of Medicine
Section of Nephrology
University of Chicago Hospitals
Chicago, Illinois

Michelle Whittier Krause, MD, MPH[1]
Associate Professor of Medicine
Division of Nephrology
University of Arkansas for Medical Sciences
Little Rock, Arkansas

Biff F. Palmer, MD, FACP, FASN[2]
Professor of Internal Medicine
Department of Internal Medicine
Nephrology Fellowship Program Director

Division of Nephrology
University of Texas Southwestern Medical Center
Dallas, Texas

Editor-in-Chief

Patrick C. Alguire, MD, FACP[1]
Director, Education and Career Development
American College of Physicians
Philadelphia, Pennsylvania

Nephrology Reviewers

Sharon Adler, MD, FACP[2]
Robert J. Anderson, MD, MACP[1]
Lee Berkowitz, MD, FACP[1]
Frantz Duffoo, MD, FACP[1]
Kent A. Kirchner, MD, FACP[1]
Richard I. Kopelman, MD, FACP[1]
Dan L. Longo, MD, FACP[1]
Mark E. Pasanen, MD, FACP[1]
Barbara L. Schuster, MD, MACP[1]
Jerry L. Spivak, MD, FACP[2]

Nephrology ACP Editorial Staff

Amanda Neiley, Staff Editor
Sean McKinney, Director, Self-Assessment Programs
Margaret Wells, Managing Editor
Charles Rossi, Senior Associate of Clinical Content
   Development
John Murray, Editorial Coordinator

ACP Principal Staff

Steven E. Weinberger, MD, FACP[2]
Deputy Executive Vice President
Senior Vice President, Medical Education and Publishing

D. Theresa Kanya, MBA[1]
Vice President, Medical Education and Publishing

Sean McKinney[1]
Director, Self-Assessment Programs

Margaret Wells[1]
Managing Editor

Charles Rossi[1]
Senior Associate of Clinical Content Development

Becky Krumm[1]
Senior Staff Editor

Ellen McDonald, PhD[1]
Senior Staff Editor

Amanda Neiley[1]
Staff Editor

Katie Idell[1]
Production Administrator/Editor

Valerie Dangovetsky[1]
Program Administrator

John Murray[1]
Editorial Coordinator

Shannon O'Sullivan[1]
Editorial Coordinator

Developed by the American College of Physicians

---

1. Has no relationships with any entity producing, marketing, re-selling, or distributing health care goods or services consumed by, or used on, patients.

2. Has disclosed relationships with entities producing, marketing, re-selling, or distributing health care goods or services consumed by, or used on, patients. See below.

Conflicts of Interest

The following contributors and ACP staff members have disclosed relationships with commercial companies:

Sharon Adler, MD, FACP
Research Grants/Contracts
Asprevia, Genzyme, Genentech, Novartis
Consultantship
Genentech

Phyllis August, MD, MPH
Stock Options/Holdings
Pfizer, Merck

Arlene Chapman, MD
Research Grants/Contracts
HALT Trial/NIH, Otsuka America Pharmaceuticals

Virginia U. Collier, MD, FACP
Stock Options/Holdings
Celgene, Pfizer, Merck, Schering-Plough, Abbott, Johnson & Johnson, Medtronic, McKesson, Amgen

Michelle A. Josephson, MD, FACP
Speakers Bureau
Roche Pharmaceuticals
Research Grants/Contracts
Astellas, Wyeth, Roche Pharmaceuticals

Biff F. Palmer, MD, FACP, FASN
Speakers Bureau
Novartis

Jerry L. Spivak, MD, FACP
Consultantship
Ortho, Roche, Novartis, Pfizer

Steven E. Weinberger, MD, FACP
Stock Options/Holdings
Abbott, GlaxoSmithKline

Acknowledgments

The American College of Physicians (ACP) gratefully acknowledges the special contributions to the development and production of the 15th edition of the Medical Knowledge Self-Assessment Program® (MKSAP 15) of Scott Thomas Hurd (Senior Systems Analyst/Developer), Ricki Jo Kauffman (Manager, Systems Development), Michael Ripca (Technical Administrator/Graphics Designer), and Lisa Torrieri (Graphic Designer). The Digital version (CD-ROM and Online components) was developed within the ACP's Interactive Product Development Department by Steven Spadt (Director), Christopher Forrest (Senior Software Developer), Ryan Hinkel (Senior Software Developer), John McKnight (Software Developer), Sean O'Donnell (Senior Software Developer), and Brian Sweigard (Senior Software Developer). Computer scoring and reporting are being performed by ACT, Inc., Iowa City, Iowa. The College also wishes to acknowledge that many other persons, too numerous to mention, have contributed to the production of this program. Without their dedicated efforts, this program would not have been possible.

Continuing Medical Education

The American College of Physicians is accredited by the Accreditation Council for Continuing Medical Education (ACCME) to provide continuing medical education for physicians.

The American College of Physicians designates this educational activity for a maximum of 166 *AMA PRA Category 1 Credits*™. Physicians should only claim credit commensurate with the extent of their participation in the activity.

AMA PRA Category 1 Credit™ is available from July 31, 2009, to July 31, 2012.

Learning Objectives

The learning objectives of MKSAP 15 are to:
• Close gaps between actual care in your practice and preferred standards of care, based on best evidence

- Diagnose disease states that are less common and sometimes overlooked and confusing
- Improve management of comorbidities that can complicate patient care
- Determine when to refer patients for surgery or care by subspecialists
- Pass the ABIM certification examination
- Pass the ABIM maintenance of certification examination

Target Audience

- General internists and primary care physicians
- Subspecialists who need to remain up-to-date in internal medicine
- Residents preparing for the certifying examination in internal medicine
- Physicians preparing for maintenance of certification in internal medicine (recertification)

How to Submit for CME Credits

To earn CME credits, complete a MKSAP 15 answer sheet. Use the enclosed, self-addressed envelope to mail your completed answer sheet(s) to the MKSAP Processing Center for scoring. Remember to provide your MKSAP 15 order and ACP ID numbers in the appropriate spaces on the answer sheet. The order and ACP ID numbers are printed on your mailing label. If you have <u>not</u> received these numbers with your MKSAP 15 purchase, you will need to acquire them to earn CME credits. E-mail ACP's customer service center at custserv@acponline.org. In the subject line, write "MKSAP 15 order/ACP ID numbers." In the body of the e-mail, make sure you include your e-mail address as well as your full name, address, city, state, ZIP code, country, and telephone number. Also identify where you have made your MKSAP 15 purchase. You will receive your MKSAP 15 order and ACP ID numbers by e-mail within 72 business hours.

Permission/Consent for Use of Figures Shown in MKSAP 15 Nephrology Multiple-Choice Questions

Figure shown in Self-Assessment Test Item 39 is modified with permission from Physician's Information and Education Resource (PIER). Philadelphia: American College of Physicians. Copyright © 2009, American College of Physicians.

Disclosure Policy

It is the policy of the American College of Physicians (ACP) to ensure balance, independence, objectivity, and scientific rigor in all its educational activities. To this end, and consistent with the policies of the ACP and the Accreditation Council for Continuing Medical Education (ACCME), contributors to all ACP continuing medical education activities are required to disclose all relevant financial relationships with any entity producing, marketing, re-selling, or distributing health care goods or services consumed by, or used on, patients. Contributors are required to use generic names in the discussion of therapeutic options and are required to identify any unapproved, off-label, or investigative use of commercial products or devices. Where a trade name is used, all available trade names for the same product type are also included. If trade-name products manufactured by companies with whom contributors have relationships are discussed, contributors are asked to provide evidence-based citations in support of the discussion. The information is reviewed by the committee responsible for producing this text. If necessary, adjustments to topics or contributors' roles in content development are made to balance the discussion. Further, all readers of this text are asked to evaluate the content for evidence of commercial bias so that future decisions about content and contributors can be made in light of this information.

Resolution of Conflicts

To resolve all conflicts of interest and influences of vested interests, the ACP precluded members of the content-creation committee from deciding on any content issues that involved generic or trade-name products associated with proprietary entities with which these committee members had relationships. In addition, content was based on best evidence and updated clinical care guidelines, when such evidence and guidelines were available. Contributors' disclosure information can be found with the list of contributors' names and those of ACP principal staff listed in the beginning of this book.

Educational Disclaimer

The editors and publisher of MKSAP 15 recognize that the development of new material offers many opportunities for error. Despite our best efforts, some errors may persist in print. Drug dosage schedules are, we believe, accurate and in accordance with current standards. Readers are advised, however, to ensure that the recommended dosages in MKSAP 15 concur with the information provided in the product information material. This is especially important in cases of new, infrequently used, or highly toxic drugs. Application of the information in MKSAP 15 remains the professional responsibility of the practitioner.

The primary purpose of MKSAP 15 is educational. Information presented, as well as publications, technologies, products, and/or services discussed, is intended to inform subscribers about the knowledge, techniques, and experiences of the contributors. A diversity of professional opinion exists, and the views of the contributors are their own and not those of the ACP. Inclusion of any material in the program does not constitute endorsement or recommendation by the ACP. The ACP does not warrant the safety, reliability, accuracy, completeness, or usefulness of and disclaims any and all liability for damages and claims that may result from the use of information, publications, technologies, products, and/or services discussed in this program.

Publisher's Information

Unauthorized Use of This Book Is Against the Law

The ACP will consider granting an individual permission to reproduce only limited portions of this publication for his or her own exclusive use. Send requests in writing to MKSAP® Permissions, American College of Physicians, 190 North Independence Mall West, Philadelphia, PA 19106-1572.

MKSAP 15 ISBN: 978-1-934465-25-7
Nephrology ISBN: 978-1-934465-38-7

Printed in the United States of America.

For order information in the U.S. or Canada call 800-523-1546, extension 2600. All other countries call 215-351-2600. Fax inquiries to 215-351-2799 or e-mail to custserv@acponline.org.

Errata and Norm Tables

Errata for MKSAP 15 will be posted at http://mksap.acponline.org/errata as new information becomes known to the editors.

MKSAP 15 Performance Interpretation Guidelines with Norm Tables, available December 31, 2010, will reflect the knowledge of physicians who have completed the self-assessment tests before the program was published. These physicians took the tests without being able to refer to the syllabus, answers, and critiques. For your convenience, the tables are available in a printable PDF file at http://mksap.acponline.org/normtables.

Table of Contents

Acute Kidney Injury

Kidney Stones

The Kidney in Pregnancy

Chronic Kidney Disease

Nephrology

Clinical Evaluation of Kidney Function

Estimation of the Glomerular Filtration Rate

The National Kidney Foundation Kidney Disease Outcomes Quality Initiative (NKF K/DOQI) guidelines define chronic kidney disease (CKD) as a decrease in the estimated glomerular filtration rate (eGFR) or as kidney damage that manifests as abnormal urinalysis findings such as proteinuria or hematuria, abnormal imaging study findings that are present for more than 3 months, or pathologic changes seen on kidney biopsy. These guidelines also recommend using the eGFR to classify patients with kidney disease (see Chronic Kidney Disease).

The glomerular filtration rate (GFR) represents the volume of water filtered from the plasma per unit of time. Estimation of this value is currently considered the best method of evaluating kidney function and ideally involves a substance that is freely filtered by the glomeruli. This substance should not be reabsorbed or secreted in the tubules, is excreted only by the kidneys, and can be measured in the plasma under steady-state conditions.

Markers for Estimating the Glomerular Filtration Rate

Serum Creatinine

Creatinine is freely filtered in the glomeruli, excreted by the kidneys, and easily measured in the blood. Measurement of this value has historically been the study of choice to evaluate kidney function.

As the GFR decreases with kidney injury, the serum creatinine level concomitantly increases. For example, a 50% reduction in the GFR is associated with an increase in the serum creatinine level from 1.0 to 2.0 mg/dL (88.4 to 176.8 μmol/L). The serum creatinine level also typically increases by 1.0 to 1.5 mg/dL (88.4 to 132.6 μmol/L) daily in patients who become anephric due to circumstances such as bilateral nephrectomy, end-stage kidney disease, or acute kidney injury. A greater rise in the serum creatinine level suggests an increase in creatinine production, which occurs in conditions such as rhabdomyolysis.

The creatinine level alone, however, is not an ideal measure of kidney function. A reduction or loss of muscle mass due to circumstances such as advanced age, liver failure, or malnutrition may cause a disproportionately low creatinine level that results in overestimation of the GFR. Furthermore, 15% to 20% of creatinine in the bloodstream is not filtered in the glomeruli but instead is secreted into the urine by the proximal tubular cells. Therefore, CKD, which may cause an increase in the proximal tubular secretion of creatinine by as much as 40% to 50%, also may be associated with an overestimation of the GFR.

Conversely, use of certain medications, such as cimetidine and trimethoprim, blocks the proximal tubular secretion of creatinine. This circumstance may result in an underestimation of the GFR, which may lead to misdiagnosis of acute kidney injury.

Equations

Because the serum creatinine level can be an inaccurate marker of the GFR, the NKF K/DOQI guidelines suggest the use of the Cockcroft-Gault and Modification of Diet in Renal Disease (MDRD) study equations as an alternative method of estimating kidney function in adults (**Table 1**). However, the serum creatinine level is used to calculate these equations, as well; therefore, these equations are subject to similar limitations as serum creatinine measurement alone.

Furthermore, the Cockcroft-Gault and MDRD equations were developed for patients with CKD and have not been shown to accurately estimate kidney function in healthy persons or in patients with acute kidney injury. Use

---

TABLE 1 Mathematical Equations for the Estimation of Kidney Function

Cockcroft-Gault Equation

$$Ccr = \frac{[(140 - age) \times weight] \times (Scr) \times 0.85 \text{ (if the patient is female)}}{72}$$

Modification of Diet in Renal Disease Study Equation

$GFR = 186 \times (Scr)^{-1.154} \times (age)^{-0.203} \times 0.742$ (if the patient is female) or $\times 1.212$ (if the patient is black)

Abbreviated Modification of Diet in Renal Disease Study Equation

$GFR = 175 \times (Scr)^{-1.154} \times (age)^{-0.203} \times 0.742$ (if the patient is female) or $\times 1.212$ (if the patient is black)

Ccr = creatinine clearance; GFR = glomerular filtration rate; Scr = serum creatinine level.

of these equations should be limited to patients with stages 3 to 5 CKD or those with an eGFR of 59 mL/min/1.73 m² or less.

Creatinine Clearance

Experts now recommend use of either a 24-hour urine collection for creatinine clearance or radionuclide kidney clearance scanning to obtain a precise estimation of kidney function, which is needed in circumstances such as the evaluation of living donor kidney transplant candidates.

Over- or undercollection of a sample obtained for 24-hour urine collection may result in an inaccurate estimation of the GFR. However, the accuracy of 24-hour urine collection can be assessed by comparing the total urine creatinine excretion with the expected value of creatinine excretion (20 to 25 mg/kg/24 h [0.18 to 0.22 mmol/kg/d] in men, 15 to 20 mg/kg/24 h [0.13 to 0.18 mmol/kg/d] in women). For example, if a complete 24-hour urine collection is obtained, the total urine creatinine excretion in a 75-kg (165-lb) female living donor kidney transplant candidate should be between 1125 and 1500 mg/24 h; a total urine creatinine excretion of 375 mg/24 h in this woman would be known to be a falsely low estimate of kidney function.

Radionuclide Kidney Clearance Scanning

Radionuclide kidney clearance scanning, also known as GFR scanning, is now considered the gold standard for the estimation of the GFR in healthy persons and in those with acute kidney injury. However, use of these studies is limited because of cost, lack of widespread availability, and operator technical difficulties.

Blood Urea Nitrogen

Blood urea nitrogen (BUN) is derived from protein waste products and freely filtered in the glomeruli. This level is often measured simultaneously with creatinine to evaluate kidney function. The normal blood urea nitrogen (BUN)-creatinine ratio is 10:1 to 15:1.

Conditions that decrease kidney perfusion, such as dehydration or heart failure, are associated with increased reabsorption of BUN in the proximal tubules and a disproportionate increase in the BUN-creatinine ratio, typically to 20:1 or higher. A high-protein diet, catabolic states, and gastrointestinal bleeding also may cause an increase in the BUN level and a subsequent underestimation of kidney function.

Conversely, decreased urea production and inadequate protein intake associated with disease states such as liver failure and malnutrition may cause a decrease in the BUN level and a subsequent overestimation of kidney function.

KEY POINTS

- Chronic kidney disease is defined as a decrease in the estimated glomerular filtration rate or as kidney damage that manifests as abnormal urinalysis findings, abnormal imaging study findings that are present for more than 3 months, or pathologic changes seen on kidney biopsy.

- Estimation of the glomerular filtration rate using the Modification of Diet in Renal Disease (MDRD) study or Cockcroft-Gault equation is currently considered the best method of evaluating kidney function.

- The accuracy of 24-hour urine collection can be assessed by comparing the total urine creatinine excretion with the expected value of creatinine excretion.

- Radionuclide kidney clearance scanning is considered the gold standard for the estimation of the glomerular filtration rate in healthy persons and in those with acute kidney injury.

Interpretation of the Urinalysis

Urinalysis, including dipstick analysis and examination of the microscopic sediment, is indicated in the clinical assessment of patients with acute kidney injury and CKD.

Dipstick Urinalysis

Specific Gravity

Urine specific gravity refers to the concentration of solutes in the urine and is typically between 1.008 and 1.015, but values outside of this range can be normal depending upon hydration status. A decreased specific gravity may be indicative of dilute urine, which may occur in patients with excessive fluid ingestion or diabetes insipidus. An increased specific gravity may be caused by dehydration (even overnight), hypovolemia, or administration of hyperosmolar solutions such as iodinated contrast dye and mannitol.

pH

Normal urine is acidic. Alkaline urine is suggestive of distal renal tubular acidosis or bacterial infection with urease-splitting organisms such as *Ureaplasma urealyticum* or *Proteus* or *Pseudomonas* species. The urine pH also is a useful parameter for monitoring patients undergoing medical therapy that requires alkalinization of the urine, which is indicated for patients as prophylactic treatment for uric acid stones.

Albumin

Albumin is the only protein that is detected on dipstick urinalysis. Dipstick urinalysis provides a qualitative assessment of albuminuria and detects albumin in patients with an albumin excretion greater than 300 to 500 mg/24 h. Quantitative measurements, rather than dipstick methodology, are recommended to detect albumin excretion less than 300 mg/24 h.

The urine dipstick cannot detect immunoglobulins; therefore, dipstick urinalysis in patients with multiple myeloma is negative for protein, but administration of sulfosalicylic acid precipitates all proteins, including light chains, or Bence Jones proteins. A 24-hour urine protein electrophoresis also identifies different types of protein, including both λ and K light chains. Urine immunofixation can identify the presence of a monoclonal paraprotein.

Glucose

Glycosuria usually is identified on dipstick urinalysis in patients whose plasma glucose level exceeds 180 mg/dL (10 mmol/L). This condition typically occurs in patients with diabetes mellitus. The presence of glycosuria in patients without diabetes suggests a disturbance in proximal tubular function of the sodium-glucose cotransporter, which may occur in Fanconi syndrome or multiple myeloma.

Ketones

Urine ketones are associated with diabetic ketoacidosis and starvation ketosis with fatty acid breakdown. Ketonuria is indicative of the presence of acetoacetic acid but not acetone or β-hydroxybutyric acid. Patients with starvation ketoacidosis in whom the ketone bodies are predominantly in the form of β-hydroxybutyric acid may have negative urine ketones but still be in a ketoacidotic state.

Blood

Dipstick urinalysis is sensitive for erythrocytes, hemoglobin, and myoglobin. Approximately 1 to 3 erythrocytes/hpf must be present for dipstick urinalysis to test positive for blood. Patients with hemolysis and rhabdomyolysis test positive for blood on dipstick urinalysis in the absence of intact erythrocytes on urine microscopy because of the cross-reactivity of hemoglobin and myoglobin using dipstick technology.

Ingestion of large dosages of ascorbic acid may result in a false-negative result for blood on dipstick urinalysis. Conversely, certain pigments found in beets and medications such as rifampin and chloroquine may cause a false-positive result for blood on this study.

Leukocyte Esterase and Nitrites

The presence of leukocyte esterase and nitrites on dipstick urinalysis is suggestive of infection. More than 3 leukocytes/hpf must be present in the urine for dipstick urinalysis to test positive for leukocyte esterase.

The reduction of nitrate to nitrite is caused by bacteria such as *Escherichia coli*, *Proteus* and *Pseudomonas* species, and *Klebsiella pneumoniae*. Detection of nitrites on dipstick urinalysis has a sensitivity for urinary tract infection of 45% to 60% and a specificity of 85% to 98%. Positive leukocyte esterase has a sensitivity for urinary tract infection of 48% to 68% but a lower specificity of 17% to 93%. Dipstick-positive urine for both nitrites and leukocyte esterase is 68% to 88% sensitive for urinary tract infection. Negative dipstick urinalysis findings for nitrites and leukocyte esterase have a high negative predictive value for urinary tract infection.

Bilirubin

Bilirubin is not present in the urine of healthy persons. The presence of bilirubin on dipstick urinalysis is suggestive of hepatic failure or obstructive jaundice.

Urobilinogen

Urobilinogen is the result of bacterial reduction of conjugated bilirubin in the small intestine. Positive dipstick urinalysis results for urobilinogen are consistent with hemolytic anemia and hepatic necrosis but not obstructive jaundice.

KEY POINTS

- Urinalysis, including dipstick analysis and examination of the microscopic sediment, is indicated in the clinical assessment of patients with acute kidney injury and chronic kidney disease.
- Albumin is the only protein that is detected on dipstick urinalysis.
- The presence of leukocyte esterase and nitrites on dipstick urinalysis is suggestive of infection.

Urine Microscopy

Microscopic analysis of the urine sediment can detect elements not seen on dipstick urinalysis. Unlike dipstick urinalysis, this study identifies and quantifies elements in the urine. Urine microscopy is indicated for all patients with acute kidney injury and suspected glomerular disease.

Leukocytes

Pyuria refers to an increased amount of leukocytes in the urine, defined as the presence of 4 leukocytes/hpf or more. The most likely cause of pyuria is urinary tract infection.

Sterile pyuria refers to pyuria associated with a negative urine culture; this condition may be caused by infection with less common causes of urinary tract infection such as *Mycobacterium tuberculosis* and viruses such as adenovirus, polyomavirus, and cytomegalovirus.

One of the most common noninfectious causes of sterile pyuria is acute interstitial nephritis, which is often caused by exposure to certain medications, particularly antibiotics or NSAIDs. In patients with chronic tubulointerstitial disease, sterile pyuria is associated with non–nephrotic-range proteinuria. Acute rejection in kidney transplant recipients also may manifest as isolated sterile pyuria.

Wright or Hansel staining of the urine sediment can reveal eosinophiluria, which may occur in patients with acute interstitial nephritis, postinfectious glomerulonephritis, acute atheroembolic disease of the kidney, septic emboli, or small-vessel vasculitis.

Erythrocytes

Hematuria refers to the presence of more than 3 erythrocytes/hpf in the urine and is a common finding on urinalysis. Hematuria that is detected on only one urine sample, known as isolated hematuria, is generally associated with infection, heavy exercise, and menstruation.

Bleeding in patients with persistent hematuria may originate anywhere along the genitourinary tract, and the location of the bleeding must be identified in order to determine the next steps in evaluation. Therefore, differentiating between glomerular and nonglomerular hematuria by urine microscopy is important (**Figure 1**).

Glomerular hematuria is characterized by the presence of dysmorphic erythrocytes or schistocytes on urine microscopy, and hematuria associated with the presence of erythrocyte casts is specifically indicative of glomerulonephritis. Urine microscopy in patients with glomerular disease also may detect intact erythrocytes; however, these elements are less

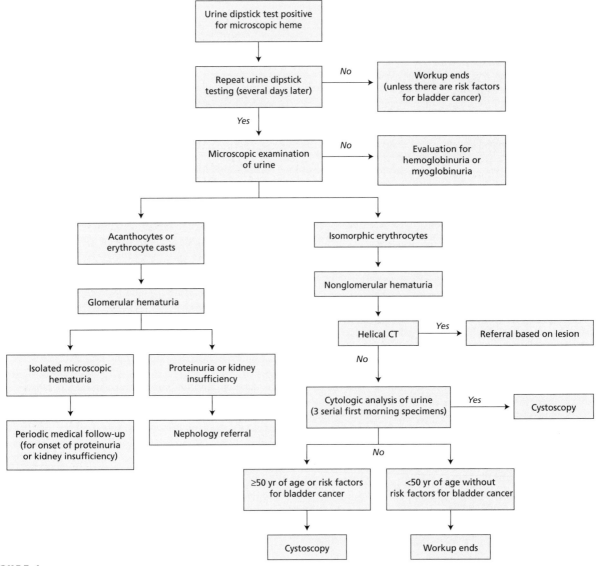

FIGURE 1.

Evaluation of microscopic hematuria.

If hematuria is determined to be nonglomerular in origin and a kidney stone is suspected, CT should be performed without contrast or first without and then with contrast. Ultrasonography should be performed instead of CT in pregnant patients and those with hypersensitivity to contrast. Risk factors for bladder cancer include cigarette smoking, occupational exposure to chemicals used in certain industries (leather, dye, rubber, or tire manufacturing), heavy phenacetin use, past treatment with high-dose cyclophosphamide, and ingestion of aristolochic acid found in some herbal weight-loss preparations.

specific for glomerular disease than dysmorphic erythrocytes or schistocytes, and evaluation for other indicators of kidney damage such as proteinuria or a reduction in kidney function is indicated in this setting.

Nonglomerular hematuria refers to blood in the urine that originates outside of the glomerulus. This condition is associated with isomorphic erythrocytes that usually appear normal on urine microscopy. The most common causes of asymptomatic nonglomerular hematuria are urinary tract infections and kidney stones.

Genitourinary tract malignancies also may cause nonglomerular hematuria, which may be transient and should always be evaluated in patients over the age of 50 years. These malignancies are more common in men and predominantly consist of prostate, bladder, renal-cell, and testicular cancers. In women, vaginal bleeding associated with cervical, uterine, and endometrial cancer may manifest as microscopic hematuria.

Renal-cell cancer may manifest as microscopic hematuria, hypertension, and flank pain or a palpable abdominal mass. Bladder cancer also may cause microscopic hematuria. Suspicion for bladder cancer particularly should be raised in patients with additional risk factors for this condition, such as cigarette smoking, benzene exposure, long-term analgesic use, or use of certain medications such as cyclophosphamide.

Microscopic hematuria also commonly occurs in patients who use anticoagulants. However, bleeding in these patients should not automatically be attributed to these agents and warrants evaluation for a genitourinary tract abnormality.

Casts

Urine microscopy is one of the only methods of identifying and characterizing urine casts. Identification of certain types of urine casts may help to suggest a diagnosis, and some casts are pathognomonic for particular disorders (**Table 2**).

KEY POINTS

- Pyuria is most likely caused by urinary tract infection.

- Sterile pyuria refers to pyuria associated with a negative urine culture and may be caused by infection, acute interstitial nephritis, chronic tubulointerstitial disease, and acute kidney transplant rejection.

- Glomerular hematuria is characterized by the presence of dysmorphic erythrocytes or schistocytes on urine microscopy, whereas nonglomerular hematuria is associated with isomorphic erythrocytes that usually appear normal on urine microscopy.

- Asymptomatic nonglomerular hematuria is most commonly caused by urinary tract infections and kidney stones but should raise suspicion for genitourinary tract malignancies in older patients.

- Erythrocyte casts are pathognomonic for acute glomerulonephritis.

TABLE 2 Conditions Associated with Urine Casts

Type of Cast	Associated Condition
Muddy brown	Acute tubular necrosis
Granular	Acute tubular necrosis
Finely granular	Chronic kidney disease
Hyaline	Volume depletion, dehydration
Waxy	Chronic kidney disease
Leukocyte	Pyelonephritis, acute interstitial nephritis
Erythrocyte	Acute glomerulonephritis (these casts are pathognomonic for this condition)

Measurement of Albumin and Protein Excretion

Urinalysis is one of the most effective methods of identifying and quantifying proteinuria. Various proteins are excreted into the urine, including albumin, tubular proteins, and immunoglobulins.

The gold standard for measuring urine protein excretion is a 24-hour urine collection; normal protein excretion using this method is defined as less than 150 mg/24 h. However, timed urine collection is a cumbersome process to perform correctly, and under- or overcollection of a sample poses the risk of an inaccurate assessment of protein excretion. The NKF K/DOQI therefore recommends use of urinary ratios on random urine samples as an alternative method of estimating proteinuria in the clinical assessment of kidney disease. Typically, a total albumin-creatinine ratio is used to measure microalbuminuria (defined as a urine albumin excretion of 30 to 300 mg/24 h), and either the total albumin-creatinine or total protein-creatinine ratio can be used to measure proteinuria (**Table 3**).

Microalbuminuria is common and has been identified as a risk factor for cardiovascular disease, peripheral vascular disease, and progressive kidney disease. Proteinuria generally is associated with a greater risk for progression of CKD, especially in patients whose urine protein excretion exceeds 500 mg/24 h. A urine protein-creatinine ratio above 3.5 mg/mg is classified as nephrotic-range proteinuria and is associated with various glomerular diseases, whereas a urine protein-creatinine ratio below 2 mg/mg is associated with chronic tubulointerstitial, renovascular, and glomerular diseases.

Isolated or transient proteinuria is common and may be associated with febrile illnesses or heavy exercise. This condition is typically benign and does not warrant further evaluation.

Protein excretion may vary based on time of collection and, in a small percentage of children and young adults, with posture. Orthostatic or postural proteinuria refers to protein excretion that increases during the day but decreases at night during recumbency. Diagnosis of orthostatic proteinuria is established by comparing the urine protein excretion during the day with findings from a separate urine collection obtained during the night. Orthostatic proteinuria is benign and has not been associated with long-term kidney disease.

TABLE 3 National Kidney Foundation Kidney Disease Outcomes Quality Initiative Definitions of Proteinuria and Albuminuria

	Urine Collection Method	Normal	Microalbuminuria	Albuminuria or Clinical Proteinuria
Total Protein	24-Hour excretion (varies with method)	<300 mg/24 h	–	>300 mg/24 h
	Spot urine dipstick	<30 mg/dL	–	>30 mg/dL
	Spot urine protein-creatinine ratio (varies with method)	<0.2 mg/mg	–	>0.2 mg/mg
Albumin	24-Hour excretion	<30 mg/24 h	30-300 mg/24 h	>300 mg/24 h
	Spot urine albumin-specific dipstick	<3 mg/dL	>3 mg/dL	–
	Spot urine albumin-creatinine ratio (varies by sex[a])	<17 mg/g (men) <25 mg/g (women)	17-250 mg/g (men) 25-355 mg/g (women)	>250 mg/g (men) >355 mg/g (women)

[a]Sex-specific cut-off values are from a single study. Use of the same cut-off value for men and women leads to higher values of prevalence for women than men. Current recommendations from the American Diabetes Association define cut-off values for spot urine albumin-creatinine ratio for microalbuminuria as 30 mg/g and 300 mg/g, respectively, without regard to sex.

Modified with permission from K/DOQI clinical practice guidelines for chronic kidney disease: evaluation, classification, and stratification. Am J Kidney Dis. 2002;39(2 Suppl 1):S1-S266. [PMID: 11904577] Copright 2002, Elsevier.

Experts recommend that at least two samples should be obtained in order to confirm a diagnosis of persistent proteinuria.

KEY POINTS

- A total albumin-creatinine ratio on a random urine sample can be used to measure microalbuminuria and either the total albumin-creatinine ratio or total protein-creatinine ratio can be used to measure proteinuria as an alternative method to 24-hour urine collection.
- A urine protein-creatinine ratio above 3.5 mg/mg is associated with glomerular diseases, whereas a urine protein-creatinine ratio below 2 mg/mg is associated with chronic tubulointerstitial, renovascular, and glomerular diseases.

Imaging Studies

Assessment of kidney function often requires imaging of the urinary tract (**Table 4**). Kidney ultrasonography is relatively inexpensive and widely available. Radiographic studies for non–kidney-related conditions commonly reveal simple-appearing cysts, which do not require further imaging studies or intervention. However, complex cystic structures or mass lesions, especially those greater than 4 cm, should raise suspicion for malignancy and warrant further evaluation with CT or MRI. Ultrasound duplex arteriography, CT arteriography, MRI, and angiotensin-converting enzyme inhibitor renography are used to evaluate renal vasculature in the presence of disrupted arterial or venous blood flow, which may be associated with atherosclerotic lesions, fibromuscular dysplasia, or thrombosis.

Kidney function should be evaluated in order to determine the most appropriate radiographic study. This evaluation is particularly important before performing studies that require use of radiocontrast agents in order to avoid contrast-induced nephropathy, which is associated with increased morbidity and

TABLE 4 Use of Radiographic Imaging Studies in the Assessment of Kidney Function and Disease

Imaging Study	Indications
Kidney ultrasonography	Urinary tract obstruction, nephrolithiasis, cysts, mass lesions, location for kidney biopsy
Ultrasound duplex arteriography	Renal artery stenosis
ACE inhibitor renography	Renal artery stenosis
Abdominal CT	Urinary tract obstruction, nephrolithiasis, mass lesions
CT arteriography	Renal artery stenosis, renal vascular lesion
MRI	Cysts, mass lesions, renal artery stenosis
Radionuclide kidney clearance scanning (GFR scanning)	GFR estimation, kidney infarcts, urinary tract obstruction

ACE = angiotensin-converting enzyme inhibitor; GFR = glomerular filtration rate.

mortality even with return of kidney function to the original baseline value.

Kidney ultrasonography is noninvasive. This study also does not require the use of radiocontrast agents and is therefore safe for use in patients with reduced kidney function and pregnant patients.

Abdominal CT may involve use of intravenous iodinated contrast agents, which are associated with a risk for contrast-induced nephropathy in patients with an eGFR of less than 60 mL/min/1.73 m². Experts therefore recommend against the use of these agents in this population group.

Recently, the incidence of nephrogenic systemic fibrosis (NSF) (formerly known as nephrogenic fibrosing dermopathy) has increased in patients with reduced kidney function who are exposed to intravenous gadolinium contrast agents during MRI. NSF is believed to be caused by a systemic inflammatory response associated with mobilization of iron that results in abnormal proliferation and deposition of fibroblasts in the dermis and connective tissue. This condition manifests as a scleroderma-like disease associated with edema, plaque-like rash, and hardening of the skin (**Figure 2**).

Patients with an eGFR of less than 40 mL/min/1.73 m² are believed to be at greatest risk for development of NSF after administration of gadolinium, and use of this agent should be avoided in this population group. Additional risk factors for NSF include the use of high-dose erythropoietin or intravenous iron as well as hyperparathyroidism.

Currently, no effective treatment regimen or intervention has been shown to resolve or improve symptoms associated with NSF except perhaps for early kidney transplantation. NSF also is associated with a high mortality rate. Experts therefore recommend that kidney function be evaluated before performing imaging studies that require use of radiocontrast agents.

Patients who are undergoing dialysis and require administration of gadolinium contrast should receive 3 consecutive days of hemodialysis treatments after this study is performed. Gadolinium is not effectively removed with peritoneal dialysis, and this intervention should not be used in place of hemodialysis to remove contrast.

KEY POINTS

- Simple-appearing cysts seen on radiographic studies of the kidneys do not require further imaging studies or intervention.

- The presence of complex cystic structures or mass lesions, especially those greater than 4 cm, seen on radiographic studies should raise suspicion for malignancy and warrant further evaluation with CT or MRI.

- In order to avoid contrast-induced nephropathy, kidney function should be evaluated before performing imaging studies that require use of radiocontrast agents.

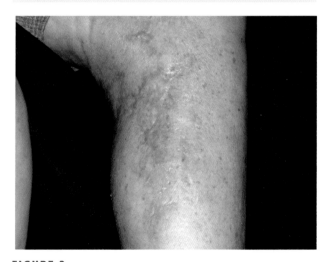

FIGURE 2.
Nephrogenic systemic fibrosis.
The patient has nephrogenic systemic fibrosis associated with an erythematous plaque, edema, and peau d'orange appearance.

Kidney Biopsy

Kidney biopsy is recommended when histologic confirmation is needed to help diagnose kidney disease, implement medical therapy, or change medical treatment. Kidney biopsy is used predominantly in patients with glomerular disease, and the most common indications for kidney biopsy include the nephrotic syndrome, acute glomerulonephritis, or kidney transplant dysfunction. Kidney biopsy is often performed under direct visualization by ultrasonography or CT.

Risks associated with kidney biopsy include hematuria and the need for blood transfusion, embolization of a bleeding vessel, or nephrectomy. Contraindications to kidney biopsy include coagulopathy, thrombocytopenia, hydronephrosis, atrophic kidney, numerous kidney cysts, acute pyelonephritis, or severe hypertension.

The presence of a solitary kidney is a relative contraindication to percutaneous kidney biopsy because of the risk for nephrectomy due to uncontrolled bleeding associated with this study. However, percutaneous kidney biopsy may be performed in this setting under direct visualization by laparoscopy.

Kidney masses or renal-cell carcinomas also are relative contraindications to kidney biopsy because these features are associated with an increased risk of bleeding and spread of malignant cells through the biopsy tract. Experts recommend partial or complete nephrectomy for diagnosis and treatment in these settings.

KEY POINTS

- The most common indications for kidney biopsy include the nephrotic syndrome, acute glomerulonephritis, and kidney transplant dysfunction.

- Contraindications to kidney biopsy include coagulopathy, thrombocytopenia, hydronephrosis, atrophic kidney, numerous kidney cysts, acute pyelonephritis, or severe hypertension.

Bibliography

DeVille WL, Yzermans JC, van Duijn NP, Bezemer PD, van der Windt DA, Bouter LM. The urine dipstick test useful to rule out infections. A meta-analysis of the accuracy. BMC Urol. 2004;4:4. [PMID: 15175113]

National Kidney Foundation. K/DOQI clinical practice guidelines for chronic kidney disease: Evaluation, classification, and stratification. Am J Kidney Dis. 2002;39(2 Suppl 1):S1-S62. [PMID: 11904577]

Poggio ED, Wang X, Greene T, Van Lente F, Hall PM. Performance of the Modification of Diet in Renal Disease and Cockcroft-Gault Equations in the Estimation of GFR in Health and in Chronic Kidney Disease. J Am Soc Nephrol. 2005;16(2):459-466. [PMID: 15615823]

Rule A, Larson T, Bergstralh E, Slezak J, Jacobsen S, Cosio F. Using Serum Creatinine To Estimate Glomerular Filtration Rate: Accuracy in Good Health and in Chronic Kidney Disease. Ann Intern Med. 2004;141(12):929-937. [PMID: 15611490]

Sarafidis PA, Bakris GL. Microalbuminuria and chronic kidney disease as risk factors for cardiovascular disease. Nephrol Dial Transplant. 2006; 21(9):2366-2374. [PMID: 16782993]

Stevens LA, Coresh J, Greene T, Levey AS. Assessing Kidney Function — Measured and Estimated Glomerular Filtration Rate. N Engl J Med. 2006;354(23):2473-2483. [PMID: 16760447]

Swaminathan S, Shah SV. New Insights into Nephrogenic Systemic Fibrosis. J Am Soc Nephrol. 2007;18(10):2636-2643. [PMID: 17855637]

Fluids and Electrolytes

Osmolality and Tonicity

Osmolality is defined as the number of solute particles per kilogram of solution. Plasma osmolality can be directly measured via an osmometer or calculated using the following equation:

$$\text{Plasma Osmolality (mosm/kg } H_2O) = 2 \times \text{Serum Sodium (meq/L)} + \text{Blood Urea Nitrogen (mg/dL)}/2.8 + \text{Plasma Glucose (mg/dL)}/18$$

The osmolal gap is the difference between the measured and calculated osmolality and is normally less than 10 mosm/kg H_2O (10 mmol/kg H_2O). An osmolal gap higher than 10 mosm/kg H_2O (10 mmol/kg H_2O) indicates the accumulation of an additional solute in the plasma (see Ethylene Glycol and Methanol Poisoning).

All particles determine the plasma osmolality, but only effective osmoles determine the plasma tonicity. Effective osmoles cannot penetrate cell membranes and therefore may affect cell volume. Conversely, ineffective osmoles such as urea and alcohols pass freely into and out of cells and do not affect cell volume. An excess of an ineffective osmole therefore would not cause a cellular shift and would be associated with a high plasma osmolality but normal plasma tonicity.

KEY POINT

- An osmolal gap higher than 10 mosm/kg H_2O (10 mmol/kg H_2O) indicates the accumulation of an additional solute in the plasma.

Disorders of Serum Sodium

Sodium is the major electrolyte constituting the extracellular fluid and the primary determinant of plasma osmolality. The serum sodium concentration is maintained within a narrow range by adjustments in water intake and kidney water excretion. Serum sodium concentration abnormalities therefore reflect disturbances in water balance.

Hyponatremia

Hyponatremia is defined as a serum sodium concentration less than 136 meq/L (136 mmol/L). Initial manifestations of hyponatremia include nausea and malaise; as this condition progresses, headache, lethargy, muscle cramps, restlessness, disorientation, and obtundation may develop.

Chronic hyponatremia refers to hyponatremia that is present for more than 48 hours and is characterized by a slowly decreasing serum sodium concentration. In patients with chronic hyponatremia, neurologic manifestations are generally minimal and the brain size remains normal. Chronic hyponatremia usually occurs in the outpatient setting.

Acute hyponatremia refers to hyponatremia that develops in less than 48 hours. Patients with acute hyponatremia frequently do have neurologic manifestations and cerebral edema. Acute hyponatremia is more common than chronic hyponatremia in hospitalized patients.

Risk Factors

Postoperative administration of hypotonic fluids is a risk factor for acute hyponatremia, because antidiuretic hormone levels remain increased for several days after a surgical procedure. Severe hyponatremia also may develop in patients undergoing bowel preparation for procedures such as colonoscopy.

Common causes of hyponatremia in the outpatient setting include overhydration, diarrhea, vomiting, central nervous system infection, extreme exercise, advanced age, liver failure, kidney failure, heart failure, and use of certain medications (**Table 5**). Hypotonic fluid intake in the setting of intense exercise, particularly during an endurance event, also frequently causes this condition. Patients with severe exercise-induced hyponatremia may collapse, and this condition can be fatal.

Thiazide diuretics are the most common cause of drug-induced hyponatremia. Thiazide-induced hyponatremia typically develops within 2 weeks of drug initiation and is most likely to occur in elderly women and when consumption of hypotonic fluids usually increases. Concomitant use of NSAIDs and selective serotonin reuptake inhibitors can further increase the risk of thiazide-induced hyponatremia.

TABLE 5 Drugs Associated with Hyponatremia

Agents That Stimulate Antidiuretic Hormone Release
Chlorpropamide
Clofibrate
Cyclophosphamide
Vincristine
Carbamazepine
Selective serotonin reuptake inhibitors
Amitriptyline
Thiothixene
Haloperidol
Thioridazine

Agents That Potentiate the Kidney Effect of Antidiuretic Hormone
Chlorpropamide
Carbamazepine
NSAIDs
Cyclophosphamide

Agents That Produce an Antidiuretic Hormone–Like Effect
Oxytocin
Desmopressin

Experts recommend routine monitoring of the serum sodium concentration 2 to 4 weeks after initiating a thiazide-containing agent. The illicit drug 3,4-methylenedioxymethamphetamine (also known as ecstasy) also can cause acute, severe hyponatremia.

Evaluation

Assessment of the plasma osmolality, urine osmolality, and effective arterial blood volume (EABV) can help to determine the cause of hyponatremia (**Figure 3**).

Plasma Osmolality

Hyponatremia is most commonly a marker of hypo-osmolality. Hyponatremia that occurs in the absence of a hypo-osmolar state (pseudohyponatremia) is generally caused by an increased serum concentration of an effective osmole or the addition of an isosmotic or near-isosmotic non–sodium-containing fluid to the extracellular space.

Common causes of pseudohyponatremia include hyperglobulinemia and hypertriglyceridemia. Because these conditions are associated with a decrease of plasma water

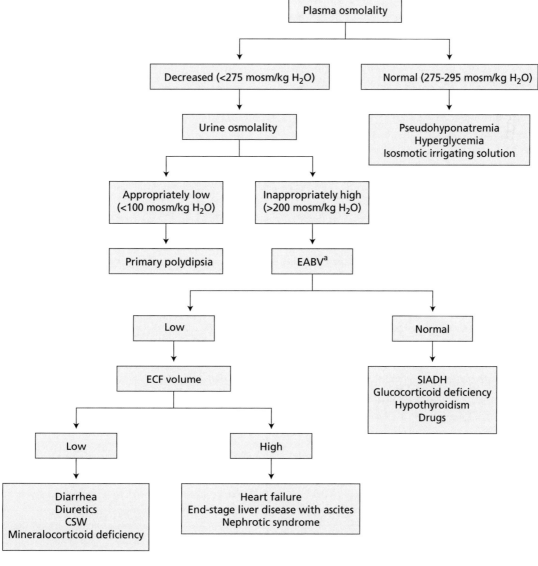

FIGURE 3.
Approach to the patient with hyponatremia.
[a]The clinical determination of EABV is usually straightforward. On physical examination, the best index of this value is the pulse and blood pressure. Urine electrolyte levels are also extremely useful in assessing the EABV. A low EABV is characterized by low urine sodium and urine chloride levels and low fractional excretions of sodium and chloride in the urine. In patients with normal serum creatinine levels, a high BUN level suggests a low EABV, whereas a low BUN level suggests a high EABV.

BUN = blood urea nitrogen; CSW = cerebral salt wasting; EABV = effective arterial blood volume; ECF = extracellular fluid; SIADH = syndrome of inappropriate antidiuretic hormone secretion.

relative to plasma solids in the blood, the amount of sodium in a given volume of blood also decreases.

True hyponatremia may be associated with an elevation in the plasma concentration of an effective osmole. This elevation results in an increase in plasma osmolality (hyperosmolar hyponatremia), which causes water to leave the cells and results in a diluted serum sodium concentration. Hyponatremia caused by these circumstances occurs in patients with hyperglycemia or, rarely, after infusion of hypertonic mannitol.

In these settings, the serum sodium concentration quickly decreases by 1.6 meq/L (1.6 mmol/L) for every 100 mg/dL (5.5 mmol/L) increase in glucose or mannitol. The increased tonicity also stimulates thirst and antidiuretic hormone secretion, which contribute to further water retention. Finally, as the plasma osmolality normalizes, the serum sodium concentration decreases by 2.8 meq/L (2.8 mmol/L) for every 100 mg/dL (5.5 mmol/L) increase in glucose, resulting in a normal plasma osmolality but a low serum sodium concentration.

Isosmotic or near-isosmotic non–sodium-containing irrigating solutions may enter the extracellular space during transurethral resection of the prostate or laparoscopic surgery. The systemic reabsorption of large amounts of these solutions, which usually contain glycine or sorbitol, can induce hyponatremia in the setting of a normal plasma osmolality.

Urine Osmolality

The presence of hyponatremia in a patient with normal kidney water excretion is suggestive of polydipsia, which is characterized by intake of water that exceeds the normal excreting capacity of the kidneys (20 to 30 L daily). These patients typically have a urine osmolality less than 100 mosm/kg H_2O (100 mmol/kg H_2O).

Hyponatremia that occurs in the absence of primary polydipsia is associated with decreased kidney water excretion and an inappropriately concentrated urine, which is characterized by a urine osmolality greater than 200 mosm/kg H_2O (200 mmol/kg H_2O).

Effective Arterial Blood Volume

The EABV refers to the part of the extracellular fluid in the arterial system that perfuses the tissues and stimulates the volume receptors. Hyponatremia can be caused by a decrease in EABV, which results in baroreceptor stimulation of antidiuretic hormone secretion and increased proximal tubular reabsorption of sodium. Consequently, distal delivery of filtrate to the tip of the loop of Henle decreases.

Hyponatremia may be associated with low extracellular fluid volume (hypovolemic hyponatremia) or high extracellular fluid volume in edematous patients (hypervolemic hyponatremia). Hyponatremia associated with a normal EABV is known as isovolemic hyponatremia.

Syndrome of Inappropriate Antidiuretic Hormone Secretion and Cerebral Salt Wasting

The syndrome of inappropriate antidiuretic hormone secretion (SIADH) and cerebral salt wasting (CSW) are two potential causes of hypo-osmolar hyponatremia that may develop several days after a neurosurgical procedure is performed. Manifestations of both SIADH and CSW include a decreased serum sodium concentration, low or low-normal plasma osmolality, and elevated urine osmolality. Because the treatment of SIADH and CSW differs, distinguishing between these conditions is imperative and is based largely on the EABV. SIADH is associated with antidiuretic hormone–mediated kidney water retention and is therefore characterized by euvolemia or a slightly volume-expanded state. Conversely, CSW is associated with kidney salt wasting, which leads to a decrease in intravascular volume.

SIADH is more common than CSW. Patients with SIADH also usually have an extremely decreased serum uric acid concentration, because volume expansion in this condition causes decreased uric acid absorption in the proximal nephron. CSW, on the other hand, is suggested by the presence of hypotension and often affects patients with subarachnoid hemorrhage. Fluid restriction is the treatment of choice in patients with SIADH, whereas intravenous normal saline is indicated for CSW.

Treatment

When treating a patient with chronic hyponatremia, the sodium concentration should be increased at the same rate at which it decreased (**Table 6**). If the extracellular fluid osmolality rapidly normalizes in a patient with chronic hyponatremia, cell shrinkage may occur and can precipitate osmotic demyelination. Limiting serum sodium correction to less than 10 to 12 meq/L (10 to 12 mmol/L) within 24 hours and less than 18 meq/L (18 mmol/L) within 48 hours helps to prevent this complication. Conversely, in patients with acute hyponatremia, sufficient time to remove osmoles from the brain has not passed. Rapid normalization of the extracellular fluid osmolality returns the brain size to normal and is therefore indicated.

Frequent monitoring of the serum sodium concentration should be used to guide therapy. When overcorrection of the sodium concentration has occurred or is likely, desmopressin acetate administered with or without hypotonic fluids may be warranted to slow the rate of correction.

The vasopressin receptor antagonists V_1 and V_2 also may be used to treat hyponatremia. These agents cause an increase in water excretion with little or no change in the urine sodium excretion.

The intravenous V_1 and V_2 receptor antagonist conivaptan and the oral V_2 receptor antagonist tolvaptan are approved for treatment of euvolemic and hypervolemic hyponatremia. Vaptan agents should not be used to treat hypovolemic hyponatremia.

TABLE 6 Treatment of Hyponatremia

ECF Volume Status	Acute Hyponatremia		Chronic Hyponatremia
	Slow	Rapid	
Normal	Fluid restriction	Hypertonic saline + furosemide	Remove cause Discontinue drug Begin corticosteroid or thyroid hormone replacement Treat cause of SIADH
Low	Normal saline	Hypertonic saline	Remove cause
High	Fluid restriction	Hypertonic saline + furosemide	Remove cause Begin demeclocycline, 600-1200 mg/d Begin intravenous conivaptan, 20 mg over 30 minutes, then 20 mg over 24 hours for no more than 4 days

ECF = extracellular fluid; SIADH = syndrome of inappropriate antidiuretic hormone secretion.

KEY POINTS

- Manifestations of hyponatremia include nausea, malaise, headache, lethargy, muscle cramps, restlessness, disorientation, and obtundation.

- Low effective arterial blood volume is associated with hypovolemic and hypervolemic hyponatremia.

- The syndrome of inappropriate antidiuretic hormone secretion is characterized by euvolemia or a slightly volume-expanded state and is treated with fluid restriction.

- Cerebral salt wasting is associated with a decrease in intravascular volume and should be treated with intravenous normal saline.

- In the treatment of chronic hyponatremia, limiting serum sodium correction to less than 10 to 12 meq/L (10 to 12 mmol/L) within 24 hours and less than 18 meq/L (18 mmol/L) within 48 hours helps to prevent osmotic demyelination.

- In patients with acute hyponatremia, rapid normalization of the extracellular fluid osmolality is indicated.

- Conivaptan and tolvaptan are approved to treat euvolemic and hypervolemic hyponatremia, but vaptan agents should not be used to treat hypovolemic hyponatremia.

Hypernatremia

Hypernatremia is defined as a serum sodium concentration greater than 145 meq/L (145 mmol/L). This relatively common condition always indicates hypertonicity and cell shrinkage and is an independent risk factor for mortality in the intensive care unit. Manifestations of hypernatremia include lethargy, weakness, fasciculations, seizures, and coma.

Evaluation

Inadequate Water Intake

Evaluation of a patient with hypernatremia should begin by assessing for a cause of inadequate water intake. Inadequate water intake usually occurs in patients in an altered state of consciousness or with impaired mental status who are unaware of thirst or unable to communicate the need for water, such as the elderly and critically ill. Infants and young children who have restricted access to water also may consume inadequate amounts of water, and a reduced sensation of thirst is a normal feature of increasing age. A specific lesion of the hypothalamus affecting the thirst center is a rare cause of hypernatremia.

Accelerated Water Loss or Increased Sodium Gain

The extracellular fluid status should then be assessed to evaluate for accelerated water loss or increased sodium gain (**Figure 4**). Hypovolemic hypernatremia results from fluid losses in which the sodium concentration is less than the plasma concentration. Conversely, hypervolemic hypernatremia is caused by administration of hypertonic saline or hypertonic sodium bicarbonate or a mineralocorticoid excess.

Isovolemic hypernatremia is caused by pure water loss via a mucocutaneous route or the kidneys. Because two thirds of pure water loss is sustained within cells, patients with isovolemic hypernatremia do not become clinically volume depleted unless the water deficit is substantial.

In patients with isovolemic hypernatremia, insensible losses of water via the respiratory tract or skin result in a concentrated urine, whereas inappropriate water loss via the kidneys due to central or nephrogenic diabetes insipidus results in a dilute urine. Kidney water loss can lead to hypernatremia in patients with impaired thirst or restricted access to water; however, these features usually are not present in patients with diabetes insipidus, who typically have polyuria, polydipsia, and a normal serum sodium concentration.

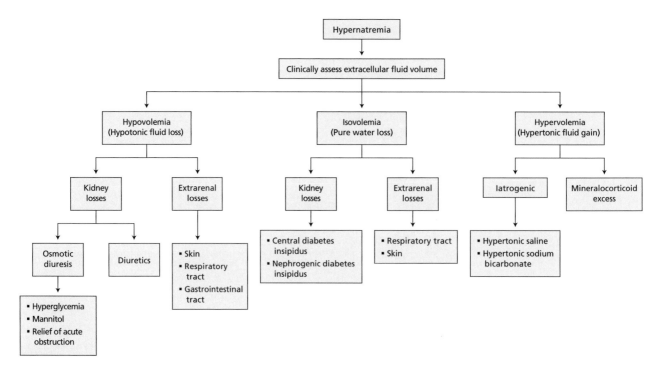

FIGURE 4.
Approach to the patient with hypernatremia.
All of these states are associated with impairment of thirst or access to water.

Assessment of Polyuria

Polyuria in adults is characterized by a urine volume that exceeds 50 mL/kg body weight daily and is associated with frequent urination. Polyuria can be caused by osmotic diuresis, also known as solute diuresis, or water diuresis. A urine osmolality greater than 300 mosm/kg H_2O (300 mmol/kg H_2O) in a patient with polyuria is suggestive of osmotic diuresis. Polyuria associated with osmotic diuresis occurs in patients with poorly controlled diabetes mellitus; mannitol administration; and high-protein enteral feeding, which is specifically associated with urea diuresis.

Once osmotic diuresis is excluded, the cause of water diuresis must be assessed. Water diuresis may represent appropriate water loss, which occurs in primary polydipsia, or inappropriate water loss, which occurs in conditions such as central or nephrogenic diabetes insipidus.

Central and nephrogenic diabetes insipidus are both characterized by severe, frequent nocturia as well as an absence of change in urine osmolality in response to water deprivation. Patients with central and nephrogenic diabetes insipidus also tend to have a mild negative water balance and a serum sodium concentration greater than 140 meq/L (140 mmol/L).

The clinical setting and urine osmolality can help to differentiate between central and nephrogenic diabetes insipidus (**Figure 5**) (**Table 7**). Central diabetes insipidus is associated with a decreased release of antidiuretic hormone, and nephrogenic diabetes insipidus is associated with a decreased kidney response to this hormone. Subcutaneous administration of antidiuretic hormone causes an increase in urine osmolality in patients with central diabetes insipidus but is not associated with a change in urine osmolality in patients with nephrogenic diabetes insipidus. Central diabetes insipidus also is characterized by an abrupt onset of symptoms, whereas symptoms in nephrogenic diabetes insipidus typically manifest gradually. In addition, patients with central diabetes insipidus often have a predilection for ice water.

Treatment

Increased extracellular fluid osmolality associated with hypernatremia initially causes cell shrinkage within the brain. This shrinkage causes cells to generate intracellular osmoles that pull water back into the cells and return brain size to normal. However, if extracellular osmolality normalizes rapidly, the additional intracellular osmoles pull water into the brain cells, resulting in cerebral edema. Therefore, hypernatremia generally should be corrected slowly by water administration at a rate that leads to half-correction in 24 hours.

The water deficit in patients with hypernatremia can be estimated using the following formula:

$$\text{Total Body Water } [0.6 \text{ in Men and } 0.5 \text{ in Women} \times \text{Body Weight (kg)}] \times [(\text{Plasma Sodium}/140) - 1]$$

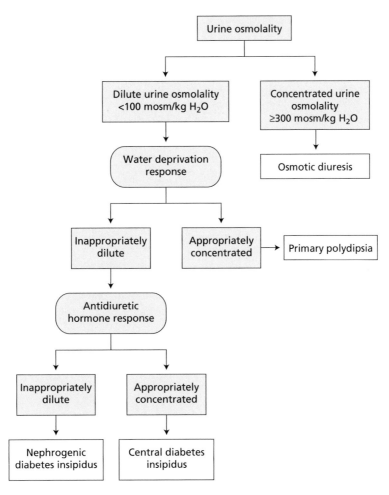

FIGURE 5.
Diagnosis of central and nephrogenic diabetes insipidus in a patient with polyuria.

TABLE 7 Common Causes of Diabetes Insipidus	
Central Diabetes Insipidus	**Nephrogenic Diabetes Insipidus**
Idiopathic	Electrolyte disturbances (hypokalemia, hypercalcemia)
Head trauma	Vasopressinase production by placenta during pregnancy leading to destruction of vasopressin
Post neurosurgery	Drugs (lithium, foscarnet, amphotericin B, demeclocycline, ifosfamide)
Cranial neoplasm	Chronic tubulointerstitial diseases (Sjögren syndrome, amyloidosis, sickle cell nephropathy, multiple myeloma, sarcoidosis)
Pituitary infiltrative diseases (histiocytosis, sarcoidosis)	
Central nervous system infections	
Sheehan pituitary necrosis	
Brain death	

However, when calculating the amount of water to administer to patients with hypernatremia, insensible losses and any ongoing losses from the urinary and gastrointestinal tracts must be taken into account. This formula also does not account for the volume of isotonic saline needed in patients who may be concomitantly volume depleted. Therefore, the serum sodium concentration should be carefully monitored to ensure an appropriate rate of correction.

- Hypovolemic hypernatremia results from fluid losses in which the sodium concentration is less than the plasma concentration.
- Hypervolemic hypernatremia results from administration of hypertonic saline or hypertonic sodium bicarbonate or a mineralocorticoid excess.
- Isovolemic hypernatremia is caused by pure water loss via a mucocutaneous route or the kidneys.
- A urine osmolality greater than 300 mosm/kg H_2O (300 mmol/kg H_2O) in a patient with polyuria is suggestive of osmotic diuresis.
- Water diuresis occurs in primary polydipsia and central or nephrogenic diabetes insipidus.
- Hypernatremia generally should be corrected slowly by water administration at a rate that leads to half-correction in 24 hours.

Disorders of Serum Potassium

Hypokalemia

Evaluation

Hypokalemia is defined as a serum potassium concentration less than 3.5 meq/L (3.5 mmol/L). The serum potassium concentration may be a misleading marker of the degree of a patient's serum potassium deficit, as patients with normal or even increased serum concentrations of potassium may have significant total body potassium depletion. The exact cause of hypokalemia can usually be established by evaluating the history, blood pressure, acid-base balance, and urine potassium concentration.

Hypokalemia Associated with Normal Total Body Potassium Content

Causes of hypokalemia associated with normal total body potassium content include a laboratory error or pseudohypokalemia, which may develop in patients with leukemia and elevated leukocyte counts. In this setting, leukocytes may extract potassium from the serum, which can lead to a decreased serum potassium concentration despite normal total body potassium content. In the absence of these circumstances, a low serum potassium concentration in the presence of normal total body potassium content and no evidence of gastrointestinal or kidney potassium losses suggests a shift of potassium from the extracellular to the intracellular space.

The kidneys are ultimately responsible for maintaining total body potassium content, but factors that modulate internal potassium balance affect the disposal of acute potassium loads. Intracellular shifting of potassium is primarily regulated by insulin and catecholamines. An excess of insulin can cause a shift of potassium into the cells that decreases the serum

potassium concentration. β-Agonists may cause a similar potassium shift. In the setting of an acute myocardial infarction, hypokalemia may develop as a sequela of high-circulating epinephrine levels. Intracellular sequestration of potassium also may occur in patients with hypothermia or in those with megaloblastic anemia who are treated with vitamin B_{12}.

Hypokalemia Associated with Decreased Total Body Potassium Content

In the absence of a cellular shift, a low serum potassium concentration can be caused by losses via the gastrointestinal tract or skin, kidney potassium losses, or inadequate dietary intake of potassium. A urine potassium concentration of less than 20 meq/L (20 mmol/L) is suggestive of extrarenal losses, whereas a concentration higher than this value is suggestive of kidney losses.

The transtubular potassium concentration gradient (TTKG), which can be calculated as follows, also has been used to determine the cause of hypokalemia that is not associated with a cellular shift:

$$TTKG = [Urine\ Potassium \div (Urine\ osmolality/Plasma\ osmolality)] \div Plasma\ Potassium$$

Using this formula, a TTKG less than 2 is suggestive of extrarenal potassium losses when accompanied by a urine potassium-creatinine ratio less than 1 mmol/mmol and a 24-hour urine potassium concentration less than 15 mmol/24 h (15 mmol/d).

Inadequate dietary intake of potassium is a rare cause of hypokalemia that is typically associated with anorexia nervosa, extreme dieting, alcoholism, and intestinal malabsorption. Increased kidney potassium excretion secondary to magnesium deficiency also may contribute to hypokalemia.

Gastrointestinal disorders are the most common clinical cause of extrarenal potassium losses. Diarrhea leads to fecal potassium wastage and is associated with a normal anion gap acidosis due to increased gastrointestinal loss of bicarbonate. Acidosis causes redistribution of potassium out of the cells, which results in a degree of hypokalemia that is less severe than the degree of total body potassium depletion.

Sweat is an unusual cause of potassium depletion. However, a substantial loss of sweat can cause hypokalemia.

Increased renal tubular distal delivery of sodium and water or increased mineralocorticoid activity may stimulate kidney potassium secretion. These two factors are influenced by EABV (**Figure 6**).

Distal sodium delivery and aldosterone secretion become coupled only when a pathophysiologic disorder is present, and this coupling is associated with kidney potassium wasting. This coupling can be caused by a primary increase in mineralocorticoid activity or a primary increase in distal sodium delivery unrelated to changes in the EABV.

Increases in mineralocorticoid activity can be caused by primary increases in renin secretion, primary increases in

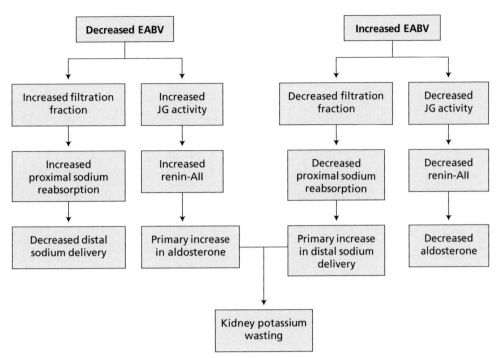

FIGURE 6.
Effective arterial blood volume and kidney potassium wasting.

AII = angiotensin II; EABV = effective arterial blood volume; JG = juxtaglomerular.

aldosterone secretion, increases in a nonaldosterone mineralocorticoid, or an increased mineralocorticoid-like effect. In these settings, extracellular fluid volume is expanded and hypertension is typically present.

Establishing a differential diagnosis in patients with hypertension, hypokalemia, and metabolic alkalosis involves measurement of the plasma renin activity and plasma aldosterone levels. Primary aldosteronism should be suspected in patients with hypertension who have low plasma renin activity and high plasma aldosterone levels. High plasma renin activity accompanied by a high aldosterone level is suggestive of renovascular hypertension, malignant hypertension, or a renin-secreting tumor.

Conditions that cause primary increases in distal sodium delivery are characterized by normal or low extracellular volume and are usually associated with normal blood pressure. Diuretics that act proximal to the cortical collecting duct are the most frequent cause of increases in distal sodium delivery. Nonreabsorbed anions such as bicarbonate, which occur with active vomiting or a type 2 proximal renal tubular acidosis, also may increase distal sodium delivery.

In addition, the inability to reabsorb β-hydroxybutyrate and acetoacetate as well as the sodium salts of penicillins in the proximal tubule can result in increased delivery of sodium to the distal nephron. These anions also escape reabsorption in the distal nephron; therefore, a more lumen-negative voltage develops, and the driving force for potassium excretion into the tubular fluid is enhanced.

Hypokalemia due to a primary increase in distal sodium delivery can best be categorized by the presence of metabolic acidosis, which is suggestive of renal tubular acidosis, or metabolic alkalosis, which is suggestive of vomiting or diuretic use.

Clinical Manifestations

Hypokalemia leads to cell hyperpolarization, which impedes impulse conduction and muscle contraction. Typically, a flaccid paralysis develops in the hands and feet that moves proximally and eventually involves the trunk and respiratory muscles. Hypokalemia also may cause a myopathy that can lead to rhabdomyolysis or may cause a smooth muscle dysfunction such as paralytic ileus.

Episodic hypokalemia occurs in hypokalemic periodic paralysis, an inherited disorder with an autosomal dominant pattern of transmission. An acquired form of this disorder occurs in patients with thyrotoxicosis, particularly in those of Japanese or Mexican descent. Hypokalemic periodic paralysis typically develops in patients between 5 and 20 years of age. Episodes of paralysis in affected patients are often precipitated by a meal containing carbohydrates, exercise, or stress and manifest as muscle weakness and paralysis lasting longer than 24 hours. Respiratory involvement in this condition can be fatal.

Electrocardiographic findings in patients with hypokalemia may include ST-segment depression, T-wave flattening, and an increased U-wave amplitude.

Hypokalemia causes a decrease in the medullary gradient and resistance of the cortical collecting tubule to antidiuretic hormone, which results in a kidney concentrating defect that leads to polyuria and polydipsia. Prolonged hypokalemia may lead to tubulointerstitial nephritis and kidney failure. Because the serum potassium concentration partially regulates insulin release, hypokalemia also may cause glucose intolerance.

Treatment

In the absence of a significant cellular shift, a decline in the serum potassium concentration from 4 to 3 meq/L (4 to 3 mmol/L) generally is associated with an intracellular potassium deficit of 200 to 300 meq/70 kg (200 to 300 mmol/70 kg) body weight; a serum potassium concentration of 2 meq/L (2 mmol/L) reflects a deficit of approximately 400 to 500 meq/70 kg (400 to 500 mmol/70 kg) body weight. Despite these guidelines, frequent monitoring of the serum potassium concentration still is indicated during potassium replacement therapy.

Oral or intravenous potassium is administered as potassium chloride. Oral administration of potassium chloride is safer than other routes and can be given in divided dosages of 100 to 150 meq/d. Liquid and tablet potassium chloride may irritate the gastric mucosa; microencapsulated or wax-matrix formulations are better tolerated.

Intravenous potassium chloride may be needed in patients who cannot take oral medications or who have a large potassium deficit associated with cardiac arrhythmias, respiratory paralysis, or rhabdomyolysis. The maximum recommended rate of administration is 20 meq/h at a maximum concentration of 40 meq/L; higher concentrations will result in phlebitis.

Replacement of potassium chloride via dextrose-containing solutions may decrease the potassium concentration further secondary to insulin release; therefore, saline solutions are preferred. Potassium bicarbonate or potassium citrate can be administered in patients with hypokalemia and concomitant metabolic acidosis.

Additional therapy for chronic hypokalemia may include potassium-sparing diuretics such as amiloride, spironolactone, or triamterene. However, these agents should be used with caution in patients with kidney insufficiency or other disorders that impair kidney potassium excretion.

KEY POINTS

- Use of β-agonists or excessive insulin can cause hypokalemia.
- In the absence of a cellular shift, a low serum potassium concentration can be caused by losses via the gastrointestinal tract or skin, kidney potassium losses, or inadequate dietary intake of potassium.
- In patients with hypokalemia caused by a primary increase in distal sodium delivery, the presence of metabolic acidosis is suggestive of renal tubular acidosis; the presence of metabolic alkalosis is suggestive of vomiting or diuretic use.
- Manifestations of hypokalemia may include a flaccid paralysis, rhabdomyolysis, smooth muscle dysfunction, polyuria, polydipsia, kidney failure, and glucose intolerance.
- Electrocardiographic findings in patients with hypokalemia may include ST-segment depression, T-wave flattening, and an increased U-wave amplitude.
- Oral administration of potassium chloride is safer than other routes and can be given in divided dosages of 100 to 150 meq/d.
- The maximum recommended rate of intravenous potassium chloride administration is 20 meq/h at a maximum concentration of 40 meq/L.

Hyperkalemia

Hyperkalemia is defined as a serum potassium concentration higher than 5 meq/L (5 mmol/L). As with hypokalemia, hyperkalemia may develop in the presence of normal or altered total body potassium content. Acute hyperkalemia usually is caused by cell shifts or tissue injury, whereas chronic hyperkalemia develops in patients with impaired kidney potassium excretion.

Evaluation

Hyperkalemia occurs when abnormalities develop in the regulatory mechanisms that excrete excess potassium quickly or redistribute excess potassium into cells until it is excreted. For example, after consumption of a high-potassium meal, the kidneys alone cannot excrete potassium at a sufficiently rapid rate to prevent life-threatening hyperkalemia; in healthy persons, rapid shifting and storage of excess potassium into the cells are needed until the kidneys have successfully excreted the potassium load.

Causes of hyperkalemia include pseudohyperkalemia, excessive dietary intake of potassium, cellular redistribution, and decreased kidney excretion of potassium.

Pseudohyperkalemia

Pseudohyperkalemia is an in vitro phenomenon caused by the mechanical release of potassium from cells during phlebotomy or specimen processing or in the setting of marked leukocytosis and thrombocytosis.

Excessive Dietary Intake

In patients with normal kidney and adrenal function, ingestion of sufficient potassium to produce hyperkalemia is rare. However, in patients with impaired kidney function, dietary potassium intake usually contributes to hyperkalemia. High-potassium dietary sources include melons, citrus juice, and some commercial salt substitutes.

Cellular Redistribution

Hyperkalemia may result from redistribution of potassium out of cells due to tissue damage associated with rhabdomyolysis, trauma, burns, massive intravascular coagulation, and tumor lysis syndrome.

Metabolic acidosis results in potassium redistribution out of cells and is determined by the type of acid present. Mineral acidosis associated with ammonium chloride or hydrochloric acid results in the greatest departure of potassium from cells because of the relative impermeability of the chloride anion. Conversely, organic acidosis associated with lactic or β-hydroxybutyric acid does not cause a significant efflux of potassium.

Increased osmolality, which occurs in conditions such as uncontrolled diabetes, also causes potassium to move out of cells. In patients with diabetic ketoacidosis, both the hypertonic state and insulin deficiency cause hyperkalemia, not metabolic acidosis.

Iatrogenic causes of hyperkalemia due to cellular redistribution include use of the depolarizing muscle relaxant succinylcholine and digitalis toxicity. β-Adrenergic–blocking agents also can interfere with disposal of acute potassium loads.

Decreased Kidney Excretion of Potassium

Decreased kidney excretion of potassium is usually a result of a primary decrease in distal delivery of salt and water, abnormal cortical collecting duct function, or a primary decrease in mineralocorticoid levels.

An acute decrease in the glomerular filtration rate (GFR) may cause a marked decrease in distal delivery of salt and water, which may secondarily decrease distal potassium secretion. In patients with oliguric acute kidney injury, distal delivery of sodium chloride and volume also is low, and hyperkalemia frequently occurs. Conversely, patients with nonoliguric acute kidney injury usually have sufficient distal delivery of sodium chloride and rarely develop hyperkalemia.

Patients with chronic kidney disease (CKD) usually do not develop hyperkalemia until the GFR decreases to less than 10 mL/min/1.73 m^2. Hyperkalemia that occurs in patients

with a GFR higher than this value should raise suspicion for a decreased aldosterone level or a specific lesion of the cortical collecting duct.

Decreased mineralocorticoid activity can result from primary disturbances of the renin-angiotensin-aldosterone system or use of drugs that interfere with this system. Hyperkalemia most commonly develops when one or more of these drugs are administered in a patient with a previously impaired renin-angiotensin-aldosterone system. NSAIDs are one of the most common causes of drug-induced hyperkalemia.

Angiotensin-converting enzyme (ACE) inhibitors and angiotensin receptor blockers (ARBs) also may cause hyperkalemia. Use of these agents is particularly challenging, because patients who have the highest risk for hyperkalemia may experience the greatest cardiovascular and kidney benefits from these agents. Therefore, in patients with CKD, the level of kidney function should not be the sole determinant of whether ACE inhibitors or ARBs are initiated or continued.

Amiloride, triamterene, and pentamidine inhibit distal sodium transport and secondarily inhibit potassium secretion; trimethoprim has a similar effect. Spironolactone and eplerenone compete with aldosterone and block the mineralocorticoid effect.

The risk for developing hyperkalemia in patients using drugs that interfere with the renin-angiotensin-aldosterone system or secondarily inhibit potassium secretion can be minimized by beginning therapy with these agents at a low dose and measuring the serum potassium concentration 1 week after initiating or increasing the dosage. An increase in serum potassium greater than 5.5 meq/L (5.5 mmol/L) warrants a decrease in the dosage or elimination of the offending drug or, in patients treated with concomitant therapy with an ACE inhibitor, ARB, or aldosterone receptor blocker, discontinuation of one of these agents. The dosage of spironolactone also should not exceed 25 mg/d when used with an ACE inhibitor or an ARB, and this combination of drugs should be avoided in patients with a GFR less than 30 mL/min/1.73 m^2.

Certain interstitial kidney diseases such as sickle cell nephropathy and lupus nephropathy can disproportionately affect the distal nephron and lead to hyperkalemia in the presence of normal aldosterone levels and only mild decreases in GFR.

Clinical Manifestations

Hyperkalemia leads to depolarization of the resting membrane; the heart is particularly sensitive to this depolarizing effect. Electrocardiographic findings in patients with hyperkalemia include peaking of T waves, lengthening of the PR and QRS intervals, development of a sine wave pattern, and eventually ventricular fibrillation and asystole. These changes usually develop at a serum potassium concentration of 6 meq/L (6 mmol/L) in patients with acute hyperkalemia, whereas electrocardiograms in patients with chronic hyperkalemia may remain normal until this value reaches 8 to 9 meq/L (8 to 9 mmol/L).

Neuromuscular manifestations associated with hyperkalemia include ascending paralysis and eventual flaccid quadriplegia. Hyperkalemic periodic paralysis is caused by mutations in the sodium channel *SCN4A* gene. This condition usually affects patients who are less than 10 years of age and manifests as attacks lasting less than 24 hours. Fasting and potassium administration may precipitate attacks of hyperkalemic periodic paralysis.

Treatment

Acute Hyperkalemia

Immediate treatment with calcium gluconate or calcium chloride is indicated for patients with life-threatening hyperkalemia. Electrocardiographic changes also warrant calcium therapy.

Combination therapy with glucose and insulin shifts potassium into cells. Administration of sodium bicarbonate helps to expand the extracellular fluid space and therefore dilutes the serum potassium concentration but also may shift potassium into cells. Inhalation of β_2-agonists and parenteral use of albuterol also may cause a significant potassium shift into cells.

However, although these therapies provide immediate relief of acute potassium toxicity, the improvement is only temporary; interventions such as administration of sodium polystyrene sulfonate and dialysis help to decrease total body potassium content.

Chronic Hyperkalemia

When possible, discontinuation of drugs that impair kidney potassium excretion is indicated for patients with chronic hyperkalemia. A low-potassium diet also should be initiated, including avoidance of potassium-containing salt substitutes.

Interventions that increase urine flow rate and distal sodium delivery may enhance kidney potassium excretion. Agents that increase kidney potassium loss may be warranted. Thiazide diuretics can be used to help treat hyperkalemia in patients with GFR above 30 mL/min/1.73 m², but loop diuretics are needed for patients with a GFR below 30 mL/min/1.73 m².

In patients with CKD associated with metabolic acidosis, sodium bicarbonate therapy is indicated. Intermittent potassium-binding resin therapy also may help in this setting but is poorly tolerated when used as chronic therapy and has been associated with gastrointestinal ulceration.

KEY POINTS

- Hyperkalemia that occurs in patients with a glomerular filtration rate higher than 10 mL/min/1.73 m² suggests a decreased aldosterone level or a lesion of the cortical collecting duct.

- An increase in serum potassium greater than 5.5 meq/L (5.5 mmol/L) in patients taking a drug known to cause hyperkalemia warrants a decrease in the dosage or elimination of the offending drug or, in patients treated with concomitant therapy with an angiotensin-converting enzyme inhibitor, angiotensin receptor blocker, or aldosterone receptor blocker, discontinuation of one of these agents.

- Electrocardiographic findings of hyperkalemia include peaking of T waves, lengthening of the PR and QRS intervals, development of a sine wave pattern, ventricular fibrillation, and asystole.

- Immediate treatment with calcium gluconate or calcium chloride is indicated for patients with life-threatening hyperkalemia or electrocardiographic changes.

- Treatment of chronic hyperkalemia may include discontinuation of drugs that can impair kidney potassium excretion, a low-potassium diet, and use of diuretics.

Disorders of Serum Phosphate

Hypophosphatemia

Hypophosphatemia is defined as a serum phosphate concentration less than 3 mg/dL (1 mmol/L). The glomerulus freely filters approximately 90% of plasma inorganic phosphate, and the proximal tubule reabsorbs nearly 80% of the filtered load. Phosphate crosses the apical membrane of the proximal tubular cell via the type IIa sodium-phosphate cotransporter. Low dietary phosphate intake and decreased parathyroid hormone levels increase cotransporter expression, whereas high dietary phosphate intake and elevated parathyroid hormone levels decrease cotransporter expression.

Hypophosphatemia is common in hospitalized patients, particularly those with sepsis and trauma. Severe symptomatic hypophosphatemia is relatively rare and most often develops in patients with chronic alcoholism.

Hypophosphatemia may manifest as severe weakness, rhabdomyolysis, hemolysis, and a leftward shift of the oxygen dissociation curve.

Evaluation

Hypophosphatemia may be caused by decreased dietary intake of phosphate, a cellular shift, decreased gastrointestinal absorption, increased kidney excretion, or a combination of these factors (**Table 8**). For example, hypophosphatemia in patients with alcoholism often develops because of poor oral intake, decreased intestinal absorption due to frequent vomiting and diarrhea, and increased kidney excretion due to the direct effect of ethanol on the tubule. Furthermore, respiratory alkalosis that develops during alcohol withdrawal and correction of alcoholic ketoacidosis shift phosphate into the cells. The administration of glucose-containing fluids stimulates the release of insulin, which further shifts phosphate into the intracellular compartment.

Glycosuria, ketonuria, and osmotic diuresis lead to decreased total body phosphate content in patients with diabetic ketoacidosis. However, the insulin deficiency and acidemia associated with diabetic ketoacidosis may cause the serum phosphate concentration in affected patients to be normal or even increased. Treatment of this condition with insulin and correction of the acidosis shifts phosphate into cells, which then unmasks the total body phosphate deficit.

Treatment

Phosphate supplementation is indicated only for patients who are symptomatic or who have a condition resulting in chronic phosphate wasting. Oral phosphate therapy is the preferred treatment of hypophosphatemia. Intravenous phosphate can precipitate with calcium and produce various adverse effects, including hypocalcemia, acute kidney injury, and potentially arrhythmias. Intravenous phosphate replacement therapy therefore should be reserved for patients with a serum phosphate level below 1.5 mg/dL (0.5 mmol/L) and warrants close monitoring of serum phosphorus levels.

KEY POINTS

- Severe symptomatic hypophosphatemia most often develops in patients with chronic alcoholism.
- Hypophosphatemia may manifest as severe weakness, rhabdomyolysis, hemolysis, and a leftward shift of the oxygen dissociation curve.
- Hypophosphatemia may be caused by decreased dietary intake of phosphate, a cellular shift, decreased gastrointestinal absorption, increased kidney excretion, or a combination of these factors.
- Hypophosphatemia in patients with diabetic ketoacidosis may only become apparent after the ketoacidosis is corrected.
- Intravenous phosphate replacement therapy should be reserved for patients with a serum phosphate concentration below 1.5 mg/dL (0.5 mmol/L).

TABLE 8 Selected Causes of Hypophosphatemia

Cellular Redistribution
Respiratory alkalosis
Administration of glucose and insulin (refeeding)
Correction of metabolic acidosis
Intestinal Malabsorption
Vitamin D deficiency
Fat malabsorption
Increased Kidney Excretion
Hyperparathyroidism
Fanconi syndrome
Vitamin D–resistant rickets
Osmotic diuresis
Decreased Phosphate Intake

Hyperphosphatemia

Hyperphosphatemia is defined as a serum phosphate concentration greater than 4.5 mg/dL (1.4 mmol/L). Acute hyperphosphatemia is typically caused by tissue breakdown, which occurs in rhabdomyolysis or tumor lysis syndrome.

Bibliography

Brunelli SM, Goldfarb S. Hypophosphatemia: clinical consequences and management. J Am Soc Nephrol. 2007;18(7):1999-2003. [PMID: 17568018]

Choi M, Ziyadeh F. The utility of the transtubular potassium gradient in the evaluation of hyperkalemia. J Am Soc Nephrol. 2008;19(3):424-426. [PMID: 18216310]

Lindner G, Funk G, Schwarz C, et al. Hypernatremia in the critically ill is an independent risk factor for mortality. Am J Kidney Dis. 2007;50(6):952-957. [PMID: 18037096]

Perianayagam A, Sterns RH, Silver SM, et al. DDAVP is effective in preventing and reversing inadvertent overcorrection of hyponatremia. Clin J Am Soc Nephrol. 2008;3(2):331-336. [PMID: 18235152]

Verbalis JG, Goldsmith SR, Greenberg A, Schrier RW, Sterns RH. Hyponatremia treatment guidelines 2007: expert panel recommendations. Am J Med. 2007;120(11 Suppl 1):S1-21. [PMID: 17981159]

Acid-Base Disorders

Evaluation of all acid-base disorders begins by determining which acid-base disorder(s) are present, the cause of each disorder, and whether adequate compensation is present. Metabolic disturbances are characterized by a pH abnormality caused by a change in the serum bicarbonate, whereas respiratory disturbances are characterized by an arterial P_{CO_2} abnormality.

Metabolic Acidosis

Diagnosis and Evaluation

Metabolic acidosis is characterized by a low serum pH, a decreased serum bicarbonate concentration, and a respiratory compensation resulting in a decreased arterial P_{CO_2} (**Table 9**). Assessment of the serum anion gap helps to further evaluate patients with metabolic acidosis (**Figure 7**). This value can be calculated using the following formula:

Anion Gap = [Sodium] – ([Chloride] + [Bicarbonate])

Normally, the anion gap is approximately 12 ± 2 meq/L (12 ± 2 mmol/L). Most unmeasured anions consist of albumin. Therefore, the presence of either a low albumin level or an unmeasured cationic light chain, which occurs in multiple myeloma, results in a low anion gap. When the primary disturbance is a metabolic acidosis, the anion gap helps to narrow the diagnostic possibilities to a high anion gap acidosis or a normal anion gap acidosis.

Normal anion gap metabolic acidosis can be of kidney or extrarenal origin. Metabolic acidosis of kidney origin such as renal tubular acidosis (RTA) is caused by abnormalities in tubular hydrogen transport (**Figure 8**). Metabolic acidosis of extrarenal origin is most commonly caused by gastrointestinal losses of bicarbonate; other extrarenal causes include the external loss of biliary and pancreatic secretions and ureteral diversion procedures.

TABLE 9 Compensation in Acid-Base Disorders	
Condition	**Expected Compensation**
Metabolic acidosis	Acute: P_{CO_2} = (1.5) [H_{CO_3}] + 8 Chronic: P_{CO_2} = [H_{CO_3}] + 15 Failure of the P_{CO_2} to decrease to expected value = complicating respiratory acidosis; excessive decrease of the P_{CO_2} = complicating respiratory alkalosis Quick check: P_{CO_2} = value should approximate last two digits of pH
Metabolic alkalosis	For each ↑ 1 meq/L in [H_{CO_3}], P_{CO_2} ↑ 0.7 mm Hg
Respiratory acidosis	Acute: 1 meq/L ↑ [H_{CO_3}] for each 10 mm Hg ↑ in P_{CO_2} Chronic: 3.5 meq/L ↑ [H_{CO_3}] for each 10 mm Hg ↑ in P_{CO_2} Failure of the [H_{CO_3}] to increase to the expected value = complicating metabolic acidosis; excessive increase in [H_{CO_3}] = complicating metabolic alkalosis
Respiratory alkalosis	Acute: ↓ 2 meq/L [H_{CO_3}] for each 10 mm Hg ↓ in P_{CO_2} Chronic: 4-5 meq/L ↓ [H_{CO_3}] for each 10 mm Hg ↓ in P_{CO_2} Failure of the [H_{CO_3}] to decrease to the expected value = complicating metabolic alkalosis; excessive decrease in [H_{CO_3}] = complicating metabolic acidosis

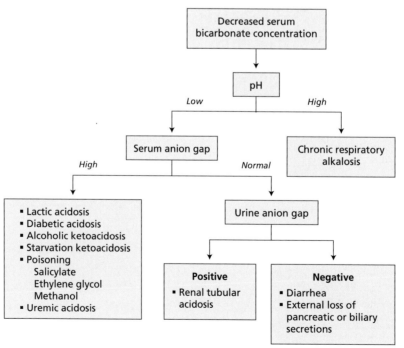

FIGURE 7.
Approach to the patient with a decreased serum bicarbonate concentration.

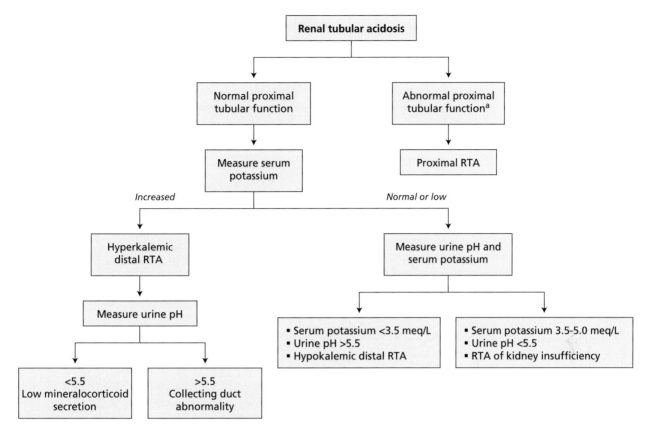

FIGURE 8.
Approach to the patient with metabolic acidosis of kidney origin.

RTA = renal tubular acidosis.

[a]Abnormal proximal tubular function refers to the finding of glycosuria in the setting of normal serum glucose levels, aminoaciduria, and uricosuria, which are features of the Fanconi syndrome.

The clinical history usually helps to distinguish between kidney and extrarenal causes of metabolic acidosis, but measuring the urine ammonium excretion can confirm the cause of this condition. Extrarenal causes of metabolic acidosis are associated with an appropriate increase in net acid excretion that is primarily reflected by high levels of urine ammonium excretion, whereas kidney causes of this condition are associated with low net acid excretion and decreased urine ammonium levels.

Urine ammonium measurement is not a commonly available study, but this value can be indirectly assessed by calculating the urine anion gap (UAG) using the following formula:

$$\text{Urine Anion Gap} = ([\text{Urine Sodium}] + [\text{Urine Potassium}]) - [\text{Urine Chloride}]$$

The UAG is normally between 30 to 50 meq/L (30 to 50 mmol/L). Metabolic acidosis of extrarenal origin is suggested by a large, negative UAG caused by significantly increased urine ammonium excretion. Conversely, metabolic acidosis of kidney origin is suggested by a positive UAG related to minimal urine ammonium excretion.

Classification

Normal Anion Gap Metabolic Acidosis of Kidney Origin

Proximal Renal Tubular Acidosis

Proximal or type 2 RTA should be suspected in patients with a normal anion gap metabolic acidosis, a normal UAG, hypokalemia, and an intact ability to acidify the urine to a pH of less than 5.5 while in a steady state. In the steady state, the serum bicarbonate concentration is usually between 16 and 18 meq/L (16 and 18 mmol/L).

Proximal RTA can be an isolated finding but most commonly is accompanied by generalized dysfunction of the proximal tubule, which manifests as glycosuria, phosphaturia, uricosuria, aminoaciduria, and tubular proteinuria and is known as Fanconi syndrome (**Table 10**). Proximal RTA is not associated with nephrolithiasis or nephrocalcinosis. However, osteomalacia can develop as a result of chronic hypophosphatemia and/or deficiency in the active form of vitamin D. Patients with proximal RTA may develop osteopenia due to acidosis-induced demineralization of bone.

Correction of acidosis in patients with proximal RTA is often not possible even with administration of large amounts of sodium bicarbonate, because bicarbonate is rapidly excreted in the urine. In addition, this therapy accelerates kidney potassium losses. The addition of a thiazide diuretic may increase the efficacy of alkali therapy by inducing volume depletion, lowering the glomerular filtration rate (GFR) and thereby decreasing the filtered load of bicarbonate. The addition of a potassium-sparing diuretic may limit the degree of kidney potassium wasting. Once therapy is initiated, close monitoring of serum electrolyte levels is indicated to prevent severe derangements in these levels.

Hypokalemic Distal Renal Tubular Acidosis
Hypokalemic distal RTA (type 1 RTA) should be considered in patients with a normal anion gap acidosis, hypokalemia, a positive UAG, and an inability to maximally decrease the urine pH; a urine pH greater than 5.5 in the setting of systemic acidosis is consistent with this condition (**Table 11**). Compared with patients with proximal RTA, the systemic acidosis in patients with hypokalemic distal RTA is usually more severe, and the serum bicarbonate concentration may be as low as 10 meq/L (10 mmol/L). Hypokalemic distal RTA also may cause severe hypokalemia that can lead to musculoskeletal weakness and symptoms of nephrogenic diabetes insipidus.

Patients with hypokalemic distal RTA frequently have nephrolithiasis and nephrocalcinosis. This predisposition to kidney calcification results from the combined effects of increased urine calcium excretion due to acidosis-induced bone mineral dissolution, a persistently alkaline urine pH, and low urine citrate excretion.

Administration of alkali therapy in an amount equal to daily acid production (usually 1 to 2 meq/kg daily) usually corrects the metabolic acidosis in patients with hypokalemic distal RTA. The potassium deficit should be corrected in these patients before correcting the acidosis. Potassium citrate is the preferred form of alkali therapy for patients with persistent hypokalemia or calcium stone disease.

TABLE 10 Causes of Proximal Renal Tubular Acidosis
Isolated Renal Tubular Acidosis
Sporadic
Familial
Disorders of carbonic anhydrase
Drug-induced
Acetazolamide
Sulfanilamide
Topiramate
Carbonic anhydrase II deficiency
Renal Tubular Acidosis Associated with Fanconi Syndrome
Systemic disease not present:
Sporadic
Familial
Systemic disease present:
Genetic disorders
Cystinosis
Wilson disease
Hereditary fructose intolerance
Lowe syndrome
Metachromatic leukodystrophy
Dysproteinemic states
Myeloma kidney
Light chain deposition disease
Primary and secondary hyperparathyroidism
Drugs or toxins
Outdated tetracycline
Ifosfamide
Gentamicin
Steptozocin
Lead
Cadmium
Mercury
Tubulointerstitial diseases
Posttransplant rejection
Balkan nephropathy
Medullary cystic disease
Other
Bone fibroma
Osteopetrosis
Paroxysmal nocturnal hemoglobinuria

TABLE 11 Causes of Hypokalemic Distal Renal Tubular Acidosis
Primary
Idiopathic
Familial
Secondary
Autoimmune disorders
Hypergammaglobulinemia
Sjögren syndrome
Primary biliary cirrhosis
Systemic lupus erythematosus
Genetic disorders
Ehlers-Danlos syndrome
Marfan syndrome
Hereditary elliptocytosis
Drugs and toxins
Amphotericin B
Toluene[a]
Disorders associated with nephrocalcinosis
Hyperparathyroidism
Hypervitaminosis D
Idiopathic hypercalciuria
Tubulointerstitial diseases
Obstructive uropathy
Kidney transplantation

[a]Found in model glue, spray paint, and paint thinners. Prolonged, repeated toluene exposure can lead to irreversible electrolyte abnormalities.

TABLE 12 Causes of Hyperkalemic Distal Renal Tubular Acidosis
Mineralocorticoid Deficiency
Low renin, low aldosterone
Diabetes mellitus
Drugs
NSAIDs
Cyclosporine A
Tacrolimus
β-Blockers
High renin, low aldosterone
Adrenal destruction
Congenital enzyme defects
Drugs
Angiotensin-converting enzyme inhibitors
Angiotensin receptor blockers
Heparin
Ketoconazole
Cortical Collecting Duct Abnormalities
Absent or defective mineralocorticoid receptor
Drugs
Spironolactone
Eplerenone
Triamterene
Amiloride
Trimethoprim
Pentamidine
Chronic tubulointerstitial disease

Hyperkalemic Distal Renal Tubular Acidosis

Hyperkalemic distal RTA (type 4 RTA) should be suspected in patients with a normal anion gap metabolic acidosis associated with hyperkalemia and a slightly positive UAG (**Table 12**). Patients in whom this condition is caused by a defect in mineralocorticoid activity typically have a urine pH higher than 5.5.

In patients with structural damage to the collecting duct, the urine pH may be alkaline. This finding reflects both impaired hydrogen secretion and decreased urine ammonium excretion.

Hyperkalemic distal RTA occurs most often in patients with diabetes mellitus who have mild-to-moderate kidney insufficiency. However, the magnitude of hyperkalemia and acidosis is disproportionately severe for the observed degree of kidney insufficiency. This condition also may occur in patients with a urinary tract obstruction.

The primary goal of treatment in patients with hyperkalemic distal RTA is to correct the hyperkalemia. A decrease in the serum potassium level often results in correction of the acidosis by restoring kidney ammonium production and therefore increasing the buffer supply for distal acidification. Alkali therapy with sodium bicarbonate may treat the acidosis and hyperkalemia in patients with hyperkalemic distal RTA.

Drugs known to interfere in the synthesis or activity of aldosterone should be discontinued. In patients who do not have hypertension or fluid overload, administration of a synthetic mineralocorticoid such as fludrocortisone is an effective treatment for aldosterone deficiency; in patients with hypertension, a thiazide diuretic would be an appropriate alternative treatment. In addition, loop diuretics are indicated in patients with an estimated GFR of less than 30 mL/min/1.73 m^2; these agents increase distal sodium delivery, which stimulates potassium and hydrogen secretion in the collecting duct.

Renal Tubular Acidosis of Kidney Insufficiency

Patients with chronic kidney disease (CKD) initially develop a normal anion gap metabolic acidosis associated with normokalemia as the GFR decreases below 30 mL/min/1.73 m². In patients with a GFR of less than 15 mL/min/1.73 m², an anion gap metabolic acidosis usually develops and reflects a progressive inability to excrete phosphate, sulfate, and the sodium salts of various organic acids. Initiation of sodium bicarbonate once the serum sodium level decreases to less than 22 meq/L (22 mmol/L) achieves correction of the metabolic acidosis in patients with CKD.

Normal Anion Gap Metabolic Acidosis of Extrarenal Origin

Diarrhea

Loss of bicarbonate in intestinal secretions distal to the stomach can cause metabolic acidosis. Hypokalemia caused by gastrointestinal losses together with a low serum pH stimulate the synthesis of ammonia in the proximal tubule. The increase in availability of ammonia allows for a maximal increase in hydrogen secretion by the distal nephron. This large increase in buffer capacity may cause the urine pH to persistently remain above 6.0 during chronic diarrheal states.

However, a normal anion gap hypokalemic metabolic acidosis associated with a urine pH greater than 5.5 is consistent with both a diarrheal state and hypokalemic distal RTA. The clinical history usually helps to distinguish between these two conditions but would not be useful in the setting of surreptitious laxative abuse; therefore, the UAG is often used to establish a definitive diagnosis (see Figure 8).

Ileal Conduits

Surgical diversion of the ureter into the intestine may lead to the development of a normal anion gap metabolic acidosis due to systemic reabsorption of ammonium and chloride from the urinary fluid and exchange of chloride for bicarbonate through activation of the chloride-bicarbonate exchanger on the intestinal lumen. The likelihood of developing metabolic acidosis associated with ileal conduits increases with the amount of time the urine is in contact with the bowel and the total surface area of bowel that is exposed to urine.

Anion Gap Metabolic Acidosis

Lactic Acidosis

Lactic acidosis develops when an imbalance occurs between the production and use of lactic acid. Lactic acidosis due to increased production of lactic acid may occur in patients who engage in extreme exercise or have tonic-clonic seizures and is usually of short duration. Patients with sustained, severe lactic acidosis have a concomitant defect in lactic acid use.

Type A lactic acidosis is associated with underperfusion of tissue or acute hypoxia, whereas patients with type B lactic acidosis do not have these features (**Table 13**).

D-Lactic Acidosis

D-Lactic acidosis is a form of metabolic acidosis that can occur in patients who have the short-bowel syndrome, which may be caused by small-bowel resection or jejunoileal bypass surgery. In these patients, the colon receives large amounts of carbohydrates that are normally extensively reabsorbed in the small intestine. In the presence of colonic bacterial overgrowth, these substrates are metabolized into D-lactate and absorbed into the systemic circulation. Accumulation of D-lactate produces an anion gap metabolic acidosis that is associated with normal serum lactate levels, because the standard test for lactate is specific for L-lactate.

Patients with D-lactic acidosis typically seek medical attention after ingesting a high-carbohydrate meal and present with neurologic abnormalities such as confusion, slurred speech, and ataxia. Management of this condition primarily involves sodium bicarbonate therapy for acute acidosis and a low-carbohydrate diet and antimicrobial therapy to decrease the degree of bacterial overgrowth.

TABLE 13 Causes of Lactic Acidosis
Type A
Cardiogenic shock
Septic shock
Hemorrhagic shock
Acute hypoxia
Carbon monoxide poisoning
Anemia
Type B
Hereditary enzyme deficiency (glucose-6-phosphate dehydrogenase deficiency)
Drugs or toxins
Phenformin
Metformin
Cyanide
Salicylates
Ethylene glycol
Methanol
Propylene glycol
Linezolid
Propofol
Nucleoside reverse transcriptase inhibitors (stavudine, didanosine)
Systemic diseases
Liver failure
Malignancy

Diabetic Ketoacidosis

Diabetic ketoacidosis is usually associated with an anion gap acidosis, but a normal anion gap acidosis may be present early in the disease course when the extracellular fluid volume is nearly normal. The degree to which the anion gap is elevated is determined by the rapidity, severity, and duration of the ketoacidosis as well as the status of the extracellular fluid volume.

Insulin and intravenous fluids to correct volume depletion are indicated in patients with diabetic ketoacidosis. Because diabetic ketoacidosis commonly causes deficiencies in potassium, magnesium, and phosphate, intravenous replacement therapy with these electrolytes also may be warranted.

Alcoholic Ketoacidosis

Ketoacidosis may develop in patients with a history of chronic ethanol abuse; decreased food intake; and, often, nausea and vomiting. The alcohol withdrawal, volume depletion, and starvation that occur in these patients significantly increase the levels of circulating catecholamines, which results in the peripheral mobilization of fatty acids that is much greater than would be associated with starvation alone. In addition, the metabolism of alcohol leads to an increase in the reduced-oxidized nicotinamide adenine dinucleotide ratio, causing a higher β-hydroxybutyrate-acetoacetate ratio.

Stimulation of insulin release leads to diminished fatty acid mobilization from adipose tissue as well as decreased hepatic output of ketoacids. Therefore, glucose administration leads to the rapid resolution of acidosis in patients with alcoholic ketoacidosis.

Ethylene Glycol and Methanol Poisoning

Ethylene glycol and methanol poisoning are characterized by a severe anion gap metabolic acidosis accompanied by an osmolal gap. An osmolal gap is present when the measured plasma osmolality exceeds the calculated plasma osmolality by >10 mosm/kg H_2O (10 mmol/kg H_2O) (see Osmolality and Tonicity in Fluids and Electrolytes).

These conditions are also associated with lactic acidosis, which contributes to the elevated anion gap.

Ethylene glycol is a component of antifreeze and solvents. Metabolism of ethylene glycol by alcohol dehydrogenase generates various acids, including glycolic, oxalic, and formic acids.

Ethylene glycol poisoning initially causes neurologic manifestations similar to ethanol intoxication, and seizures and coma can rapidly develop. If this condition is not treated, noncardiogenic pulmonary edema and cardiovascular collapse may occur. Approximately 24 to 48 hours after ethylene glycol ingestion, patients may develop flank pain and kidney failure that is often accompanied by calcium oxalate crystals in the urine.

Methanol is also metabolized by alcohol dehydrogenase and forms formaldehyde, which is then converted to formic acid. Clinical manifestations of methanol ingestion include acute inebriation followed by an asymptomatic period lasting 24 to 36 hours. Abdominal pain caused by pancreatitis, seizures, and coma may then develop. Because formic acid is toxic to the retina, blindness also may occur. Furthermore, methanol intoxication is associated with hemorrhage in the white matter and putamen, which can lead to a parkinsonian syndrome.

Management of ethylene glycol and methanol poisoning involves supportive measures such as stabilization of the respiratory system, treatment of acidosis, reducing the metabolism of these compounds, and accelerating the removal of the alcohol from the body through methods such as hemodialysis. Fomepizole is the agent of choice to inhibit alcohol dehydrogenase and prevent formation of toxic metabolites.

Salicylate Poisoning

Aspirin poisoning leads to increased lactic acid production. The accumulation of lactic acid, salicylic acid, ketoacids, and other organic acids results in an anion gap metabolic acidosis. Salicylates also have a concomitant direct stimulatory effect on the respiratory center. Increased ventilation lowers the arterial P_{CO_2}, which contributes to the development of a respiratory alkalosis.

Salicylate poisoning manifests as either a respiratory alkalosis or an anion gap metabolic acidosis in adults, whereas affected children usually only have an anion gap metabolic acidosis. Clinical manifestations of salicylate poisoning in adults may include tinnitus, tachypnea, tachycardia, excessive sweating, and nausea and vomiting. Patients with severe toxicity may develop hyperthermia, pulmonary edema, hematemesis, and mental status changes.

In addition to supportive therapy, initial management of salicylate poisoning includes correcting the systemic acidemia and increasing the urine pH. Increasing the systemic pH leads to an increase in the ionized fraction of salicylic acid, which results in decreased accumulation of the drug in the central nervous system. An alkaline urine pH also favors increased urine excretion of the salicylate. Hemodialysis is warranted in patients with serum salicylate concentrations above 80 mg/dL (5.8 mmol/L) or in the setting of severe clinical toxicity.

Pyroglutamic Acidosis

Pyroglutamic acidosis occurs in critically ill patients who receive therapeutic doses of acetaminophen; in this setting, acetaminophen metabolism and oxidative stress associated with critical illness lead to a decrease in glutathione levels, which causes pyroglutamic acid to accumulate. Pyroglutamic acidosis manifests as an anion gap metabolic acidosis accompanied by mental status changes ranging from confusion to coma. An unexplained anion gap metabolic acidosis in the presence of recent acetaminophen ingestion should raise suspicion for this condition.

Mixed Metabolic Disorders

The process for determining if a complicating metabolic disturbance is present along with an anion gap metabolic acidosis involves calculating the corrected bicarbonate level. If the corrected bicarbonate level is less than 24 + 2 meq/L (24 + 2 mmol/L), a coexisting normal anion gap metabolic acidosis is present; conversely, if the corrected bicarbonate level is greater than 24 + 2 meq/L (24 + 2 mmol/L), a coexisting metabolic alkalosis is present.

The corrected bicarbonate level is obtained using the following formula:

$$\text{Corrected Bicarbonate} = [\text{Measured HCO}_3] + [\text{Anion Gap} - 12]$$

This formula is based upon the assumption that the measured anion gap represents in part the bicarbonate that was consumed in attempting to compensate for the process producing the anion gap metabolic acidosis. If the measured anion gap is added to the measured bicarbonate concentration and the normal anion gap of 12 is subtracted, then the result should represent the bicarbonate concentration if the anion gap acidosis were not present, hence the name "corrected bicarbonate." Finding an abnormal bicarbonate concentration after this correction is made suggests the presence of an additional normal anion gap acidosis if the corrected bicarbonate level is lower than normal or a metabolic alkalosis if the corrected bicarbonate level is higher than normal.

KEY POINTS

- Treatment of proximal renal tubular acidosis may require sodium bicarbonate, and the addition of a thiazide diuretic may be warranted.
- Treatment of hypokalemic distal renal tubular acidosis includes correction of hypokalemia followed by administration of alkali therapy.
- The primary treatment of hyperkalemic distal renal tubular acidosis is to correct the hyperkalemia.
- Accumulation of D-lactate produces an anion gap metabolic acidosis that is associated with normal serum lactate levels.
- Ethylene glycol and methanol poisoning are characterized by a severe anion gap metabolic acidosis accompanied by an osmolal gap greater than 10 mosm/kg H_2O (10 mmol/kg H_2O).
- Fomepizole is the agent of choice to inhibit alcohol dehydrogenase and prevent formation of toxic metabolites in patients with ethylene glycol and methanol poisoning.
- An unexplained anion gap metabolic acidosis in the presence of recent acetaminophen ingestion should raise suspicion for pyroglutamic acidosis.

Metabolic Alkalosis

Metabolic alkalosis develops when a decrease in acid or increase in alkali results in the addition of new bicarbonate, which may be generated by kidney or extrarenal mechanisms, to the blood. To maintain a metabolic alkalosis, the capacity of the kidney to correct the alkalosis must be impaired or the capacity to reabsorb bicarbonate must be enhanced, and at least one of the following features is usually required: decreased effective arterial blood volume (EABV), hypokalemia, or hypochloremia (**Figure 9**). Treatment is focused on correction of the mechanism responsible for metabolic alkalosis.

Metabolic alkalosis is generally benign. However, alkalemia can lead to respiratory depression and decreased delivery of oxygen to the tissues and a high blood pH can cause decreased tissue perfusion. Therefore, aggressive correction of the alkalosis is particularly important in critically ill patients, in whom perfusion of the heart and brain is essential.

Classification and Evaluation

Assessment of the EABV can help to determine whether a metabolic alkalosis is saline resistant (**Table 14**). If the EABV can be restored with saline, the metabolic alkalosis can be easily corrected; however, numerous types of metabolic alkalosis respond poorly to saline. Saline-resistant metabolic alkalosis is generally maintained by a combination of increased mineralocorticoid levels, increased distal sodium delivery, and hypokalemia.

Saline-Responsive Metabolic Alkalosis Associated with a Decreased Effective Arterial Blood Volume

Gastrointestinal Acid Loss

Vomiting or nasogastric suction can cause a loss of gastric acid that generates a metabolic alkalosis. This alkalosis is maintained by volume contraction due to loss of sodium chloride in the gastric fluid. During active vomiting, the plasma bicarbonate concentration is usually higher than the threshold for reabsorption in the proximal nephron. The resultant bicarbonaturia leads to increased excretion of sodium and potassium bicarbonate, which results in further total body sodium depletion and the development of potassium depletion.

During this active phase, the urine chloride level is typically less than 15 meq/L (15 mmol/L) and is accompanied by elevated urine sodium and potassium levels and a urine pH

TABLE 14 Classification of Metabolic Alkalosis

	Low EABV	Low EABV	High EABV
Urine Chloride (meq/L)	<15	>15	>15
Response to Saline	Saline responsive	Saline resistant	Saline resistant

EABV = effective arterial blood volume.

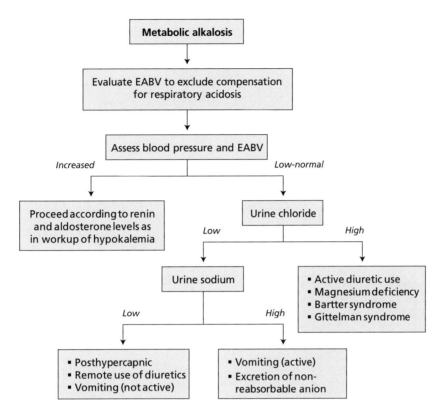

FIGURE 9.
Approach to the patient with metabolic alkalosis.

EABV = effective arterial blood volume.

between 7 and 8. When the patient stops vomiting, an equilibrium is established such that the bicarbonaturia resolves; however, a metabolic alkalosis is maintained by the volume contraction, potassium depletion, and reduced GFR. Among these factors, the decreased EABV is primarily responsible for maintaining the metabolic alkalosis, and administration of saline results in bicarbonaturia and correction of the metabolic alkalosis.

Diuretic Use
Thiazide and loop diuretics commonly cause a metabolic alkalosis that is generated in the distal nephron by the combination of high aldosterone levels and enhanced distal delivery of sodium. If diuretics are stopped and the patient remains on a low-sodium diet, the alkalosis will be maintained because the patients are usually volume contracted and hypokalemic. Saline infusion is indicated to correct this condition.

Saline-Resistant Metabolic Alkalosis Associated with a Decreased Effective Arterial Blood Volume
In some forms of metabolic alkalosis, the alkalosis is maintained by a decreased EABV as well as additional factors, such as increased distal delivery of sodium and a mineralocorticoid effect (**Table 15**). Saline infusions in these settings may

TABLE 15 Treatment of Saline-Resistant Metabolic Alkalosis	
Cause	**Treatment**
Decreased EABV	
Thiazide and loop diuretics	Discontinue causative drug; replete EABV
Magnesium deficiency	Replete magnesium deficit
Gitelman syndrome	Amiloride, triamterene, or spironolactone; potassium supplements and magnesium supplements
Bartter syndrome	Amiloride, triamterene, or spironolactone; potassium supplements; magnesium supplements if needed
Increased EABV	
Renin-secreting tumor	Remove tumor
Primary hyperaldosteronism	Remove tumor; spironolactone for BAH
Glucocorticoid-remediable aldosteronism	Dexamethasone
Liddle syndrome	Amiloride or triamterene
BAH = bilateral adrenal hyperplasia; EABV = effective arterial blood volume.	

decrease the metabolic alkalosis but will not completely resolve this condition.

Saline-Resistant Metabolic Alkalosis Associated with an Increased Effective Arterial Blood Volume

Metabolic alkalosis that is associated with a high EABV is both generated and maintained by increased mineralocorticoid activity accompanied by increased distal delivery of sodium. Potassium deficiency also occurs in this setting and exacerbates the alkalosis.

The preferred treatment of metabolic alkalosis in patients with volume expansion and primary mineralocorticoid excess is to remove the underlying cause. When this intervention is not possible, therapy is directed at blocking the actions of the mineralocorticoid at the level of the kidney (see Table 15).

KEY POINTS

- Saline-responsive metabolic alkalosis is characterized by a low effective arterial blood volume and a urine chloride level less than 15 meq/L (15 mmol/L).
- The preferred treatment of metabolic alkalosis in patients with volume expansion is to remove the underlying cause of the persistent mineralocorticoid activity or block actions of mineralocorticoid at the level of the kidney.

Respiratory Alkalosis

Primary respiratory alkalosis is characterized by an arterial PCO_2 of less than 35 mm Hg. Liver failure is a common cause of primary respiratory alkalosis. Salicylate poisoning and elevated progesterone levels associated with pregnancy also may cause this condition. In hospitalized patients, respiratory alkalosis is the presenting manifestation of gram-negative sepsis.

Classification and Evaluation

Primary respiratory alkalosis must be differentiated from secondary respiratory alkalosis, which is a compensatory mechanism in the setting of primary metabolic acidosis (see Table 9).

Acute respiratory alkalosis is characterized by an acute decrease in the arterial PCO_2, which results in a bicarbonate-chloride shift in the erythrocytes and a decrease in the serum bicarbonate concentration by 2 meq/L (2 mmol/L) for every 10 mm Hg decrease in the arterial PCO_2.

Chronic respiratory alkalosis is characterized by a 2- to 3-day process during which a transient bicarbonate diuresis occurs. At steady state, the serum bicarbonate concentration decreases by 4 to 5 meq/L (4 to 5 mmol/L) for each 10 mm Hg decrease in the arterial PCO_2.

In order to maintain a normal extracellular fluid volume in the setting of increased urinary loss of sodium bicarbonate, the kidney retains sodium chloride. Patients with chronic respiratory alkalosis therefore typically have hyperchloremia. These patients also have a 3- to 5-meq/L (3- to 5-mmol/L) increase in the serum anion gap because of the greater fixed negative charge on serum albumin as well as an increased serum lactate concentration; this increase in lactate production is caused by the stimulatory effect of high serum pH on phosphofructokinase, which regulates the rate of glycolysis.

Clinical Manifestations

Both primary and secondary respiratory alkalosis often initially manifest as tachypnea. Acute hypocapnia decreases cerebral blood flow and causes binding of free calcium to albumin in the blood. Mild respiratory alkalosis may cause lightheadedness and palpitations. More profound respiratory alkalosis may cause symptoms that resemble those of hypocalcemia, including paresthesias of the extremities and circumoral area and carpopedal spasm. Patients with ischemic heart disease may occasionally develop cardiac arrhythmias, ischemic electrocardiographic changes, and angina pectoris.

Management

Primary respiratory alkalosis is treated by correcting the underlying cause. Reassurance is indicated for patients with respiratory alkalosis associated with the hyperventilation syndrome. In addition, rebreathing into a paper bag or other closed system causes the arterial PCO_2 to increase, resulting in partial correction of hypocapnia and symptomatic improvement.

Respiratory alkalosis frequently develops as a complication of the hypoxia that occurs at high altitudes. Administration of oxygen or a return to lower altitudes can reverse the respiratory alkalosis that develops in this setting.

KEY POINTS

- Acute compensation for respiratory alkalosis is characterized by a 2 meq/L (2 mmol/L) decrease in serum bicarbonate for each 10 mm Hg decrease in the arterial PCO_2.
- Chronic compensation for respiratory alkalosis is characterized by a 5 meq/L (5 mmol/L) decrease in serum bicarbonate for each 10 mm Hg decrease in arterial PCO_2.
- Respiratory alkalosis may cause lightheadedness and palpitations and symptoms that resemble those of hypocalcemia, including paresthesias and carpopedal spasm.
- Reassurance and rebreathing into a paper bag or other closed system are indicated for patients with respiratory alkalosis associated with the hyperventilation syndrome.

Respiratory Acidosis

Primary respiratory acidosis is characterized by the presence of acidemia and hypercapnia. The development of respiratory acidosis is usually multifactorial. Major causes of carbon dioxide retention include disease or a disorder of a component of the respiratory system, including the central and peripheral nervous systems, respiratory muscles, thoracic cage, pleural space, airways, and lung parenchyma.

Diagnosis

Acute respiratory acidosis is associated with an increase in the plasma bicarbonate concentration by 1 meq/L (1 mmol/L) for every 10 mm Hg elevation in the arterial P_{CO_2}. After 24 to 48 hours, proximal tubular cells increase hydrogen secretion, which results in accelerated bicarbonate reabsorption and increased kidney excretion of sodium chloride. Chronic respiratory acidosis is characterized by a 3.5 meq/L (3.5 mmol/L) increase in bicarbonate for each 10 mm Hg elevation in the arterial P_{CO_2}. Serum bicarbonate concentrations higher or lower than these values suggest the presence of a mixed respiratory and metabolic acid-base disorder.

Primary respiratory acidosis develops as a result of ineffective alveolar ventilation and is suggested by a P_{CO_2} higher than 45 mm Hg. However, a P_{CO_2} less than this value may indicate respiratory acidosis in a patient with primary metabolic acidosis that is not adequately compensated by alveolar ventilation. This condition must be differentiated from primary respiratory acidosis. The differential diagnosis of acute and chronic respiratory acidosis includes various conditions of the respiratory system (**Table 16**).

Clinical Manifestations

Carbon dioxide diffuses and equilibrates across the blood-brain barrier much more rapidly than bicarbonate, which results in a more rapid decrease in cerebrospinal fluid and cerebral interstitial pH. Therefore, acute respiratory acidosis is typically significantly more symptomatic than acute metabolic acidosis.

Respiratory acidosis may manifest as hypercapnic encephalopathy, a clinical syndrome with initial symptoms that include irritability, headache, mental cloudiness, apathy, confusion, anxiety, and restlessness that can progress to asterixis, transient psychosis, delirium, somnolence, and coma. Severe hypercapnia may cause decreased myocardial contractility, arrhythmias, and peripheral vasodilatation, particularly when the serum pH decreases below 7.1.

Treatment

Patients with acute respiratory acidosis are primarily at risk for hypoxemia rather than hypercapnia or acidemia. Therefore, initial therapy should focus on establishing and securing a patent airway in order to provide adequate oxygenation.

Excessive oxygen may worsen hypoventilation in patients with chronic respiratory acidosis and should be avoided in this population. When mechanical ventilation is required, the arterial P_{CO_2} should be decreased slowly and with caution to minimize the risk of inducing posthypercapnic metabolic alkalosis due to the high serum bicarbonate concentration. In order to normalize the acid-base status, the kidneys must excrete this bicarbonate. However, this excretion will not occur when the EABV is reduced either because of sodium depletion secondary to restricted salt intake or diuretic therapy or because of a sodium-retentive state, such as heart failure or cirrhosis. Correction of the superimposed metabolic alkalosis can usually be achieved with saline and discontinuation of loop diuretics if these agents are being used. However, patients with edema and with heart failure may require acetazolamide to correct the alkalosis.

KEY POINTS

- Primary respiratory acidosis is characterized by the presence of acidemia and hypercapnia.
- Serum bicarbonate concentrations higher or lower than the expected compensation suggest the presence of a mixed respiratory and metabolic acid-base disorder.
- Patients with acute respiratory acidosis are primarily at risk for hypoxemia rather than hypercapnia or acidemia.
- Excessive oxygen may worsen hypoventilation in patients with chronic respiratory acidosis.
- Correction of induced posthypercapnic metabolic alkalosis can usually be achieved with saline and discontinuation of loop diuretics if these agents are being used.

Bibliography

Colussi G, Bettinelli A, Tedeschi S, et al. A thiazide test for the diagnosis of renal tubular hypokalemic disorders. Clin J Am Soc Nephrol. 2007;2(3):454-460. [PMID: 17699451]

Fenves AZ, Kirkpatrick HM 3rd, Patel VV, Sweetman L, Emmett M. Increased anion gap metabolic acidosis as a result of 5-oxoproline

TABLE 16 Differential Diagnosis of Respiratory Acidosis
Inhibition of the medullary respiratory center
Disorders of the chest wall and the respiratory muscles
Airway obstruction
Disorders affecting gas exchange across the pulmonary capillaries
Increased carbon dioxide production
Mechanical ventilation

(pyroglutamic acid): a role for acetaminophen. Clin J Am Soc Nephrol. 2006;1(3):441-447. [PMID: 17699243]

Kraut JA, Madias NE. Serum anion gap: its uses and limitations in clinical medicine. Clin J Am Soc Nephrol. 2007;2(1):162-174. [PMID: 17699401]

Sabatini S, Kurtzman NA. Bicarbonate therapy in severe metabolic acidosis. J Am Soc Nephrol. 2009;20(4):692-695. [PMID: 18322160]

Walsh SB, Shirley DG, Wrong OM, Unwin RJ. Urinary acidification assessed by simultaneous furosemide and fludrocortisones treatment: an alternative to ammonium chloride. Kidney Int. 2007; 71(12):1310-1316. [PMID: 17410104]

Hypertension

Epidemiology

Hypertension affects one in four adults worldwide, and poorly controlled hypertension is the leading cause of death globally. Hypertension is more prevalent in non-Hispanic black persons and older persons than in the general population. Approximately 67% of patients older than 60 years of age and more than 75% of patients older than 80 years of age have hypertension.

Associated Complications

Blood pressure measurements higher than 120/80 mm Hg place patients at increased risk for cardiovascular disease. Although hypertension is more strongly associated with risk for stroke than risk for coronary heart disease, the risks for both stroke and coronary heart disease begin to increase at a systolic pressure of approximately 115 mm Hg and double for every 20/10 mm Hg increase in blood pressure.

Additional conditions associated with hypertension include heart failure, progressive atherosclerosis, kidney failure, and dementia. Furthermore, risk factors for cardiovascular disease other than hypertension, diabetes mellitus, and obesity often coexist with hypertension and compound the risk for cardiovascular disease.

Pulse pressure, defined as the difference between the systolic and diastolic blood pressure, may help to determine a patient's risk for cardiovascular disease. A high pulse pressure indicates the presence of stiffer, less-compliant arteries. Elderly persons with a higher pulse pressure are considered to be at particularly high risk for cardiovascular disease. However, whether increased pulse pressure is an independent risk factor for cardiovascular events remains uncertain.

KEY POINT

- Blood pressure measurements higher than 120/80 mm Hg place patients at increased risk for cardiovascular disease.

Evaluation

Blood Pressure Measurement

Office Measurement

Blood pressure is most often measured during a visit to the office using a mercury sphygmomanometer, an aneroid sphygmomanometer, or the oscillometric technique. Mercury sphygmomanometers provide the most accurate measurement but are being eliminated in the United States and are currently the least commonly used method of blood pressure measurement. Aneroid and oscillometric devices are accurate but must be maintained and calibrated.

Experts recommend that multiple blood pressure measurements be obtained. In adults, classification of hypertension is based on an average of two or more readings obtained more than 1 minute apart at two or more visits.

Ambulatory Blood Pressure Monitoring

Ambulatory blood pressure monitoring provides multiple blood pressure readings over a prolonged period of time. This method evaluates mean 24-hour blood pressure; mean daytime blood pressure; mean nighttime blood pressure; the average difference between waking and sleeping blood pressure to evaluate for nocturnal dipping (which may be defined as a decrease in mean arterial blood pressure of >10% during sleep); and blood pressure variability.

Prediction of Cardiovascular Risk

Ambulatory blood pressure monitoring is a better predictor of cardiovascular events than office measurement. Experts are uncertain as to whether the 24-hour mean blood pressure or the mean daytime blood pressure is the best predictor of these events, but the mean 24-hour blood pressure is the most widely used. Failure of the blood pressure to decrease by at least 10% during sleep, known as nondipping, as well as an excessive morning surge in blood pressure have been associated with increased cardiovascular risk, particularly for stroke.

Diagnostic thresholds for ambulatory blood pressure monitoring based on outcomes data for cardiovascular risk suggest that a daytime awake average blood pressure measurement of 130 to 135/85 mm Hg is considered the normal threshold and corresponds to an office reading of approximately 140/90 mm Hg (**Table 17**).

Other Uses

Because ambulatory blood pressure monitoring demonstrates the efficacy of blood pressure control over a 24-hour period, this method of monitoring can help to guide pharmacologic therapy for hypertension. This method of monitoring also helps to prevent overtreatment of hypertension, particularly in elderly patients who are prone to symptomatic episodes of low blood pressure. Ambulatory blood pressure monitoring can be beneficial, but its use is limited by cost, the patient's

TABLE 17 Diagnostic Thresholds for Ambulatory Blood Pressure Monitoring Based on 10-Year Cardiovascular Risk[a]

Category	Office Measurement (mm Hg)	Mean 24-Hour Measurement (mm Hg)	Mean Daytime Measurement (mm Hg)	Mean Nighttime Measurement (mm Hg)
Optimal	120/80	115/75	120/80	100/65
Normal	130/85	125/75	130/85	110/70
Hypertension	140/90	130/80	140/85	120/70

[a]These thresholds were derived from 24-hour ambulatory blood pressure monitoring performed in 5682 participants enrolled in prospective population studies in Europe and Japan. In multivariate analyses, ambulatory blood pressure thresholds yielded 10-year cardiovascular risks similar to those associated with optimal, normal, and high blood office measurements.

Modified with permission from Kikuya M, Hansen TW, Thijs L, et al; International Database on Ambulatory blood pressure monitoring in relation to Cardiovascular Outcomes Investigators. Circulation. 2007;115(16):2145-2152. [PMID: 17420350] Copyright 2007, American Heart Association, Inc.

willingness to undergo this monitoring, and the availability of adequate equipment in routine office settings.

Blood pressure variability and the ambulatory arterial stiffness index have been shown to be independent correlates of cardiovascular morbidity and mortality. The ambulatory arterial stiffness index can be obtained by plotting the systolic blood pressures against the diastolic blood pressures obtained via ambulatory blood pressure monitoring over a 24-hour period, calculating the regression slope, and subtracting 1 from this calculated figure.

Small studies have shown that home blood pressure monitoring compares favorably with ambulatory blood pressure monitoring regarding prediction of adverse cardiovascular events. If ambulatory blood pressure measurement is not available or is prohibitively expensive, home blood pressure monitoring may be considered a reasonable substitute.

Physical Examination and Laboratory Studies

A careful history should be obtained in patients with hypertension to evaluate for secondary hypertension. In addition, all patients with hypertension should be evaluated for target organ damage such as heart disease, cerebrovascular disease, kidney disease, and peripheral vascular disease; familial disorders; and lifestyle factors that may exacerbate hypertension.

Physical examination of a patient with hypertension should include measurement of vital signs, BMI, cardiopulmonary examination, auscultation of the major blood vessels to identify bruits, funduscopic examination, abdominal examination, neurologic examination, and evaluation of the extremities for edema and circulatory abnormalities.

A complete blood count, lipid and biochemical profiles, urinalysis, and electrocardiography can help to suggest the presence of secondary hypertension and provide evidence of target organ damage. The European Hypertension Society guidelines also recommend evaluation for microalbuminuria, but guidelines from the Seventh Report of the Joint National Committee on Prevention, Detection, Evaluation and Treatment of High Blood Pressure (JNC 7) advocate that this testing remain optional.

Echocardiography helps to monitor patients with manifestations of hypertensive heart disease, such as left ventricular

hypertrophy, diastolic dysfunction, and heart failure, but is not recommended for all patients with hypertension.

KEY POINTS

- In adults, classification of hypertension is based on an average of two or more blood pressure readings obtained more than 1 minute apart at two or more visits.

- A daytime awake average blood pressure measurement of 130 to 135/85 mm Hg is considered the normal threshold for ambulatory blood pressure monitoring and corresponds to an office reading of approximately 140/90 mm Hg.

- Ambulatory blood pressure measurement can help to guide pharmacologic therapy for hypertension and helps to prevent overtreatment of hypertension.

- All patients with hypertension should be evaluated for target organ damage, familial disorders, and lifestyle factors that may exacerbate hypertension.

Classification

JNC 7 guidelines define normal blood pressure as less than 120/80 mm Hg and hypertension as 140/90 mm Hg or higher (**Table 18**).

Prehypertension

According to JNC 7 guidelines, prehypertension is defined as a systolic blood pressure of 120 to 139 mm Hg or a diastolic blood pressure of 80 to 89 mm Hg. Lifestyle modifications and pharmacologic therapy have been evaluated as a means of *preventing* hypertension in patients who meet these criteria.

The Trials of Hypertension Prevention (TOHP) study demonstrated small blood pressure reductions and a decrease in the incidence of overt hypertension with lifestyle modifications in patients with prehypertension. The Trial of Preventing Hypertension study evaluated the effects of a 2-year period of drug treatment followed by placebo in 809 patients with prehypertension. Findings of this study showed a small reduction in the incidence of hypertension after 4

TABLE 18 Seventh Report of the Joint National Committee on Prevention, Detection, Evaluation and Treatment of High Blood Pressure Classification of Blood Pressure for Adults 18 Years and Older

Category	Systolic (mm Hg)		Diastolic (mm Hg)
Normal[a]	<120	and	<80
Prehypertension[b]	120-139	or	80-89
Stage 1 hypertension	140-159	or	90-99
Stage 2 hypertension	≥160	or	≥100

[a]This blood pressure measurement is defined as "optimal" by all other hypertension societies, such as the British Hypertension Society, European Society of Hypertension/European Society of Cardiology, and the World Health Organization/International Society of Hypertension.

[b]Guidelines from other hypertension societies classify a systolic or diastolic blood pressure within this range as high normal.

Modified with permission from the U.S. Department of Health and Human Services. Seventh Report of the Joint National Committee on Prevention, Detection, Evaluation, and Treatment of High Blood Pressure (JNC 7). www.nhlbi.nih.gov/guidelines/hypertension/phycard.pdf. Published May, 2003. Accessed July 10, 2009.

years in the treatment group, but use of pharmacologic therapy in patients with prehypertension remains controversial.

Essential Hypertension

Pathogenesis

More than 90% of patients with hypertension who are evaluated in the primary care setting have essential, or primary, hypertension. Essential hypertension is a heterogeneous, polygenic disorder resulting from dysregulation of hormones, proteins, and neurogenic factors involved in blood pressure regulation as well as factors such as diet and activity level.

Impaired kidney sodium excretion has a central role in the pathogenesis of hypertension. Approximately 30% to 60% of blood pressure variability is inherited, but common genes that significantly affect blood pressure have not yet been identified. Polymorphisms in alleles at many different loci interact with behavioral and environmental factors to contribute to the final disease trait. Rare monogenic forms of hypertension also have been identified (**Table 19**).

Nearly all genes identified in the pathogenesis of hypertension cause alterations in kidney sodium handling, which confirms the importance of kidney sodium excretion in the development of this condition. Studies also have identified potential mechanisms in essential hypertension, such as alterations in with-no-lysine (WNK) kinases, aldosterone synthase, and the epithelial sodium channel.

Management

The goal of treatment of hypertension is to reduce cardiovascular morbidity and mortality by lowering blood pressure. Lowering blood pressure has definitively been shown to reduce stroke, myocardial infarction, heart failure, and overall cardiovascular mortality. The relative risk reduction associated with lowering blood pressure is similar across all categories of baseline risk, but the reduction in absolute risk is greater and the number needed to treat smaller in those with a higher baseline absolute risk, such as older patients with higher blood pressure and multiple cardiovascular risk factors.

JNC 7 guidelines recommend lifestyle modifications and drug treatment for all patients with stage 1 or greater hypertension, regardless of absolute risk. Lifestyle modifications help to lower blood pressure and modify additional cardiovascular risk factors, such as obesity, diabetes, and dyslipidemia (**Table 20**). The PREMIER trial showed that lifestyle modifications such as maintaining weight loss and participating in a regular exercise program for 18 months were associated with sustained blood pressure control and a reduced risk for chronic cardiovascular disease.

Evidence obtained from clinical trials suggests that the goal of antihypertensive treatment is to reduce blood pressure to below 140/90 mm Hg in the general population. The American Heart Association recommends a blood pressure target of 130/80 mm Hg for those with coronary artery disease, carotid artery disease, peripheral artery disease, abdominal aortic aneurysm, and a Framingham 10-year risk score of 10% or greater. However, data clearly demonstrate a linear, progressive increased risk of ischemic heart disease and stroke in patients with blood pressures higher than 115/75 mm Hg, which suggests that these targets may be too high. Clinical trials addressing lower blood pressure targets are currently being planned.

Choosing an Antihypertensive Agent

Most antihypertensive agents reduce blood pressure by 15% to 20%, and all classes of antihypertensive drugs effectively reduce cardiovascular morbidity and mortality compared with placebo. Angiotensin-converting enzyme (ACE) inhibitors and angiotensin receptor blockers (ARBs) are indicated in patients with heart failure and proteinuric kidney disease. Diuretics are indicated in patients with salt-sensitive hypertension and may be particularly effective in the elderly and those with reduced GFR. β-Blockers should be used for those with coronary artery disease or migraine headaches. Clinical trials have shown that achieving appropriate blood pressure targets is more important in reducing morbidity and mortality than the choice of antihypertensive therapy. Achieving blood pressure targets is particularly critical in patients with evidence of target organ damage and those who are at greater risk for target organ damage, such as black patients.

TABLE 19 Monogenic Forms of Hypertension

Disorder	Pathogenesis	Clinical Features	Treatment
Liddle syndrome	Autosomal dominant; gain of function of epithelial sodium channel	Elevated blood pressure, hypokalemic metabolic alkalosis, low renin and aldosterone levels, excess sodium retention	Amiloride, thiazide diuretics, spironolactone
Glucocorticoid-remediable aldosteronism	Autosomal dominant; regulation of aldosterone secretion by ACTH	Elevated blood pressure, hypokalemic metabolic alkalosis, low renin levels, moderately high aldosterone levels	Aldosterone blockade, corticosteroids
Apparent mineralocorticoid excess	Autosomal recessive; activation of mineralocorticoid receptor by cortisol	Elevated blood pressure, younger age at presentation, hypokalemic metabolic alkalosis, low renin and aldosterone levels	Thiazide diuretics, aldosterone blockade
Type 2 pseudohypoaldosteronism (Gordon syndrome)	Autosomal dominant; mutations in WNK kinases 1 and 4	Elevated blood pressure, hyperkalemia, hyperchloremic metabolic acidosis, low renin and aldosterone levels	Thiazide diuretics
Mineralocorticoid receptor activation	Mutation in mineralocorticoid receptor	Elevated blood pressure, younger age, low renin and aldosterone levels, mineralocorticoid receptor activation by steroids such as progesterone, exacerbation in pregnancy	Thiazide diuretics
Mutations in peroxisome-activated receptor-γ	Autosomal dominant; loss of function mutation in peroxisome proliferator–activated receptor-γ	Insulin resistance, hypertension	Lifestyle modification, antihypertensive agents, insulin-sensitizing agents
Hypertension and brachydactyly	Autosomal dominant	Short stature, mechanism of hypertension unknown	Antihypertensive agents

ACTH = adrenocorticotropic hormone; WNK kinase = with-no-lysine kinase.

Choosing an antihypertensive agent with minimum adverse effects is important. Patient characteristics, including comorbid conditions, age, race, and history of efficacy and adverse reactions to previously used drugs, also should help to determine the most appropriate therapy (**Table 21**). For example, the treatment regimen for patients with hypertension who have a history of diabetic nephropathy or other proteinuric kidney diseases should include an ACE inhibitor or ARB.

Calcium channel blockers and diuretics are more effective in lowering blood pressure in patients who are likely to be sodium sensitive, such as older patients, black patients, and those with lower pretreatment plasma renin activity. Conversely, ACE inhibitors or β-blockers may be more

TABLE 20 Lifestyle Modifications Recommended for All Persons with Hypertension

Modification	Approximate Systolic Blood Pressure Reduction
Reduce weight	5-20 mm Hg/10 kg (22 lb) weight loss
Follow DASH diet[a]	8-14 mm Hg after 8 weeks
Participate in aerobic physical activity for 30 to 34 minutes most days	4-9 mm Hg
Reduce sodium intake to <100 mmol/24 h[b]	2-8 mm Hg
Limit daily alcohol consumption to two drinks for men and one drink for women	2-4 mm Hg
Smoking cessation	No effect but recommended for cardiovascular protection

DASH = Dietary Approaches to Stop Hypertension.

[a]The DASH diet is rich in fruits, vegetables, and low-fat dairy products with a reduced content of saturated and total fat.

[b]This amount is equivalent to 2.4 g of sodium or 6 g of sodium chloride.

Modified with permission from the U.S. Department of Health and Human Services. The Seventh Report of the Joint National Committee on Prevention, Detection, Evaluation and Treatment of High Blood Pressure. www.nhlbi.nih.gov/guidelines/hypertension/express.pdf. December, 2003. Accessed July 10, 2009.

TABLE 21 Compelling Indications, Contraindications, and Side Effects for Antihypertensive Drugs

Class of Drug	Compelling Indications	Contraindications	Side Effects
Thiazide diuretics	Heart failure, advanced age, volume-dependent hypertension, low-renin hypertension, systolic hypertension	Gout	Hypokalemia, hyperuricemia, glucose intolerance, hypercalcemia, impotence
Aldosterone antagonists	Primary aldosteronism, resistant hypertension, sleep apnea	Reduced GFR, hyperkalemia	Hyperkalemia, increased creatinine level, painful gynecomastia, menstrual irregularities, gastrointestinal distress
ACE inhibitors	Heart failure, left ventricular dysfunction, proteinuria, diabetic nephropathy, chronic kidney disease, post–myocardial infarction	Pregnancy, hyperkalemia	Cough, angioedema, hyperkalemia, potential increased creatinine level in patients with bilateral renal artery stenosis, rash, loss of taste, leukopenia (captopril)
Angiotensin receptor blockers	Same as ACE inhibitors; useful when ACE inhibitors are not tolerated	Pregnancy, hyperkalemia	Angioedema (rare), hyperkalemia, potential increased creatinine level in patients with bilateral renal artery stenosis
Calcium channel blockers	Systolic hypertension, cyclosporine-induced hypertension, angina, coronary heart disease	Heart block (for nondihydropyridine calcium channel blockers verapamil and diltiazem)	Headache, flushing, gingival hyperplasia, edema, constipation
β-Blockers	Angina, heart failure, post–myocardial infarction, migraine, tachyarrhythmias	Asthma and COPD, heart block	Bronchospasm, bradycardia, heart failure, impaired peripheral circulation, insomnia, fatigue, decreased exercise tolerance, hypertriglyceridemia
α-Blockers	Prostatic hyperplasia	Orthostatic hypotension	Headache, drowsiness, fatigue, weakness, postural hypotension

ACE = angiotensin-converting enzyme; COPD = chronic obstructive pulmonary disease; GFR = glomerular filtration rate.

effective in younger patients, white patients, and those with higher pretreatment plasma renin activity.

Some evidence suggests that β-blockers do not perform as well as comparator drugs, particularly in preventing stroke, and are no longer universally recommended as first-line agents in the absence of a compelling indication. However, JNC 7, the European Society of Hypertension, and the World Health Organization/International Society of Hypertension guidelines continue to recommend these agents for patients with a history of myocardial infarction and heart failure.

Finally, a reevaluation of findings from the Antihypertensive and Lipid-Lowering Treatment to Prevent Heart Attack Trial (ALLHAT) has shown that thiazide diuretics are superior to α-blockers, ACE inhibitors, and calcium channel blockers as initial therapy for reducing cardiovascular and kidney risk in patients with hypertension. Thiazide diuretics also were shown to be superior in preventing heart failure, and new-onset diabetes associated with use of these agents was not found to increase cardiovascular disease outcomes.

Combination Therapy

Patients with hypertension should be evaluated approximately every month until blood pressure targets are achieved. Monotherapy is effective in approximately 40% of unselected patients with hypertension. However, if single-agent therapy is ineffective after 1 to 3 months of treatment, switching to or adding a drug with a complementary mechanism of action is indicated; for example, a diuretic or calcium channel blocker can be added to an ACE inhibitor or an ARB.

Monotherapy is unlikely to be effective in patients whose blood pressure is more than 20 mm Hg above the blood pressure goal, and initial treatment with two antihypertensive agents may particularly be warranted in this setting. Patients with stage 2 or higher hypertension also often require treatment with more than one agent.

Novel Antihypertensive Agents

Aliskiren is a direct renin inhibitor that reversibly binds to the catalytic site of the enzyme and prevents cleavage of angiotensinogen. This agent lowers blood pressure moderately and is expected to be effective in patients in whom ACE inhibitors and ARBs also would be effective. Specific clinical advantages of renin inhibition compared with ACE inhibitors or ARBs have not been demonstrated.

Nebivolol is a third-generation β_1-blocker that is believed to stimulate production of nitric oxide. This agent may have a more favorable metabolic profile compared with other β-blockers, but whether this additional property is associated with clinically relevant benefits remains uncertain.

- Guidelines from the Seventh Report of the Joint National Committee on Prevention, Detection, Evaluation and Treatment of High Blood Pressure define normal blood pressure as less than 120/80 mm Hg and hypertension as 140/90 mm Hg or higher.

- Lifestyle modifications and drug treatment are indicated for all patients with stage 1 or greater hypertension.

- The goal of antihypertensive treatment is to reduce blood pressure to below 140/90 mm Hg in the general population.

- If single-agent antihypertensive therapy is ineffective after 1 to 3 months of treatment, switching to or adding a drug with a complementary mechanism of action is indicated.

- Initial treatment with two antihypertensive agents may particularly be warranted for patients whose blood pressure is more than 20 mm Hg above the blood pressure goal, and those with stage 2 or higher hypertension often require treatment with more than one agent.

Secondary Hypertension

Approximately 10% of cases of hypertension occur secondary to an underlying kidney or endocrine condition or exogenous substances such as oral contraceptives, NSAIDs, calcineurin inhibitors, sympathomimetic agents, and epoetin alfa. Secondary hypertension should be considered in patients with hypertension who have atypical clinical features and are resistant to antihypertensive therapy.

In patients with secondary hypertension, identifying specific abnormalities that cause elevated blood pressure can help to resolve this condition or determine more specific therapy. The most common causes of renovascular hypertension include kidney disease, primary aldosteronism, renovascular disease, and pheochromocytoma.

Kidney Disease

Hypertension is more common in patients with kidney disease than in the general population, and experts recommend lower blood pressure targets for patients with kidney disease. Target blood pressure measurements of less than 130/80 mm Hg are recommended for those with minimal proteinuria (defined as a 24-hour urine protein level below 1 g/24 h) and less than 125/75 mm Hg for those with significant proteinuria (defined as a 24-hour urine protein level above 1 g/24 h).

Primary Aldosteronism

Pathophysiology and Epidemiology

Primary aldosteronism consists of a heterogeneous group of disorders characterized by mineralocorticoid hypertension (hypertension in the setting of hypokalemic metabolic alkalosis and suppressed plasma renin activity) accompanied by anatomic abnormalities of the adrenal glands. Primary aldosteronism affects approximately 5% to 15% of patients with hypertension and may be the most common curable endocrine form of hypertension.

Diagnosis

Spontaneous hypokalemia is strongly suggestive of primary aldosteronism, but many patients with this condition have normal serum potassium levels. The plasma aldosterone-plasma renin ratio (ARR) is a screening test for primary aldosteronism that is useful even in patients who are taking antihypertensive agents except for aldosterone blockers. However, experts recommend that this study be performed after correction of hypokalemia and hypovolemia.

Patients with very low serum renin levels regardless of the aldosterone level almost always have an elevated ARR; therefore, in these patients, the ARR is helpful only if the serum aldosterone level is above 15 ng/dL (414 pmol/L). The normal range of the ARR varies among institutions because renin and aldosterone assays may differ, but an ARR above 25 is generally considered abnormal.

An elevated ARR alone is not diagnostic of primary aldosteronism unless nonsuppressible or autonomous aldosterone excess is demonstrated by the presence of a urine aldosterone excretion of 12 μg/24 h (33.2 nmol/d) or higher obtained after correction of hypokalemia and adherence to a high-sodium diet for 3 days. In some patients, administering an intravenous saline infusion also may demonstrate nonsuppressible serum aldosterone levels.

Once nonsuppressible or autonomous aldosterone production is demonstrated, adrenal imaging is indicated to reveal the adrenal anatomy and identify patients with unilateral disease such as an aldosterone-producing adenoma (Conn syndrome) or primary unilateral adrenal hyperplasia. High-resolution CT with thin cuts of the upper abdomen is the preferred imaging technique in these patients but may not accurately distinguish between a unilateral aldosterone-producing adenoma and bilateral idiopathic hyperaldosteronism. MRI may be more sensitive but is less specific for these conditions and should be reserved for patients with contraindications to CT scanning.

After biochemical confirmation of hyperaldosteronism, localization procedures differentiate aldosterone-producing adenomas or unilateral hyperplasia from bilateral hyperplasia. Adrenal vein sampling is considered the gold standard for demonstrating lateralization of aldosterone secretion and is recommended for patients who are candidates for adrenalectomy. However, adrenal vein sampling is technically difficult and may not be helpful if both adrenal veins are not successfully cannulated.[131] I-Iodocholesterol scintigraphy is an alternative method of demonstrating lateralization of hyperfunctioning adrenal tissue but is not widely used because of low sensitivity and lack of availability of the radiotracer.

Management

Unilateral aldosterone-producing adenoma; unilateral adrenal hyperplasia; and, rarely, aldosterone-producing carcinoma can be resolved with surgery. Laparoscopic adrenalectomy without previous adrenal vein sampling may be warranted in patients less than 40 years of age if nonsuppressible hyperaldosteronism is documented and if CT scanning demonstrates unilateral adrenal abnormalities and a normal contralateral gland.

Adrenalectomy improves blood pressure control in most patients and is associated with an average long-term cure rate between 30% and 72%. In patients with primary aldosteronism, surgical cure is associated with younger age and shorter duration of hypertension; these findings demonstrate the importance of early identification of this condition. Hypertension that persists after adrenalectomy is most likely caused by coexisting essential hypertension and correlates with older age, a longer duration of hypertension, an increased serum creatinine level, and a strong family history of hypertension.

Bilateral adrenal adenomas or hyperplasia cannot be resolved with surgery. Glucocorticoid-remediable aldosteronism, a rare form of nonprimary aldosteronism that can cause hypertension, also is not able to be cured surgically. This autosomal dominant familial disorder is characterized by excess aldosterone production that can be suppressed by exogenous corticosteroids.

If surgery is not indicated, aldosterone inhibition with spironolactone or eplerenone may be used to treat primary aldosteronism. Eplerenone is believed to have fewer adverse antiandrogenic effects than spironolactone, but trials comparing the efficacy of these agents have not been reported. Additional therapy with long-acting calcium channel blockers, ACE inhibitors, ARBs, or thiazide diuretics may be necessary to achieve optimal blood pressure control.

Renovascular Hypertension

Pathophysiology, Epidemiology, and Risk Factors

Renovascular hypertension is defined as hypertension caused by narrowing of one or more of the renal arteries. Underperfusion and ischemia of the kidneys leads to stimulation of the renin-angiotensin system. Sodium retention and increased volume may contribute to hypertension in patients with bilateral disease and/or renal parenchymal disease. However, not all patients with renal artery stenosis have renovascular hypertension.

Renovascular hypertension due to fibromuscular dysplasia, a nonatherosclerotic, noninflammatory renovascular disease, is most commonly caused by medial fibroplasia of the renal artery (**Figure 10**). Fibromuscular dysplasia is a disease of unknown cause and most commonly involves the renal and carotid arteries.

Hypertension caused by fibromuscular disease is more common in women and usually affects patients between 15 and 30 years of age. Catheter-based angiography is the most

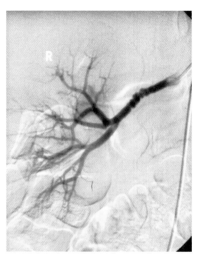

FIGURE 10.
Angiogram of the renal artery in a patient with fibromuscular dysplasia.
On imaging studies, the lesion associated with this condition resembles a string of beads.

Reprinted with permission from Physician's Information and Education Resource (PIER). Philadelphia: American College of Physicians. Copyright 2009, American College of Physicians.

accurate method of diagnosis of this condition. This study is indicated for patients whose clinical presentation raises strong suspicion for fibromuscular disease–related hypertension, such as those with severe resistant hypertension and high plasma renin activity. Furthermore, revascularization with angioplasty may be performed at the same time as diagnostic angiography.

Renal artery stenosis is associated with advancing age, cigarette smoking, dyslipidemia, and diabetes mellitus. This condition is detected in 14% to 30% of patients who undergo coronary angiography. The clinical significance of incidentally detected renal artery stenosis depends on whether the patient's clinical and laboratory features are consistent with renovascular hypertension. In the absence of a clear indication for imaging the renal vasculature, such as resistant hypertension and a rising serum creatinine level, additional imaging of the renal arteries is not recommended during routine coronary angiography procedures.

Atherosclerotic renovascular disease is usually associated with widespread atherosclerosis, peripheral vascular disease, cardiovascular disease, and ischemic target organ damage. Because individuals with atherosclerotic renal artery stenosis are usually older and older patients have a high prevalence of essential hypertension, determining the degree to which reduced renal perfusion distal to a stenotic lesion contributes to either elevated blood pressure or CKD is difficult. In addition, most imaging studies cannot demonstrate a functional relationship between the anatomic kidney lesion and a patient's blood pressure or level of kidney function.

Management

Renal revascularization only improves hypertension in patients with an anatomic lesion that is hemodynamically significant and sufficiently severe to activate the renin-angiotensin system. Revascularization of anatomic lesions without functional significance usually does not improve blood pressure and may be associated with significant morbidity due to complications of angioplasty or surgery.

At present, no clinical trials or guidelines adequately address optimal therapy for obstructive renal artery lesions in patients with atherosclerotic disease. Angioplasty rarely cures hypertension in these patients and only improves blood pressure in 30% to 50% of affected patients. Evaluation of renal artery stenosis in patients with suspected atherosclerotic renovascular hypertension should only be considered in patients with accelerated, resistant hypertension and possibly in those with evidence of atherosclerosis whose serum creatinine levels acutely increase after treatment with renin-angiotensin system blockers.

In appropriate candidates with fibromuscular disease–associated hypertension, percutaneous angioplasty is associated with less morbidity than surgery and is therefore the preferred method of revascularization. However, surgery may be needed if this intervention is not successful. Restenosis after balloon angioplasty occurs in 7% to 27% of patients and usually develops within 6 months.

Medical therapy for patients with atherosclerotic renovascular disease should include aggressive control of cardiovascular risk factors through interventions such as smoking cessation and lipid control. Antihypertensive therapy with multiple agents also is usually necessary. Renin-angiotensin system inhibition with either ACE inhibitors or ARBs may significantly improve blood pressure, but patients with severe stenoses or unilateral renal artery stenosis in a solitary kidney may still experience acute declines in kidney function.

Few randomized controlled trials have compared renal angioplasty and surgery or renal artery revascularization with medical therapy in patients with renovascular hypertension. These interventions have been associated with dramatic improvements in blood pressure control and kidney function in carefully selected individuals, particularly those with the recent onset of uncontrolled hypertension and decreased kidney function; however, early identification of these patients is challenging.

Variability in patient selection and in the definitions of renovascular hypertension and outcomes has made interpretation of the few randomized clinical trials comparing renal artery revascularization with medical therapy difficult. Available observational and clinical trial data suggest that, among patients who undergo revascularization, blood pressure and kidney function improve or remain unchanged in up to 75% of subjects and may worsen in as many as 25% to 30% of subjects. In a recent clinical trial comparing renal angioplasty with stenting versus medical therapy in patients with impaired kidney function, revascularization was shown to have no benefit with respect to preservation of kidney function.

Serious complications of revascularization, such as cholesterol embolization, bleeding, post procedure myocardial infarction or stroke, or death may occur. A recent meta-analysis evaluating observational data as well as randomized controlled trials of medical therapy compared with revascularization concluded that available evidence does not clearly support one particular approach. Clinical trials addressing this area are nearing completion, but identifying the subgroup of individuals who will benefit from revascularization procedures remains challenging.

Complications associated with renal angioplasty include hemorrhage; vessel dissection; diffuse atheroembolic disease; kidney failure; and, in patients with a high risk for cardiovascular events, myocardial infarction, and stroke. Restenosis rates ranged between 14% and 18%.

Renovascular Hypertension and Chronic Kidney Disease

Atherosclerotic renovascular disease may be caused by ischemic nephropathy, which is defined as the combined effects of nephrosclerosis, prolonged ischemia, and atheroembolic disease and is frequently accompanied by CKD. The frequency with which ischemic nephropathy results in end-stage kidney disease is unknown. Currently, the best known predictors of progression to end-stage kidney disease are the glomerular filtration rate at presentation and the degree of fibrosis detected on kidney biopsy.

Pheochromocytoma

Pathophysiology

Pheochromocytomas, also known as paragangliomas, are rare tumors that develop in the adrenal medulla or extra-adrenal chromaffin tissue. The endocrine cells of the sympathoadrenal system synthesize and secrete catecholamines. Excessive production of these catecholamines can cause sustained or paroxysmal hypertension, diaphoresis, headache, and anxiety. Approximately 8% of patients with a pheochromocytoma are completely asymptomatic, and 5% of incidentally discovered adrenal tumors have been shown to be pheochromocytomas.

Complications of pheochromocytomas can be fatal and include myocardial infarction, stroke, and cardiovascular collapse. Approximately 10% of patients with a pheochromocytoma have metastatic disease, and approximately 15% to 20% of patients with this condition have associated germline mutations in genes known to cause the genetic forms of pheochromocytoma. Familial pheochromocytoma occurs in multiple endocrine neoplasia type II; von Hippel-Lindau disease; neurofibromatosis; familial paraganglioma; and, rarely, multiple endocrine neoplasia type I.

Diagnosis and Evaluation

Diagnosis of pheochromocytoma requires confirmation of excess catecholamine production supported by positive findings on certain imaging studies. Fractionated catecholamines and metanephrines can be measured in the serum or via a 24-hour urine collection. Some experts recommend measurement of fractionated plasma metanephrines, which are 96% to 100% sensitive for pheochromocytoma; however, these metanephrines are only 85% to 89% specific for pheochromocytoma, and positive results may require additional diagnostic testing to exclude false-positive results. Measurement of fractionated metanephrines and catecholamines via 24-hour urine collection has a sensitivity and specificity of 98%, but urine collection is more difficult than serum testing.

MRI or CT scanning can localize the tumor in patients with a pheochromocytoma. Metaiodobenzylguanidine adrenal scanning is highly specific for pheochromocytomas, is helpful in diagnosing extra-adrenal tumors, and can be used to confirm positive findings on CT and MRI scanning. Metaiodobenzylguanidine scanning also may be used when a patient's clinical presentation raises strong suspicion for pheochromocytoma and biochemical testing demonstrates excess catecholamine production but results on CT or MRI are negative.

Management

Surgical resection is the treatment of choice for pheochromocytoma and can resolve associated hypertension. Beginning 10 to 14 days before surgery, α- and β-blockers are indicated to control blood pressure and pulse rate during the preoperative period and to prevent massive outpouring of catecholamines during surgical manipulation. Catecholamine-induced vasoconstriction and pressure natriuresis can cause a decrease in plasma volume, and institution of a high-sodium diet and avoidance of diuretics are indicated to restore volume.

The long-acting α-blocker phenoxybenzamine should be started first. The dosage of this agent should be titrated upward to achieve blood pressure control and until adverse effects such as nasal congestion, postural hypotension, fatigue, and diarrhea develop. After 1 to 2 weeks of this therapy, small doses of β-blockers may be added to control tachycardia; however, use of β-blockers alone may exacerbate hypertension due to unopposed α tone and is not indicated.

Metyrosine inhibits catecholamine synthesis and reduces tumor stores of catecholamines. This agent should be used when both α- and β-blockers are insufficient to control symptoms or are not tolerated, or when significant intraoperative manipulation of the tumor is anticipated.

KEY POINTS

- Secondary hypertension should be considered in patients with hypertension who have atypical clinical features and are resistant to antihypertensive therapy.

- An elevated plasma aldosterone-plasma renin ratio accompanied by unsuppressed aldosterone excretion after correction of hypokalemia and adherence to a high-sodium diet for 3 days is diagnostic of primary aldosteronism.

- In patients with primary aldosteronism who cannot be treated surgically, aldosterone inhibition with spironolactone or eplerenone may be used.

- Catheter-based angiography is the most accurate method of diagnosing renovascular hypertension caused by fibromuscular disease.

- Medical therapy for patients with atherosclerotic renovascular disease should include aggressive control of cardiovascular risk factors and treatment with a renin-angiotensin system inhibitor.

- Diagnosis of pheochromocytoma requires confirmation of excess catecholamine production supported by positive findings on MRI or CT scanning.

- Surgical resection is the treatment of choice for pheochromocytoma and can resolve associated hypertension.

White Coat Hypertension

White coat hypertension is characterized by at least three separate office blood pressure measurements above 140/90 mm Hg with at least two sets of measurements below 140/90 mm Hg obtained in nonoffice settings, accompanied by the absence of target organ damage. Ambulatory blood pressure measurement is considered the gold standard for diagnosing this condition.

Patients with white coat hypertension have a lower risk for cardiovascular events compared with those with sustained hypertension but also have a greater risk for developing sustained hypertension than those without this condition. Pharmacologic treatment of white coat hypertension has not been shown to reduce morbid events.

KEY POINTS

- White coat hypertension is characterized by at least three separate office blood pressure measurements above 140/90 mm Hg with at least two sets of measurements below 140/90 mm Hg obtained in nonoffice settings, accompanied by the absence of target organ damage.

- Ambulatory blood pressure measurement is considered the gold standard for diagnosing white coat hypertension.

Masked Hypertension

Masked hypertension is characterized by a normal office blood pressure measurement and high ambulatory blood pressure measurement. This condition may affect up to 10 million persons in the United States. Patients with masked hypertension have a definite increased risk for cardiovascular events compared with patients with normal office and ambulatory blood pressure measurements. Suspicion for masked hypertension is usually raised when the physician is informed of discrepancies between office and home blood pressure readings. Ambulatory blood pressure monitoring can be used to confirm this diagnosis.

There are no clinical trials addressing treatment of masked hypertension. However, treatment is indicated for patients with an elevated average 24-hour ambulatory blood pressure measurement.

> **KEY POINT**
>
> - Masked hypertension is characterized by a normal office blood pressure measurement and high ambulatory blood pressure measurement.

Resistant Hypertension

Epidemiology and Risk Factors

Resistant hypertension is defined as blood pressure that remains above goal despite treatment with the optimal dosages of three antihypertensive agents of different classes, including a diuretic. Determining the prevalence of true resistant hypertension is difficult, because patients with uncontrolled hypertension secondary to poor medication adherence or inadequate treatment or those with white coat hypertension are not considered to have resistant hypertension. Ambulatory blood pressure monitoring can differentiate true resistant hypertension from a white coat effect that misleadingly suggests resistance to therapy.

Patient characteristics more likely to be associated with resistant hypertension include older age, BMI above 30, higher baseline blood pressure, diabetes, and black race. Excessive consumption of dietary sodium and alcohol contributes to resistant hypertension. Resistant hypertension also may be associated with use of certain medications that variably increase blood pressure.

A high proportion of patients with resistant hypertension have secondary hypertension due to either primary aldosteronism or renovascular hypertension; therefore, these conditions should be excluded in patients with suspected resistant hypertension. Sleep apnea and obesity also are prevalent in patients with resistant hypertension.

Approximately 50% to 60% of patients with sleep apnea have hypertension, and 50% of patients with hypertension may have sleep apnea. This association is particularly strong in patients with resistant hypertension. A combination of the following factors may contribute to the association between sleep apnea and resistant hypertension: excessive sodium volume, nocturnal hypoxemia–mediated sustained increases in sympathetic nervous system activity, insulin resistance associated with obesity, and excess aldosterone production.

Management

Management of resistant hypertension should include appropriate lifestyle modifications, discontinuation of medications that may increase blood pressure, and correction of secondary causes of hypertension. Patients with suspected sleep apnea should be referred for a formal sleep evaluation, and those diagnosed with this condition should consider treatment with continuous positive airway pressure.

Because patients with resistant hypertension often have excessive volume expansion, adequate diuretic therapy is recommended in this setting. Chlorthalidone has a long duration of action and may be more effective than hydrochlorothiazide. Mineralocorticoid receptor antagonists such as spironolactone, amiloride, and eplerenone also are particularly effective in treating patients with resistant hypertension, including those with obesity and sleep apnea. Loop diuretics should be used in patients with resistant hypertension and CKD, and shorter-acting loop diuretics such as furosemide should be administered at least twice daily.

> **KEY POINTS**
>
> - Resistant hypertension is defined as blood pressure that remains above goal despite treatment with the optimal dosages of three antihypertensive agents of different classes, including a diuretic.
> - Ambulatory blood pressure monitoring can differentiate true resistant hypertension from a white coat effect that misleadingly suggests resistance to therapy.
> - Secondary hypertension should be excluded in patients with suspected resistant hypertension.
> - Management of resistant hypertension should include appropriate lifestyle modifications; discontinuation of medications that may increase blood pressure; correction of secondary causes of hypertension; and, when appropriate, diuretic therapy.

Hypertension in Special Populations

Women

Diagnosis and treatment of hypertension is similar in men and women, but women have a higher prevalence of adverse effects associated with certain medications. Elderly women in particular are at greater risk for hyponatremia associated with thiazide diuretics.

Patients with Diabetes Mellitus

In patients with diabetes mellitus, hypertension significantly contributes to the risk of diabetic vascular disease and death. Furthermore, compared with the general population, patients with hypertension are more likely to have impaired glucose tolerance, insulin resistance, and obesity and are at increased risk for the development of diabetes.

All hypertension guidelines emphasize the importance of aggressively decreasing blood pressure to below 130/80 mm Hg in patients with diabetes by using any major classes of antihypertensive agents. However, the role of antihypertensive therapy in exacerbating glucose intolerance should be considered.

Several clinical trials have shown differences in the rates of new cases of diabetes among various treatment groups; generally, renin-angiotensin system inhibitors have been associated with a lower incidence of diabetes compared with diuretics and β-blockers. In addition, in a recent meta-analysis, new-onset diabetes was lowest in those using ACE inhibitors and ARBs, followed by calcium channel blockers, β-blockers, and diuretics.

These results are consistent with earlier studies reporting a reduction in new-onset diabetes with ACE inhibitors and ARBs and an increased incidence of new-onset diabetes with β-blockers and diuretics. However, the Diabetes Reduction Assessment with Ramipril and Rosiglitazone Medication (DREAM) trial revealed contrasting evidence. In this trial, patients with impaired fasting glucose levels or impaired glucose tolerance were randomly assigned to either ramipril or placebo. After 3 years, no significant difference in the incidence in new-onset diabetes was detected. Nevertheless, because the primary goal of antihypertensive therapy is to lower blood pressure, favoring the use of renin-angiotensin system blockers in patients at high risk for type 2 diabetes is reasonable. Most patients with diabetes require two or more antihypertensive medications to achieve desired blood pressure targets.

Older Patients

Patients with hypertension who are less than 50 years of age usually have an elevated diastolic blood pressure. In persons older than 50 years, systolic blood pressure continues to increase whereas diastolic blood pressure usually decreases; therefore, in this population group, isolated systolic hypertension is prevalent and an elevated systolic blood pressure is the most useful outcome predictor of cardiovascular morbidity and mortality.

In a meta-analysis of eight trials of various antihypertensive regimens in over 15,000 patients older than 60 years with a systolic blood pressure above 160 mm Hg and diastolic blood pressure below 95 mm Hg, drug treatment was associated with improvements in total mortality (13%) and in mortality due to cardiovascular disease (18%), stroke (30%), and coronary heart disease (23%). Compared with placebo, antihypertensive therapy also has recently been shown to reduce stroke and cardiovascular disease mortality in patients over 80 years of age with hypertension.

JNC guidelines recommend similar treatment thresholds for elderly patients with hypertension as for the general population (that is, all patients with a blood pressure of 140/90 mm Hg or higher should be treated with lifestyle modifications and drug therapy). However, elderly patients are more likely to have wide variances in blood pressure compared with younger individuals and may develop orthostatic hypotension if medications are titrated to higher doses too rapidly.

Furthermore, clinical trials have shown that patients who have preexisting coronary disease who achieve low diastolic blood pressure (defined as <70 mm Hg) may have an increased incidence of cardiovascular events. Older patients in particular are at higher risk for this phenomenon, which is known as the J-shaped curve because the risk for these events declines as diastolic blood pressure decreases but increases as pressure decreases below the determined measurement for low diastolic blood pressure.

KEY POINTS

- All hypertension guidelines emphasize the importance of aggressively decreasing blood pressure to below 130/80 mm Hg in patients with diabetes.

- Generally, renin-angiotensin system inhibitors have been associated with a lower incidence of diabetes compared with diuretics and β-blockers.

- An elevated systolic blood pressure is the most useful outcome predictor of cardiovascular morbidity and mortality in patients older than 50 years of age.

- Elderly patients are more likely to have wide variances in blood pressure compared with younger individuals and may develop orthostatic hypotension if medications are titrated to higher doses too rapidly.

Bibliography

Balk E, Raman G, Chung M, et al. Effectiveness of management strategies for renal artery stenosis: a systematic review. Ann Intern Med. 2006;145(12):901-912. [PMID: 17062633]

Bax L, Woittiez AJ, Kouwenberg HJ, et al. Stent placement in patients with atherosclerotic renal artery stenosis and impaired renal function: a randomized trial. Ann Intern Med. 2009;150(12):840-848. [PMID: 19414832]

Beckett NS, Peters R, Fletcher AE, et al; HYVET Study Group. Treatment of hypertension in patients 80 years of age or older. N Engl J Med. 2008;358(18):1887-1898. [PMID: 18378519]

Chapman N, Dobson A, Wilson S, et al; Anglo-Scandinavian Cardiac Outcomes Trial Investigators. Effect of spironolactone on blood pressure in subjects with resistant hypertension. Hypertension. 2007;49(4): 839-845. [PMID: 17309946]

Elliott WJ, Meyer PM. Incident diabetes in clinical trials of antihypertensive drugs: a network meta-analysis [erratum in Lancet. 2007;369(9572):1518]. Lancet. 2007;369(9557): 201-207. [PMID: 17240286]

Julius S, Nesbitt SD, Egan BM, et al, for the Trial of Preventing Hypertension (TROPHY) Study Investigators. Feasibility of treating prehypertension with an angiotensin-receptor blocker. N Engl J Med. 2006;354(16):1685-1697. [PMID: 16537662]

Levin A, Linas S, Luft FC, Chapman AB, Textor S; ASN HTN Advisory Group. Controversies in renal artery stenosis: a review by the American Society of Nephrology Advisory Group on Hypertension. Am J Nephrol. 2007;27(2):212-220. [PMID: 17377375]

The Trials of Hypertension Prevention Collaborative Research Group. Effects of weight loss and sodium reduction intervention on blood pressure and hypertension incidence in overweight people with high-normal blood pressure. The Trials of Hypertension Prevention, phase II. Arch Intern Med. 1997;157(6):657-667. [PMID: 9080920]

Williams B, Lacy PS, Thom SM, et al; CAFE Investigators; Anglo-Scandinavian Cardiac Outcomes Trial Investigators; CAFE Steering Committee and Writing Committee. Differential impact of blood pressure-lowering drugs on central aortic pressure and clinical outcomes: principal results of the Conduit Artery Function

Evaluation (CAFE) study. Circulation. 2006;113(9):1213-1225. [PMID: 16476843]

Wright JT Jr, Probstfield JL, Cushman WC, et al; ALLHAT Collaborative Research Group. ALLHAT findings revisited in the context of subsequent analyses, other trials, and meta-analyses. Arch Intern Med. 2009;169(9):832-842. [PMID: 19433694]

Tubulointerstitial Disorders

Pathophysiology

Regardless of the cause of tubulointerstitial disease, antigens on tubular proteins or tubular epithelial cells are believed to cause the inciting kidney injury associated with this disease.

Tubulointerstitial disease can occur as a primary disorder that affects the function of the tubules, the interstitium, or the genitourinary tract with relative sparing of the glomeruli. Tubulointerstitial disease also may develop secondary to glomerular or vascular diseases. The degree of tubulointerstitial fibrosis in patients with secondary tubulointerstitial disease correlates with the risk for progressive loss of kidney function and the development of end-stage kidney disease (ESKD) that requires kidney replacement therapy.

KEY POINT

- Tubulointerstitial disorders are characterized by diseases that affect the vascular and interstitial compartments of the kidney with relative sparing of the glomeruli.

Clinical Manifestations

Primary chronic tubulointerstitial disease is characterized by a syndrome of chronic kidney disease (CKD) that slowly progresses to ESKD. Patients with primary chronic tubulointerstitial disease also may have polyuria and nocturia. Older patients and women have an increased risk for the development of CKD.

Acute tubulointerstitial disease is characterized by pyuria, eosinophilia, eosinophiluria, and acute kidney injury (see Acute Kidney Injury).

KEY POINTS

- Primary chronic tubulointerstitial disease is characterized by a syndrome of chronic kidney disease that slowly progresses to end-stage kidney disease.
- Acute tubulointerstitial disease is characterized by pyuria, eosinophilia, eosinophiluria, and acute kidney injury.

Diagnosis and Evaluation

The diagnosis of tubulointerstitial disease can be established in patients with slowly progressive CKD associated with a bland urine sediment and urine protein excretion that is typically less than 2 g/24 h. Low-molecular-weight tubular proteins such as β_2-microglobulin, uromodulin (Tamm-Horsfall mucoprotein), and light chains are primarily excreted in these patients; urine albumin excretion is typically absent. Patients with tubulointerstitial disease also may have a decreased estimated glomerular filtration rate (eGFR) and a non–anion gap metabolic renal tubular acidosis.

Ultrasonography of the kidneys in patients with chronic tubulointerstitial disease reveals atrophic, echogenic kidneys consistent with CKD. Characteristic kidney biopsy findings in patients with tubulointerstitial disease include lymphocytic infiltration and fibrosis in the interstitium with tubular atrophy, arteriosclerosis, and global glomerulosclerosis.

Patients with established tubulointerstitial disease should be evaluated for conditions and factors associated with this disease (**Table 22**). Serial measurement of the eGFR is indicated as these patients progress to ESKD. In addition, ultrasonography or CT of the genitourinary tract should be performed to exclude urinary tract obstruction.

Causes of Primary Chronic Tubulointerstitial Disease

One of the most common causes of chronic tubulointerstitial disease is chronic hypertension with resultant nephrosclerosis. Chronic primary tubulointerstitial disease also may be caused by immunologic or infectious diseases, medications, malignancies, metabolic factors, or obstruction.

Immunologic Diseases

Sjögren Syndrome

Sjögren syndrome is one of the most common immunologic causes of tubulointerstitial disease. Approximately 20% to 50% of patients with Sjögren syndrome have kidney involvement that primarily manifests as tubular defects such as distal renal tubular acidosis, a decrease in urine concentrating ability, and a reduced eGFR. Rarely, patients with Sjögren syndrome have glomerular disorders such as membranous nephropathy or membranoproliferative glomerulonephritis.

Sarcoidosis

Approximately 25% of patients with sarcoidosis have kidney involvement that predominantly occurs as a result of tubulointerstitial disease caused by noncaseating granulomatous inflammation and fibrosis. Patients with sarcoidosis may have an elevated serum 1,25-dihydroxyvitamin D_3 level that leads to hypercalcemia and hypercalciuria; these patients also may have an increased risk for nephrolithiasis and nephrocalcinosis. Furthermore, individuals with sarcoidosis and

TABLE 22 Causes of Primary Tubulointerstitial Diseases
Immunologic
Sjögren syndrome
Sarcoidosis
Systemic lupus erythematosus
Infectious
Viral (polyomavirus BK virus, JC virus, cytomegalovirus, adenovirus, Epstein-Barr virus, hepatitis C virus)
Mycobacterial (*Mycobacterium tuberculosis, Mycobacterium avium* complex)
Bacterial (chronic pyelonephritis, *Rickettsia*, leptospirosis, schisotosomiasis)
Inherited
Polycystic kidney disease
Medullary sponge kidney
Uromodulin (Tamm-Horsfall mucoprotein)–related kidney disease (type 2 medullary cystic kidney disease, familial juvenile hyperuricemic nephropathy, sickle cell disease)
Malignancy
Multiple myeloma
Leukemia
Medications
Combination analgesics (phenacetin, aspirin, caffeine, NSAIDs)
Calcineurin inhibitors (cyclosporine, tacrolimus)
Lithium
Metabolic
Heavy metals (lead, mercury, cadmium)
Hyperuricemia
Cystinosis
Obstructive
Prostatic hyperplasia
Urinary reflux nephropathy
Nephrolithiasis
Malignancies

tubulointerstitial disease have polyuria and a decreased ability to concentrate and acidify the urine.

Systemic Lupus Erythematosus

Primary tubulointerstitial disease associated with systemic lupus erythematosus (SLE) is relatively uncommon. Up to 33% of patients with SLE have interstitial inflammation and fibrosis, which may be caused by deposition of immune complexes within the interstitium. These patients have a normal eGFR and do not have a significant loss of kidney function, whereas those with secondary tubulointerstitial disease with lupus glomerulonephritis do have significantly decreased kidney function.

Infectious Diseases

Inflammatory changes and fibrosis of the kidneys in patients with primary tubulointerstitial disease resulting from an infection are believed to be caused directly by the infecting organism or to occur secondary to systemic inflammation. Epstein-Barr virus, cytomegalovirus, and the polyomavirus BK virus in particular may cause progressive loss of kidney function in patients with compromised immune systems, such as kidney transplant recipients or those with HIV infection.

Malignancy

Multiple myeloma is one of the most common malignancies associated with CKD. Approximately 50% of patients with multiple myeloma have reduced kidney function at the time of diagnosis, and approximately 10% of these individuals have chronic tubulointerstitial disease (see Multiple Myeloma in MKSAP 15 Hematology and Oncology).

Medications

Analgesics

Analgesics are one of the most common classes of medications associated with tubulointerstitial disease. Use of combination analgesics such as acetaminophen and aspirin with caffeine or codeine and aspirin with phenacetin is particularly associated with an increased risk of analgesic nephropathy.

According to the National Analgesic Nephropathy Study (NANS), patients who use more than 1 kg of aspirin over a lifetime or have a total analgesic ingestion of 0.3 kg or more yearly have an increased risk of ESKD. However, these findings were primarily seen in patients using dual therapy with phenacetin and aspirin. The incidence of analgesic nephropathy has decreased since phenacetin-containing compounds were removed from the market in Europe and the United States.

A history of chronic analgesic use, elevations in the blood urea nitrogen and serum creatinine levels, and a bland urine sediment that may contain occasional granular casts or leukocytes are diagnostic of analgesic nephropathy. This condition also may be associated with genitourinary tract malignancies, and urine cytology and cystoscopy are recommended in patients with analgesic nephropathy and persistent hematuria. The presence of small, indented, calcified kidneys (SICK) also is diagnostic of analgesic nephropathy; however, these findings are usually not seen on noncontrast CT. Therefore, routine use of this study does not help to diagnose this condition.

Calcineurin Inhibitors

On kidney biopsy obtained 5 and 10 years after kidney transplantation, approximately 66% and 90% of kidney transplant recipients, respectively, have evidence of a striped pattern of fibrosis caused by calcineurin inhibitor toxicity. Calcineurin inhibitors also have been shown to cause ESKD in approximately 10% of patients who have undergone transplantation of organs other than the kidneys.

Lithium

Chronic tubulointerstitial disease associated with lithium typically involves the distal tubules and cortical collecting ducts. Kidney disease caused by lithium is more common in patients with repeated toxicity and high serum lithium levels.

Manifestations of lithium-induced disease include a reduced eGFR, nephrogenic diabetes insipidus, and distal renal tubular acidosis.

Metabolic Factors

Lead

Lead nephropathy is an often unrecognized cause of CKD, especially in those with concomitant gout caused by decreased urine uric acid excretion. Patients with heavy lead exposure such as painters, welders, battery workers, and makers of home-brewed whiskey in lead pipes are at risk for the development of this condition.

Lead nephropathy typically involves the proximal tubular cells and manifests as anemia and the Fanconi syndrome. Serum lead levels are an insensitive marker for lead toxicity, and calcium disodium ethylenediaminetetraacetic acid (EDTA) mobilization testing should be performed if lead nephropathy is suspected. A 24-hour urine collection of more than 600 µg/ 24 h (3 µmol/d) of lead is diagnostic of lead toxicity.

Hyperuricemia

Some experts believe that hyperuricemia directly causes chronic tubulointerstitial disease, whereas others believe that hyperuricemia is a secondary effect of reduced glomerular filtration rather than a tubular toxin. In patients with hyperuricemia, reduction of serum uric acid levels with allopurinol has failed to demonstrate significant renoprotective effects.

Obstruction

The most common obstructive causes of chronic tubulointerstitial diseases are prostatic disease in men, cervical cancer in women, and urinary reflux in children and young adults. Prompt diagnosis of obstruction via radiographic imaging studies is essential to relieve obstruction and reverse acute kidney injury. Obstruction that is present for longer than 8 to 12 weeks typically results in irreversible kidney failure.

KEY POINTS

- Diagnosis of tubulointerstitial disease can be established in patients with slowly progressive chronic kidney disease associated with a bland urine sediment and urine protein excretion that is typically less than 2 g/24 h.

- Ultrasonography of the kidneys in patients with chronic tubulointerstitial disease reveals atrophic, echogenic kidneys consistent with chronic kidney disease.

- Epstein-Barr virus, cytomegalovirus, and the polyomavirus BK virus may cause progressive loss of kidney function in patients with compromised immune systems.

- A history of chronic analgesic use, elevations in the blood urea nitrogen and serum creatinine levels, and a bland urine sediment that may contain occasional granular casts or leukocytes are diagnostic of analgesic nephropathy.

- The most common obstructive causes of chronic tubulointerstitial diseases are prostatic disease in men, cervical cancer in women, and urinary reflux in children and young adults.

Management

There is no cure for chronic tubulointerstitial disease, but treatment of underlying causes of this condition may slow the progression to ESKD. Discontinuation of the inciting agent(s) in patients with medication-induced tubulointerstitial disease is indicated to prevent further kidney injury but is unlikely to improve kidney function once interstitial fibrosis with a decreased eGFR develops. In addition, concomitant use of nephrotoxic medications and intravenous contrast agents should be avoided in all patients with tubulointerstitial disease.

KEY POINTS

- There is no cure for chronic tubulointerstitial disease, but treatment of underlying causes of this condition may slow the progression to end-stage kidney disease.

- Concomitant use of nephrotoxic medications and intravenous contrast agents should be avoided in all patients with tubulointerstitial disease.

Bibliography

Henrich W, Clark R, Kelly J, et al. Non–Contrast-Enhanced Computerized Tomography and Analgesic-Related Kidney Disease: Report of the National Analgesic Nephropathy Study. J Am Soc Nephrol. 2006;17(5):1472-1480. [PMID: 16611714]

Nankivell B, Borrows R, Fung C, O'Connell P, Allen R, Chapman J. The National History of Chronic Allograft Nephropathy. N Engl J Med. 2003;349(24):2326-2333. [PMID: 14668458]

Patel SR, Dressler GR. BMP7 signaling in renal development and disease. Trends Mol Med. 2005;11(11):512-518. [PMID: 16216558]

Glomerular Diseases

Pathophysiology

Glomeruli are bundles of capillaries interposed between afferent and efferent arterioles in the kidneys. These bundles are composed of several cell types, including mesangial cells that support the glomerular capillary wall and endothelial and epithelial cells located on opposite sides of the glomerular basement membrane (GBM) (**Figure 11**).

Damage to the glomerular epithelial cells (known as podocytes) or the GBM alters the permeability of the capillary

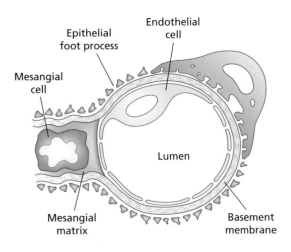

FIGURE 11.
Normal glomerular capillary.

wall and results in proteinuria. Rupture of the capillary wall or proliferation of the glomerular mesangial cells causes hematuria.

Rupture of the GBM leads to necrosis and crescent formation. The inflammatory infiltrations into Bowman's space are caused by damage to the capillary wall. These infiltrates become crescents consisting of coagulation proteins, macrophages, T cells, fibroblasts, and epithelial cells that irreversibly replace Bowman's space, which can result in a rapidly progressive glomerulonephritis associated with acute kidney injury.

Clinical Manifestations

Glomerular disease can produce clinical patterns of kidney disease classified as either the nephrotic syndrome or the nephritic syndrome, and patients with glomerular disease often have characteristics of both syndromes. Kidney biopsy is considered the best means of establishing a diagnosis and distinguishing between the nephrotic and nephritic syndromes (**Figure 12**).

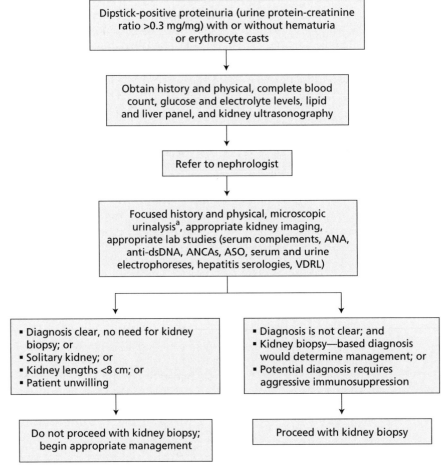

FIGURE 12.
Approach to the patient with glomerular disease.

ANA = antinuclear antibodies; anti-dsDNA = anti–double-stranded DNA antibodies; ASO = antistreptolysin O antibodies; VDRL = Venereal Disease Research Laboratory testing.

[a]The presence of erythrocyte casts and/or dysmorphic erythrocytes indicates a glomerular process. Acutely deteriorating kidney function warrants prompt kidney biopsy to determine whether aggressive immunosuppressive therapy is needed.

The Nephrotic Syndrome

The nephrotic syndrome is characterized by a urine protein-creatinine ratio above 3.5 mg/mg, hypoalbuminemia, hyperlipidemia, lipiduria, edema, and hypercoagulability. This syndrome may manifest as a primary kidney disease or occur secondary to a systemic disease. The nephrotic syndrome is usually caused by injury exclusively to the podocyte or GBM.

The Nephritic Syndrome

The nephritic syndrome, also known as glomerulonephritis, is often caused by immune-complex deposition in the glomerular capillaries and results in protein and erythrocytes escaping into Bowman's space. This condition is characterized by hematuria, oliguria, hypertension, and kidney insufficiency caused by glomerular inflammation. Urinalysis usually reveals pyuria and cellular and granular casts, and nephrotic-range proteinuria is often present.

Some patients with the nephritic syndrome have dermal inflammation that manifests as palpable purpura, necrosis, ulcers, or nodules. These patients may have kidney-dermal syndromes such as systemic lupus erythematosus (SLE), Henoch-Schönlein purpura (HSP), ANCA-associated vasculitis, and cryoglobulinemia. Kidney-pulmonary syndromes also may develop in patients with the nephritic syndrome. Assays for anti-GBM antibodies; ANCAs; and markers for immune complex diseases such as antinuclear antibodies, anti–double-stranded DNA antibodies, cryoglobulins, hepatitis B or C virus antibodies, and complement levels may further refine the diagnosis.

KEY POINTS

- The nephrotic syndrome is characterized by a urine protein-creatinine ratio above 3.5 mg/mg, hypoalbuminemia, hyperlipidemia, lipiduria, edema, and hypercoagulability.
- The nephritic syndrome is characterized by hematuria, oliguria, hypertension, kidney insufficiency, and proteinuria caused by glomerular inflammation.
- Features of the nephrotic and nephritic syndrome often overlap, and kidney biopsy is used to distinguish between these conditions.

Conditions that Cause the Nephrotic Syndrome

Primary Nephrotic Syndrome

Primary nephrotic syndrome is usually diagnosed when a secondary cause for the nephrotic syndrome not been identified. Because the degree of kidney function, hematuria, and proteinuria is often similar among all causes of primary nephrotic syndrome, kidney biopsy is needed to establish a definitive diagnosis, determine the most appropriate treatment, and evaluate patient prognosis.

Minimal Change Disease

Pathophysiology and Epidemiology

Minimal change disease accounts for 10% to 20% of all cases of primary nephrotic syndrome in adults. This condition is usually idiopathic but may develop secondary to use of NSAIDs or lithium. Hodgkin lymphoma and other less-common lymphomas or leukemias; thymoma; and malignancies of the kidney cells, duodenum, and pancreas also may be associated with minimal change disease.

Approximately one third of patients with minimal change disease have only one episode followed by a long-term remission. However, most patients have a relapsing disease course, and the initial relapse usually occurs within the first 6 months.

Diagnosis and Evaluation

A diagnosis of minimal change disease can be established in patients with effacement or flattening of the podocytes seen on electron microscopy and normal findings on light and immunofluorescence microscopy.

Clinical Manifestations

Minimal change disease manifests as sudden proteinuria that may be significant; for example, the urine protein-creatinine ratio may exceed 9 mg/mg. Microscopic hematuria and hyperlipidemia also may be present. Occasionally, acute kidney injury develops in adult patients with minimal change disease who have atherosclerosis and a rapid onset of severe proteinuria or edema. Hypertension and progression to end-stage kidney disease (ESKD) are rare in minimal change disease.

Management

Daily or alternate-day therapy with prednisone, 60 mg for 4 weeks followed by 40 mg/m² every other day for 4 weeks, is indicated to initially treat minimal change disease. Patients whose urine protein-creatinine ratio decreases below 0.3 mg/mg are considered to have a full response to treatment and should experience resolution of minimal change disease–associated acute kidney injury.

Approximately 10% of patients with minimal change disease become corticosteroid-dependent or are treatment resistant. Resistance is defined as a lack of full response to this treatment despite 8 weeks of therapy, or, in older adults, 12 to 16 weeks of daily therapy. Immunosuppressive agents such as cyclophosphamide, cyclosporine, tacrolimus, and mycophenolate mofetil have been used in corticosteroid-dependent or -resistant patients and in those who have frequent relapses.

Focal Segmental Glomerulosclerosis

Pathophysiology and Epidemiology

Focal segmental glomerulosclerosis (FSGS) is the most common cause of idiopathic nephrotic syndrome in adults and the most common cause of the nephrotic syndrome in black adults. This condition also is the most common primary glomerular disease that causes end-stage kidney disease in the United States.

FSGS may be idiopathic or familial or occur secondary to other conditions. A structural adaptation to nephron loss may cause FSGS, as occurs in reflux nephropathy, chronic pyelonephritis, or interstitial diseases. Additional causes of FSGS include obesity, sleep apnea, or an unidentified circulating permeability factor. However, primary podocyte dysfunction is the inciting event in most patients with FSGS.

Clinical Manifestations

FSGS is a more indolent form of the nephrotic syndrome than minimal change disease. Patients with primary FSGS usually present with microscopic hematuria, hypertension, and kidney insufficiency. Patients with secondary FSGS have minimal edema and rarely have the full spectrum of the nephrotic syndrome, such as nephrotic-range proteinuria.

Diagnosis

The primary biopsy finding in FSGS is a focal scarring lesion that involves only a few glomeruli and segments of the glomerular tuft. Immunofluorescence microscopy in affected patients reveals coarse deposits of immunoglobulins in segmentally scarred glomerular areas, C3, and usually fibrin trapped in the involved glomeruli. Electron microscopy shows diffuse obliteration of the podocytes and foam cells that often occupy the lumina of collapsed capillaries.

Morphologic variants of FSGS have been defined. The collapsing variant is characterized by collapse and sclerosis of the entire glomerular tuft and prominence of the visceral epithelial cells and has a worse prognosis than other variants. The tip variant has the defining pathologic lesion located at the tip of the glomerulus near the proximal tubule, appears to be more responsive to corticosteroids, and has a better overall prognosis. The perihilar variant (perihilar sclerosis and hyalinosis) often occurs in patients with secondary disease. A cellular variant also may occur, but some experts believe that this variant is intermediate in severity between collapsing FSGS and the tip variant.

Management

Treatment is usually necessary to reduce proteinuria or achieve remission in patients with FSGS. In nonnephrotic patients, angiotensin-converting enzyme (ACE) inhibitors or angiotensin receptor blockers (ARBs) are indicated. Patients with FSGS and persistent nephrotic syndrome require daily or alternate-day prednisone, cyclosporine, or mycophenolate mofetil for 16 weeks in addition to an ACE inhibitor or an ARB.

A randomized, controlled trial demonstrated that cyclosporine was useful in achieving remission in up to 70% of corticosteroid-resistant patients with FSGS. However, relapse occurred in nearly 40% of these patients when cyclosporine therapy was discontinued.

Corticosteroid therapy alone is associated with complete remission in 30% to 60% of patients with FSGS, no response in 40% to 50%, and partial remission in others. Cyclo-phosphamide may be effective in cortisosteroid-sensitive patients with FSGS but is usually not useful in those with corticosteroid-resistant disease.

Prognosis

Up to 50% of patients with FSGS and persistent nephrotic-range proteinuria develop ESKD within 5 years. The presence of massive proteinuria (urine protein-creatinine ratio above 10 mg/mg) in particular is associated with a poor prognosis. Remission of proteinuria is a significant predictor of kidney survival, and even partial remission is associated with a slower rate of kidney function decline and a reduced risk of kidney failure.

Membranous Nephropathy

Pathophysiology and Epidemiology

Approximately 15% to 33% of adults with proteinuria and the nephrotic syndrome have membranous nephropathy. This condition has a 2:1 male predominance and typically develops in patients between 30 and 50 years of age.

Membranous nephropathy is usually idiopathic but may occur secondary to conditions such as hepatitis B or C virus infection, malaria, syphilis, systemic lupus erythematosus, diabetes, and rheumatoid arthritis; use of drugs such as NSAIDs, captopril, and penicillamine; and malignancies of the breast, colon, stomach, kidney, and lung. Obtaining an antinuclear antibody assay to screen for lupus and serologic testing for hepatitis B and C virus infections are useful to exclude these potential secondary causes. In addition to age- and sex-appropriate screening, screening for other malignancies based on the patient's clinical presentation also is warranted.

This glomerulopathy is named for the electron-dense immune complex deposits arranged within the GBM that are visible on light microscopy in affected patients. These deposits are believed to be derived from an antigen deposited in the GBM and are associated with subsequent antibody-antigen interaction. This in situ immune complex formation activates the complement cascade that causes glomerular capillary wall permeability and proteinuria in animal studies.

Clinical Manifestations

Membranous nephropathy usually manifests as the nephrotic syndrome, but some patients may have asymptomatic proteinuria. Microscopic hematuria and an absence of erythrocyte casts also are common. Factors such as the baseline serum creatinine level and degree of proteinuria determine the rate of disease progression.

Management

The clinical features and risk for disease progression should determine the most appropriate management in patients with membranous nephropathy (**Figure 13**).

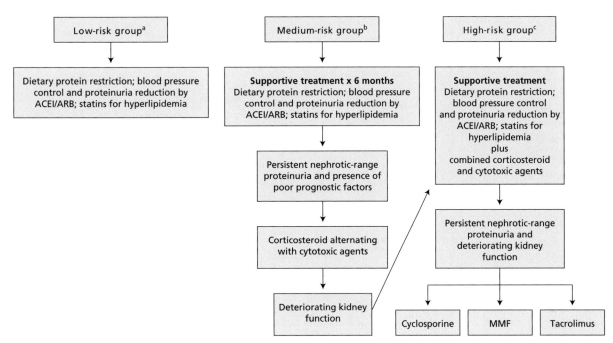

FIGURE 13.
Treatment of idiopathic membranous nephropathy.

ACEI = angiotensin-converting enzyme inhibitor; ARB = angiotensin receptor blocker; MMF = mycophenolate mofetil.

[a]Urine protein excretion less than 4 g/24 h with normal kidney function.

[b]Urine protein excretion between 4 and 8 g/24 h with normal kidney function.

[c]Urine protein excretion of 8 g/24 h or higher with impaired kidney function.

Reprinted with permission from Lai KN. Membranous nephropathy: when and how to treat. Kidney Int. 2007;71:841-3. [PMID: 17457329] Copyright © 2007, Macmillan Publishers.

Prognosis
Factors associated with a poor prognosis include male sex, older age, abnormal kidney function, a urine protein-creatinine ratio greater than 6 mg/mg sustained over 6 months, lack of complete remission with treatment, and the presence of tubulointerstitial lesions on kidney biopsy.

Immunotactoid and Fibrillary Glomerulonephritis

Pathophysiology and Epidemiology
Fibrillary and immunotactoid glomerulonephritis are relatively rare conditions caused by the deposition of randomly arranged fibrils derived from immunoglobulins that accumulate in the glomeruli. These deposited fibrils are larger than those associated with amyloidosis and do not react with Congo red staining or other agents used to diagnose amyloidosis. Fibrillary glomerulonephritis accounts for 85% to 90% of these conditions.

Fibrillary and immunotactoid glomerulonephritis are usually idiopathic, but immunotactoid glomerulonephritis can occur secondary to lymphocytic leukemia or B-cell lymphomas.

This condition also may be associated with hepatitis C virus infection, cryoglobulinemia, and SLE.

Clinical Manifestations
The mean age of presentation in patients with fibrillary and immunotactoid glomerulonephritis is 55 to 60 years. Common manifestations of these conditions include kidney dysfunction, proteinuria that is usually in the nephrotic range, microscopic hematuria, and hypertension. Nearly 50% of affected patients progress to ESKD within 10 years of diagnosis. Fibrillary and immunotactoid glomerulonephritis can recur in kidney transplantation recipients.

Management
No controlled trials have been performed in patients with fibrillary and immunotactoid glomerulonephritis, but plasmapheresis, prednisone, cytotoxic agents, NSAIDs, and colchicine have been used to manage these conditions. In addition, patients whose kidney disease is related to an underlying malignancy may benefit from therapy directed at the underlying disorder.

- Minimal change disease is characterized by the sudden onset of proteinuria that may be significant, the effacement or flattening of the podocytes seen on electron microscopy, and normal findings on light and immunofluorescence microscopy.

- Daily or alternate-day therapy with prednisone, 60 mg for 4 weeks followed by 40 mg/m² every other day for 4 weeks, is indicated to initially treat minimal change disease.

- Nonnephrotic patients with focal segmental glomerulosclerosis should undergo treatment with angiotensin-converting enzyme inhibitors or angiotensin receptor blockers; those with persistent nephrotic syndrome are also treated with prednisone, cyclosporine, or mycophenolate mofetil.

- Membranous nephropathy commonly manifests as the nephrotic syndrome and microscopic hematuria, but some patients may have asymptomatic proteinuria.

- In addition to age- and sex-appropriate screening, screening for other malignancies based on the patient's clinical presentation is warranted in patients with membranous nephropathy.

- Common manifestations of fibrillary and immunotactoid glomerulonephritis include kidney dysfunction, proteinuria that may be nephrotic range, microscopic hematuria, and hypertension.

- Plasmapheresis, prednisone, cytotoxic agents, NSAIDs, and colchicine have been used to manage fibrillary and immunotactoid glomerulonephritis.

Secondary Nephrotic Syndrome

Diabetic Nephropathy

Epidemiology and Risk Factors

Diabetic nephropathy develops in patients with a 10- to 20-year history of type 1 diabetes mellitus or a 5- to 10-year history of type 2 diabetes. This condition affects approximately 30% of patients with type 1 diabetes and 5% to 30% of those with type 2 diabetes.

Diabetic nephropathy is significantly more prevalent in American Indian, Mexican-American, and black patients compared with white patients. Additional risk factors for this condition include older age of onset of diabetes, increased blood pressure, poor glycemic control, cigarette smoking, and a family history of kidney disease and hypertension.

Screening

Screening for microalbuminuria is strongly recommended for all patients with diabetes. The American Diabetes Association 2009 guidelines specifically recommend annual measurement of the urine albumin excretion for patients who have had type 1 diabetes for 5 years or more and for all patients with type 2 diabetes beginning at the time of diagnosis.

Screening for microalbuminuria usually involves obtaining an albumin-creatinine ratio on a first morning void urine sample, a random sample, or a timed urine collection. Microalbuminuria is confirmed when two of three samples obtained within a 6-month period reveal a urine albumin-creatinine ratio between 30 and 300 mg/g. However, factors such as urinary tract infection, heavy exercise, high dietary protein intake, heart failure, acute febrile illness, menstruation, and vaginal discharge may confound these results; testing should be postponed if any of these factors is present.

Clinical Manifestations and Evaluation

Manifestations of diabetic nephropathy include proteinuria, a decline in kidney function, and hypertension. Classically, patients with this condition have nephrotic-range proteinuria and nodular sclerosis seen on kidney biopsy.

In patients with type 1 diabetes, early diabetic nephropathy is characterized by an elevated glomerular filtration rate or hyperfiltration that usually develops several years after diabetes is first diagnosed. Microalbuminuria is the first easily detectable sign of diabetic nephropathy and usually occurs 5 to 15 years after the diagnosis of diabetes. Microalbuminuria also is a predictor for increased mortality due to cardiovascular disease in patients with type 1 and 2 diabetes. Approximately 10 to 15 years after the diagnosis of diabetes, macroalbuminuria (urine albumin-creatinine ratio above 300 mg/g) can be detected on urine dipstick and is accompanied by decreasing kidney function and increased blood pressure.

In patients with type 1 diabetes, kidney failure caused by diabetic nephropathy usually occurs 15 to 30 years after diabetes is diagnosed. Whether this same rate of progression occurs in patients with type 2 diabetes or in those who have initiated early disease modification interventions remains uncertain.

Patients with diabetes who present with albuminuria and/or a reduced glomerular filtration rate may have kidney disorders other than diabetic nephropathy. Many patients with type 2 diabetes are at risk for nonproteinuric chronic kidney disease that may be caused by hypertension and atherosclerosis. However, the presence of retinopathy in patients with diabetes who have proteinuria is strongly suggestive of diabetic nephropathy.

Management

Hemoglobin A_{1c} levels correlate with the severity of kidney and retinal diabetic microvascular disease, and glycemic control in patients with diabetes delays or prevents the progression of diabetic nephropathy. Decreasing proteinuria in these patients involves use of renin-angiotensin system inhibitors and decreasing the blood pressure to below 130/80 mm Hg in all patients with diabetes and to less than 125/75 mm Hg in patients with diabetes who have a urine protein-creatinine ratio above 1 mg/mg. In addition, ACE inhibitors or ARBs should be used to reduce proteinuria, even if the patient is at target blood pressure (see Hypertension).

ACE inhibitors and ARBs also have been shown to slow the progression of diabetic kidney disease; however, a recent study revealed that administration of these agents to patients with normal urine albumin excretion, a normal glomerular filtration rate, and normal blood pressure did not prevent development of diabetic retinopathy. Nevertheless, these agents are still recommended for patients with hypertension regardless of their level of urine albumin and for those with albuminuria.

ACE inhibitors and ARBs both slow the decline of the glomerular filtration rate and have an equivalent renoprotective effect. Results from the ONTARGET study, which involved elderly patients at high risk for cardiovascular events, indicate that use of combination ACE and ARB therapy does not reduce morbidity and mortality and furthermore increases adverse side effects compared with usage of ACE inhibitors alone. Further studies are warranted before combination therapy can be recommended.

Kidney transplantation is the preferred kidney replacement therapy for patients with ESKD secondary to diabetes. However, diabetic nephropathy may recur many years after transplantation. Therefore, careful management of blood pressure, plasma glucose levels, and cardiovascular risk factors post transplantation is important. Simultaneous kidney-pancreas transplantation prevents recurrence of diabetic nephropathy.

Amyloidosis

Clinical Manifestations and Diagnosis
Amyloidosis refers to numerous conditions caused by deposition of abnormal fibrillary structures that are composed of precursor proteins. Manifestations of amyloidosis vary with the organ or site involved. In patients with kidney amyloidosis, proteinuria and kidney dysfunction are typically severe, but mild disease may occur. More than 25% of these patients have the nephrotic syndrome at the time of diagnosis. Biopsy of abdominal fat or rectal or duodenal mucosa is indicated if there is suspicion for systemic amyloidosis. Each of these studies is readily available in most medical centers, is 70% to 80% sensitive, and poses limited risk to the patient. Affected tissues stained with Congo red should reveal characteristic apple-green birefringence under polarized microscopy (see Immunoglobulin Light-Chain (AL) Amyloidosis in MKSAP 15 Hematology and Oncology).

Classification
Amyloidosis is classified according to the type of protein deposited. AL amyloidosis is the most common type of systemic amyloidosis in the United States. This condition is a primary disorder associated with deposition of an immunoglobulin light chain or a fragment of a light chain. Heavy chain deposition is rare and is associated with multiple myeloma, plasma cell disorders, and lymphomas.

Detection of monoclonal immunoglobulin in serum, blood, or tissues differentiates AL amyloidosis from other forms of amyloidosis.

AA amyloidosis accounts for 45% of cases of systemic amyloidosis worldwide and is more common in developing countries. This condition is caused by deposition of the amyloid A protein that is a fragment of serum amyloid A, which is an acute phase reactant produced by the liver. AA amyloidosis develops secondary to chronic inflammatory states and is associated with numerous disorders as well as injection drug use (**Table 23**). The diagnosis of amyloidosis should be considered in patients with long-standing, chronic inflammatory disease who develop a pattern of multiorgan dysfunction, especially if the kidneys, liver, or bowel is involved.

Familial (AF) amyloidosis is an autosomal-dominant disorder that may be caused by deformities of transthyretin. Disorders of the fibrinogen A alpha chain also can cause hereditary amyloidosis. AF amyloidosis should be considered in patients with signs and symptoms of AL or AA amyloidosis with a clear-cut inheritance pattern.

Management
Management of kidney amyloidosis involves removal of previously deposited amyloid fibrils and inhibiting production of additional precursor fibroids. AL amyloidosis can be treated with chemotherapeutic regimens such as high-dose melphalan and autologous peripheral stem-cell transplantation.

Control of the underlying infection is usually indicated for patients with AA amyloidosis; eprodisate (low-molecular-weight anionic sulfonate) also appears to slow kidney disease progression in patients with AA amyloidosis but has not yet been approved for clinical use by the U.S. Food and Drug Administration. Colchicine may be effective for amyloidosis secondary to familial Mediterranean fever. Liver transplantation is used for patients with ATTR amyloidosis.

TABLE 23 Conditions Associated with AA Amyloidosis
Chronic inflammatory arthritides
Rheumatoid arthritis
Juvenile idiopathic arthritis
Bronchiectasis
Infection in paraplegic patients
Osteomyelitis
Tuberculosis
Familial Mediterranean fever
Crohn disease
Castleman disease
Lymphoma
Vasculitis

Multiple Myeloma

Pathophysiology

Myeloma-related kidney disorders occur when coprecipitation of immunoglobulin light chains and Tamm-Horsfall proteins causes cast formation in the distal nephron. Tubular reabsorption of filtered light chains results in cellular protein overload, which ultimately causes inflammation and fibrosis.

Clinical Manifestations

Myeloma-related kidney disease manifests as mild to severe kidney dysfunction and proteinuria that is generally minimal. Between 20% and 25% of patients with multiple myeloma have established kidney insufficiency at the time of diagnosis.

Patients with myeloma-related kidney disease may have tubular dysfunction, including acid-base and concentration abnormalities and the Fanconi syndrome. Less than 15% to 25% of those with multiple myeloma have the nephrotic syndrome. Kidney disorders associated with multiple myeloma include acute kidney injury, light chain or AL amyloidosis, monoclonal immunoglobulin deposition, cast nephropathy (also known as myeloma kidney), cryoglobulinemic glomerulonephritis, and proliferative glomerulonephritis. Rarely, treatment with bisphosphonates for skeletal complications of multiple myeloma causes FSGS and acute tubular necrosis.

Cast nephropathy occurs in 30% to 50% of patients with multiple myeloma and is particularly associated with severe kidney dysfunction. Nearly 50% of these patients have acute kidney injury that is caused by dehydration, infection, hypercalcemia, or radiocontrast agent or NSAID use. Monoclonal immunoglobulin deposition occurs in 25% of patients with myeloma-related kidney disease, light chain deposition in 2% to 3%, and amyloidosis in 4% to 5%.

Diagnosis and Evaluation

Urine dipstick does not reveal albuminuria in patients with myeloma-related kidney disorders, but the addition of sulfosalicylic acid to the urine will precipitate all nonalbumin proteins, including light chains. Kidney biopsy is recommended to confirm multiple myeloma in the absence of other tissue diagnoses and to exclude other kidney disorders.

Management

Patients with multiple myeloma and ESKD are as responsive to chemotherapy as other patients, and management of myeloma-related kidney disorders should include systemic chemotherapy and autologous stem-cell transplantation to resolve the underlying disorder. Melphalan and prednisone should be used in patients who are not eligible for autologous stem-cell transplantation. Kidney transplantation has been successful in patients with multiple myeloma who have achieved full remission, but recurrence of light chain nephropathy and kidney failure has been reported.

In patients with cast nephropathy, volume expansion, alkalinization of the urine, discontinuation of nephrotoxic agents, and avoidance of radiocontrast agents is important. In addition, treatment of concomitant hypercalcemia is indicated to decrease the risk for intratubular cast formation and progressive kidney failure. Plasmapheresis is no longer recommended in patients with multiple myeloma who have kidney failure.

Prognosis

Kidney function is one of the most important determinants of survival in patients with multiple myeloma. Patients with serum creatinine levels below 1.5 mg/dL (132.6 µmol/L) have a 1-year survival rate of 80%, whereas those with levels above 2.3 mg/dL (203.3 µmol/L) have a 1-year survival rate of 50%.

Patients who attain remission with autologous stem-cell transplantation have a median survival of 40 months to 89 months compared with 26 months in those who are unresponsive to this therapy. Approximately 24% of patients with multiple myeloma new to dialysis who have undergone successful autologous stem-cell transplantation regain sufficient kidney function to discontinue dialysis.

HIV-Associated Nephropathy

Pathophysiology and Epidemiology

HIV-associated nephropathy (HIVAN) accounts for 33% of biopsy-proven glomerulopathies in patients with HIV infection. This condition primarily affects black patients and is the third leading cause of ESKD in this population group. HIVAN is not associated with a particular opportunistic infection or stage of infection with HIV. Patients with this condition have evidence of direct viral infection of glomerular visceral epithelial cells.

Clinical Manifestations and Diagnosis

HIVAN is characterized by the nephrotic syndrome, kidney insufficiency, and rapid progression to ESKD. Patients with HIVAN usually do not have edema or hypertension due to sodium wasting caused by proximal tubular lesions. On ultrasonography, the kidneys are typically large and highly echogenic. Kidney biopsy in patients with HIVAN may reveal segmental glomerulosclerosis, but tubular cystic lesions are pathognomonic of this condition. The presence of tubular reticular bodies seen on electron microscopy of a biopsy specimen further supports the diagnosis.

Many patients initially diagnosed with HIVAN already have advanced disease, but better screening practices are causing earlier detection of HIV-related kidney disease. Use of highly active antiretroviral therapy (HAART) has led to a decreased incidence of proteinuria in patients with HIV infection from 20% to 5% and a reduction in new-onset ESKD. However, even in patients undergoing HAART, the severity of HIVAN correlates with CD4 cell count and viral load.

Other forms of glomerular disease that can develop in patients due to infection with HIV include membranoproliferative glomerulonephritis, IgA nephropathy, lupus-like syndromes, and thrombotic microangiopathies such as hemolytic uremic syndrome (HUS) and thrombotic thrombocytopenic purpura (TTP). Furthermore, approximately 22% of patients with HIV infection who have proteinuria may develop an HIV-specific disorder known as HIV immune complex kidney disease. Finally, long-term survivors of HIV infection may develop chronic medical conditions associated with CKD and ESKD, including diabetes, hypertension, and atherosclerosis.

Management

Therapies that attempt to slow the progression of HIVAN include antiretroviral therapy and renin-angiotensin-aldosterone system inhibition with ACE inhibitors and ARBs. Limited evidence suggests a possible benefit of high-dose corticosteroids; however, the benefit of these interventions should be weighed against the risks of infection. HAART is typically used in this setting and helps to delay kidney disease progression. Patients with HIV infection also are eligible for kidney transplantation.

Hepatitis B Virus–Associated Kidney Disease

Membranous Nephropathy

Lamivudine therapy results in improved kidney outcome in patients with hepatitis B virus infection–induced membranous nephropathy who have a urine protein-creatinine ratio greater than 3 mg/mg. This therapy helps to decrease proteinuria and stop progression to ESKD independent of blood pressure control. Potential resistance to lamivudine therapy because of YMDD mutations of hepatitis B virus may require use of other, potentially nephrotoxic, agents such as adefovir. Patients with hepatitis B virus infection–induced membranous nephropathy have a worse kidney prognosis than those with idiopathic membranous nephropathy.

KEY POINTS

- Manifestations of diabetic nephropathy include proteinuria, a decline in kidney function, and hypertension that develops in patients with a 10- to 20-year history of type 1 diabetes or a 5- to 10-year history of type 2 diabetes.
- Renin-angiotensin system inhibitors should be used to decrease the blood pressure to below 130/80 mm Hg in all patients with diabetes and to less than 125/75 mm Hg in patients with diabetes who have a urine protein-creatinine ratio above 1 mg/mg.
- Patients with kidney amyloidosis typically have severe proteinuria and kidney dysfunction.
- Urine dipstick does not reveal albuminuria in patients with myeloma-related kidney disorders, but the addition of sulfosalicylic acid to the urine will precipitate all nonalbumin proteins, including light chains.
- HIV-associated nephropathy primarily affects black patients and is the third leading cause of end-stage kidney disease in this population group.

- HIV-associated nephropathy manifests as the nephrotic syndrome; large, highly echogenic kidneys seen on ultrasonography; kidney insufficiency; and rapid progression to end-stage kidney disease.
- Management of HIV-associated nephropathy may include highly active antiretroviral therapy, renin-angiotensin-aldosterone system inhibition, and kidney transplantation.
- Lamivudine therapy results in improved kidney outcome in patients with hepatitis B virus infection–induced membranous nephropathy who have a urine protein-creatinine ratio greater than 3 mg/mg.

Diseases That Cause the Nephritic Syndrome

IgA Nephropathy

Pathophysiology and Epidemiology

IgA nephropathy is the most common cause of glomerulonephritis worldwide. In the United States, approximately 5% of all kidney biopsies and 10% of biopsies of patients with glomerulonephritis reveal IgA nephropathy. IgA nephropathy is rare in black patients but common in American Indian individuals.

IgA nephropathy is caused by defective mucosal immunity in which IgA molecules react to as-yet unidentified antigens. These IgA antibodies are abnormally glycosylated and are therefore not effectively removed by the reticuloendothelial system. Once deposited, these immune complexes incite an inflammatory response that stimulates circulating factors such as platelet-derived growth factor that results in mesangial cell proliferation and mesangial matrix expansion. IgA nephropathy may have a genetic propensity, but most cases are sporadic.

Clinical Manifestations and Evaluation

IgA nephropathy may only involve the kidney or occur as part of a syndrome that includes skin or liver disease as well as other disorders such as inflammatory bowel disease; celiac disease; ankylosing spondylitis; and infections. IgA nephropathy also may develop in patients with Henoch-Schönlein purpura.

Approximately 30% to 40% of patients with IgA nephropathy present with an episode of macroscopic or gross hematuria that is usually associated with a concomitant pharyngitic or gastrointestinal infection. Complete resolution of hematuria in these patients is usually associated with infrequent disease recurrence, prolonged periods of disease quiescence, and excellent long-term prognosis.

Approximately 40% of patients with IgA nephropathy have persistent asymptomatic microscopic hematuria and proteinuria. In this setting, hypertension is much more common, kidney function impairment develops over time, and remission is rare. Some patients with IgA nephropathy present with the nephrotic syndrome caused by either diffuse proliferative glomerulonephritis or, rarely, the presence of a concomitant unrelated glomerulopathy such as minimal change disease.

Management

Conservative management with an ACE inhibitor or an ARB is indicated for patients with IgA nephropathy who have good prognostic indicators such as normal kidney function, normal blood pressure, and a urine protein-creatinine ratio less than 1 mg/mg. Those with more progressive disease who have elevated serum creatinine levels should receive pulse corticosteroid therapy or, if kidney insufficiency is present, corticosteroids and an alkylating agent.

Fish oil supplementation has been reported to be somewhat beneficial in IgA nephropathy. However, meta-analyses of published studies have concluded that only minor benefits are likely.

KEY POINTS

- IgA nephropathy may only involve the kidney or occur as part of a syndrome that includes skin or liver disease and other disorders such as inflammatory bowel disease, celiac disease, ankylosing spondylitis, and infections.
- Angiotensin-converting enzyme inhibitor or angiotensin receptor blocker therapy is indicated for patients with IgA nephropathy who have normal kidney function, normal blood pressure, and urine protein-creatinine ratio less than 1 mg/mg.
- Patients with progressive IgA nephropathy or a urine protein-creatinine ratio above 1 mg/mg should receive pulse corticosteroid therapy or, if kidney insufficiency is present, corticosteroids and an alkylating agent.

Membranoproliferative Glomerulonephritis

Pathophysiology and Epidemiology

Idiopathic membranoproliferative glomerulonephritis is a relatively uncommon cause of glomerulonephritis that usually manifests as a nephritic syndrome with hematuria and mild to moderate proteinuria. This condition is caused by immune complex deposition in the glomeruli; mesangial and endothelial cell proliferation; expansion of the mesangial matrix; thickening of the peripheral capillary walls by subendothelial immune and/or intramembranous dense deposits; and mesangial cell interposition into the capillary wall, which causes thickening of the GBM on light microscopy.

Membranoproliferative glomerulonephritis is most often associated with autoimmune diseases such as SLE or Sjögren syndrome, infections such as hepatitis C virus or poststreptococcal or infective endocarditis, or certain malignancies.

Clinical Manifestations

Membranoproliferative glomerulonephritis frequently manifests as glomerular hematuria, which is suggested by dysmorphic erythrocytes and erythrocyte casts seen on urinalysis. However, some patients may not have evidence of glomerular hematuria, and the urine protein-creatinine ratio can range from less than 1.5 mg/mg to nephrotic-range proteinuria. Additional findings include a low C3 level with a normal C4 level.

Classification

Type I membranoproliferative glomerulonephritis is the most commonly diagnosed form of this disease. Type I membranoproliferative glomerulonephritis can be a primary disorder or occur secondary to hepatitis B or C virus infection (with or without mixed cryoglobulinemia), mixed cryoglobulinemia, SLE, poststreptococcal infection, or infective endocarditis. Affected patients have immune deposits in the mesangium and subendothelial space.

Type II membranoproliferative glomerulonephritis rarely occurs in adults. This condition is usually diagnosed in children between 4 and 15 years of age who present with hematuria accompanied by proteinuria, acute nephritic syndrome, or the nephrotic syndrome. Drusen deposition in the retina and acquired partial lipodystrophy also may be present. Kidney biopsy reveals dense ribbon-like deposits along the basement membrane, tubules, and Bowman's capsule of the kidneys; because of these findings, type II membranoproliferative glomerulonephritis also is known as dense deposit disease.

Type III membranoproliferative glomerulonephritis is a disorder in which the immune complexes are located on the subepithelial and subendothelial aspects of the GBM. This condition may occur as an inherited disorder.

Management

Idiopathic membranoproliferative glomerulonephritis regardless of type has been treated with corticosteroids and other immunosuppressive agents, antiplatelet agents, anticoagulants, antithrombolytic agents, plasmapheresis, and plasma exchange. The two main treatment approaches have been corticosteroids and antiplatelet agents, but the efficacy of these approaches has not been adequately evaluated.

Treatment of the underlying disorder is an effective means of managing patients with secondary membranoproliferative disease. When membranoproliferative glomerulonephritis is associated with hepatitis C virus infection, pegylated interferon-alfa 2a and ribavirin therapy may decrease proteinuria and improve kidney function.

Prognosis

More than 50% of patients with idiopathic membranoproliferative glomerulonephritis progress to ESKD. Poor prognostic signs include nephrotic-range proteinuria, kidney insufficiency, hypertension, and the presence of crescents or tubulointerstitial disease on biopsy. Patients with asymptomatic hematuria, proteinuria, and focal abnormalities on kidney biopsy tend to have a better prognosis.

Hepatitis C Virus–Associated Kidney Disease

Clinical Manifestations

Hepatitis C virus–associated kidney disease most often manifests as membranoproliferative glomerulonephritis and mixed cryoglobulinemia.

Mesangioproliferative glomerulonephritis also may be associated with cryoglobulinemia in patients with hepatitis C virus infection. In the absence of cryoglobulins, patients with hepatitis C virus infection may develop membranous glomerulonephropathy and polyarteritis nodosa that may be associated with hypocomplementemia.

Hypertension is present in 25% to 75% of patients with membranoproliferative glomerulonephritis and cryoglobulinemia, and edema is present in most patients. Nephritic sediment is common in these patients, whereas nephrotic-range proteinuria occurs in approximately 20% of patients.

Rapidly progressive glomerulonephritis develops in 20% of patients with membranoproliferative glomerulonephritis and cryoglobulinemia, but terminal kidney disease is rare. Patients with active hepatitis C virus infection and cardiovascular disease tend to have a poor prognosis.

Management

Treatment of hepatitis C virus infection includes antiviral therapy with interferon alfa or pegylated interferon. The addition of ribavirin to these agents has been shown to improve kidney outcome in patients with membranoproliferative glomerulonephritis associated with hepatitis C virus infection and mixed cryoglobulinemia, but treatment response is decreased in those with advanced kidney failure. In addition, ribavirin-induced hemolytic anemia may develop in patients with poor kidney function and requires treatment with iron and erythropoietin.

Hepatitis B Virus–Associated Kidney Disease

Polyarteritis Nodosa

Only 1% to 5% of patients with hepatitis B virus infection have polyarteritis nodosa, but 30% of patients with polyarteritis nodosa have hepatitis B virus infection. Patients with hepatitis B virus infection and polyarteritis nodosa usually demonstrate complement activation. Clinical features include hypertension, variable kidney insufficiency, and occasionally kidney infarction bleeding caused by renal artery microaneurysm rupture. Urinalysis may show hematuria and subnephrotic proteinuria.

Approximately 50% of patients treated with interferon alfa and plasma exchange experience eradication of hepatitis B virus and resolution of polyarteritis nodosa. Combination therapy with prednisolone, interferon alfa, and lamivudine is effective in 70% to 100% of patients with hepatitis B virus–associated polyarteritis nodosa.

Poststreptococcal Glomerulonephritis

Poststreptococcal glomerulonephritis initially manifests as sudden-onset edema, hematuria, and kidney insufficiency that develop 2 or 3 weeks after the onset of streptococcal pharyngitis or cellulitis. Hypertension and acute kidney insufficiency also may develop but rapidly resolve. Diuresis begins within 1 week, and kidney function returns to baseline after 3 or 4 weeks. Most patients, particularly children, achieve complete clinical resolution after an initial episode.

Some patients with severe glomerular damage have persistent proteinuria and hypertension that require long-term therapy. Repeated episodes of poststreptococcal glomerulonephritis are rare and are probably caused by antibodies to the nephritogenic streptococcal antigen.

Approximately 70% of patients with poststreptococcal glomerulonephritis have elevated antistreptolysin O antibody titers, and 90% of patients with this condition have anti-DNAse B antibodies. Testing for both of these antibodies is the most effective method of diagnosing poststreptococcal glomerulonephritis.

Therapy is supportive, and these patients usually do not require immunosuppressive therapy.

Lupus Nephritis

Clinical Manifestations and Diagnosis

Kidney biopsy results in patients with World Health Organization (WHO) class I or II lupus nephritis may be normal or reveal minimal mesangial deposits or a mesangioproliferative glomerulonephritis. These patients typically have hematuria and/or proteinuria and usually do not have kidney insufficiency. Class III or IV disease is associated with focal or diffuse nephritis and manifests as acute nephritis with hematuria and proteinuria. Typically, erythrocyte casts are seen on urinalysis. Depending on the number of glomeruli involved, these patients also may have kidney insufficiency. Patients with membranous lupus nephritis (class V) typically have proteinuria that is within the nephrotic range. Those with class VI disease have lesions restricted to the tubulointerstitial space with inflammatory infiltrates.

Management

Disease severity should determine treatment in lupus nephritis. Class I and II disease is generally associated with an excellent prognosis, and immunosuppressive therapy in these patients is not indicated unless the disease progresses. Six consecutive months of once-monthly intravenous cyclophosphamide therapy with additional cyclophosphamide therapy administered every 3 months for up to 2 years has been shown to provide long-term improvement in kidney function in patients with class III and IV disease. Prednisone alone does not provide equivalent kidney protection over a 10-year period.

Because cyclophosphamide is associated with severe side effects, including major infection, mutagenesis, and premature ovarian failure in women, alternative therapies are under investigation. As induction therapy, mycophenolate mofetil appears equivalent to intravenous cyclophosphamide in patients with diffuse proliferative glomerulonephritis. Furthermore, mycophenolate mofetil has been shown to be superior to intravenous cyclophosphamide in maintaining disease remission when intravenous cyclophosphamide was used for 6 months for induction, followed by either mycophenolate mofetil, azathioprine, or intravenous cyclophosphamide for a period of up to 48 months.

Mycophenolate mofetil and azathioprine also were superior in maintaining remission with fewer side effects compared with intravenous cyclophosphamide. However, disease recrudescence is significantly more common after discontinuation of mycophenolate mofetil than after intravenous cyclophosphamide. Finally, whether these less-toxic therapies prevent ESKD over decades of use remains uncertain.

Multiple monoclonal antibody therapies have been instituted in patients with class III and IV lupus nephritis with variable success. Rituximab in particular had shown promise in patients with class III or IV lupus nephritis resistant to cyclophosphamide therapy, but recent clinical trials have not demonstrated a significant therapeutic benefit.

Prognosis

The following factors help to determine outcome in patients with lupus nephritis: poor kidney function at the time of presentation; the severity of disease found on kidney histology; the presence of interstitial fibrosis, which indicates scarring; and the presence of crescents, which indicate active, aggressive glomerulonephritis. In addition, black race is an independent predictor of ESKD in patients with class IV disease.

Anti–Glomerular Basement Membrane Antibody Disease

Pathophysiology and Epidemiology

Anti-GBM antibody disease is caused by antibodies to a noncollagenous portion of type IV collagen. This condition may involve only the kidneys or both the kidneys and the lungs. The pulmonary-kidney presentation of anti-GBM antibody disease is known as Goodpasture syndrome and typically affects young men, whereas older women typically have involvement of only the kidneys.

Clinical Manifestations

Rapidly progressive glomerulonephritis is the most common feature of anti-GBM antibody disease. Approximately 70% of patients with Goodpasture syndrome have alveolar hemorrhage. Clinical manifestations of this condition include dyspnea and cough. Approximately 30% of patients with Goodpasture syndrome have ANCA-associated vasculitis that may involve sites outside of the lungs and kidneys, and relapse is common in this setting.

Management

Corticosteroids and cyclophosphamide are indicated to induce disease remission in patients with anti-GBM antibody disease. Because relapse rarely occurs, cyclophosphamide may be discontinued after 3 to 6 months. In addition, pulmonary hemorrhage is a medical emergency requiring immediate plasmapheresis to remove the causative antibody.

Prognosis

The promptness of therapy and the serum creatinine level at the time of diagnosis largely determine patient and kidney survival. Patients who require dialysis or who have a serum creatinine level greater than 5 to 6 mg/dL (442 to 530 μmol/L) have a significantly lower chance of kidney survival than those with normal kidney function.

KEY POINTS

- The pulmonary-kidney presentation of anti–glomerular basement membrane antibody disease is known as Goodpasture syndrome and typically affects young men, whereas older women typically have involvement of only the kidneys.
- Corticosteroids and cyclophosphamide are indicated to induce disease remission in patients with anti–glomerular basement antibodies.

Small- and Medium-Vessel Vasculitis

Clinical Manifestations

Kidney disease in patients with systemic vasculitis frequently manifests as a rapidly progressive glomerulonephritis and is usually diagnosed approximately 15 months after the onset of symptoms. Small-vessel kidney vasculitides include Wegener granulomatosis, microscopic polyangiitis, and Churg-Strauss syndrome. Patients with these conditions usually present with nonspecific signs and symptoms such as weight loss, decreased appetite, polymyalgia, hematuria, and proteinuria. More than 90% of patients with microscopic polyangiitis have kidney involvement, and older patients are more likely to have severe kidney vasculitis. Vasculitis of the medium-sized vessels includes polyarteritis nodosa and typically causes ischemia of the tissues supported by the involved vessels.

Extrarenal involvement in patients with these vasculitides may occur in any organ system.

Diagnosis

Diagnosis of Wegener granulomatosis or microscopic polyangiitis involves antibody assays and kidney biopsy. Most patients are ANCA positive. Antiproteinase-3 (anti-PR3) antibodies are usually detected in patients with Wegener granulomatosis, whereas antimyeloperoxidase (anti-MPO) antibodies are usually found in those with microscopic polyangiitis. Serial ANCA testing should not be used to monitor disease activity or to guide treatment decisions in patients with Wegener granulomatosis.

To establish a diagnosis of Wegener granulomatosis, microscopic polyangiitis, polyarteritis nodosa, or Churg-Strauss syndrome with kidney involvement, kidney biopsy must reveal the presence of a necrotizing crescentic glomerulonephritis or necrotizing vasculitis of microscopic vessels such as the small arteries, arterioles, capillaries, or venules.

Management

A study performed by the European Vasculitis Study Group showed that patients with severe Wegener granulomatosis who underwent plasma exchange in addition to immunosuppressive therapy with daily cyclophosphamide and high-dose oral methylprednisolone had a 24% risk reduction for progression to ESKD compared with those who received immunosuppressive therapy alone.

Combination therapy with cyclophosphamide and high-dose corticosteroids results in remission in 75% to 90% of patients with microscopic polyangiitis–related kidney disease at 6 months. However, elderly patients may have a poorer prognosis because of medication-related side effects and complications such as infection.

At 5 years, relapse occurs in approximately 33% of patients with microscopic polyangiitis and is significantly more likely in patients with anti-PR3 antibodies or upper and/or lower respiratory tract disease. Therefore, maintenance therapy with agents such as aspirin, methotrexate, or leflunomide and mycophenolate motefil is indicated. New alternative therapies that may be effective include rituximab, N-acetylcysteine, and tumor necrosis factor-α inhibitors and may permit reduction in other strong immunosuppressive therapies.

Indefinite follow-up is recommended for patients with microscopic polyangiitis, with continued ANCA positivity a predictor of relapse. Furthermore, plasma exchange may delay or eliminate the need for dialysis in patients with microscopic polyangiitis–related kidney disease who have undergone induction therapy and are now on maintenance therapy.

The 1-year survival rate of patients with ANCA-associated glomerulonephritis is 73% to 76%. In addition, serious adverse events develop in approximately 50% of patients treated for small- and medium-vessel vasculitis.

More than 80% of patients with Churg-Strauss syndrome or polyarteritis nodosa achieve remission with appropriate therapy. Immunosuppressive therapy benefits these patients. Corticosteroids alone can be used in patients without poor prognostic factors with immunosuppressive agents added in case of treatment failure. However, most patients require combination therapy with corticosteroids and immunosuppressive agents, particularly pulse cyclophosphamide. Adjuvant therapy with plasma exchange also is indicated for patients with severe kidney involvement. Once remission is achieved, maintenance therapy with at least 18 months of azathioprine or methotrexate can replace cyclophosphamide.

KEY POINTS

- Kidney disease in patients with systemic vasculitis frequently manifests as a rapidly progressive glomerulonephritis.

- Most patients with polyarteritis and microscopic polyangiitis are ANCA positive; antiproteinase-3 (anti-PR3) antibodies are usually detected in patients with Wegener granulomatosis, whereas antimyeloperoxidase (anti-MPO) antibodies are usually found in those with microscopic polyangiitis.

- In patients with severe Wegener granulomatosis, plasma exchange in addition to immunosuppressive therapy has a 24% risk reduction for progression to end-stage kidney disease compared with those who received immunosuppressive therapy alone.

- Plasma exchange may delay or eliminate the need for dialysis in patients with microscopic polyangiitis–related kidney disease who have undergone induction therapy and are receiving maintenance therapy.

Thrombotic Microangiopathy

Thrombotic microangiopathy is a clinical syndrome that affects multiple organ systems but is always characterized by thrombocytopenia and microangiopathic hemolytic anemia. Thrombotic microangiopathy may manifest as thrombotic thrombocytopenic purpura (TTP) or hemolytic-uremic syndrome (HUS).

Pathophysiology and Clinical Manifestations

Patients with TTP often have increased levels of ultra-large von Willebrand factor multimers, which bind to platelets and induce platelet agglutination. Normally, these multimers are not present in the circulation because of cleavage by the von Willebrand factor–cleaving protease ADAMTS13. Most patients with TTP have a severe deficiency of ADAMTS13. Although most cases of TTP are idiopathic, some patients have an associated disease known to cause TTP; for example, TTP is present in 5% of patients with disseminated malignancy.

HUS is usually caused either by infection with Shiga toxin–producing *Escherichia coli* or by complement dysregulation caused by genetic mutations. Rarely, HUS develops in the postpartum period in women who have had preeclampsia antepartum. In children, this condition usually develops after a diarrheal illness. HUS commonly manifests as acute kidney injury accompanied by thrombocytopenia and microangiopathic hemolytic anemia.

TTP and HUS may be accompanied by other manifestations, including neurologic abnormalities, kidney dysfunction, and fever; however, the presence of only microangiopathic hemolytic anemia and thrombocytopenia without another apparent cause is considered a sufficient criterion for institution of treatment. Patients with TTP generally have a higher incidence of neurologic symptoms, whereas patients with HUS have a higher incidence of kidney involvement. Nevertheless, these conditions have considerable clinical overlap (see Thrombotic Microangiopathies in MKSAP 15 Hematology and Oncology).

Management and Prognosis

Empiric plasma exchange therapy is indicated for patients with a clinical presentation compatible with thrombotic microangiopathy. Patients with untreated TTP have a mortality rate above 85%, whereas those who undergo plasma exchange have a mortality rate between 10% and 30%.

In patients with TTP, the identification of severe ADAMTS 13 deficiency is predictive of relapse. For patients with HUS not associated with diarrhea, identification of mutations in factor H and I and membrane cofactor protein is important for predicting response to kidney transplantation once kidney failure occurs.

KEY POINTS

- Thrombotic microangiopathy is a clinical syndrome characterized by multiple organ involvement, thrombocytopenia, and microangiopathic hemolytic anemia.

- Empiric plasma exchange therapy is indicated for patients with a clinical presentation compatible with thrombotic thrombocytopenic purpura-hemolytic uremic syndrome.

Bibliography

Barnett AH, Bain SC, Bouter P, et al; Diabetics Exposed to Telmisartan and Enalapril Study Group. Angiotensin-receptor blockade versus converting-enzyme inhibition in type 2 diabetes and nephropathy [erratum in N Engl J Med. 2005;352(16):1731]. N Engl J Med. 2004; 351(19):1952-1961. [PMID: 15516696]

Dember LM, Hawkins PN, Hazenberg BP, et al; Eprodisate for AA Amyloidosis Trial Group. Eprodisate for the treatment of renal disease in AA amyloidosis. N Engl J Med. 2007;356(23):2349-2360. [PMID: 17554116]

Ginzler EM, Dooley MA, Aranow C, et al. Mycophenolate mofetil or intravenous cyclophosphamide for lupus nephritis. N Engl J Med. 2005;353(21):2219-2228. [PMID: 16306519]

Kamar N, Rostaing L, Alric L. Treatment of hepatitis C-virus-related glomerulonephritis. Kidney Int 2006; 69(3):436-439. [PMID: 16514428]

Jayne DR, Gaskin G, Rasmussen N, et al; European Vasculitis Study Group. Randomized trial of plasma exchange or high-dosage methylprednisolone as adjunctive therapy for severe renal vasculitis. J Am Soc Nephrol. 2007;18(7):2180-2188. [PMID: 17582159]

Lai KN. Membranous nephropathy: when and how to treat. Kidney Int. 2007;71(9):841-843. [PMID: 17457329]

Mauer M, Zinman B, Gardiner R, Suissa S, Sinaiko A, Strand T, et al. Renal and retinal effects of enalapril and losartan in type 1 diabetes. N Engl J Med. 2009;361:40-51. [PMID: 19571282]

Moranne O, Watier L, Rossert J, Stengel B; GN-Progress Study Group. Primary glomerulonephritis: an update on renal survival and determinants of progression. QJM. 2008;101(3):215-224. [PMID: 18245806]

Nishi S, Alchi B, Imai N, Gejyo F. New advances in renal amyloidosis. Clin Exp Nephrol. 2008;12(2):93-101. [PMID: 18175051]

Genetic Disorders and Kidney Disease

Cystic Disorders

Autosomal-Dominant Polycystic Kidney Disease

Autosomal-dominant polycystic kidney disease (ADPKD) is the most common heritable kidney disease. This condition is caused by mutations in *PKD1* or *PKD2* genes; disease caused by mutations in the *PKD1* gene is more common and has a more severe course than that caused by *PKD2* gene mutations. The hallmark of ADPKD is gradual kidney cyst growth that results in massive kidney enlargement, which leads to loss of kidney function.

Clinical Manifestations

Kidney manifestations of ADPKD include massive kidney enlargement, back and flank pain, kidney stones, urinary tract infections, hypertension, and hematuria. Proteinuria in patients with ADPKD is associated with a greater risk for end-stage kidney disease (ESKD). Overt proteinuria is uncommon, and a urine protein-creatinine ratio above 1 mg/mg suggests the presence of another kidney disease. Larger kidney size is associated with loss of kidney function, and most patients with ADPKD develop kidney failure by the fifth or sixth decade of life.

Extrarenal manifestations of ADPKD include cysts in the liver, pancreas, spleen, thyroid, seminal vesicles, and arachnoidea mater. By age 35 years, most patients with ADPKD have liver cysts detectable on MRI, and severe hepatic cystic disease occurs predominantly in women. Intracranial aneurysms occur in approximately 5% of these patients, and 50% of these cysts may rupture. The most important risk factor for the development of intracranial aneurysms in patients with ADPKD is a family member with an intracranial aneurysm.

Screening and Diagnosis

Ultrasonography is the imaging method of choice for diagnosing ADPKD. The number of kidney cysts seen on ultrasonography that are required to establish a diagnosis varies based on the patient's age, PKD genotype, and whether a family history of ADPKD is present.

Simple kidney cysts are rare in patients less than 20 years of age, and the appearance of a single cyst in an at-risk individual in this population less than 30 years of age is specific for ADPKD. However, more than eight bilateral cysts must be present in individuals older than 60 years of age to establish a diagnosis, because simple cysts are common in older patients.

In individuals 15 to 30 years of age with a family history of a *PKD1* mutation, a normal ultrasound confers an 80% to 95% likelihood of not inheriting ADPKD; this likelihood increases to more than 95% in patients older than 30 years. In individuals 15 to 30 years of age with a family history of a *PKD2* mutation, a normal ultrasound conveys a 67% likelihood of not inheriting ADPKD. Genetic testing also is helpful, particularly during early disease when imaging studies are less reliable.

Confirmation of the presence of a mutation in *PKD1* or *PKD2* via genetic testing in at-risk family members is indicated in individuals less than 30 years of age considering kidney donation, if clinical and radiologic diagnosis is uncertain, or if desired for family planning.

Management

Hypertension in patients with ADPKD is common, develops early, and is associated with poor kidney outcomes. The blood pressure target in patients with ADPKD is less than 125/75 mm Hg. An angiotensin-converting enzyme inhibitor or angiotensin receptor blocker should be used as first-line therapy to achieve this goal.

Infection of kidney cysts may manifest as flank pain and fever accompanied by a bland urinalysis and a negative urine culture. The treatment of cyst infection in patients with ADPKD requires antibiotics that are capable of penetrating the cyst, including fluoroquinolones, chloramphenicol, and trimethoprim-sulfamethoxazole; therapy should be continued for at least 2 to 4 weeks.

Patients with ADPKD who have cyst hemorrhage commonly develop low-grade fever and gross hematuria. These episodes are most often self-limited, and bed rest and increased fluid intake shorten the duration of gross hematuria. Cyst hemorrhage in the absence of gross hematuria is often painful due to acute cyst expansion.

Approximately 25% of patients with ADPKD have kidney stones and are associated with microscopic hematuria; flank pain; and, infrequently, fever. The type of stone should determine the most appropriate treatment independent of the presence of ADPKD (see Kidney Stones).

- Kidney manifestations of autosomal-dominant poly-cystic kidney disease include kidney enlargement, back and flank pain, kidney stones, urinary tract infections, hypertension, hematuria, and mild proteinuria.

- Extrarenal manifestations of autosomal-dominant polycystic kidney disease include cysts of the liver, pancreas, spleen, thyroid, seminal vesicles, and arachnoidea mater as well as intracranial aneurysms.

- Ultrasonography is the imaging method of choice for diagnosing autosomal-dominant polycystic kidney disease.

- Patients with autosomal-dominant polycystic kidney disease should be treated to a blood pressure target of less than 125/75 mm Hg using an angiotensin-converting enzyme inhibitor or angiotensin receptor blocker.

- The treatment of cyst infection in patients with autosomal-dominant polycystic kidney disease requires antibiotics that are capable of penetrating cysts, including fluoroquinolones, chloramphenicol, and trimethoprim-sulfamethoxazole; this therapy should be continued for at least 2 to 4 weeks.

Autosomal-Recessive Polycystic Kidney Disease

Autosomal-recessive polycystic kidney disease (ARPKD) is a rare condition that manifests in infancy and typically causes kidney failure within the first two decades of life.

Clinical Manifestations

Tubular dilatation is the hallmark of ARPKD and is associated with massive kidney enlargement at birth, abdominal masses, and respiratory distress. Difficult-to-control hypertension and growth retardation also are common.

Congenital hepatic fibrosis is a universal feature of ARPKD, and hepatic fibrosis and portal hypertension predominate the clinical picture in patients in their second and third decades of life.

Management

Hypertension in patients with ARPKD should be treated with salt restriction and an angiotensin-converting enzyme inhibitor, and dialysis should be considered when needed. Patients with ARPKD are candidates for kidney or combined liver and kidney transplantation, as indicated.

Tuberous Sclerosis

Diagnosis

Tuberous sclerosis is an autosomal-dominant disorder caused by mutations in the *TSC1* and *TSC2* genes. A definitive diagnosis of tuberous sclerosis entails the presence of any two major features or one major feature and two minor features (**Table 24**). Kidney angiomyolipomas occur in 70% to 80%

of affected patients and are detected by CT or MRI based on their fat content. Complications of these lesions include pain and hemorrhage and commonly occur once lesions reach 4 cm (1.6 in) in diameter. Hemorrhage from these lesions is the most common cause of kidney failure and death in adults with tuberous sclerosis.

TABLE 24 Revised Diagnostic Criteria for Tuberous Sclerosis Complex

Major Features

1. Facial angiofibromas or forehead plaque
2. Nontraumatic ungual or periungual fibroma
3. Hypomelanotic macules (three or more)
4. Shagreen patch (connective tissue nevus)
5. Multiple retinal nodular hamartomas
6. Cortical tuber[a]
7. Subependymal nodule
8. Subependymal giant cell astrocytoma
9. Cardiac rhabdomyoma, single or multiple
10. Lymphangiomyomatosis[b]
11. Renal angiomyolipoma[b]

Minor Features

1. Multiple, randomly distributed pits in dental enamel
2. Hamartomatous rectal polyps[c]
3. Bone cysts[d]
4. Cerebral white matter radial migration lines[a, d, e]
5. Gingival fibromas
6. Nonrenal hamartoma[c]
7. Retinal achromic patch
8. "Confetti" skin lesions
9. Multiple renal cysts[c]

Definite Tuberous Sclerosis Complex

Either two major features or one major feature plus two minor features

Probable Tuberous Sclerosis Complex

One major plus one minor feature

Possible Tuberous Sclerosis Complex

Either one major feature or two or more minor features

[a]When cerebral cortical dysplasia and cerebral white matter migration tracts occur together, they should be counted as one rather than two features of tuberous sclerosis.

[b]When both lymphangiomyomatosis and renal angiomyolipomas are present, other features of tuberous sclerosis should be present before a definite diagnosis is assigned.

[c]Histologic confirmation is suggested.

[d]Radiographic confirmation is sufficient.

[e]One panel member (M.R.G.) felt strongly that three or more radial migration lines should constitute a major sign.

Reprinted with permission from Roach ES, Gomez MR, Northrup H. Tuberous sclerosis complex consensus conference: revised clinical diagnostic criteria. J Child Neurol. 1998;13(12):624-628. [PMID: 9881533] Copyright Sage Publications, 1998.

Management

Case reports have demonstrated significant reductions in kidney angiomyolipomas over a short period of time with use of rapamycin. Arterial embolization is a frequently used kidney-sparing measure to reduce the size of kidney angiomyolipomas, and successful embolization prevents regrowth of these tumors.

KEY POINTS

- Hepatic fibrosis and portal hypertension predominate the clinical picture in patients with autosomal-recessive polycystic kidney disease in their second and third decades of life.
- Hypertension in patients with autosomal-recessive polycystic kidney disease should be treated with salt restriction and an angiotensin-converting enzyme inhibitor.
- Kidney angiomyolipomas may develop in patients with tuberous sclerosis and are detected via CT or MRI.
- Rapamycin and arterial embolization may help treat kidney angiomyolipomas in patients with tuberous sclerosis.

Noncystic Disorders

Noncystic genetic diseases of the kidney primarily affect the glomerular basement membrane, transportation of fluid and electrolytes, and deposition of sphingomyelin compounds.

Alport Syndrome

Alport syndrome, also known as hereditary nephritis, is an X-linked disorder in approximately 80% of patients and an auto-somal-recessive disorder in about 10% of patients. Mutations in the α5 chain of type IV collagen on chromosome Xq22 cause the X-linked, or classic, form of this disease, whereas mutations in the α3 and α4 chains of type IV collagen cause the autosomal-recessive form.

Alport syndrome commonly manifests as nephrotic-range proteinuria and progressive kidney insufficiency. Disruption in the basement membrane of the middle ear and the ocular lenses also causes sensorineural hearing loss and visual abnormalities associated with anterior lenticonus.

Men with Alport syndrome develop hematuria, proteinuria, and progressive chronic kidney disease early, usually in the second or third decade of life. Women with X-linked Alport syndrome have a milder disease course that usually manifests as microscopic hematuria. Age of onset of ESKD is highly variable in women and can be in the fifth or sixth decade of life.

The lack of normal α5 type IV collagen on skin biopsy is diagnostic of Alport syndrome in affected men; however, in affected women, the presence of α5 type IV collagen is less consistent due to lyonization of the X chromosome and is therefore less accurate.

Thin Basement Membrane Nephropathy

Thin basement membrane nephropathy, also known as benign familial hematuria, is an inherited disorder caused by mutations in the α3 and α4 chains of type IV collagen. Unlike Alport syndrome, thin basement membrane nephropathy usually does not cause kidney failure. This condition usually initially manifests during childhood and is characterized by microscopic or gross hematuria, and a family history of hematuria is suggestive of the condition.

KEY POINTS

- Alport syndrome commonly manifests as nephrotic-range proteinuria and progressive kidney insufficiency and may cause sensorineural hearing loss and visual abnormalities.
- Thin basement membrane nephropathy, also known as benign familial hematuria, initially manifests during childhood and is characterized by microscopic or gross hematuria.

Fabry Disease

Fabry disease is an X-linked disorder caused by deficiency of the α-galactosidase A enzyme. This condition causes globotriaosylceramide to accumulate in multiple tissues throughout the body.

Clinical manifestations of Fabry disease include mild nephrotic-range proteinuria, slow deterioration in kidney function, cutaneous angiokeratomas, painful paresthesias of the hands, and premature coronary artery disease. Progression to ESKD during the third or fourth decade of life is the most common complication in affected men and the primary cause of premature death in all patients with Fabry disease.

Biochemical or genetic screening for Fabry disease is recommended for family members of affected patients. Intravenous replacement with recombinant human α-galactosidase A is effective in treating Fabry disease.

KEY POINTS

- Clinical manifestations of Fabry disease include mild proteinuria, slow deterioration in kidney function, cutaneous angiokeratomas, painful paresthesias of the hands, and premature coronary artery disease.
- Intravenous replacement with recombinant human α-galactosidase A is effective in treating Fabry disease.

Bibliography

Ortiz A, Oliveira JP, Wanner C, Brenner BM, Waldek S, Warnock DG. Recommendations and guidelines for the diagnosis and treatment of Fabry nephropathy in adults. Nat Clin Pract Nephrol. 2008;4(6):327-336. [PMID: 18431378]

Ravine D, Gibson RN, Walker RG, Sheffield LJ, Kincaid-Smith P, Danks DM. Evaluation of ultrasonographic diagnostic criteria for autosomal dominant polycystic kidney disease 1. Lancet. 1994;343(8901):824-827. [PMID: 7908078]

Siroky BJ, Czyzyk-Krzeska MF, Bissler JJ. Renal involvement in tuberous sclerosis complex and von Hippel-Lindau disease: shared disease mechanisms? Nat Clin Pract Nephrol. 2009;5(3):143-156. [PMID: 19240728]

Acute Kidney Injury

Pathophysiology and Epidemiology

Acute kidney injury (AKI), formerly known as acute renal failure, is characterized by an abrupt decline in kidney function that occurs over hours to days. Consensus on an operational definition of AKI has not yet been reached, but one expert panel recommends the following criteria: an absolute increase in the serum creatinine level of 0.3 mg/dL (26.5 µmol/L) or above from baseline within 48 hours; an increase in the serum creatinine level of 50% or more, or urine output less than 0.5 mL/kg/h for more than 6 hours. Risk factors for AKI include preexisting chronic kidney disease (CKD), diabetic nephropathy, heart failure, liver disease, hypovolemia, and age over 50 years.

Growing evidence demonstrates that kidney injury associated with little or no change in the glomerular filtration rate (GFR) may still cause significant clinical sequelae. AKI is associated with an increased risk for mortality up to 90 days post hospital discharge even in patients with transient disease associated with a rapid return to baseline kidney function. Recent evidence suggests that this condition, independent of the cause, contributes to excess mortality.

KEY POINTS

- Acute kidney injury is a common condition characterized by an abrupt decline in kidney function that occurs over hours to days.
- Risk factors for acute kidney injury include preexisting chronic kidney disease, diabetic nephropathy, heart failure, liver disease, hypovolemia, and age over 50 years.

Clinical Manifestations and Evaluation

Frequent manifestations of AKI include retention of metabolic waste products such as urea and creatinine and failure to regulate the content of the extracellular fluid that may result in metabolic acidosis, hyperkalemia, disturbances in body fluid homeostasis, and secondary end-organ dysfunction.

Patients with suspected AKI should undergo a thorough history including evaluation of any nephrotoxic exposures such as iodinated contrast agents, NSAIDs, angiotensin-converting enzyme (ACE) inhibitors, angiotensin receptor blockers, and cyclooxygenase-2 inhibitors. Physical examination should include evaluation of volume status and a search for extrarenal manifestations that may suggest a cause of the AKI;

for example, the presence of palpable purpura is suggestive of a vasculitic cause.

Analysis of the urine sediment is essential (**Figure 14**). The fractional excretion of sodium (FE_{Na}) also is useful and can be calculated using the following equation:

$$FE_{Na} = \frac{[Urine\ Sodium]/[Serum\ Sodium] \times 100\%}{[Urine\ Creatinine]/[Serum\ Creatinine]}$$

In patients with oliguric AKI, a FE_{Na} of less than 1% reflects avid tubular sodium reabsorption and suggests a diagnosis of prerenal azotemia in the absence of urine sediment abnormalities. A FE_{Na} above 2% in these patients should raise suspicion for acute tubular necrosis. However, the FE_{Na} should be interpreted with caution in patients with preexisting CKD because these individuals have a decreased capacity for tubular sodium reabsorption. For example, the FE_{Na} may be 2% in a patient with CKD with superimposed prerenal azotemia.

Kidney ultrasonography is indicated for all patients with AKI to define kidney anatomy and echogenicity and to exclude hydronephrosis. Patients with underlying kidney parenchymal disease usually show increased echogenicity on kidney ultrasonography.

Kidney biopsy should be considered when the diagnosis remains unclear after excluding prerenal and postrenal disease. Biopsy also may be warranted to help guide therapy or provide prognostic information.

KEY POINTS

- Evaluation of patients with suspected acute kidney injury should include a history of nephrotoxic exposures.
- Kidney ultrasonography is indicated for all patients with acute kidney injury, and kidney biopsy should be considered when the diagnosis remains unclear after excluding prerenal and postrenal disease.

Classification

Prerenal Azotemia

Prerenal azotemia develops when autoregulation of kidney blood flow can no longer maintain GFR. This condition generally occurs in patients with a mean arterial pressure below 60 mm Hg but may occur at higher pressures in individuals with CKD or in those who take medications that can alter local glomerular hemodynamics, such as NSAIDs.

Patients with prerenal azotemia may have a history of fluid losses and decreased fluid intake accompanied by physical examination findings consistent with extracellular fluid volume depletion, such as postural hypotension. However, these findings are absent in up to 50% of patients with this condition, and prerenal azotemia also may develop in patients with normal or

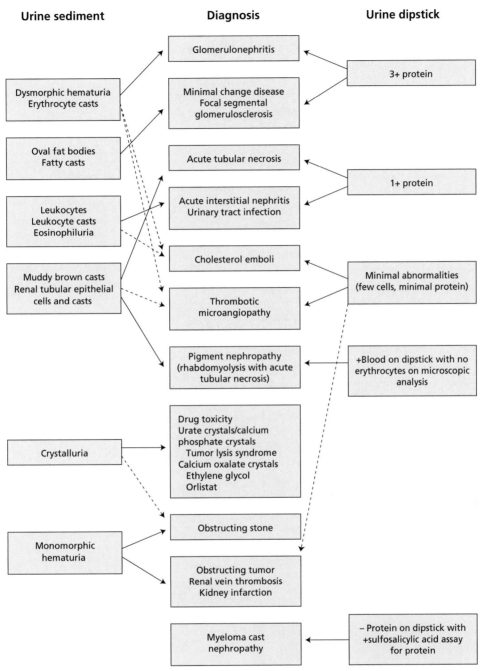

FIGURE 14.
Urinalysis findings in acute kidney injury.

—— = most common findings; ---- = less common findings.

increased extracellular fluid volume caused by changes in glomerular hemodynamics. For example, patients with heart failure or liver disease have a decreased effective circulating blood volume (defined as the part of the circulation that effectively perfuses the tissues and hence the kidneys) but may have edema and total body fluid overload.

KEY POINT

- Physical examination findings consistent with extracellular fluid volume depletion are absent in up to 50% of patients with prerenal azotemia, and this condition may develop in patients with normal or increased extracellular fluid volume.

Intrarenal Disease

Acute Tubular Necrosis

Acute tubular necrosis is the most common form of intrarenal disease that causes AKI in hospitalized patients. Onset of this condition usually occurs after a sustained period of ischemia or exposure to nephrotoxic agents. Acute tubular necrosis may resolve over 1 to 3 weeks or result in permanent end-stage kidney disease, depending on the duration and severity of the ischemic or nephrotoxic insult.

Urinalysis in approximately 75% of patients with acute tubular necrosis reveals muddy brown casts, and most patients have a FE_{Na} above 2% (**Figure 15**).

A mean arterial pressure of at least 65 mm Hg is a reasonable target to guide titration of fluid and vasopressor agents in most patients with shock and acute tubular necrosis, but a precise target has yet to be established in clinical trials. The clinical setting also should help to guide therapy; for example, a lower mean arterial pressure may be appropriate for patients with left ventricular dysfunction.

Trials of pharmacologic therapy directed toward ameliorating the severity or hastening recovery of acute tubular necrosis have been largely disappointing. Low-dose dopamine has been shown to have no benefit in improving outcomes or mortality. Two small pilot studies showed that fenoldopam may help to ameliorate early acute kidney dysfunction but require further validation. Loop diuretics are of no benefit in preventing AKI or improving outcomes in oliguric patients, but diuretic agents are a useful adjunct in the management of fluid overload and hyperkalemia complicating acute tubular necrosis before initiation of dialysis.

A 2007 study showed that approximately 81% of surviving patients with acute tubular necrosis who had preexisting normal kidney function and no longer required dialysis at discharge had well-preserved kidney function at 7-year follow-up. However, patients with acute tubular necrosis associated with multiorgan failure have a 50% to 80% mortality rate.

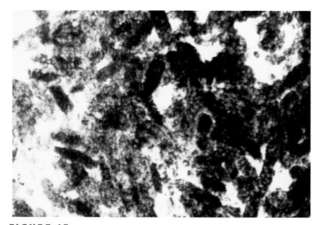

FIGURE 15.
Muddy brown casts seen on urine microscopy in a patient with acute tubular necrosis.

Contrast-Induced Nephropathy

Pathophysiology and Epidemiology

Contrast-induced nephropathy is characterized by an increase in the serum creatinine level 24 to 48 hours after contrast administration. Most patients with contrast-induced nephropathy have nonoliguric kidney injury with recovery of kidney function within 1 to 2 weeks.

Risk Factors

Patients undergoing coronary angiography who have a serum creatinine level of 1.5 mg/dL (132.6 µmol/L) or higher or a GFR below 60 mL/min/1.73 m² have the greatest risk of developing contrast-induced nephropathy, especially if concurrent diabetes mellitus is present. Additional risk factors for contrast-induced nephropathy also have been identified, and a tool to calculate a patient's risk for developing this condition is available at www.zunis .org/Contrast-Induced%20Nephropathy%20Calculator2.htm.

Primary Prevention

The most effective intervention to decrease the incidence and severity of contrast-induced nephropathy is volume expansion with either isotonic saline or sodium bicarbonate (**Figure 16**). The Contrast-Induced Nephropathy Consensus Working Panel specifically recommends that patients receive isotonic crystalloid at a rate of 1.0 to 1.5 mL/kg/h for 3 to 12 hours before contrast is administered, continuing for 6 to 24 hours afterward. Numerous small studies have shown superior outcomes with isotonic sodium bicarbonate compared with isotonic saline, but a recent well-powered randomized controlled trial demonstrated no advantage of isotonic sodium bicarbonate over isotonic saline.

Before contrast administration, NSAIDs and metformin should be discontinued. Metformin can cause lactic acidosis in patients with kidney insufficiency. Patients with stable kidney function who have undergone long-term use of ACE inhibitors or angiotensin receptor blockers may continue these agents. Whether *N*-acetylcysteine therapy prevents contrast-induced nephropathy is uncertain, but this agent has a relatively favorable risk profile and can be considered in high-risk patients.

Finally, use of either low-osmolar (500 to 850 mosm/kg) or iso-osmolar (approximately 290 mosm/kg) nonionic contrast agents is associated with a lower risk of contrast-induced nephropathy in high-risk patients.

Alternatives to Iodinated Contrast Agents

Gadolinium-containing compounds had been used as an alternative to iodinated contrast in patients with CKD but are now believed to be nephrotoxic in high-risk individuals. Furthermore, gadolinium may be associated with nephrogenic systemic fibrosis in patients with kidney dysfunction and therefore is not recommended for individuals at highest risk for contrast-induced nephropathy, especially those with a GFR below 30 mL/min/1.73 m².

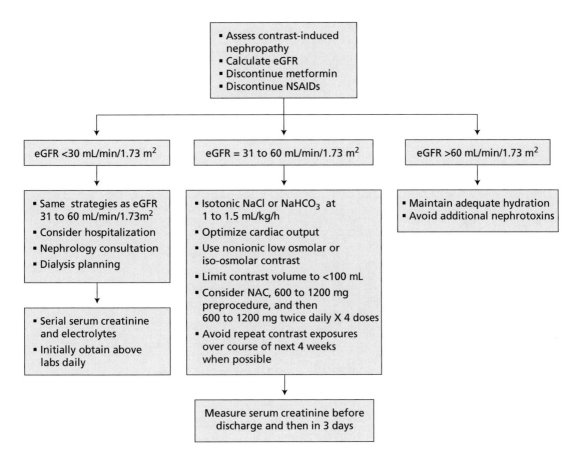

FIGURE 16.
Management of patients receiving iodinated contrast media.

eGFR = estimated glomerular filtration rate; NAC = N-acetylcysteine.

Modified with permission from McCullough PA, Stacul F, Davidson C, Becker CR, Adam A, Lameire N, Tumlin JA; CIN Consensus Working Panel. Overview. Am J Cardiol. 2006; 98:2K-4K. Copyright © 2006, Elsevier.

Digital subtraction angiography with carbon dioxide contrast is an appropriate alternative imaging study in high-risk patients. However, this technique cannot be used for imaging above the diaphragm because of the risk of cerebral toxicity.

Rhabdomyolysis and Pigment Nephropathy

Rhabdomyolysis develops when muscle injury leads to the release of myoglobin and other intracellular muscle contents into the circulation. Myoglobin is known to cause nephrotoxicity by induction of kidney ischemia and tubular obstruction that results in a form of AKI known as pigment nephropathy. Approximately 46% of patients with rhabdomyolysis develop AKI.

Rhabdomyolysis most commonly develops after exposure to myotoxic drugs, infection, excessive exertion, or prolonged immobilization (**Table 25**). Use of alcohol and illicit drugs such as cocaine are important leading causes of this condition, and the risk of rhabdomyolysis is particularly high in patients using more than one potentially myotoxic agent.

A diagnosis of rhabdomyolysis should be considered in patients with a serum creatine kinase level above 5000 U/L (83.5 μkat/L) who demonstrate heme positivity on urine dipstick testing in the absence of hematuria. Complications of rhabdomyolysis include hypocalcemia, hyperphosphatemia, hyperuricemia, metabolic acidosis, acute muscle compartment syndrome, and limb ischemia.

Expansion of the extracellular fluid volume with isotonic saline is the most effective intervention to limit nephrotoxicity in patients with rhabdomyolysis. Calcium repletion therapy should be reserved only for hypocalcemic patients with this condition who have cardiac or neuromuscular irritability, because this therapy can cause rebound hypercalcemia in the recovery phase.

TABLE 25 Causes of Rhabdomyolysis

Nontraumatic	Nontraumatic (*continued*)
Strenuous exercise, especially in unconditioned individuals	Toxins
Heat stroke	Multiple bee and wasp stings
Sickle cell disease and trait following exertion	Snake bites
Seizures	Toxic shock syndrome
Myopathies	Carbon monoxide poisoning
Neuroleptic malignant syndrome	Infections
Malignant hyperthermia	Viral (HIV, influenza, coxsackievirus, cytomegalovirus, Epstein-Barr virus, varicella, dengue, herpes simplex virus, parainfluenza virus, adenovirus, echovirus)
Alcohol abuse	Bacterial (*Staphylococcus, Salmonella, Clostridium, Pneumococcus,* and *Legionella* species; leptospirosis, Q fever, Rocky Mountain spotted fever)
Medications[a]	Malaria
Antipsychotics	Electrolyte abnormalities
Selective serotonin reuptake inhibitors	Endocrinopathies
Zidovudine	Thyroid disease (hypo- and hyperthyroidism)
Lithium	Pheochromocytoma
Antihistamines	Inflammatory myopathies
Statins (increased risk with exertion or concurrent use of colchicine)	**Trauma or Compression**
Fibric acid derivatives	Prolonged surgery (orthopedic, vascular, urologic, bariatric)
Daptomycin	Immobilization
Propofol	Burns
Valproic acid	Multiple trauma
Dietary supplements	Crush injuries
Ephedrine	
Creatine	
Illicit drugs	
Cocaine	
Ecstasy (3,4-methylenedioxymethamphetamine)	

[a]Increased incidence with polypharmacy.

Acute Interstitial Nephritis

Acute interstitial nephritis is most commonly caused by a hypersensitivity reaction to a medication, and proton pump inhibitors are now believed to be a common cause of drug-induced acute interstitial nephritis. Acute interstitial nephritis also may be caused by certain infections or autoimmune conditions (**Table 26**).

Drug-induced acute interstitial nephritis may manifest as rash, pruritus, eosinophilia, and fever; however, these features may be absent, particularly in acute interstitial nephritis due to use of NSAIDs and proton pump inhibitors.

Urinalysis findings in patients with acute interstitial nephritis may include leukocyte casts, eosinophils, and a urine protein-creatinine ratio usually less than 2.5 mg/mg. Kidney biopsy is often required to establish a definitive diagnosis because of the lack of sensitivity and specificity of eosinophiluria or gallium scanning. In patients with suspected drug-induced acute interstitial nephritis, discontinuing the inciting agent and monitoring for improvement in kidney function over the next 2 to 3 weeks are often sufficient. Indications for biopsy generally include diagnostic uncertainty, advanced kidney failure,

consideration of potentially toxic treatment, or lack of spontaneous recovery following cessation of drug therapy.

Management of drug-induced interstitial nephritis includes withdrawing the inciting medication. Corticosteroids may be used in patients with aggressive disease, such as those with persistent or worsening azotemia despite discontinuation of the inciting agent, and biopsy may be particularly warranted if this therapy is being considered. Patients demonstrating active inflammation in the absence of significant chronic damage seen on biopsy are more likely to benefit from corticosteroids. However, data regarding the efficacy of corticosteroids in this setting have been limited to retrospective trials.

Thrombotic Microangiopathies

The thrombotic microangiopathies are a spectrum of disorders that develop in various clinical settings (**Table 27**) (see Thrombotic Microangiopathies in MKSAP 15 Hematology and Oncology and in Glomerular Diseases). These conditions are believed to result from endothelial damage that allows plasma constituents to enter the intima of arteries, the walls of arterioles, and the subendothelial

TABLE 26 Causes of Acute Interstitial Nephritis
Medications
NSAIDs
Cyclooxygenase-2 inhibitors
Antibiotics
Penicillins
Cephalosporins
Fluoroquinolones
Antituberculous medications (rifampin, isoniazid, ethambutol)
Sulfonamides
Miscellaneous
Allopurinol
Phenytoin
Proton pump inhibitors
Indinavir
Autoimmune
Sarcoidosis
Sjögren syndrome
Systemic lupus erythematosus
Toxins
Chinese herb nephropathy
Heavy metal toxicity
Myeloma cast nephropathy
Infiltrative
Leukemia
Lymphoma
Infections
Legionella
Cytomegalovirus
HIV
Toxoplasmosis
Polyomavirus BK virus (in kidney transplantation recipients)

TABLE 27 Causes of Thrombotic Microangiopathy	
Infections	
Escherichia coli O157:H7	*Shigella*
Pseudomonas	Symptomatic HIV
Drugs	
Mitomycin	Cisplatin and bleomycin
Gemcitabine	Cyclosporine
Tacrolimus	Ticlopidine
Clopidogrel	Quinine
Valacyclovir	Oral contraceptives
Autoimmune diseases	
Scleroderma renal crisis	
Systemic lupus erythematosus	
Antiphospholipid antibody syndrome	
Hematopoietic stem cell transplantation	
Pregnancy and post partum	
Malignant hypertension	
Idiopathic	

zone of glomerular capillaries. These vessels subsequently develop narrow lumens often occluded with thrombi that lead to ischemic kidney injury.

Manifestations of the thrombotic microangiopathies may include AKI that is usually accompanied by microangiopathic hemolytic anemia. Approximately 50% of patients have low C3 levels. The urine sediment usually shows minimal or no abnormalities and is nondiagnostic; rarely, erythrocyte or muddy brown casts may be seen.

Scleroderma renal crisis is a form of thrombotic microangiopathy characterized by severe hypertension and AKI that often improves after ACE inhibitor therapy (see Systemic Sclerosis in MKSAP 15 Rheumatology).

KEY POINTS

- Acute tubular necrosis usually occurs after a sustained period of ischemia or exposure to nephrotoxic agents and is most commonly associated with muddy brown casts on urinalysis and a fractional excretion of sodium above 2%.
- Contrast-induced nephropathy is characterized by an increase in the serum creatinine level 24 to 48 hours after contrast administration and is usually associated with recovery of normal kidney function in 1 to 2 weeks.
- The most effective intervention to decrease the incidence and severity of contrast-induced nephropathy is volume expansion with either isotonic saline or sodium bicarbonate.
- Rhabdomyolysis most commonly develops after exposure to myotoxic drugs, infection, excessive exertion, or prolonged immobilization.
- Expansion of the extracellular fluid volume with isotonic saline is the most effective intervention to limit nephrotoxicity in patients with rhabdomyolysis.
- Urinalysis findings in patients with acute interstitial nephritis may include leukocyte casts, eosinophils, and a protein-creatinine ratio below 2.5 mg/mg.
- Acute kidney injury in patients with scleroderma renal crisis often improves after angiotensin-converting enzyme inhibitor therapy.

Postrenal Disease

Urinary Tract Obstruction

Urinary tract obstruction accounts for approximately 5% of cases of AKI. Obstruction can cause intrarenal vasoconstriction, ischemic tubular injury, and interstitial fibrosis that may lead to end-stage kidney disease if uncorrected.

Although patients with complete obstruction have significantly decreased urine output, those with partial obstruction may have polyuria caused by loss of tubular function or excretion of excess retained solute. Obstruction also should be strongly suspected in patients with AKI who have known obstructive prostatic disease or pelvic malignancy.

Kidney ultrasonography in most patients with obstruction reveals hydronephrosis; however, this finding may be absent in those with retroperitoneal fibrosis, which causes encasement of the collecting system in fibrotic tissue that may prevent dilation of the collecting system. Retroperitoneal fibrosis should be suspected in patients with AKI who present with flank or abdominal pain in whom prerenal and kidney parenchymal disease have been excluded, particularly in patients with lymphoma. Noncontrast CT of the abdomen and pelvis is the preferred imaging modality to establish a diagnosis.

Patients with AKI caused by urinary tract obstruction have a favorable prognosis when obstruction is relieved within 1 week of onset.

KEY POINTS

- Urinary tract obstruction should be strongly suspected in patients with acute kidney injury who have known obstructive prostatic disease or pelvic malignancy and may manifest as significantly decreased urine output or polyuria.
- Kidney ultrasonography in most patients with urinary tract obstruction reveals hydronephrosis.
- Patients with acute kidney injury caused by urinary tract obstruction have a favorable prognosis when obstruction is relieved within 1 week of onset.

Acute Kidney Injury in Specific Clinical Settings

The Critical Care Setting

AKI is particularly common in the intensive care unit and has a mortality rate of 50% or higher in this setting. Acute tubular necrosis is the leading cause of AKI in the critical care setting and typically occurs in patients with shock or after major surgery or nephrotoxic exposures.

Abdominal Compartment Syndrome

Abdominal compartment syndrome is a form of AKI that occurs most commonly in patients in the surgical intensive care unit who have intra-abdominal hemorrhage, severe pancreatitis, or ileus or those who have undergone massive fluid resuscitation or recent abdominal surgery. The cause of kidney dysfunction in this setting is unclear but may be related to increased renal venous pressure.

Abdominal compartment syndrome may manifest as acute kidney dysfunction that is often accompanied by decreased cardiac output, increased systemic vascular resistance, and high pulmonary capillary wedge pressures. Diagnosis of abdominal compartment syndrome is established in patients with an intravesicular pressure greater than 20 mm Hg as measured through a bladder catheter who also have new-onset organ system failure. Surgical decompression of the abdomen is usually required and often promptly improves kidney function.

KEY POINTS

- Diagnosis of abdominal compartment syndrome is established in patients who have an intravesicular pressure greater than 20 mm Hg as measured through a bladder catheter who also have new-onset organ system failure.
- Surgical decompression of the abdomen is usually required in patients with abdominal compartment syndrome and often promptly improves kidney function.

Cardiovascular Disease

Cardiorenal Syndrome

Cardiorenal syndrome refers to kidney dysfunction that develops in the setting of acute decompensated heart failure. Approximately one third of patients hospitalized with decompensated heart failure have cardiorenal syndrome, which can lead to longer hospitalization periods and a sevenfold increase in mortality.

Nesiritide has been shown to lower pulmonary capillary wedge pressure and improve congestive symptoms in patients with acute decompensated heart failure. However, this agent also is associated with a higher incidence of acute kidney dysfunction in these patients and therefore should not replace conventional therapy, including diuretics, in this setting.

Numerous trials have investigated the use of isolated ultrafiltration using a peripherally inserted ultrafiltration device that does not require central access, specialized nursing, or admission to the intensive care unit in patients with decompensated heart failure. This intervention has been shown to achieve lower weight more rapidly and to decrease hypokalemia but did not improve mortality or decrease the length of hospitalization. Furthermore, trials demonstrating superiority of this procedure to management with diuretics have yet to be published. Therefore, ultrafiltration should be reserved primarily for patients with persistent symptomatic volume overload who are unresponsive to drug therapy.

Cholesterol Crystal Embolization

Cholesterol crystal embolization may cause AKI in patients with aortic atherosclerotic plaques. This condition may occur spontaneously but most often develops after coronary or kidney angiography or aortic surgery. Anticoagulation with heparin, warfarin, or thrombolytic agents is believed to help incite this condition, but a definitive causal relationship has not been clearly demonstrated.

Kidney injury in patients with cholesterol crystal embolization usually has a subacute onset with a stuttering course over several weeks. Cutaneous manifestations develop in approximately 10% to 15% of patients and may include livedo reticularis, skin ulceration, and nodules (**Figure 17**). Extrarenal manifestations include abdominal pain, gastrointestinal bleeding, pancreatitis, and retinal artery emboli (known as Hollenhorst plaques) (**Figure 18**).

Patients with cholesterol crystal embolization typically have a bland urine sediment but may have dysmorphic hematuria and erythrocyte casts. If present, an elevated erythrocyte sedimentation rate, eosinophilia, and hypocomplementemia usually develop early in the disease course and resolve after 1 week.

The prognosis in patients with cholesterol crystal embolization is poor, and therapy should be directed toward management of risk factors such as dyslipidemia and hypertension and should include smoking cessation and glycemic control in patients with diabetes. In addition, invasive arterial procedures should be avoided in high-risk patients.

KEY POINTS

- Cardiorenal syndrome refers to kidney dysfunction that develops in the setting of acute decompensated heart failure.
- Cholesterol crystal embolization may cause acute kidney injury in patients with aortic atherosclerotic plaques and most often develops after angiography or aortic surgery.
- Patients with cholesterol crystal embolization may have cutaneous manifestations, abdominal pain, gastrointestinal bleeding, pancreatitis, and retinal artery emboli.
- Management of risk factors such as dyslipidemia and hypertension as well as smoking cessation and glycemic control in patients with diabetes are indicated for individuals with cholesterol crystal embolization.

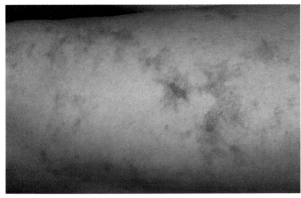

FIGURE 17.
Livedo reticularis.

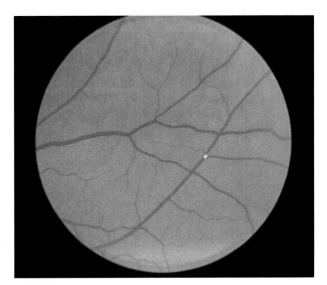

FIGURE 18.
Hollenhorst plaque.
This cholesterol crystal embolus is visible in a branch of a retinal artery.

Liver Disease

AKI frequently complicates advanced cirrhosis and acute hepatic failure. Because liver dysfunction is usually associated with impaired kidney perfusion and kidney vasoconstriction, patients in this setting have an increased risk for acute tubular necrosis. Prerenal azotemia may occur in patients with gastrointestinal bleeding, diuretic use, or large-volume paracentesis.

Hepatorenal Syndrome

Hepatorenal syndrome manifests as azotemia caused by significantly impaired kidney perfusion in patients with worsening liver dysfunction (see Complications of Liver Disease in MKSAP 15 Gastroenterology and Hepatology). Recently updated diagnostic criteria state that hepatorenal syndrome can be diagnosed in the setting of bacterial infection in the absence of septic shock (**Table 28**).

TABLE 28 Diagnostic Criteria for Hepatorenal Syndrome

1. Cirrhosis with ascites

2. Serum creatinine >1.5 mg/dL (>133 μmol/L)

3. No improvement of serum creatinine (decrease to a level of ≤1.5 mg/dL [133 μmol/L]) after at least 2 days after diuretic withdrawal and volume expansion with albumin. The recommended dose of albumin is 1 g/kg of body weight daily up to a maximum of 100 g/d.

4. Absence of shock

5. No current or recent treatment with nephrotoxic drugs

6. Absence of intrarenal disease as indicated by proteinuria >500 mg/24 h, microhematuria (>50 erythrocytes/hpf), and/or abnormal kidney ultrasound

Modified with permission from Salerno F, Gerbes A, Ginès P, Wong F, Arroyo V. Diagnosis, prevention and treatment of hepatorenal syndrome in cirrhosis. Gut. 2007;56(9):1310-1318. [PMID: 17389705] Copyright 2007, BMJ Publishing Group Ltd.

Type I hepatorenal syndrome is characterized by a 50% decline in the GFR to a value less than 20 mL/min/1.73 m^2 or a doubling of the serum creatinine level to above 2.5 mg/dL (221.0 µmol/L) in a period of less than 2 weeks. Type I hepatorenal syndrome most commonly occurs in patients with fulminant hepatic failure or after variceal bleeding, spontaneous bacterial peritonitis, sepsis, overly aggressive diuresis, or large-volume paracentesis. Albumin infusions are recommended for patients with spontaneous bacterial peritonitis to decrease the risk of this condition. Type II hepatorenal syndrome develops more insidiously in the setting of refractory ascites.

Liver transplantation is the treatment of choice for transplant-eligible patients with hepatorenal syndrome. In patients with suspected hepatorenal syndrome, volume expansion should be performed with albumin, 1 g/kg daily up to a maximum dosage of 100 g/d. Improvement of kidney function after this intervention suggests a component of prerenal azotemia. Vasopressors such as norepinephrine alone or midodrine in conjunction with octreotide, albumin infusions, and other supportive measures should be initiated until liver transplantation can be performed in eligible patients. The vasopressin analogue terlipressin is widely used in Europe, but clinical trials using this agent in the United States are ongoing.

Transjugular intrahepatic portosystemic shunt (TIPS) should be considered in patients who fail to respond to vasopressors but should only be used in individuals with severe hepatic dysfunction because of the associated risk for encephalopathy. Patients with hepatorenal syndrome who are not eligible for liver transplantation are generally poor candidates for chronic dialysis because of their poor prognosis and propensity for infectious complications and hypotension.

KEY POINTS

- Hepatorenal syndrome manifests as azotemia caused by significantly impaired kidney perfusion in patients with worsening liver dysfunction.
- Albumin infusions are recommended for patients with spontaneous bacterial peritonitis to decrease the risk of hepatorenal syndrome.
- In patients with suspected hepatorenal syndrome, volume expansion with albumin should be performed to assess whether there is a component of prerenal azotemia.
- Vasopressors can be used as adjunctive therapy for patients with hepatorenal syndrome until liver transplantation can be performed in eligible patients.

Malignancy

AKI is a frequent complication in patients with malignancy and can be caused by the underlying malignancy or be related to treatment (**Table 29**). Tumor lysis syndrome and myeloma

TABLE 29 Causes of Acute Kidney Injury in Patients with Malignancy

Prerenal Diseases
Hypercalcemia
Gastrointestinal losses during chemotherapy
Hepatic sinusoidal obstruction syndrome following hematopoietic stem cell transplantation
Intrarenal Diseases

Acute tubular necrosis
   Cisplatin
   Ifosfamide

Acute interstitial nephritis
   Lymphomatous infiltrates
   Leukemic infiltrates

Tubular obstruction
   Myeloma cast nephropathy
   Tumor lysis syndrome
   Methotrexate

Thrombotic microangiopathy
   Mitomycin
   Cisplatin and bleomycin
   Gemcitabine
   Cyclosporine
   Hematopoietic stem cell transplantation

Postrenal Disease
Bladder outlet obstruction
Retroperitoneal tumor or lymphadenopathy
Retroperitoneal fibrosis
Vascular
Renal vein tumor or thrombus

cast nephropathy in particular are associated with a high morbidity and mortality rate.

Tumor Lysis Syndrome

Pathophysiology

Tumor lysis syndrome usually develops after initiation of chemotherapy and occasionally occurs spontaneously in patients with a high tumor burden (see Tumor Lysis Syndrome in MKSAP 15 Hematology and Oncology). Kidney dysfunction in this setting is caused by urate deposition as well as calcium phosphate precipitation within the renal tubules. Tumor lysis syndrome manifests as acute oliguric kidney injury accompanied by increased serum uric acid, phosphorus, and potassium levels.

Primary Prevention

Allopurinol prophylaxis significantly reduces the risk of urate deposition in the kidneys in patients with a high tumor burden who are undergoing induction chemotherapy. The recombinant-urate oxidase inhibitor rasburicase is U.S. Food and Drug Administration approved for use in the prevention of urate nephropathy in pediatric patients with severe hyperuricemia who receive chemotherapy that is expected to cause tumor lysis syndrome. This agent also has been shown to decrease serum uric acid levels and reduce the incidence of AKI in small, uncontrolled trials of adult patients. Candidates for rasburicase prophylaxis are patients at increased risk for tumor lysis syndrome, including those with serum uric acid levels higher than 7.5 mg/dL (0.4 mmol/L), high-turnover tumors (such as hematologic malignancies) with elevated serum lactate dehydrogenase levels, decreased intravascular volume status, and tumor infiltration of the kidneys, and patients undergoing aggressive-intensity cytoreductive therapy.

Generally, patients most at risk for tumor lysis syndrome are hospitalized because of the severity of their symptoms or because the treatment requires inpatient management. Intravenous hydration is indicated for all patients with high tumor burden undergoing induction chemotherapy. Those with an elevated serum lactate dehydrogenase or serum uric acid levels or heavy tumor burden should be admitted for hydration and close monitoring of kidney function and levels of serum potassium, phosphorus, and uric acid levels.

Patients with a preexisting reduction in GFR, oliguria and/or acidic urine, and volume depletion also should be hospitalized.

A consensus panel also recently proposed guidelines for stratifying risk for tumor lysis syndrome (**Table 30**). According to these guidelines, patients at low risk for tumor lysis syndrome should receive hydration but do not require hypouricemic therapy. Intermediate-risk patients should receive allopurinol rather than rasburicase for prophylaxis in the absence of pretreatment hyperuricemia. Finally, high-risk patients should be hospitalized for aggressive intravenous hydration and prophylactic rasburicase.

Management
Urinary alkalinization has historically been used to treat tumor lysis syndrome but has been shown to increase the risk of calcium phosphate deposition in the renal tubules, leading to worsening kidney dysfunction. Hydration with isotonic saline is therefore preferred.

Early intervention with dialysis is indicated in patients with tumor lysis syndrome who are oliguric or have life-threatening hyperkalemia. Continuous kidney replacement therapy may be advantageous in patients with higher levels of serum uric acid and phosphorus. Rasburicase has not yet been compared with dialysis in the treatment of established tumor lysis syndrome.

Myeloma Cast Nephropathy
Approximately 20% of patients with multiple myeloma have kidney disease (see Multiple Myeloma). Light chains produced in patients with multiple myeloma can induce tubular obstruction and AKI, a condition known as myeloma cast nephropathy, or myeloma kidney. The diagnosis of myeloma cast nephropathy should be suspected in patients over 40 years of age with unexplained AKI. In patients with a negative dipstick urinalysis for protein, sulfosalicylic acid testing of the urine may detect light chains and is an important clue to the diagnosis of this condition. Patients with suspected

TABLE 30 Stratification of Patients at Risk for Tumor Lysis Syndrome

Type of Cancer	Risk		
	High	Intermediate	Low
Non-Hodgkin lymphoma	Burkitt lymphoma, lymphoblastic, Burkitt acute lymphoblastic leukemia	Diffuse large B-cell lymphoma	Indolent non-Hodgkin lymphoma
Acute lymphoblastic leukemia	Leukocyte count ≥100,000/µL (100 × 10⁹/L)	Leukocyte count 50,000-100,000/µL (50-100 × 10⁹/L)	Leukocyte count ≤50,000/µL (50 × 10⁹/L)
Acute myeloid leukemia	Leukocyte count ≥50,000/µL (50 × 10⁹/L) monoblastic	Leukocyte count 10,000-50,000/µL (10-50 × 10⁹/L)	Leukocyte count ≤10,000/µL (10 × 10⁹/L)
Chronic lymphocytic leukemia	—	Leukocyte count 10,000-100,000/µL (10-100 × 10⁹/L) treated with fludarabine	Leukocyte count ≤10,000/µL (10 × 10⁹/L)
Other hematologic malignancies (including chronic myeloid leukemia and multiple myeloma) and solid tumors	—	Rapid proliferation with expected rapid response to therapy	Remainder of patients

myeloma cast nephropathy should undergo serum protein electrophoresis, serum free light chain measurement, and a 24-hour urine collection for protein electrophoresis and immunofixation.

Plasmapheresis combined with chemotherapy has historically been used to treat myeloma cast nephropathy. A randomized controlled trial showed that patients who received plasmapheresis had improved kidney function but no survival benefit. Therefore, this therapy is still recommended for individuals with either biopsy-proven myeloma cast nephropathy or those with a high likelihood of this disorder because of the reduction in dialysis dependency among those patients who survive.

Bisphosphonates should be used with caution in patients with myeloma and kidney dysfunction. Pamidronate has been reported to induce AKI and the nephrotic syndrome in patients with multiple myeloma. In addition, zoledronic acid has been reported to induce acute tubular necrosis, particularly when an 8-mg dose of this agent is infused in less than 15 minutes. Oral bisphosphonates are generally contraindicated when the estimated GFR is below 30 mL/min/1.73 m^2.

Chemotherapy-Induced Disease

Cisplatin has direct tubular toxicity that can be attenuated through pretreatment with theophylline. Ifosfamide, etoposide, and carboplatin also can cause acute tubular injury, and pretreatment hydration is indicated to limit nephrotoxicity. Methotrexate precipitates within the tubules, but pretreatment hydration and urine alkalinization can help to decrease this effect. Gemcitabine and bleomycin can induce a thrombotic microangiopathy that is unresponsive to plasmapheresis. Bevacizumab and other vascular endothelial growth factor inhibitors also may cause thrombotic thrombocytopenic purpura.

KEY POINTS

- Tumor lysis syndrome usually develops after initiation of chemotherapy and occasionally occurs spontaneously in patients with a high tumor burden.

- Allopurinol or off-label usage of rasburicase may help to prevent tumor lysis syndrome in at-risk patients.

- Hydration with isotonic saline is the most appropriate management of tumor lysis syndrome, and early intervention with dialysis is indicated in patients who are oliguric or have life-threatening hyperkalemia.

- In patients with a negative dipstick urinalysis for protein, sulfosalicylic acid testing of the urine may detect light chains and is an important clue to the diagnosis of myeloma cast nephropathy.

- Bisphosphonates should be used with caution in patients with myeloma and kidney dysfunction.

HIV Infection

Patients with HIV infection have an increased risk of AKI caused by various factors. In one series of 111 episodes of AKI in 77 patients with HIV infection, 39% were caused by prerenal disease, 43% were caused by intrarenal disease mostly related to ischemia and drugs, 8% were caused by postrenal disease, and 9% were of unknown cause.

Opportunistic infection with *Pneumocystis jiroveci* can induce AKI by direct infection and obstruction of the glomerular and peritubular capillaries. HIV infection also is known to induce thrombotic thrombocytopenic purpura, and therapy should include highly active antiretroviral therapy (HAART) in addition to plasmapheresis. Patients with HIV infection also may develop acute interstitial nephritis secondary to infection with this virus or with Epstein-Barr virus, cytomegalovirus, BK virus, aspergillosis, zygomycosis, histoplasmosis, and *Cryptococcus* and *Nocardia* species. Patients with HIV infection also may develop rhabdomyolysis and have an increased incidence of false-positive results on ANCA and antiglomerular basement membrane antibody assays.

Although certain antiretroviral agents are nephrotoxic, AKI in patients with HIV infection is usually unrelated to use of HAART. Moreover, use of HAART may slow the progression of HIV-associated nephropathy and has improved survival in this setting. Indinavir can induce intratubular precipitation of crystals and interstitial nephritis. Tenofovir, adefovir, didanosine, lamivudine, and stavudine are known to cause proximal tubular injury and also may cause mitochondrial toxicity and lactic acidosis.

KEY POINTS

- Patients with HIV infection have an increased risk of acute kidney injury most often caused by certain opportunistic infections.

- Highly active antiretroviral therapy may slow the progression of HIV-associated nephropathy and usually does not cause acute kidney injury.

Newly Described Nephrotoxic Acute Kidney Injury

Several therapeutic agents have recently been reported to induce AKI. Orlistat may cause acute oxalate nephropathy. Intravenous immune globulin therapy can induce AKI through osmotic tubular injury in preparations containing additives such as sucrose, maltose, and glycine.

Sodium phosphate–containing cathartic agents that are frequently used in preparation for colonoscopy have been associated with AKI in patients who have risk factors for acute phosphate nephropathy, such as reduced GFR; advanced age; and use of ACE inhibitors, angiotensin receptor blockers, NSAIDs, and diuretics. However, acute phosphate nephropathy also may occur in patients receiving sodium phosphate solutions for bowel preparation who have normal kidney function and no apparent risk factors. This condition is most likely related to a rapid elevation in the serum phosphate level and subsequent deposition of calcium phosphate crystals in the renal tubules. Acute and chronic kidney injury then develops days or months after administration of sodium phosphate preparations. Sodium phosphate–containing bowel preparation solutions therefore should be avoided, particularly because of the availability of safer alternatives such as polyethylene glycol electrolyte solution.

KEY POINTS

- Orlistat and intravenous immune globulin therapy using preparations containing additives such as sucrose, maltose, and glycine may cause acute kidney injury.

- Sodium phosphate–containing bowel preparation solutions may cause acute kidney injury and should be avoided, particularly because of the availability of safer alternatives such as polyethylene glycol electrolyte solution.

Bibliography

Chertow GM, Burdick E, Honour M, Bonventre JV, Bates DW. Acute kidney injury, mortality, length of stay, and costs in hospitalized patients. J Am Soc Nephrol. 2005;16(11):3365-3370. [PMID: 16177006]

Clark WF, Stewart AK, Rock GA, et al; Canadian Apheresis Group. Plasma exchange when myeloma presents as acute renal failure: a randomized, controlled trial [erratum in Ann Intern Med. 2007;146(6):471]. Ann Intern Med. 2005;143(11):777-784. [PMID: 16330788]

Coiffier B, Altman A, Pui CH, Younes A, Cairo MS. Guidelines for the management of pediatric and adult tumor lysis syndrome: an evidence-based review. J Clin Oncol. 2008;26(16):2767-2778. [PMID: 18509186]

Franceschini N, Napravnik S, Eron JJ Jr, Szczech LA, Finn WF. Incidence and etiology of acute renal failure among ambulatory HIV-infected patients. Kidney Int. 2005;67(4):1526-1531. [PMID: 15780107]

Liano F, Felipe C, Tenorio MT, et al. Long-term outcome of acute tubular necrosis: A contribution to its natural history. Kidney Int. 2007;71(7): 679-686. [PMID: 17264879]

Maioli M, Toso A, Leoncini M, et al. Sodium bicarbonate versus saline for the prevention of contrast-induced nephropathy in patients with renal dysfunction undergoing coronary angiography or intervention. J Am Coll Cardiol. 2008;52(8):599-604. [PMID: 18702961]

Malli G, Chaudhry V, Cornblath DR. Rhabdomyolysis-an evaluation of 475 hospitalized patients. Medicine (Baltimore). 2005;84(6):377-385. [PMID: 16267412]

McCullough PA, Stancul F, Becker CR, et al. Contrast-induced nephropathy (CIN) consensus working panel: executive summary. Rev Cardiovasc Med 2006;7(4):177-197. [PMID: 17224862]

Kidney Stones

Pathophysiology and Epidemiology

Kidney stones can be composed of calcium oxalate, calcium phosphate, uric acid, struvite, and cystine. Approximately 80% of kidney stones are composed of calcium oxalate, whereas less than 10% are composed of calcium phosphate.

A low fluid intake promotes stone formation, and persons who consume more than 2500 mL of fluid daily are 30% less likely to develop kidney stones compared with those who consume lower amounts.

Calcium Oxalate Stones

Risk Factors and Prevention

Hypercalciuria

Hypercalciuria is the most common metabolic abnormality in patients with calcium-containing stones (**Table 31**). Paradoxically, an increase in dietary calcium intake decreases the risk of calcium oxalate stone formation and recurrence because dietary calcium binds to gastrointestinal oxalate and thus prevents oxalate absorption. Thiazide diuretics also may be considered in patients with hypercalciuria and recurrent calcium-containing kidney stones to help lower the rate of kidney stone recurrence.

Hyperoxaluria

Enteric and primary hyperoxaluria occur in 10% of patients with calcium oxalate stones. Enteric hyperoxaluria is associated with malabsorption syndromes that allow fatty acids to bind with calcium in the intestinal lumen and results in an increased gastrointestinal absorption of oxalate; the kidneys then eliminate oxalate into the urine, where it binds with urine calcium and forms calcium oxalate stones. Similarly, primary hyperoxaluria is an inherited genetic disorder of metabolism that can lead to calcium oxalate stone formation by causing excess oxalate secretion into the urine.

In patients with hyperoxaluria, dietary calcium intake should be increased to 1 to 4 g daily. Foods high in oxalate such as rhubarb, peanuts, spinach, beets, and chocolate also should be avoided.

TABLE 31 Causes of Hypercalciuria

Genetic
Absorptive hypercalcemia
Familial distal renal tubular acidosis
Bartter syndrome
Familial hypocalciuric hypocalcemia
Vitamin D excess
Vitamin D supplementation
Sarcoidosis
Malignancy associated with bone resorption and parathyroid hormone–related protein secretion
Primary hyperparathyroidism

Hypocitraturia

A decrease in citric acid, which binds to urine calcium and inhibits calcium oxalate stone formation, is another risk factor for calcium oxalate nephrolithiasis. Potassium citrate supplementation or intake of foods high in citrate such as lemon juice helps to decrease the risk of recurrent stones.

Struvite Stones

Approximately 10% of patients with kidney stones develop struvite stones, which may be composed of magnesium ammonium phosphate, calcium carbonate-apatite, or a combination of these components. Women with recurrent urinary tract infections with urease-splitting *Klebsiella* and *Proteus* species in particular have an increased risk for this condition.

If not adequately treated, struvite stones may develop into staghorn calculi that can fill the entire kidney pelvis. Antibiotic therapy and referral for stone removal are the management of choice for infected struvite stones.

Cystine Stones

Cystine stones account for only 1% to 3% of all kidney stones. More than 50% of patients with these stones have cystinuria, an autosomal-recessive disorder that results in increased urine cystine excretion. Clues that suggest cystine stones include large branched calculi or kidney stones that occur in childhood or adolescence. In patients with cystinuria, urine alkalinization is indicated to increase the solubility of cystine. Penicillamine and captopril also should be used to decrease serum cystine levels.

Uric Acid Stones

Approximately 10% of kidney stones are composed of uric acid, and an estimated 10% to 15% of patients with gout develop uric acid stones. Patients with hyperuricosuria, especially those with urine uric acid levels greater than 1000 mg/24 h (5.9 mmol/d), have an increased risk of uric acid stone formation. In addition, tumor lysis syndrome can cause intratubular crystallization of uric acid that can contribute to acute kidney injury and is another risk factor for uric acid stones.

In individuals with gout and hyperuricosuria, urine alkalinization increases the solubility of uric acid and decreases the formation of kidney stones. Allopurinol also may be warranted in recurrent uric acid stone formers to decrease urine uric acid excretion if increased fluid intake and alkalinization of the urine fail to decrease the rate of uric acid stone formation. The hyperuricosuric effects of probenecid may exacerbate stone disease, and this agent should be avoided in patients with gout who have a history of uric acid stones.

KEY POINTS

- Hypercalciuria is the most common metabolic abnormality in patients with calcium-containing stones.

- An increase in dietary calcium intake paradoxically decreases the risk of calcium oxalate stone formation and recurrence, and thiazide diuretics can further decrease the recurrence of these stones in selected individuals.

- Women with recurrent urinary tract infections with urease-splitting *Klebsiella* and *Proteus* species have an increased risk for struvite stones.

- Patients with hyperuricosuria, especially those with urine uric acid levels greater than 1000 mg/24 h (5.9 mmol/d), have an increased risk of uric acid stone formation.

Clinical Manifestations

Some patients with kidney stones are completely asymptomatic and only incidentally notice gravel or a stone after urinating. Nevertheless, symptoms eventually develop in approximately 33% to 50% of patients with asymptomatic kidney stones.

Acute renal colic is characterized by the sudden onset of unilateral flank pain. Acute renal colic also may cause nausea and vomiting, and patients with stones located in the ureters or urethra may have irritative symptoms such as urinary urgency and frequency.

Approximately 90% of kidney stones less than 5 mm in diameter pass spontaneously with supportive treatment, whereas only 50% of stones between 5 and 7 mm in diameter spontaneously pass. Spontaneous passage is unlikely in stones over 7 mm in diameter.

KEY POINT

- Approximately 90% of kidney stones less than 5 mm in diameter pass spontaneously with supportive treatment.

Diagnosis and Evaluation

Laboratory Studies

Laboratory studies used in the evaluation of patients with kidney stones include kidney function studies; measurement of serum calcium, phosphorus, bicarbonate, and uric acid levels; and urinalysis with microscopic analysis of the urine sediment. Measurement of the serum parathyroid hormone level also is warranted if hypercalcemia or hypophosphatemia is present.

Patients with kidney stones usually have intact kidney function, and the presence of acute kidney injury is suggestive of bilateral obstruction, obstruction in a solitary kidney, volume depletion, or sepsis. Hematuria is seen in most patients but may be intermittent.

In patients with crystalluria, analysis of the urine sediment may help to characterize the type of kidney stone that is present (**Figure 19**). However, even patients without kidney stones may have crystalluria, and the gold standard to determine stone composition is to obtain the stone by straining the urine and then performing stone analysis.

Patients who have kidney stones and either have a family history of stone disease or chronic medical conditions favoring stone formation or who are white males should undergo additional laboratory studies to evaluate for metabolic abnormalities that can contribute to stone formation. These studies consist of three 24-hour urine collections for urine volume, pH, creatinine, sodium, calcium, uric acid, oxalate, and citrate excretion.

Imaging Studies

Most kidney stones are radiopaque and are easily visualized on plain radiographs of the abdomen, which are inexpensive, non-invasive, and widely available. However, false-negative results may occur in patients with small stones, radiolucent stones that are composed of uric acid or related to use of indinavir, and interference of the overlying bowel. Similarly, vascular calcification and phleboliths may cause false-positive results for kidney stones. As such, plain abdominal radiography has a low sensitivity and specificity for the diagnosis of this condition.

Kidney ultrasonography has a low sensitivity for kidney stones but a higher specificity than plain abdominal radiography. This study is relatively inexpensive, widely available,

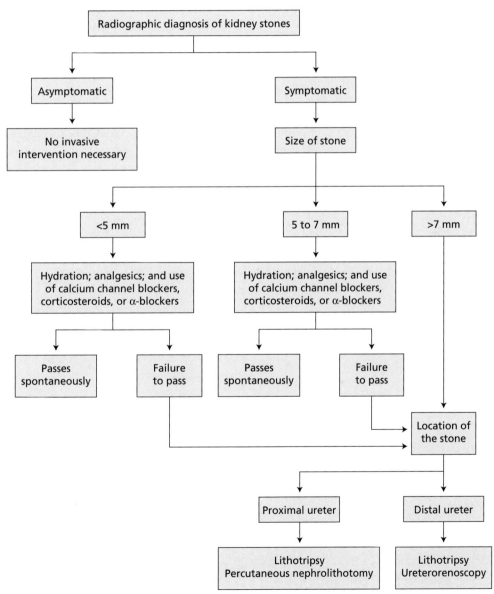

FIGURE 19.
Management of kidney stones.

and provides a functional assessment of the severity of the stone disease. Kidney ultrasonography also can detect urinary tract obstruction with associated hydronephrosis but may not reveal small stones or stones in the ureters and urethra.

Intravenous pyelography has a high sensitivity and specificity in the diagnosis of kidney stones. However, this study requires bowel preparation and the use of intravenous iodinated contrast agents, which are contraindicated in patients with acute kidney injury and chronic kidney disease.

Noncontrast helical abdominal CT has replaced intravenous pyelography as the gold standard for diagnosing kidney stones. This study reveals urinary tract obstruction with hydronephrosis, can detect stones as small as 1 mm in diameter, and can help evaluate other potential causes of abdominal pain and hematuria. However, noncontrast helical abdominal CT is expensive and has a higher radiation exposure than other imaging studies.

KEY POINTS

- Patients with kidney stones usually have intact kidney function, and the presence of acute kidney injury is suggestive of bilateral obstruction, obstruction in a solitary kidney, volume depletion, or sepsis.

- The gold standard to determine kidney stone composition is to obtain the stone by straining the urine and then performing stone analysis.

- Noncontrast helical abdominal CT is the gold standard for diagnosing kidney stones.

Management

Management of kidney stones is determined by whether the stone is symptomatic, stone size, and stone location (see Figure 19). Asymptomatic kidney stones found on imaging studies do not require urgent stone removal and treatment but may warrant further evaluation as to the cause of the stone as well as consideration for possible interventions to prevent recurrent stone formation. Stone removal also may be warranted in patients with urinary tract obstruction.

Approximately 80% of symptomatic kidney stones pass spontaneously within 2 to 3 days with supportive hydration. Stones that do not pass within 1 to 2 months are unlikely to pass spontaneously. NSAIDs or narcotic agents also can be used to relieve associated pain, but the former should be avoided in individuals with a decreased glomerular filtration rate. Use of calcium channel blockers to dilate ureteral smooth muscle and corticosteroids to decrease inflammation and ureteral edema or α-blockers to possibly increase ureteral contraction has been shown to increase the rate of spontaneous stone passage and may be warranted in patients with an acute attack. In a recent meta-analysis, the use of medical therapy with either calcium channel blockers or α-blockers resulted in a 65% greater stone passage rate than conservative medical therapy. Further clinical trials are required to determine the

superiority of calcium channel blocking agents versus α-blockers in the medical treatment of acute renal colic.

Extracorporeal shock-wave lithotripsy (ESWL) is indicated for stones less than 1 cm in diameter located in the kidney and upper urinary tract and in conjunction with percutaneous nephrolithotomy to help break apart large stones or staghorn calculi. Cystine stones are usually resistant to this intervention.

Percutaneous nephrolithotomy is indicated for stones larger than 1 cm in diameter, staghorn calculi, and cystine stones that are resistant to ESWL. This intervention also is indicated for patients with urinary tract abnormalities such as horseshoe kidney. Percutaneous nephrolithotomy is 95% effective in stone removal, and repeated interventions are rarely necessary. However, this procedure is more invasive than ESWL and requires the use of general anesthesia.

Ureterorenoscopy is recommended to remove stones in the distal ureter or to remove stone fragments caused by ESWL. This procedure allows visualization of the stone or stone fragments but is more invasive than ESWL and also may require repeated interventions for complete stone removal.

Open stone surgery is indicated only when all other interventions have failed.

KEY POINTS

- Asymptomatic kidney stones found on imaging studies do not require urgent stone removal.

- In patients with an acute attack of kidney stones, NSAIDs or narcotic agents can be used to relieve pain and a calcium channel blocker or α-blockers may help to increase the rate of spontaneous stone passage.

- Extracorporeal shock-wave lithotripsy is indicated for stones less than 1 cm in diameter located in the kidney and upper urinary tract.

- Percutaneous nephrolithotomy is indicated for stones larger than 1 cm in diameter, staghorn calculi, and cystine stones that are resistant to extracorporeal shock-wave lithotripsy and in patients with urinary tract abnormalities.

- Ureterorenoscopy is recommended to remove kidney stones in the distal ureter or to remove stone fragments caused by extracorporeal shock-wave lithotripsy.

Prognosis and Follow-up

Stone disease recurs in 30% to 50% of patients, particularly those with metabolic and genetic factors that favor stone development. After one stone recurrence, the incidence of future stone formation increases to nearly 90%. The best prevention of recurrent stone disease is consumption of more than 2 L of fluids daily and modification of identifiable metabolic factors and diet.

A causal association may exist between kidney stones and progression to chronic kidney disease or end-stage kidney disease. In a 2004 study of patients without hypertension, a history of kidney stones was associated with a threefold increased risk for chronic kidney disease, a sixfold increased risk for diabetic nephropathy, and a ninefold increased risk for interstitial nephritis. Whether the increased risk of chronic kidney disease in kidney stone formers is caused solely by the presence of stones or by factors associated with stones such as recurrent urinary tract obstruction, infection, and possible hyperuricemia with resultant tubulointerstitial disease is not yet known.

KEY POINTS

- The best prevention of recurrent kidney stone disease is consumption of more than 2 L of fluids daily and modification of identifiable metabolic factors and diet.
- A causal association may exist between kidney stones and progression to chronic kidney disease or end-stage kidney disease.

Bibliography

Kaufman D, Kelly J, Curhan G, et al. Oxalobacter formigenes may reduce the risk of calcium oxalate kidney stones. J Am Soc Nephrol. 2008;19(6):1197-1203. [PMID: 18322162]

Parsons JK, Hergan LA, Sakamoto K, Lankin C. Efficacy of alpha-Blockers for the Treatment of ureteral stones. J Urol. 2007;177(3):983-987. [PMID: 17296392]

Singh A, Alter HJ, Littlepage A. A systematic review of medical therapy to facilitate passage of ureteral calculi. Ann Emerg Med. 2007;50(5):552-563. [PMID: 17681643]

Taylor EN, Curhan GC. Diet and fluid prescription in stone disease. Kidney Intern. 2006;70(5):835-839. [PMID: 16837923]

Vupputuri S, Soucie JM, McClellan W, Sandler DP. History of kidney stones as a possible risk factor for chronic kidney disease. Ann Epidemiol. 2004;14(3):222-228. [PMID: 15036227]

The Kidney in Pregnancy

Kidney Anatomy and Physiology in the Pregnant Patient

Changes in the Urinary Tract

During normal gestation, blood flow to the kidneys significantly increases coincidentally with increased levels of estrogen, progestin, and relaxin. Dilatation of kidney calices, pelvices and the ureters also occurs in conjunction with these changes. Ureteric dilatation dramatically increases during the second trimester and can be mistaken for obstructive nephropathy on imaging studies.

Hemodynamic Changes and Volume Regulation

Pregnancy is characterized by marked and sustained systemic vasodilatation and reduced systemic vascular resistance that can be detected by 6 weeks of pregnancy. The kidney plasma flow and glomerular filtration rate (GFR) remain increased throughout gestation but peak during the first trimester. The increase in the GFR causes a decrease in the serum creatinine level. The ratio of GFR to kidney plasma flow, otherwise known as the filtration fraction, slightly decreases during pregnancy.

Urine protein excretion increases during pregnancy to 150 to 300 mg/24 h. Sodium reabsorption and total body water also increase, resulting in an increase in plasma volume. The increased renin release associated with pregnancy leads to an increase in aldosterone production, sodium retention and a slight decrease in serum potassium levels. Increases in cardiac output and plasma volume that occur in the second and third trimester contribute to the anemia of pregnancy.

Acid-Base Regulation

During pregnancy, hypocapnia and chronic respiratory alkalosis with an average arterial PCO_2 of 30 mm Hg develop. A compensatory increase in urine bicarbonate excretion and a decrease in serum bicarbonate levels of approximately 4 meq/L (4 mmol/L) also occur.

Water Metabolism

Pregnant women typically have a plasma osmolality 5 to 10 mosm/kg H_2O (5 to 10 mmol/kg H_2O) lower than nongravid women. Pregnant women also have decreased osmotic thresholds for thirst and arginine vasopressin release.

KEY POINTS

- Ureteric dilatation that occurs during normal pregnancy can resemble obstructive nephropathy.
- Pregnancy causes an increase in urine protein excretion to 150 to 300 mg/24 h and a decrease in the serum creatinine level.

Hypertensive Disorders Associated with Pregnancy

Preeclampsia

Pathophysiology and Epidemiology

Preeclampsia is characterized by new-onset hypertension, at least 1+ protein on dipstick urinalis, and a urine protein excretion of 300 mg/24 h or higher. This condition can develop anytime after 20 weeks of pregnancy but usually occurs close to term. Preeclampsia associated with seizures is known as eclampsia.

Preeclampsia is more common in nulliparous women, those with multiple gestations, and individuals at the extremes of reproductive age. Patients with preexisting kidney disease, hypertension, diabetes mellitus, obesity, hydatidiform mole, thrombophilic disorders, and the antiphospholipid antibody syndrome also have an increased risk of preeclampsia.

Clinical Manifestations and Diagnosis

Clinical manifestations of preeclampsia may include headache, visual disturbances, liver dysfunction, and fetal growth restriction. The HELLP syndrome (Hemolysis, Elevated Liver enzymes, Low Platelets) is a variant of preeclampsia.

Early diagnosis of preeclampsia is critical to initiate appropriate management. Patients with preeclampsia usually have a serum creatinine level from 0.8 to 1.2 mg/dL (70.7 to 106.1 μmol/L), which is normal for nonpregnant patients but elevated for pregnant individuals. A serum uric acid level above 4.5 mg/dL (0.3 mmol/L) and marked hypocalciuria (characterized by urine calcium excretion below 100 mg/24 h [2.5 mmol/d]) also should raise suspicion for preeclampsia.

Prevention and Management

Low-dose aspirin (75 to 150 mg/d) is associated with a 10% to 15% relative risk reduction in preventing preeclampsia and reducing adverse maternal and fetal outcomes. Calcium supplements reduce hypertension and preeclampsia modestly only in women consuming a baseline low-calcium diet.

Management of patients with preeclampsia typically includes bed rest, antihypertensive therapy, close monitoring of maternal and fetal conditions, and prevention of convulsions. Hospitalization is recommended except in patients with extremely mild disease.

Because clinical manifestations of preeclampsia resolve within days to weeks of delivery, definitive management of this condition is delivery of the fetus. Women with preeclampsia remote from term may require preterm delivery, which can be associated with fetal morbidity and mortality. Delivery should be considered in all patients who develop preeclampsia at term and in patients with signs of impending eclampsia such as hyperreflexia, headaches, and epigastric pain or those with uncontrollable hypertension. A platelet count below 100,000/μL (100×10^9/L) and/or elevated liver enzymes, which are features of the HELLP syndrome, may require immediate delivery.

Lowering mildly elevated blood pressure neither resolves preeclampsia nor prevents adverse maternal consequences of accelerated hypertension. No consensus exists for a target blood pressure in women with preeclampsia and severe hypertension, but levels that exceed 150/100 mm Hg may be hazardous in those with previously low-normal blood pressure. Parenteral antihypertensive therapy is recommended when delivery is likely to take place in the next 24 hours, whereas oral therapy is recommended if delivery can safely be postponed (**Table 32**).

Magnesium sulfate has been shown to prevent and treat eclampsia and is superior to phenytoin and diazepam in managing seizures. Furthermore, this agent mildly decreases blood pressure levels in some women. Because convulsions are most likely to occur in the immediate postpartum period, magnesium sulfate therapy is usually initiated immediately after delivery.

KEY POINTS

- Preeclampsia is characterized by new-onset hypertension, at least 1+ protein on dipstick urinalysis, and a urine protein excretion of 300 mg/24 h or higher that develops anytime after 20 weeks of pregnancy.

- Low-dose aspirin has a 10% to 15% relative risk reduction in preventing preeclampsia and reducing adverse maternal and fetal outcomes.

- Management of patients with preeclampsia typically includes bed rest, antihypertensive therapy, close monitoring of maternal and fetal conditions, prevention of convulsions, and hospitalization.

- Delivery should be considered in all patients who develop preeclampsia at term; in patients with signs of impending eclampsia such as hyperreflexia, headaches, and epigastric pain or those with uncontrollable hypertension; and in those with a platelet count below 100,000/μL (100×10^9/L) and/or elevated liver enzymes.

- Magnesium sulfate has been shown to prevent and treat eclampsia and is usually initiated immediately after delivery.

Gestational Hypertension

Gestational hypertension refers to high blood pressure that first develops at 20 weeks of pregnancy or later and is not associated with proteinuria. This condition may be confused with chronic hypertension in women whose blood pressure often decreases in early pregnancy but later increases.

Approximately 15% to 45% of women initially diagnosed with gestational hypertension develop preeclampsia. Risk factors for the development of preeclampsia in patients with gestational hypertension include onset of gestational hypertension before 20 weeks of pregnancy, a previous pregnancy complicated by hypertension, and higher blood pressure.

No evidence exists showing that targeted blood pressure control prevents preeclampsia, and antihypertensive therapy in patients with gestational hypertension should focus on preventing maternal consequences of severe hypertension (**Table 33**).

KEY POINTS

- Gestational hypertension refers to high blood pressure that first develops at 20 weeks of pregnancy or later and is not associated with proteinuria or other laboratory features of preeclampsia.

- No evidence exists showing that targeted blood pressure control prevents preeclampsia, and antihypertensive therapy in patients with gestational hypertension should focus on preventing maternal consequences of severe hypertension.

TABLE 32 Drugs for Urgent Control of Severe Hypertension in Pregnancy

Drug	U.S. FDA Pregnancy Category	Comments[a]
Labetalol	C	Due to a lower incidence of maternal hypotension and other side effects, use of this agent now supplants that of hydralazine; avoid in women with asthma or heart failure
Hydralazine	C	A drug of choice according to NHBPEP; long experience of safety and efficacy
Nifedipine	C	The authors prefer long-acting preparations; obstetric experience with short-acting agents has been favorable but is not U.S. FDA approved for management of hypertension
Diazoxide	C	Use is waning; may arrest labor; causes hyperglycemia
Nitroprusside	C[b]	Possible cyanide toxicity if used for >4 hours; agent of last resort

FDA = Food and Drug Administration; NHBPEP = National High Blood Pressure Education Program.

[a]Adverse effects for all agents, except as noted, may include headache, flushing, nausea, and tachycardia.

[b]This agent would be classified as a U.S. FDA category D agent in pregnancy; there is positive evidence of human fetal risk, but the benefits from use in pregnant women may be acceptable despite the risk.

Data from Briggs GG, Freeman RK, Yaffe SJ. Drugs in Pregnancy and Lactation. 8th ed. Philadelphia: Lippincott Williams & Wilkins; 2008.

Chronic Hypertension

Essential Hypertension

During pregnancy, blood pressure levels typically decrease early in the first trimester and may remain lower than non-pregnant levels until term. Therefore, most women with stage 1 essential hypertension do well during pregnancy.

However, pregnant women with more severe hypertension; a longer duration of hypertension; and cormorbidities such as diabetes mellitus, chronic kidney disease (CKD), and vasculitis have a higher incidence of complications than the general population. During pregnancy, up to 25% of women with chronic or preexisting hypertension develop superimposed preeclampsia.

Maintaining blood pressure levels close to normal has not been shown to prevent the development of superimposed preeclampsia. In women with chronic hypertension

TABLE 33 Drugs for Gestational or Chronic Hypertension in Pregnancy[a]

Drug	U.S. FDA Pregnancy Risk Category	Comments
Preferred Agent		
Methyldopa	B	Drug of choice according to NHBPEP; safety after first trimester well documented, including 7-year follow-up of offspring
Second-Line Agents		
Labetalol	C	May be associated with fetal growth restriction
Nifedipine	C	May inhibit labor and have synergistic action with magnesium sulfate in lowering blood pressure; little experience with other calcium channel blockers
Hydralazine	C	Few controlled trials; long experience with few adverse events documented; useful in combination with sympatholytic agents; may cause neonatal thrombocytopenia
β-Receptor antagonists	C	May decrease uteroplacental blood flow; may impair fetal response to hypoxic stress; risk of growth restriction when started in first or second trimester with use of atenolol; may be associated with neonatal hypoglycemia at higher dosages
Hydrochlorothiazide	C[b]	Most controlled studies were performed in normotensive pregnant women rather than hypertensive patients; can cause volume contraction and electrolyte disorders; may be useful in combination with methyldopa and a vasodilator to mitigate compensatory fluid retention

FDA = U.S. Food and Drug Administration; NHBPEP = National High Blood Pressure Education Program.

[a]No antihypertensive agent has been proven safe for use during the first trimester.

[b]Classified by Briggs et al. as a U.S. FDA category D agent in pregnancy; there is positive evidence of human fetal risk, but the benefits from use in pregnant women may be acceptable despite the risk.

Data from Briggs GG, Freeman RK, Yaffe SJ. Drugs in Pregnancy and Lactation. 8th ed. Philadelphia, PA: Lippincott Williams & Wilkins; 2008.

who had mild to moderately elevated blood pressure before pregnancy, physiologic vasodilatation may cause a decrease in blood pressure early in pregnancy. Furthermore, in the absence of known target organ damage, discontinuation of antihypertensive medications and close monitoring may be sufficient in these patients. Therapy can then be initiated if the blood pressure increases to 140 to 150/90 to 100 mm Hg, but a slightly lower threshold for treatment may be warranted in women with CKD.

Standard dosages of oral antihypertensive agents can be used during pregnancy (see Table 33). Early first-trimester exposure to angiotensin-converting enzyme inhibitors and angiotensin receptor blockers has been associated with mild fetal cardiac abnormalities, and exposure later in pregnancy is associated with severe adverse fetal effects such as kidney agenesis and neonatal anuric kidney failure. Therefore, these agents are contraindicated in pregnancy and should be discontinued before conception when possible.

Secondary Hypertension

Kidney disease is the most common cause of secondary hypertension. Pregnant women with stage 3 or higher CKD, especially when hypertension is present, have a high incidence of preeclampsia and preterm birth.

Pheochromocytoma and renovascular hypertension are associated with poor maternal and fetal prognoses. Accelerated hypertension, superimposed preeclampsia, and fetal demise in particular are more common in patients with these disorders. Conversely, women with primary aldosteronism, and particularly those with stage 1 hypertension, may have relatively uncomplicated pregnancies.

If women are first evaluated after conception for secondary hypertension, laboratory studies can be performed to exclude pheochromocytoma and to screen for primary aldosteronism (see Hypertension). However, stimulation of the renin-angiotensin-aldosterone system that occurs in normal pregnancy complicates interpretation of the plasma renin and aldosterone levels and makes diagnosis of hyperaldosteronism extremely difficult.

Renovascular hypertension is similarly difficult to diagnose during pregnancy. Magnetic resonance angiography can help to diagnose renal artery lesions. Kidney angioplasty also has been performed successfully in the early second trimester and should be considered in women with severe, poorly controlled hypertension.

KEY POINTS

- In pregnant women with chronic hypertension who had mild to moderately elevated blood pressure before pregnancy, discontinuation of antihypertensive medications and close monitoring may be sufficient in the absence of known target organ damage.

- Therapy can be initiated in pregnant women with chronic hypertension if the blood pressure increases to 140 to 150/90 to 100 mm Hg, but a slightly lower threshold for treatment may be warranted in women with chronic kidney disease.

- Angiotensin-converting enzyme inhibitors and angiotensin receptor blockers are contraindicated in pregnancy and should be discontinued before conception when possible.

- Pheochromocytoma and renovascular hypertension are associated with poor maternal and fetal prognoses, whereas women with primary aldosteronism may have relatively uncomplicated pregnancies.

Kidney Disease in the Pregnant Patient

The greater the degree of kidney function impairment and high blood pressure, the less likely a patient is to have a successful pregnancy.

Among women with moderate or severe kidney dysfunction (characterized by a serum creatinine level above 1.5 mg/dL [132.6 μmol/L] or stage 3 or higher CKD), 40% of pregnancies are complicated by hypertension, worsening proteinuria, or deterioration in kidney function that may be irreversible. Women without hypertension who have minimal proteinuria are significantly less likely to develop irreversible deterioration in kidney function during pregnancy. The presence of hypertension, and particularly severe hypertension at any time during pregnancy, also is associated with premature delivery.

In pregnant women with underlying kidney disease, the urine protein excretion may significantly increase. This increased proteinuria is associated with worse fetal prognosis, but the increase in proteinuria does not necessarily reflect worsening of the underlying kidney disease.

Diabetes Mellitus

One of the most common medical disorders in pregnant patients is diabetes mellitus, which is usually caused by gestational diabetes or, less commonly, type 1 diabetes.

Women with type 1 diabetes who have only microalbuminuria associated with well-preserved kidney function and normal blood pressure have pregnancy outcomes similar to those in the general population as well as a low risk for deterioration in kidney function. Nevertheless, these patients have an increased risk for preeclampsia and urinary tract infection.

Strict glucose control is associated with improved fetal outcome (see Diabetes during Pregnancy in MKSAP 15 Endocrinology and Metabolism). Patients taking angiotensin-converting enzyme inhibitors or angiotensin receptor blockers should be switched before conception to alternative agents such as methyldopa or a dihydropyridine calcium channel blocker.

Systemic Lupus Erythematosus

Systemic lupus erythematosus (SLE) is associated with significant maternal and fetal risk and tends to become more active during pregnancy. Generally, women who become pregnant who have SLE, and particularly those with active disease, have an increased risk for mortality, preeclampsia, and preterm delivery compared with the general population. Maternal and fetal outcomes are even worse when SLE is active at conception and in patients who have kidney involvement. Conception is therefore not recommended in patients with SLE unless their disease has been inactive for the preceding 6 months.

Women with SLE may have elevated titers of antiphospholipid antibodies and lupus anticoagulant, which are associated with spontaneous fetal loss, hypertensive syndromes indistinguishable from preeclampsia, and thrombotic events. Aspirin, 80 to 325 mg/d, is recommended if anticardiolipin antibody titers are elevated or the lupus anticoagulant is detected; the lupus anticoagulant also should be treated. Combination therapy with subcutaneous heparin and aspirin is recommended in patients with a history of thrombotic events. Emergency delivery may be necessary in patients with progressively active SLE-related kidney disease whose kidney function continues to decline despite immunosuppressive therapy and supportive care.

Appropriate therapy for lupus nephritis during pregnancy includes corticosteroids and azathioprine. Patients contemplating pregnancy despite counseling to the contrary who are already using agents that are potentially toxic to a fetus, such as cyclophosphamide and mycophenolate mofetil, should switch to azathioprine and corticosteroids.

Chronic Glomerulonephritis

CKD may be first diagnosed during pregnancy because pregnant patients undergo frequent blood pressure measurements and urinalyses. Chronic glomerulonephritis should be suspected when hypertension, proteinuria, or an elevated serum creatinine level are detected during the first antepartum visit.

The presence of significant kidney dysfunction (characterized by a serum creatinine level above 1.5 mg/dL [132.6 μmol/L] or stage 3 or higher CKD) with or without proteinuria is more consistent with glomerulonephritis than preeclampsia. Chronic glomerulonephritis also should be suspected when kidney dysfunction and proteinuria develop in normotensive women.

Whether histologic subtyping of a kidney biopsy specimen can help to determine prognosis for pregnancy is uncertain. Therefore, kidney biopsy in pregnant patients usually is deferred until after delivery unless acute deterioration in kidney function or nephrotic syndrome is present. However, patients with normal kidney function without hypertension generally have a favorable prognosis.

Autosomal-Dominant Polycystic Kidney Disease

Overall, fertility in women with autosomal-dominant polycystic kidney disease (ADPKD) is the same as in the general population. The presence of preexisting hypertension and kidney dysfunction in patients with ADPKD who become pregnant poses an increased risk for complications such as preeclampsia, preterm delivery, and intrauterine growth retardation. Ciliary abnormalities related to ADPKD also may pose an increased risk for ectopic pregnancy.

Chronic Pyelonephritis

Chronic pyelonephritis is characterized by recurrent urinary tract infections that are often associated with urinary tract abnormalities such as vesicoureteral reflux and may be exacerbated by pregnancy-related dilatation and stasis in the urinary tract. Management of patients with chronic pyelonephritis should include high fluid intake and frequent screening for bacteriuria, which, if left untreated, may contribute to preterm labor.

Acute Kidney Injury

Acute kidney injury (AKI) in pregnant patients usually develops between 35 weeks of pregnancy and the puerperium and is primarily caused by severe preeclampsia, bleeding complications, or urinary tract obstruction. AKI that develops between 12 and 18 weeks of pregnancy usually is associated with septic abortion or prerenal azotemia caused by hyperemesis gravidarum.

Management of AKI that occurs during pregnancy or immediately post partum is similar to that in nongravid patients (see Acute Kidney Injury). Because urea and other metabolites that accumulate in kidney failure traverse the placenta, dialysis should be performed early with the goal of maintaining a blood urea nitrogen level below 50 mg/dL (17.9 mmol/L).

Preeclampsia and the Thrombotic Microangiopathies

Preeclampsia causes a decrease in the GFR and in kidney blood flow, but kidney function in this setting usually remains within the normal range for nonpregnant patients. Therefore, preeclampsia is only rarely associated with severe AKI and is usually only present in patients with AKI when accompanied by the HELLP syndrome.

The thrombotic microangiopathies, thrombotic thrombocytopenic purpura and hemolytic-uremic syndrome, also are rare but important pregnancy-related causes of AKI. Manifestations of these conditions may resemble pregnancy-specific disorders such as the HELLP syndrome and acute fatty liver of pregnancy (see Pregnancy-Related Liver Disease in MKSAP 15 Gastroenterology and Hepatology).

Delivery and supportive care are indicated to treat preeclampsia and the HELLP syndrome, and kidney function usually returns to normal within days to a few weeks of delivery. Kidney biopsy may be appropriate if kidney function does not improve within 1 to 3 weeks of delivery but warrants caution because of the low platelet count and increased risk for bleeding associated with the thrombotic microangiopathies.

Pregnant patients with thrombotic thrombocytopenic purpura-hemolytic uremic syndrome may be managed with plasma exchange and other interventions used in nonpregnant patients. Hemolytic uremic syndrome is often associated with kidney failure and may be resistant to treatment with plasma infusion or exchange.

Obstruction

Although unilateral dilatation and partial obstruction of the right ureter are common in pregnancy, AKI caused by obstruction is rare and most often occurs in the setting of significant polyhydramnios, multiple gestations, bilateral nephrolithiasis, or intra-abdominal adhesions.

Management of bilateral ureteric obstruction in pregnant patients may include temporary placement of retrograde or percutaneous ureteral stents until the fetus reaches maturity. In addition, management of polyhydramnios helps to delay the onset of preterm labor and reduces obstruction.

KEY POINTS

- Pregnant women with underlying kidney disease may experience a significant increase in urine protein excretion that is associated with worse fetal prognosis but does not necessarily reflect worsening of their disease.

- Women with type 1 diabetes who have only microalbuminuria associated with well-preserved kidney function and normal blood pressure have pregnancy outcomes similar to those in the general population and a low risk for deterioration in kidney function.

- Conception is not recommended in patients with systemic lupus erythematosus unless their disease has been inactive for the preceding 6 months.

- Chronic glomerulonephritis should be suspected in pregnant women when hypertension, proteinuria, or an elevated serum creatinine level is detected during the first antepartum visit.

- Management of pregnant patients with chronic pyelonephritis should include high fluid intake and frequent screening for bacteriuria, which, if left untreated, may contribute to preterm labor.

- Delivery and supportive care are indicated to treat preeclampsia and the HELLP syndrome (Hemolysis, Elevated Liver enzymes, Low Platelets) in pregnant patients, and kidney function in patients with these disorders usually returns to normal within days to a few weeks of delivery.

- Management of bilateral ureteric obstruction in pregnant patients may include temporary placement of retrograde or percutaneous ureteral stents until the fetus reaches maturity.

Management of End-Stage Kidney Disease During Pregnancy

Dialysis

Pregnancy rarely occurs in women on dialysis. However, improved management of anemia and an increase in the number of women of childbearing potential undergoing dialysis have led to an increase in fertility rates in women with end-stage kidney disease (ESKD).

Possible maternal complications of dialysis include accelerated hypertension, cerebrovascular accidents, and mortality. Common fetal complications of this therapy include extremely low birth weight and intrauterine growth restriction. Polyhydramnios-related preterm labor also can result in premature delivery. Furthermore, the increased blood urea nitrogen level associated with dialysis may cause fetal osmotic diuresis beginning at 19 weeks of pregnancy.

Successful pregnancy in patients undergoing dialysis depends on an increase in weekly hours of dialysis from 12 to more than 20, minimal weight gain between dialysis sessions, and aggressive management of anemia.

Kidney Transplantation

Women with ESKD may have a successful pregnancy after undergoing kidney transplantation. However, these patients should wait 1 to 2 years post transplantation before conceiving, and pregnancy is not recommended if the serum creatinine level is above 2 mg/dL (177 μmol/L).

Complications in kidney transplantation recipients who become pregnant include impaired glucose tolerance, hypertension, increased risk for infection, ectopic pregnancy, and uterine rupture. Fetal complications in these patients include a higher incidence of premature delivery, intrauterine growth restriction, congenital anomalies, hypoadrenalism, thrombocytopenia, and infection.

KEY POINTS

- Successful pregnancy in patients undergoing dialysis depends on an increase in weekly hours of dialysis from 12 to more than 20, minimal weight gain between dialysis sessions, and aggressive management of anemia.

- Kidney transplantation recipients should wait 1 to 2 years post transplantation before conceiving, and pregnancy is not recommended if the serum creatinine level is above 2 mg/dL (177 μmol/L).

Bibliography

Andrade R, Sanchez ML, Alarcon GS, et al; LUMINA Study Group. C. Adverse pregnancy outcomes in women with systemic lupus erythematosus from a multiethnic US cohort: LUMINA (LVI) [erratum in Clin Exp Rheumatol. 2008;26(3):511]. Clin Exp Rheumatol. 2008;26(2):268-274. [PMID: 18565248]

Armenti VT, Radomski JS, Moritz MJ, Gaughan WJ, McGrory CH, Coscia LA. Report from the National Transplantation Pregnancy

Registry (NTPR): outcomes of pregnancy after transplantation. Clin Transpl. 2003:131-41. [PMID: 15387104]

Fischer MJ, Lehnerz SD, Hebert JR, Parikh CR. Kidney disease is an independent risk factor for adverse fetal and maternal outcomes in pregnancy. Am J Kidney Dis. 2004;43(3):415-423. [PMID: 14981599]

Imbasciati E, Gregorinin G, Cabiddu G, et al. Pregnancy in CKD stages 3 to 5: fetal and amternal outcomes. Am J Kidney Disease. 2007;49(6):753-762. [PMID: 17533018]

Podymow T, August P. Update on the use of antihypertensive drugs in pregnancy. Hypertension. 2008;51(4):960-969. [PMID: 18259046]

Williams D, Davison J. Chronic kidney disease in pregnancy. BMJ. 2008;336(7637):211-215. [PMID: 18219043]

Chronic Kidney Disease

Chronic kidney disease (CKD) is characterized by either kidney damage or a glomerular filtration rate (GFR) less than 60 mL/min/1.73 m² that persists for 3 months or more. Kidney damage in this setting refers to structural or functional abnormalities of the kidney that may manifest as abnormalities in kidney pathology, results of laboratory studies such as urinalysis, or imaging studies of the kidneys. CKD is classified according to the degree of functional impairment in GFR as estimated by the Modification of Diet in Renal Disease Study equation (**Table 34**).

Pathophysiology and Epidemiology

Approximately 16% of the U.S. population has CKD. The prevalence is increasing, possibly because of the increased incidence of major risk factors for CKD such as diabetes mellitus, hypertension, obesity, and the metabolic syndrome. CKD is more prevalent among individuals with lower socioeconomic status.

Patients with CKD typically experience a progressive decline in the GFR. The rate at which this value decreases ranges from less than 1 mL/min/1.73 m² yearly to over 12 mL/min/1.73 m² yearly in patients with untreated diabetic nephropathy.

Clinical features predictive of accelerated disease progression in patients with CKD include the degree of proteinuria, hypertension, and black race.

KEY POINTS

- Chronic kidney disease is characterized by either kidney damage or a glomerular filtration rate less than 60 mL/min/1.73 m² that persists for 3 months or more.
- Major risk factors for chronic kidney disease include diabetes mellitus, hypertension, obesity, and the metabolic syndrome.
- Clinical features predictive of accelerated disease progression in patients with chronic kidney disease include degree of proteinuria, hypertension, and black race.

Screening

Screening high-risk patients for CKD allows for early detection of this condition and the implementation of effective interventions to slow progression of kidney disease and treat the manifestations of CKD. All patients should be assessed for the presence of risk factors for CKD (**Table 35**). A personal history of diabetes, hypertension, or cardiovascular disease carries the highest risk for developing this condition. In patients with risk factors for this condition, screening with urinalysis, a urine protein- or albumin-creatinine ratio from a first morning voided specimen, and serum creatinine level measurement with corresponding estimation of the GFR is indicated.

Use of the patient-centered tool known as SCreening for Occult REnal Disease (SCORED) survey also may help to stratify risk for CKD (**Figure 20**)(see page 84). When using a cutoff value of four points in a community population, this screening tool was most accurate in excluding occult kidney disease with a sensitivity of 92%, specificity of 68%, positive predictive value of 18%, and negative predictive value of 99%.

TABLE 34 Stages of Chronic Kidney Disease

Stage	Description	GFRª (mL/min/1.73 m²)	Action
1	Kidney damage with normal GFR	≥90	Treatment of comorbid condition, interventions to slow disease progression, reduction of risk factors for cardiovascular disease
2	Kidney damage with mildly decreased GFR	60-89	Estimate disease progression
3	Moderately decreased GFR	30-59	Evaluation and treatment of disease complications (such as anemia, renal osteodystrophy)
4	Severely decreased GFR	15-29	Preparation for kidney replacement (dialysis, transplantation)
5	Kidney failure	<15 (or dialysis)	Kidney replacement therapy if uremia is present

GFR = Glomerular filtration rate; MDRD = Modification of Diet in Renal Disease Study.

ªMDRD equation: GFR (mL/min/1.73 m²) = 186 × [serum creatinine]$^{-1.154}$ × (age)$^{-0.203}$ × 0.742 (if female) × 1.21 (if black)

Modified with permission from Alguire, PC. Internal Medicine Essentials for Clerkship Students 2007-2008. Philadelphia: American College of Physicians; 2007.

TABLE 35 Risk Factors for Chronic Kidney Disease

Diabetes mellitus
Hypertension
Hyperlipidemia
Cardiovascular disease
Obesity
Metabolic syndrome
Age >60 years
Malignancy
Family history of chronic kidney disease
Smoking
HIV infection
Hepatitis C virus infection
Kidney stones
Autoimmune disease
Recurrent urinary tract infection
Recovery from acute kidney injury
Exposure to nephrotoxic drugs, such as NSAIDs and cyclooxygenase-2 inhibitors

KEY POINTS

- A personal history of diabetes, hypertension, or cardiovascular disease carries the highest risk for developing chronic kidney disease.

- In patients with risk factors for chronic kidney disease, screening with urinalysis, a urine protein- or albumin-creatinine ratio from a first morning voided specimen, serum creatinine level measurement, and estimation of the glomerular filtration rate is indicated.

Clinical Manifestations

The underlying cause and stage of CKD determine the clinical manifestations of this condition. Patients with stages 1 and 2 CKD are often asymptomatic; for example, patients with incipient diabetic nephropathy may present with asymptomatic microalbuminuria. However, those with advanced diabetic nephropathy associated with nephrotic-range proteinuria often have evidence of retinopathy and neuropathy. Patients with stages 3 and 4 CKD usually have progressive cardiovascular disease, abnormalities in bone and mineral metabolism, and anemia.

Diagnosis and Evaluation

The clinical presentation of CKD is frequently subtle. Many patients with CKD seek medical attention for the first time late in the disease course for nonspecific symptoms of fatigue caused by progressive anemia and azotemia. Often, CKD remains undiagnosed until the GFR decreases to 5 to 10 mL/min/1.73 m^2, at which time kidney replacement therapy is needed.

All patients with CKD should undergo evaluation for a specific diagnosis (**Table 36**). A careful history and physical examination often help to reveal the cause of CKD. For example, patients with long-standing diabetes complicated by both microalbuminuria and diabetic retinopathy most likely have diabetic nephropathy, whereas an absence of diabetic retinopathy in this setting suggests another cause for CKD.

Evaluation of patients with CKD should include measurement of the serum electrolytes, including sodium, potassium, chloride, bicarbonate, calcium, and phosphorus. Untimed or spot urine samples are usually used to detect and monitor proteinuria. In addition, antinuclear antibody assays, serum complement level measurement, and protein electrophoresis and/or immunofixation may be helpful in patients with systemic vasculitis, proteinuria, and/or hematuria.

A detailed urine sediment analysis and kidney ultrasonography are indicated for all patients with CKD (**Figure 21**) (see page 85). Finally, referral to a nephrologist and kidney biopsy are often needed to establish a specific diagnosis. Biopsy also should be considered in patients with CKD who have evidence of glomerular disease in the absence of diabetes or in patients with diabetes with atypical features, such as the absence of retinopathy or the development of sudden-onset nephrotic syndrome or glomerular hematuria.

KEY POINTS

- Evaluation of all patients with chronic kidney disease should include urinalysis, evaluation of urine sediment, kidney ultrasonography, and measurement of the serum electrolytes and a random urine protein-creatinine ratio.

- Biopsy should be considered in patients with chronic kidney disease who have evidence of glomerular disease in the absence of diabetes or in patients with diabetes with atypical features, such as the absence of retinopathy or the development of sudden-onset nephrotic syndrome or glomerular hematuria.

Complications

Cardiovascular Disease

Recent epidemiologic studies have shown that patients with CKD are more likely to die of cardiovascular complications before reaching end-stage kidney disease (ESKD). Patients with CKD have an excess burden of cardiovascular disease and mortality as well as an increased incidence of risk factors for cardiovascular disease. In addition, low GFR and proteinuria are independent risk factors for cardiovascular disease. Furthermore, as CKD progresses, both the number of cardiovascular risk factors a patient has and the cardiovascular mortality rate increase.

TABLE 36 Differential Diagnosis of Chronic Kidney Disease

Disease	Notes
Diabetic kidney disease	Diabetic kidney disease is the primary cause of CKD in the United States. Diabetic kidney disease, particularly type 1, usually follows a characteristic course that first manifests as microalbuminuria, then clinical proteinuria, hypertension, and declining GFR. Diabetic nephropathy is often accompanied by diabetic retinopathy, particularly in patients with type 1 diabetes mellitus. In patients with type 2 diabetes, the presence of retinopathy strongly suggests coexisting diabetic nephropathy. Diabetic nephropathy is likely even in the absence of retinopathy, but an evaluation for other causes of proteinuria is reasonable.
Nondiabetic kidney disease	
Glomerular disease	May manifest as a "nephritic" picture with hematuria, variable proteinuria, and hypertension, often with other systemic manifestations. Common causes include postinfectious glomerulonephritis, IgA nephropathy, and membranoproliferative glomerulonephritis. Nephrotic syndrome refers to high-grade proteinuria (often >3 g/24 h), hypoalbuminemia, and edema. Common causes include minimal change disease, focal segmental glomerulosclerosis, membranous nephropathy, and amyloidosis. SLE commonly affects the kidneys and may cause nephritis or nephritic syndrome. A kidney biopsy is often needed to establish a specific diagnosis and guide therapy.
Tubulointerstitial disease	Affected patients generally have bland urinalyses but may have proteinuria, a concentrating defect, pyuria, casts, or radiologic abnormalities. Analgesic nephropathy, lead nephropathy, chronic obstruction, and reflux nephropathy are examples.
Vascular disease	The clinical presentation depends on the type of blood vessels involved (small, medium, or large). Patients with small-vessel disease often have hematuria, proteinuria, and an associated systemic illness. Patients with vasculitis can present with a rapidly progressive glomerulonephritis. Examples include sickle cell disease and hemolytic uremic syndrome. Hypertension is an example of medium-vessel disease and is the second most common cause of CKD in the United States. Hypertensive disease is generally slowly progressive and leads to stage 5 CKD in the minority of patients. Black patients have more aggressive CKD caused by hypertension. Renal artery stenosis is an example of large-vessel disease.
Cystic disease	Affected patients can have normal findings on urinalyses. Diagnosis is usually made by imaging techniques and family history. Simple kidney cysts are common, particularly in older persons. Autosomal-dominant polycystic kidney disease types 1 and 2 are the most common forms.
Transplantation	CKD in the kidney transplant recipient may be caused by chronic rejection, drug toxicity, or recurrence of native kidney disease. A careful history, measurement of serum drug levels, and often kidney biopsy are required for diagnosis.

CKD = chronic kidney disease; GFR = glomerular filtration rate; SLE = systemic lupus erythematosus.

Modified with permission from Alguire, PC. Internal Medicine Essentials for Clerkship Students 2007-2008. Philadelphia: American College of Physicians; 2007.

A decrease in GFR correlates with a decrease in vascular compliance and aortic elasticity, which are associated with increased cardiovascular mortality and increased vascular calcification. A decrease in GFR also inversely correlates with an increased risk for heart failure and associated mortality, with every $10 \text{ mL}/\text{min}/1.73 \text{ m}^2$ decrease in GFR resulting in a 7% increase in mortality risk.

Patients with CKD who have an acute myocardial infarction are less likely to have chest pain but are more likely to have atypical symptoms such as dyspnea. Recent evidence suggests that acute coronary syndrome is undertreated in patients with CKD. For example, patients with CKD who have had an acute myocardial infarction are less likely to receive reperfusion therapy on hospital admission or to be prescribed β-blockers, statins, angiotensin-converting enzyme (ACE) inhibitors, and aspirin on hospital discharge.

Fibrinolysis also is more likely to be delayed in patients with CKD, but use of fibrinolytic agents most likely does not pose an increased risk of bleeding complications in this setting.

In the Arterial Revascularization Therapies Study (ARTS), the mortality rate and rates of myocardial infarction and stroke were similar in patients treated with either percutaneous bare-metal stenting or surgical revascularization. However, the percutaneous intervention group were more likely to require secondary revascularization.

Patients with CKD have been largely excluded from secondary cardiovascular prevention trials. Atorvastatin therapy was found to have no survival benefit in patients undergoing hemodialysis who have type 2 diabetes. Post hoc analyses of large clinical trials, however, suggest that use of statins in patients with stages 2 to 4 CKD is associated with a decreased rate of adverse cardiovascular events. In one randomized controlled trial, patients on hemodialysis who used carvedilol had a statistically improved mortality rate.

Treatment of hypertension in patients with CKD protects against progressive CKD and cardiovascular disease. Prophylaxis against cardiovascular disease with low-dose aspirin also should be considered in patients with CKD.

Find out if you might have silent chronic kidney disease now. Check each statement that is true for you. If a statement is not true or you are not sure, put a zero. Then add up all the points for a total.

• Age:	
1. I am between 50 and 59 years of age	Yes 2 _____
2. I am between 60 and 69 years of age	Yes 3 _____
3. I am 70 years old or older	Yes 4 _____
• I am a woman	Yes 1 _____
• I had/have anemia	Yes 1 _____
• I have high blood pressure	Yes 1 _____
• I am diabetic	Yes 1 _____
• I have a history of heart attack or stroke	Yes 1 _____
• I have a history of heart failure	Yes 1 _____
• I have circulation disease in my legs	Yes 1 _____
• I have protein in my urine	Yes 1 _____
Total _____	

If You Scored 4 or More Points

You have a 1 in 5 chance of having chronic kidney disease. At your next office visit, a simple blood test should be checked. Only a professional health care provider can determine for sure if you have kidney disease.

If You Scored 0-3 Points

You probably do not have kidney disease now, but at least once a year, you should take this survey.

FIGURE 20.
The SCreening for Occult REnal Disease (SCORED) survey.

Modified with permission from Bang H, Vupputuri S, Shoham DA, Klemmer PJ, Falk RJ, Mazumdar M, et al. SCreening for Occult REnal Disease (SCORED): a simple prediction model for chronic kidney disease. Arch Intern Med. 2007;167:374-81. [PMID: 17325299] Copyright © 2007, American Medical Association.

Anemia

Anemia is associated with decreased quality of life, left ventricular hypertrophy, and cardiovascular complications in patients with CKD. The anemia of CKD is primarily caused by reduced production of erythropoietin and usually becomes apparent in stages 4 and 5 CKD (see Anemia of Kidney Disease in MKSAP 15 Hematology and Oncology). Anemia of CKD is a diagnosis of exclusion, and the presence of other causes of anemia such as gastrointestinal bleeding, vitamin B_{12} deficiency, or hemolysis should be investigated. Measurement of the serum erythropoietin level does not usually help to discriminate among other causes of anemia or to guide treatment decisions and is therefore not recommended.

Use of erythropoietin-stimulating agents (ESAs) such as epoetin and darbepoietin alfa can correct erythropoietin deficiency and should be considered for patients with CKD who have hemoglobin levels below 10 g/dL (100 g/L). This therapy helps to decrease symptoms of anemia and may reduce the need for transfusions. However, results of both the Correction of Hemoglobin Outcomes in Renal Insufficiency

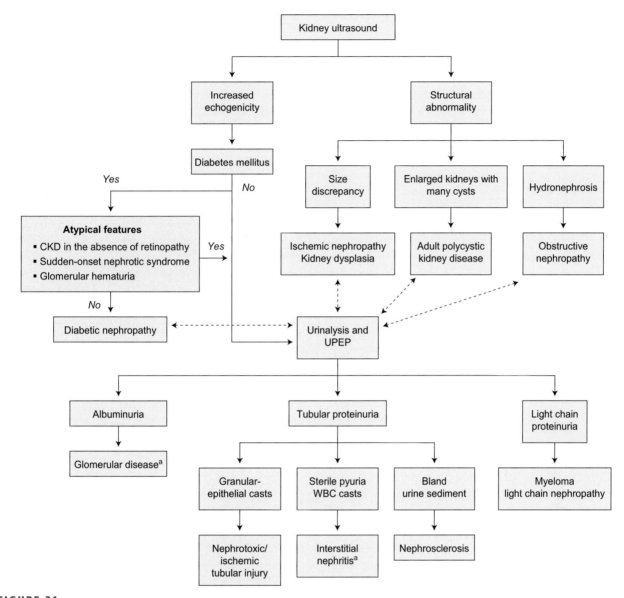

FIGURE 21.
Diagnostic evaluation of chronic kidney disease.
Dotted lines emphasize that urinalysis and urine sediment analysis should be performed in all patients.

CKD = chronic kidney disease; WBC = white blood cell; UPEP = urine protein electrophoresis.

[a]Consider kidney biopsy.

(CHOIR) study and the Normal Hematocrit study showed that patients randomized to receive therapy to obtain hemoglobin levels above 13 g/dL (130 g/L) had a higher mortality rate that was approaching statistical significance. Other studies have demonstrated increased cerebrovascular and thrombotic events and hypertension as well as flu-like symptoms and headache in patients with a target hemoglobin level above 13 g/dL (130 g/L).

The 2007 National Kidney Foundation Kidney Disease Outcomes Quality Initiative (NKF-K/DOQI) clinical practice guidelines recommended a hemoglobin level targeted to 11 to 12 g/dL (110 to 120 g/L), but not exceeding 13 g/dL (130 g/L), in dialysis and nondialysis patients with

CKD receiving ESAs. Achieving the suggested targeted hemoglobin range is particularly difficult because considerable fluctuations in hemoglobin levels commonly occur despite use of stable ESA doses. Furthermore, the hemoglobin level should increase by less than 1 g/dL (10 g/L) over a 2-week period in order to decrease the risk of ESA-associated hypertension.

Many experts recommend that hemoglobin levels should be monitored every 2 to 4 weeks after ESA therapy is initiated. Dose adjustment may be required to achieve the target hemoglobin levels and should be performed by either reducing the dose or increasing the dosing interval when the hemoglobin level increases above 12 g/dL (120 g/L). ESA therapy should be withheld when the hemoglobin level exceeds 13 g/dL (130 g/L) and should be resumed at a decreased dose once the hemoglobin decreases to below 12 g/dL (120 g/L).

In patients with anemia undergoing ESA therapy, iron stores should be maintained with oral or parenteral iron to achieve a transferrin saturation of 20% or higher and a serum ferritin level above 100 ng/mL (100 µg/L). Parenteral iron in particular is generally required for those undergoing hemodialysis. Patients who do not achieve the target hemoglobin level despite ESA therapy should be evaluated for iron deficiency, sources of blood loss including menstrual bleeding, infection, secondary hyperparathyroidism, nutritional deficiencies, hemolysis, and malignancy. Finally, because ESA therapy may be associated with increased blood pressure, close monitoring of blood pressure is indicated for patients undergoing this therapy.

Chronic Kidney Disease-Mineral and Bone Disorder

CKD is associated with progressive alterations in mineral and bone metabolism that interact with vascular biology. The term CKD-mineral and bone disorder refers to a syndrome of bone and extraskeletal calcification that occurs in patients with CKD.

Secondary hyperparathyroidism and bone disease affect almost all patients with CKD. Hyperphosphatemia, hypocalcemia, and deficiency of 1,25-dihydroxyvitamin D stimulate parathyroid hormone secretion. In patients with CKD, fragments of parathyroid hormone containing various lengths of carboxyterminal parts of the molecule accumulate. To obtain an accurate measurement of the serum parathyroid hormone level in patients with CKD, the NKF K/DOQI clinical practice guidelines recommend use of the "two-site" intact parathyroid hormone assays, which have improved sensitivity and specificity compared with "one-site" radioimmunoassays.

In patients with stages 2 and 3 CKD, increased parathyroid hormone secretion helps to maintain the serum calcium level through increased mobilization from bone and decreased urine calcium excretion. Patients with stage 3 CKD demonstrate transient postprandial hypocalcemia and hyperphosphatemia, which contribute to the increase in parathyroid hormone that precedes the onset of sustained hyperphosphatemia that characterizes stages 4 and 5 CKD. This hyperphosphatemia directly stimulates parathyroid hormone secretion and reduces 1-α-hydroxylase activity, which further exacerbates the 1,25-dihydroxyvitamin D deficiency.

According to observational studies, elevated serum phosphorus levels are associated with increased progression of CKD and increased mortality in patients with ESKD. Some experts also propose that altered calcium-phosphorus metabolism is a possible risk factor for cardiovascular disease.

An increase in the calcium-phosphorus product leads to increased medial vascular calcification, which can decrease vascular compliance and may contribute to excess cardiovascular mortality. Use of vitamin D analogs and calcium supplements in patients with CKD can lead to hypercalcemia, elevations in

the calcium-phosphorus product, and vascular calcification. Therefore, maintaining the optimal balance between treatment of vitamin D deficiency in CKD and preventing extraosseous calcification is challenging.

The optimal management of CKD-mineral and bone disorder remains uncertain. NKF K/DOQI clinical practice guidelines are available at the following Web address but are largely opinion based: www.kidney.org/professionals/KDOQI/guidelines_bone/index.htm.

In 2006, the Kidney Disease: Improving Global Outcomes (KDIGO) workgroup recommended maintaining serum phosphorus levels within the normal range in patients undergoing hemodialysis by means of dietary phosphate restriction and oral phosphate binders. Serum calcium levels should also be monitored and maintained within the normal range.

Intact serum parathyroid hormone levels also should be regularly monitored at least every 4 months with therapy directed to avoid both high and low levels of this hormone. However, achieving target levels of phosphorus and calcium should be prioritized over the management of the serum parathyroid hormone level. Intact serum parathyroid hormone levels below 100 pg/mL (100 ng/L) should be avoided, and levels above 500 pg/mL (500 ng/L) should be treated if accompanied by symptoms or clinical signs of hyperparathyroidism.

Vitamin D analogs can be used in the treatment of secondary hyperparathyroidism but should be discontinued when serum parathyroid hormone levels decrease below target levels, or if calcium or phosphate levels increase above target levels. Parathyroidectomy should be considered if standard treatments are unsuccessful and serum intact parathyroid hormone levels are persistently elevated and accompanied by systemic complications.

From a physiologic perspective, the ideal treatment of CKD-related mineral disorders would prevent the onset of parathyroid hyperplasia in stages 2 to 4 CKD before the onset of irreversible parathyroid gland growth. According to the NKF-K/DOQI practice guidelines, control of the serum parathyroid hormone and phosphorus levels is critical. Dietary phosphorus restriction, including avoidance of phosphorus-rich foods such as dairy products and processed foods, as well as the use of phosphate binders is recommended.

To date, no randomized controlled outcome trials have been performed that address the relative benefits and risks of the NKF-K/DOQI guidelines for bone and mineral metabolism in patients with CKD who have not yet started dialysis. One observational trial showed a mortality benefit associated with use of the vitamin D analog paricalcitol in patients undergoing hemodialysis.

Vitamin D compounds also have not been shown to consistently reduce parathyroid hormone levels in patients with CKD. Furthermore, vitamin D analogs can induce hypercalcemia and hyperphosphatemia and therefore should be used with caution. In order to avoid positive calcium balance, the total dose of elemental calcium in patients with stage 5 CKD who are using calcium-based phosphate binders should not exceed 1000 mg/d. Careful monitoring of the serum calcium, phosphorus, and parathyroid hormone levels in order to detect hypercalcemia, hyperphosphatemia, or oversuppression of the serum parathyroid hormone may be warranted every 4 to 8 weeks and then can be performed quarterly.

Calcimimetic agents lower serum parathyroid hormone levels and the levels of both components of the calcium-phosphorus product. The calcimimetic agent cinacalcet is approved for use only in the treatment of secondary hyperparathyroidism in patients with CKD who are receiving dialysis. The role of cinacalcet in patients with CKD and secondary hyperparathyroidism who have not yet begun dialysis has not yet been validated in randomized controlled trials.

Renal Osteodystrophy

Renal osteodystrophy specifically refers to abnormalities in bone morphology associated with CKD. This condition may manifest as osteitis fibrosa cystica, osteomalacia, adynamic bone disease, mixed uremic osteodystrophy, osteoporosis, and amyloidosis.

Most of these conditions are characterized by osteopenia. Adynamic bone disease and mixed osteodystrophy are the most common forms of renal osteodystrophy.

Bone biopsy may be performed when a specific diagnosis is required to guide therapy. Biopsy in this setting requires use of tetracycline labeling protocols and should be performed by an experienced clinician. In addition, biopsy specimens should be sent to a laboratory that sections specimens without previous decalcification.

Osteitis Fibrosa Cystica

Persistent secondary hyperparathyroidism results in a form of high-turnover bone disease known as osteitis fibrosa cystica. Affected patients are frequently asymptomatic during early disease but later may develop bone pain and increased risk for fractures.

Radiographs in patients with osteitis fibrosa cystica reveal subperiosteal bone reabsorption, particularly in the phalanges and distal clavicles, as well as areas of sclerosis mixed with osteopenia in the dorsal spine known as rugger jersey spine (**Figure 22**).

Severe secondary hyperparathyroidism also typically causes an elevation in bone-specific serum alkaline phosphatase levels. In addition, rapid osteoclastic activity and peritrabecular fibrosis associated with osteitis fibrosa cystica result in erosive osteolytic lesions called Brown tumors that may mimic neoplastic lesions.

Treatment of osteitis fibrosa cystica and secondary hyperparathyroidism is directed toward control of the serum parathyroid hormone levels with use of vitamin D analogs, cinacalcet, or control of hyperphosphatemia. Surgical parathyroidectomy also may be considered in these patients.

Osteomalacia

Osteomalacia is a form of low-turnover bone disease characterized by increased unmineralized osteoid. This condition is primarily caused by vitamin D deficiency and profound hypocalcemia. In patients with CKD, osteomalacia is usually accompanied by concurrent high-turnover bone disease and is referred to as mixed osteodystrophy.

Adynamic Bone Disease

The low-turnover condition known as adynamic bone disease is one of the leading causes of bone disease in patients with stage 5 CKD. Functional hypoparathyroidism due to excess use of vitamin D supplements and/or calcium loading may cause this condition. Adynamic bone disease also may develop as a result of excess removal of functional parathyroid tissue after parathyroidectomy.

Patients with adynamic bone disease may have serum parathyroid hormone levels below 100 pg/mL (100 ng/L) as well as frequent fractures and bone pain. Risk factors for this condition include advanced age, diabetes, poor nutrition, and oversuppression of serum parathyroid hormone with therapeutic agents.

Discontinuation of vitamin D analogs and calcium-based binders is indicated for patients with adynamic bone disease and/or severe hyperphosphatemia. Cinacalcet also should be discontinued when the intact serum parathyroid hormone level decreases below 150 pg/mL (150 ng/L). In patients who have undergone parathyroidectomy who have hypoparathyroidism, reimplantation of remnant parathyroid tissue into the bone is indicated to restore anabolic parathyroid activity in the bone.

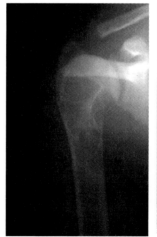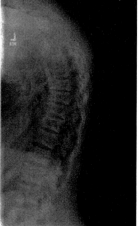

FIGURE 22.
Osteitis fibrosa cystica.
The left image shows a radiograph of the proximal humerus that reveals characteristic cystic bone lesions. The right image demonstrates a radiograph of the lateral spine in a patient with long-standing end-stage kidney disease. The band-like regions of increased opacity visible at the superior and inferior margins of the vertebral bodies are typical of rugger jersey spine.

Osteoporosis

Osteoporosis commonly occurs in patients with CKD, but diagnosis of this condition is complicated by the presence of other bone lesions. Measurement of bone mineral density via dual energy x-ray absorptiometry does not reliably predict fracture risk in patients with stages 3 to 5 CKD or distinguish between forms of renal osteodystrophy.

Osteoporosis should be suspected in patients with CKD presenting with bone pain and fractures who have risk factors for this condition, such as a history of corticosteroid use, hypogonadism, poor nutrition, or sustained vitamin D deficiency. Plain films of the bones are nonspecific and demonstrate osteopenia.

In stages 1 and 2 CKD, histologic changes of renal osteodystrophy are likely to be minimal, if present. Therefore, dual energy x-ray absorptiometry would be a reasonable modality to diagnose osteoporosis. No evidence-based recommendations are available regarding the use of bisphosphonates in patients with CKD who have osteoporosis. However, many experts believe that indications for bisphosphonate therapy in patients with stages 1 and 2 CKD should mirror those of the general population.

If advanced osteoporosis is suspected in patients with stage 3 to 5 CKD, bone biopsy should be considered before bisphosphonate therapy. Furthermore, experts recommend that 1 year of bisphosphonate therapy should only be considered when bone biopsy establishes the diagnosis of osteoporosis and fractures are present.

Because bisphosphonates are eliminated by the kidneys, the dose should be adjusted downward as CKD progresses. Once the GFR falls to less than 30 mL/min/1.73 m^2, bisphosphonates should be discontinued to prevent adynamic bone disease, unless a compelling indication such as fractures and bone biopsy–proven osteoporosis is present.

Acute kidney injury (AKI) may be associated with infusions of zoledronic acid performed in less than 15 minutes. Oral bisphosphonates have not been reported to induce AKI, but concern exists that all bisphosphonates may contribute to the development of adynamic bone disease in patients with stages 4 and 5 CKD.

KEY POINTS

- Complications associated with chronic kidney disease include cardiovascular disease, anemia, and chronic kidney disease-mineral and bone disorder.

- Treatment of hypertension in patients with chronic kidney disease protects against both progressive chronic kidney disease and cardiovascular disease.

- Anemia of chronic kidney disease is a diagnosis of exclusion, and the presence of other causes of anemia such as gastrointestinal bleeding, vitamin B$_{12}$ deficiency, or hemolysis should be investigated.

- Use of erythropoietin-stimulating agents such as epoetin and darbepoietin alfa can correct erythropoietin deficiency and should be considered for patients with chronic kidney disease who have hemoglobin levels below 10 g/dL (100 g/L).

- Patients with chronic kidney disease and anemia should be treated to a target hemoglobin level from 11 to 12 g/dL (110 to 120 g/L), and hemoglobin levels should not exceed 13 g/dL (130 g/L).

- Management of chronic kidney disease-mineral and bone disorders involves controlling the serum parathyroid hormone and phosphorus levels, restriction of phosphorus-rich foods, and the use of phosphate binders.

- Patients with chronic kidney disease may develop renal osteodystrophy that manifests as osteitis fibrosa cystica, osteomalacia, adynamic bone disease, mixed uremic osteodystrophy, osteoporosis, and amyloidosis.

Management

General Management

General management of patients with CKD should attempt to delay disease progression, treat symptoms, and reduce risk factors for disorders that have an increased prevalence in patients with CKD, such as cardiovascular disease. Therapeutic targets to delay progression of CKD are largely centered on controlling the underlying disease process, treating hypertension, and inhibiting the renin-angiotensin-aldosterone system.

The underlying cause of CKD and the need for immunosuppressive therapy in patients with glomerulonephritis and systemic vasculitis should be addressed whenever possible. Metabolic acidosis should be treated to maintain a serum bicarbonate level between 20 and 26 meq/L (20 and 26 mmol/L) to ameliorate protein catabolism and maintain 1-α-hydroxylation of vitamin D. Although correction of acidosis in CKD is reasonable from a physiologic standpoint, only limited clinical trial data are available to confirm a benefit.

Dietary protein restriction has been shown to delay progression of CKD in animal models, but its benefit in humans remains unproved. Dietary protein restriction to 0.6 to 0.8 g/kg daily accompanied by ketoacid supplementation may help to delay the onset of uremic symptoms in patients who choose to forego dialysis but carries a risk of protein-calorie malnutrition.

Maintaining glycemic control is important in patients with CKD who have diabetes. Intensified glycemic control delays the progression from normal urine albumin excretion to microalbuminuria, clinical proteinuria, and overt nephropathy. Ideally, the hemoglobin A$_{1c}$ level should be maintained near 7.0 to 7.9%.

Nephrotoxic agents such as magnesium- and phosphate-containing cathartics, NSAIDs, selective cyclooxygenase-2 inhibitors, and iodinated contrast are not recommended for patients with CKD. Metformin should be discontinued once the estimated GFR decreases below 50 mL/min/1.73 m^2.

Most patients also should discontinue use of bisphosphonates once the estimated GFR decreases below 30 mL/min/1.73 m^2 to avoid the potential risk of adynamic bone disease.

Gadolinium should be not administered to patients with ESKD and should be avoided in patients with a GFR below 30 mL/min/1.73 m^2 to prevent nephrogenic systemic fibrosis.

Management of Hypertension

Lowering blood pressure targets is indicated for all patients with kidney disease and is critical in the management of CKD regardless of the underlying disease cause. This intervention helps to decrease cardiovascular risk and may help to prevent progression to ESKD. Experts recommend blood pressure targets of less than 130/80 mm Hg for patients with minimal proteinuria and less than 125/75 mm Hg for patients with significant proteinuria (>1 g/24 h).

ACE inhibitors or angiotensin receptor blockers (ARBs) are the preferred antihypertensive agents in patients with CKD,

especially in those with proteinuria. Furthermore, continued use of ACE inhibitor therapy in patients with stages 3 and 4 CKD has been associated with a sustained renoprotective effect.

ACE inhibitors and ARBs reduce efferent arteriolar resistance and lower intraglomerular pressure and therefore may be associated with a slight increase in the serum creatinine level in patients with reduced GFR. An increase in the serum creatinine of up to 30% after initiation of these agents is acceptable. Use of these agents also may cause hyperkalemia.

Initially, once-daily administration of a low-dose ACE inhibitor is indicated to limit the risk of hyperkalemia in this setting. Serum potassium and creatinine levels also should be measured 3 to 5 days after initiation of therapy with an ACE inhibitor or ARB and every 2 to 3 months thereafter. In asymptomatic patients, the dose of the preferred antihypertensive agents should be titrated weekly until the target blood pressure is achieved.

Hyperkalemia often can be managed with restriction of dietary potassium to 60 meq/d, adequate hydration, and loop diuretics (**Figure 23**). ACE inhibitor or ARB therapy should be discontinued only if medical measures fail to maintain the serum potassium in a safe range.

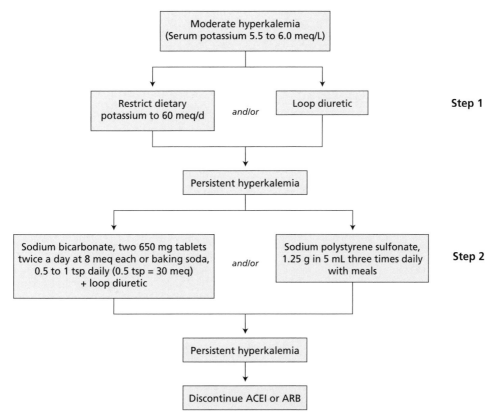

FIGURE 23.

Management of moderate hyperkalemia in patients with chronic kidney disease using angiotensin-converting enzyme inhibitor or angiotensin receptor blocker therapy.

ACEI = angiotensin-converting enzyme inhibitor; ARB = angiotensin receptor blocker.

Most patients with advanced CKD require at least two antihypertensive agents to achieve blood pressure goals. In addition, restriction of sodium to less than 2.4 g/d and adding a diuretic, particularly furosemide, can enhance the antihypertensive and antiproteinuric effects of antihypertensive agents. However, thiazide diuretics are less effective in patients with stages 4 and 5 CKD.

The patient's condition also should help determine the choice of antihypertensive therapy. For example, patients with angina may benefit from use of a β-blocker.

Treatment of End-Stage Kidney Disease

Management of ESKD consists of dialysis or kidney transplantation. Almost all patients with ESKD initially undergo at least some dialysis.

Discussions regarding the need for kidney replacement therapy should begin at least 1 year before the anticipated start of dialysis or when the GFR decreases below 30 mL/min/1.73 m². At this time, the most appropriate method of dialysis as well as a patient's suitability for transplantation should be determined.

KEY POINTS

- General management of patients with chronic kidney disease should attempt to delay disease progression, treat symptoms, and reduce risk factors for disorders that have an increased prevalence in patients with this disease.

- Ideally, the hemoglobin A_{1c} level in patients with chronic kidney disease who have diabetes should be maintained between 7% and 7.9%.

- Nephrotoxic agents such as magnesium- and phosphate-containing cathartics, NSAIDs, selective cyclooxygenase-2 inhibitors, and iodinated contrast are not recommended for patients with chronic kidney disease, and metformin and bisphosphonates should be used with caution.

- Experts recommend blood pressure targets of less than 130/80 mm Hg for patients with chronic kidney disease and less than 125/75 mm Hg for patients with proteinuria greater than 1 g/24 h.

- Angiotensin-converting enzyme inhibitors or angiotensin receptor blockers are the preferred antihypertensive agents in patients with chronic kidney disease.

- Most patients with advanced chronic kidney disease require at least two antihypertensive agents to achieve blood pressure goals, and restriction of sodium to less than 2.4 g/d and adding furosemide can enhance the effects of antihypertensive agents.

- Discussions regarding the need for kidney replacement therapy should begin at least 1 year before the anticipated start of dialysis or when the glomerular filtration rate decreases below 30 mL/min/1.73 m².

Dialysis vs. Kidney Transplantation

Kidney transplantation is the treatment of choice for most patients with ESKD. Outcomes with transplantation are more favorable in all groups when compared with dialysis, and transplantation also allows patients to have a more normal lifestyle compared with dialysis. Transplant recipients have a lower mortality rate than those who remain on dialysis. This benefit persists even when only patients eligible for transplantation are considered, which suggests that selection bias is not responsible for this difference.

Although many cardiovascular risk factors are more prevalent after transplantation, the risk for cardiovascular mortality in kidney transplant recipients is much lower than in patients who undergo dialysis.

Patients with diabetes also gain the greatest survival advantage by transplantation.

KEY POINT

- Kidney transplantation is the treatment of choice for most patients with end-stage kidney disease.

Dialysis

Preparation for Dialysis

To preserve veins for dialysis access, venipuncture and intravenous cannulation above the level of the hands ideally should be avoided once the GFR decreases below 60 mL/min/1.73 m². Peripherally inserted central venous catheters also may impair the creation or function of arteriovenous fistulas and are discouraged in patients with CKD who are considering dialysis. Therefore, the internal jugular site is preferred when central venous access is required.

Initiation of Dialysis

Exactly when to initiate dialysis and whether early initiation is beneficial remain unclear. Dialysis should be initiated before symptoms of advanced uremia develop, and certain characteristic complications of CKD may prompt initiation of therapy before patients reach stage 5 CKD (**Table 37**). However, starting dialysis when the patient is asymptomatic introduces unneeded therapy and places the patient at risk for potential complications.

Methodology

The main forms of dialysis are hemodialysis and peritoneal dialysis. Factors that influence the choice of modality include local availability, patient preference, the presence of cardiovascular disease precluding volume shifts, and difficult vascular access. In addition, peritoneal dialysis requires an intact peritoneum. Both methods require a surgical procedure, and patients who choose hemodialysis ideally should have a functioning, permanent vascular access at the time dialysis begins. In the United States, significantly more patients undergo hemodialysis than peritoneal dialysis.

TABLE 37 Indications for Dialysis

Relative	Absolute
Nausea, vomiting, and poor nutrition caused by decreased appetite	Uncontrollable hyperkalemia
Metabolic acidosis	Uncontrollable hypervolemia
Altered mental status (lethargy, malaise), asterixis	Altered mental status, somnolence
Worsening kidney function with glomerular filtration rate below 15 to 20 mL/min/1.73 m²	Pericarditis
	Bleeding diathesis from uremia-induced platelet dysfunction

Hemodialysis

Options for hemodialysis access consist of an arteriovenous fistula, an arteriovenous graft, or a catheter (**Table 38**). Access via an arteriovenous fistula entails anastomosing a vein to an artery to allow for arterialization of the vein. Use of an arteriovenous graft involves interposing a synthetic conduit between an artery and a vein. Catheter access involves placement of a large-gauge tunneled cuffed central venous catheter.

Native arteriovenous fistulas have excellent long-term patency rates and are consistently associated with the lowest mortality risk among all forms of vascular access. Because fistula maturation requires 3 to 6 months, referral for vascular surgery should be considered once the GFR approaches 25 to 30 mL/min/1.73 m², the serum creatinine level is greater than 4 mg/dL (354 µmol/L), or within 1 year of an anticipated need for dialysis. The rate of decline in the GFR also should be accounted for when planning the timing of fistula placement, and earlier placement is indicated for patients with more rapidly progressing disease.

Peritoneal Dialysis

In patients who undergo peritoneal dialysis, a catheter is placed into the peritoneum in order to deliver and drain dialysate on a chronic basis. Ideally, peritoneal dialysis catheters should be placed approximately 1 month before therapy is initiated. In patients with catheters, one episode of peritonitis occurs every 3 years on average; the majority of these episodes are successfully treated with outpatient intraperitoneal antibiotics.

Complications

Most medical complications seen in patients on dialysis are similar to those in individuals with stage 4 CKD. However, patients with ESKD on dialysis have some additional complications.

Cardiovascular Disease

Cardiovascular disease accounts for almost 50% of deaths in patients with ESKD. Patients undergoing dialysis who experience an acute myocardial infarction have a poor long-term survival. Poor outcome in these patients may partially be related to the increase in comorbidities found in patients undergoing dialysis compared with patients who are not dialysis dependent. For example, patients on dialysis in one study had a lower incidence of current cigarette smoking, hypercholesterolemia, and family history of cardiovascular disease but were more likely to have diabetes, a history of hypertension, heart failure, previous coronary artery bypass graft, and stroke.

Furthermore, electrocardiography in patients on dialysis may be less diagnostic than in the general population, which makes these patients less eligible for reperfusion therapies. In addition, electrolyte abnormalities associated with CKD predispose patients to arrhythmias and sudden death.

Acquired Cystic Disease and Cancer of the Kidneys and Urinary Tract

Acquired kidney cystic disease occurs frequently in patients on dialysis, and there is a correlation between the length of time a patient has undergone dialysis and the likelihood of cyst formation. These cysts generally develop in the renal cortex and medulla.

TABLE 38 Types of Dialysis Access Modalities

Type of Access	When to Place	Advantages	Disadvantages
AV fistula	1 to 6 months before dialysis initiation	Excellent patency; lower rate of infection and stenosis	Long maturation time; failure to develop
AV graft	Between 1 day and 2 to 3 weeks before dialysis, depending on the synthetic material used	Large surface area; easy cannulation; short maturation time; easy surgical handling	Higher rates of infection, thrombosis, and stenosis
Catheter	Immediately before use	Immediate use	Highest rate of infection, venous stenosis, poor flow rates

AV = arteriovenous.

Cysts in patients with CKD are generally asymptomatic and are usually found incidentally on imaging studies of the kidneys. However, patients with cysts may develop secondary polycythemia, infection, hemorrhage, kidney rupture, nephrolithiasis, and renal cell carcinoma.

KEY POINTS

- To preserve veins for dialysis access, venipuncture and intravenous cannulation above the level of the hands ideally should be avoided once the GFR decreases below 60 mL/min/1.73 m^2.
- Peripherally inserted central venous catheters are discouraged in patients with chronic kidney disease who are considering dialysis.
- Dialysis should be initiated before symptoms of advanced uremia develop.
- End-stage kidney disease is associated with an increased risk for cardiovascular disease, acquired cystic disease, and cancer of the kidneys.

Kidney Transplantation

Evaluation of Transplant Candidates

Preemptive transplantation before initiation of dialysis and transplantation performed after shorter periods of dialysis are associated with both patient and allograft survival advantages. Timely referral of patients with progressive CKD is therefore critical in order to facilitate identification of potential living donors.

When deciding whether to pursue kidney transplantation, whether the patient is a suitable candidate for this procedure must be decided. Criteria for acceptable candidates vary among transplant centers, but the following factors are common contraindications to transplantation: recent or metastatic malignancy, current untreated infection, severe irreversible extrarenal disease, a history of nonadherence, inability to give informed consent, active use of illicit drugs, and primary oxalosis without plans for liver transplantation.

A pretransplantation evaluation helps patients to assess and compare the risks and benefits of this procedure. In addition, candidates who are not currently eligible for transplantation may learn during evaluation that they can become eligible once certain issues are resolved. For example, patients considered ineligible for transplantation because of a recent diagnosis of cancer may become eligible after a specified number of years in remission.

Methodology

Transplanted kidneys come from either deceased or living donors. One- and 5-year graft survival with living donor kidney transplantation is significantly higher than with deceased donor transplantation (**Table 39**). Nevertheless, donor shortage is significant and is a major reason why many potentially eligible kidney transplant recipients undergo dialysis for at least a limited time. Living donation allows patients to avoid the deceased donor waiting list, but not every candidate has an eligible living donor.

Immunosuppressive Therapy

In the absence of kidney donation from an identical twin, immunosuppression is needed in kidney transplant recipients to prevent the immune system from rejecting the transplanted organ. Various immunosuppressive agents are available, and numerous regimens can be used. Most regimens combine different agents at lower doses in order to promote synergy and minimize side effects (**Table 40**).

Induction Therapy

The risk of acute rejection is greatest in the first weeks or months after transplantation. Induction immunosuppressive therapy involves the use of an intensive immunosuppressive regimen during the perioperative period in order to reduce the risk of early rejection.

Induction therapy often includes the use of polyclonal or monoclonal antibodies to achieve rapid and profound early immunosuppression. Antibody-based induction therapy helps to delay the introduction of specific immunosuppressive agents, particularly nephrotoxic agents such as calcineurin inhibitors.

Maintenance Therapy

Maintenance therapy refers to immunosuppression used on a chronic basis for the life of the kidney transplant. A combination of immunosuppressive agents is used to target different pathways and reduce the dose and therefore the side effects of particular agents. The goal of maintenance therapy is to prevent rejection but avoid unwanted side effects.

TABLE 39 Types of Kidney Transplantation						
Transplantation Type	**Advantages**	**Disadvantages**	**1-Year Graft Survival**	**1-Year Patient Survival**	**5-Year Graft Survival**	**5-Year Patient Survival**
Deceased donor	No need for living donor	Unscheduled; quality of kidney may not be optimal	89.0%	94.5%	66.5%	81.9%
Living donor	Scheduled; more likely to allow for preemptive transplantation	Nephrectomy risks in the donor	95.1%	97.9%	79.7%	90.2%

TABLE 40 Immunosuppressive Agents Used After Kidney Transplantation

Agent	Type of Antibody	Target	Action	Common Side Effects
Induction Therapy				
Thymoglobulin	Polyclonal	Various receptors	Depletes lymphocytes	Chills, fevers, arthralgia, thrombocytopenia, leukopenia, serum sickness, susceptibility to infection
IL-2 receptor antibodies (daclizumab, basiliximab)	Monoclonal	IL-2 receptor	Causes functional lymphocyte arrest	None
Alemtuzumab	Monoclonal	CD52	Depletes lymphocytes	Fever, chills, anemia, hypotension, rash, risk of infection
Muromonab-CD3	Monoclonal	CD3	Depletes lymphocytes	Cytokine release syndrome, fever, chills, pulmonary edema, headache, encephalopathy, susceptibility to infection and malignancy
Maintenance Therapy				
Tacrolimus	Calcineurin inhibitor	FK binding protein	Prevents the phosphatase activity of calcineurin, which prevents IL-2 production	Nephrotoxicity, glucose intolerance, hypertension, tremor, hair loss, hyperuricemia and gout, susceptibility to infection, increased susceptibility to certain cancers
Cyclosporine	Calcineurin inhibitor	Cyclophylin	Prevents the phosphatase activity of calcineurin, which prevents IL-2 production	Nephrotoxicity, hyperkalemia, glucose intolerance, tremor, hirsutism, gingival hyperplasia, hyperlipidemia, hypertension, hyperuricemia and gout, susceptibility to infection and malignancy
Rapamycin	mTOR inhibitor	FK binding protein	Blocks IL-2–dependent T lymphocyte proliferation	Leukopenia, hyperlipidemia, proteinuria, glucose intolerance, poor wound healing, oral ulcers, peripheral edema, pulmonary infiltrates, susceptibility to infection
Azathioprine	Antiproliferative	Replicating DNA	Interferes with DNA synthesis	Leukopenia, thrombocytopenia, hepatitis and cholestasis, susceptibility to infection and malignancy
Mycophenolate mofetil and mycophenolic acid	Antiproliferative	IMPDH	Interferes with the de novo pathway of purine synthesis	Leukopenia, anemia, thrombocytopenia, gastrointestinal disorders, susceptibility to infection and malignancy
Prednisone	Anti-inflammatory	Multiple sites	Prevents T-cell and antigen-presenting cell cytokine production and cytokine-receptor expression	Glucose intolerance, hypertension, bone loss, osteonecrosis, cataracts, hyperlipidemia, acne, centripetal obesity, easy bruising, susceptibility to infection, psychological effects

IL-2 = interleukin-2; IMPDH = inosine monophosphate dehydrogenase; mTOR = mammalian target of rapamycin.

Specific Regimens

The most commonly prescribed maintenance immunosuppressive regimen currently used immediately after transplantation is tacrolimus, mycophenolate mofetil, and a corticosteroid. Often, regimens are determined based on expected or existing drug toxicities or perceived immunologic risk. Using fewer drugs or lower doses also often helps to avoid cardiovascular, infectious, neoplastic, or nephrotoxic side effects as well as to avoid specific cosmetic sequelae such as unwanted hair growth, hair loss, acne, and centripetal fat distribution.

Agents that induce cytochrome P450 3A lower the effective immunosuppression and place transplant recipients at risk for rejection. Conversely, drugs that compete for cytochrome P450 3A metabolism decrease calcineurin inhibitor and mammalian target of rapamycin (mTOR) inhibitor metabolism and lead to increased levels of these agents and may potentially cause drug toxicity. Common agents that decrease calcineurin inhibitor levels include rifampin, isoniazid, phenytoin, barbiturates, St. John wort, intravenous trimethoprim, cephalosporins, and ciprofloxacin. Common agents that increase these levels include verapamil, diltiazem, amlodipine, metronidazole, fluconazole, sirolimus, methylprednisolone, erythromycin, azithromycin, indinavir, and ritonavir. Grapefruit and grapefruit juice also may increase calcineurin inhibitor levels.

Risks of Transplantation

The main causes of death after kidney transplantation are cardiovascular complications, infectious disease, and malignancy. Kidney transplantation is associated with an increased prevalence of cardiovascular risk factors such as diabetes, obesity, hypercholesterolemia, and anemia. The risk for cardiovascular mortality in kidney transplant recipients also is significantly increased compared with that of the general population. In addition, the prevalence of hypertension does not decrease after kidney transplantation.

The incidence of infectious disease after transplantation has decreased because of improvements in immunosuppression and infection prophylaxis, but infection remains a serious problem. Over 50% of transplant recipients have at least one infection in the first year after transplantation.

The risk for infection in an individual transplant recipient depends on the net state of immunosuppression and epidemiologic exposures. Urinary tract infections in particular are common in kidney transplant recipients, and infection with cytomegalovirus is especially problematic for these patients. Presenting features of cytomegalovirus infection may include fever, headache, diarrhea, or pulmonary symptoms. Elevated liver chemistry study results, leukopenia, and thrombocytopenia are common in affected patients.

Kidney transplant recipients have a high risk for skin cancer, particularly squamous cell carcinoma. The risk for other malignancies, including Kaposi sarcoma, Hodgkin and non-Hodgkin lymphoma, leukemia, and multiple myeloma, also is increased after kidney transplantation.

Special Considerations in Transplant Recipients

Disease Recurrence

Several common diseases that cause ESKD may recur after kidney transplantation (**Table 41**). Focal segmental glomerulosclerosis in particular commonly recurs early in the post-transplantation period.

Bone Disease

Kidney transplantation reverses certain mineral and bone metabolism disorders associated with ESKD but does not always completely reverse or resolve these conditions. Within the first 6 months after transplantation, corticosteroid use is associated with early, rapid bone loss that contributes to an increased incidence of fractures. Transplant recipients also may have abnormalities in bone quality that manifest as high-turnover, low-turnover, and mineralization defects as well as disturbances in bone quantity evidenced by low bone mineral density. In addition, vitamin D deficiency is common after kidney transplantation, particularly in individuals with darkly pigmented skin.

Pregnancy

Pregnancy in a transplant recipient is possible but is considered high risk (see The Kidney in Pregnancy). Fertility returns after transplantation, and female transplant recipients of child-bearing age are at risk for pregnancy. These patients should undergo counseling before and after transplantation regarding the increased likelihood of becoming pregnant after the procedure is complete. During counseling, the importance of contraception and planning for a pregnancy if desired also should be stressed.

Transplant recipients who plan on becoming pregnant should receive counseling about how to manage hypertension and kidney dysfunction during pregnancy and which immunosuppressive regimens are safe during pregnancy. A multidisciplinary team that incorporates maternal-fetal medicine and nephrology can help to manage pregnant transplant recipients.

Vaccinations

If possible, vaccinations in transplant recipients should be updated before kidney transplantation and immunosuppression begin. Vaccinations generally can be restarted by 6 months after transplantation once immunosuppression reaches baseline levels. Because of immunosuppression, transplant recipients

---

TABLE 41 Underlying Kidney Diseases That May Recur after Kidney Transplantation

Disease	Likelihood of Recurrence	Timing of Recurrence	Interventions
FSGS	High	Early	Plasmapheresis
IgA nephropathy	Moderate	Late	Fish oil, ACE inhibitors
Diabetic nephropathy	High	Late	ACE inhibitors, glucose and blood pressure control
Lupus nephritis	Low	Variable	As with primary disease
Membranous nephropathy	Variable	Variable	As with primary disease
Hemolytic uremic syndrome	Diarrhea-associated or typical disease does not usually recur; atypical disease recurs frequently	Early	High-dose fresh frozen plasma with plasma exchange; avoid living donor transplantation in those with atypical disease

ACE = angiotensin-converting enzyme; FSGS = focal segmental glomerulosclerosis

may have a blunted response to vaccines. Live virus vaccines are contraindicated after transplantation.

Nonadherence

Nonadherence is an underappreciated issue in all areas of medicine but is particularly concerning in transplant recipients. In this population group, nonadherence may adversely affect allograft outcome and should be addressed. Reasons for nonadherence may include medication side effects, forgetfulness, or the inability to afford medications.

KEY POINTS

- Preemptive kidney transplantation before initiation of dialysis and transplantation performed after shorter periods of dialysis are associated with both patient and allograft survival advantages.

- Common contraindications to kidney transplantation include recent or metastatic malignancy, current untreated infection, severe irreversible extrarenal disease, a history of nonadherence, inability to give informed consent, active use of illicit drugs, and primary oxalosis without plans for liver transplantation.

- One- and 5-year graft survival with living donor kidney transplantation is significantly higher than with deceased donor transplantation.

- In the absence of kidney donation from an identical twin, immunosuppression with both induction and maintenance therapy is needed in kidney transplant recipients to prevent the immune system from rejecting the transplanted organ.

- Kidney transplant recipients have an increased risk for cardiovascular disease, infection, and malignancy; in addition, focal segmental glomerulosclerosis commonly recurs early in the posttransplantation period.

- Kidney transplant recipients may have an increased risk of fractures caused by corticosteroid use, bone quality abnormalities, and vitamin D deficiency.

- Pregnancy in a transplant recipient is possible but is considered high risk.

Bibliography

Aoki J, Ong AT, Hoye A, et al. Five year clinical effect of coronary stenting and coronary artery bypass grafting in renal insufficient patients with multivessel coronary artery disease: insights from ARTS trial. Eur Heart J. 2005;26(15):1488-1493. [PMID: 15860519]

Bang H, Vupputuri S, Shoham DA, et al. SCreening for Occult REnal Disease (SCORED): A Simple Prediction Model for Chronic Kidney Disease. Arch Intern Med. 2007;167(4):374-381. [PMID: 17325299]

Besarab A, Goodkin DA, Nissenson AR; Normal Hematocrit Cardiac Trial Authors. The normal hematocrit study—follow-up. N Engl J Med. 2008;358(4):433-434. [PMID: 18216370]

Drawz P, Rahman M. In the clinic. Chronic kidney disease. Ann Intern Med. 2009;150(3):ITC2-1-15; quiz ITC2-16. [PMID: 19189903]

Jindal K, Chan CT, Deziel C, et al; Canadian Society of Nephrology Committee for Clinical Practice Guidelines. Hemodialysis clinical practice guidelines for the Canadian Society of Nephrology. Am Soc Nephrol. 2006;17(3 Suppl 1):S1-S27. [PMID: 16497879]

Kunz R, Friedrich C, Wolbers M, Mann JF. Meta-analysis: effect of monotherapy and combination therapy with inhibitors of the renin angiotensin system on proteinuria in renal disease. Ann Intern Med. 2008;148(1):30-48. [PMID: 17984482]

Palmer SC, McGregor DO, Macaskill P, Craig JC, Elder GJ, Strippoli GF. Meta-analysis: vitamin D compounds in chronic kidney disease. Ann Intern Med. 2007;147(12):840-853. [PMID: 18087055]

Rahman M, Pressel S, Davis BR, et al; ALLHAT Collaborative Research Group. Cardiovascular outcomes in high-risk hypertensive patients stratified by baseline glomerular filtration rate. Ann Intern Med. 2006;144(3):172-180. [PMID: 16461961]

Singh AK, Szczech L, Tang KL, et al; CHOIR Investigators. Correction of anemia with epoetin alfa in chronic kidney disease. N Engl J Med. 2006;355(20):2085-2098. [PMID: 17108343]

Smith GL, Lichtman JH, Bracken MB, et al. Renal impairment and outcomes in heart failure: systematic review and meta-analysis. J Am Coll Cardiol. 2006;47(10):1987-1996. [PMID: 16697315]

Self-Assessment Test

This self-assessment test contains one-best-answer multiple-choice questions. Please read these directions carefully before answering the questions. Answers, critiques, and bibliographies immediately follow these multiple-choice questions. The American College of Physicians is accredited by the Accreditation Council for Continuing Medical Education (ACCME) to provide continuing medical education for physicians.

The American College of Physicians designates MKSAP 15 Nephrology for a maximum of 14 *AMA PRA Category 1 Credits*™. Physicians should only claim credit commensurate with the extent of their participation in the activity. Separate answer sheets are provided for each book of the MKSAP program. Please use one of these answer sheets to complete the Nephrology self-assessment test. Indicate in Section H on the answer sheet the actual number of credits you earned, up to the maximum of 14, in ¼-credit increments. (One credit equals one hour of time spent on this educational activity.)

Use the self-addressed envelope provided with your program to mail your completed answer sheet(s) to the MKSAP Processing Center for scoring. Remember to provide your MKSAP 15 order and ACP ID numbers in the appropriate spaces on the answer sheet. The order and ACP ID numbers are printed on your mailing label. If you have *not* received these numbers with your MKSAP 15 purchase, you will need to acquire them to earn CME credits. E-mail ACP's customer service center at custserv@acponline.org. In the subject line, write "MKSAP 15 order/ACP ID numbers." In the body of the e-mail, make sure you include your e-mail address as well as your full name, address, city, state, ZIP code, country, and telephone number. Also identify where you have made your MKSAP 15 purchase. You will receive your MKSAP 15 order and ACP ID numbers by e-mail within 72 business hours.

CME credit is available from the publication date of July 31, 2009, until July 31, 2012. You may submit your answer sheets at any time during this period.

Self-Scoring Instructions: Nephrology

Compute your percent correct score as follows:

Step 1: Give yourself 1 point for each correct response to a question.

Step 2: Divide your total points by the total number of questions: 72.

The result, expressed as a percentage, is your percent correct score.

	Example	Your Calculations
Step 1	61	
Step 2	61 ÷ 72	÷ 72
% Correct	85%	%

Item 1

A 35-year-old woman is evaluated for a 1-month history of progressive bilateral lower-extremity edema. She was diagnosed with type 1 diabetes mellitus 10 years ago. At her last office visit 4 months ago, the urine albumin-creatinine ratio was 100 mg/g. Medications are enalapril, insulin glargine, insulin aspart, and low-dose aspirin.

On physical examination, vital signs are normal except for a blood pressure of 162/90 mm Hg. Cardiopulmonary and funduscopic examinations are normal. There is 3+ pitting edema of the lower extremities to the level of the thighs bilaterally.

Laboratory studies:

Hemoglobin A_{1c}	7.1%
Albumin	3 g/dL (30 g/L)
Serum creatinine	1.1 mg/dL (97.2 µmol/L)
Urinalysis	3+ protein; 2+ blood; 8-10 dysmorphic erythrocytes/hpf; 2-5 leukocytes/hpf; few erythrocyte casts
Urine protein-creatinine ratio	5.2 mg/mg

On kidney ultrasound, the right kidney is 12.2 cm and the left kidney is 12.7 cm. There is no hydronephrosis, and no kidney masses are seen.

Which of the following is the most appropriate next step in this patient's management?

(A) Cystoscopy
(B) Kidney biopsy
(C) Spiral CT of the abdomen and pelvis
(D) Observation

Item 2

A 26-year-old man is evaluated in the emergency department for a 1-day history of acute abdominal pain that has progressively worsened. He has pain in the left flank that radiates to the groin. He also has nausea and vomiting. Ibuprofen has not provided relief.

On physical examination, temperature is normal, blood pressure is 168/98 mm Hg, pulse rate is 100/min, and respiration rate is 18/min. BMI is 28. Abdominal examination reveals left costovertebral angle tenderness.

Laboratory studies:

Serum creatinine	1.5 mg/dL (132.6 µmol/L)
Urinalysis	pH 5.0; 2+ blood; no protein; 1+ leukocyte esterase; 2-5 leukocytes/hpf; 25-50 erythrocytes/hpf; no bacteria

Noniodinated contrast CT of the abdomen reveals a 4-mm calculus in the mid left ureter and mild hydronephrosis.

In addition to an analgesic, which of the following is the most appropriate management for this patient?

(A) Extracorporeal shock-wave lithotripsy
(B) Intravenous cephalexin
(C) Intravenous saline
(D) Percutaneous nephrostomy

Item 3

A 76-year-old woman is evaluated for a 2-week history of exertional chest pain, dyspnea, orthopnea, and edema. She also has stage 2 chronic kidney disease, type 2 diabetes mellitus, and hypertension. Medications are enalapril, metformin, metoprolol, hydrochlorothiazide, and low-dose aspirin.

On physical examination, temperature is normal, blood pressure is 162/94 mm Hg, pulse rate is 86/min, and respiration rate is 24/min. Jugular venous distention is present. Breathing is labored. Crackles are heard in both lung fields. Cardiac examination reveals an S_3 gallop but no murmurs.

Laboratory studies show a serum creatinine level of 1.3 mg/dL (114.9 µmol/L) and trace protein on urinalysis. Chest radiograph reveals cardiomegaly and pulmonary edema. An electrocardiogram shows left ventricular hypertrophy with nonspecific ST changes. Cardiac catheterization is scheduled.

In addition to discontinuing metformin, which of the following is the most appropriate next step in this patient's management?

(A) Begin fenoldopam
(B) Begin furosemide
(C) Begin isotonic bicarbonate
(D) Discontinue enalapril

Item 4

A 25-year-old black man is evaluated in the emergency department for swelling of the feet and legs. He has a 5-year history of HIV infection for which he has refused treatment.

On physical examination, temperature is normal, blood pressure is 128/74 mm Hg, pulse rate is 88/min, and respiration rate is 12/min. BMI is 23. Cardiopulmonary examination is normal. Abdominal examination is normal. There is 2+ presacral and 3+ bilateral lower-extremity edema.

Laboratory studies:

CD4 cell count	140/µL
HIV RNA viral load	120,000 copies/mL
Hepatitis B surface antigen (HBsAg)	Negative
Antibodies to hepatitis C virus (anti-HCV)	Negative
VDRL	Negative
Antinuclear antibodies	Negative
Blood urea nitrogen	18 mg/dL (6.4 mmol/L)
Serum creatinine	1.1 mg/dL (97.2 µmol/L)
Urinalysis	4+ protein; 2-3 erythrocytes/hpf; 1-2 leukocytes/hpf
Urine protein-creatinine ratio	12 mg/mg

Kidney ultrasound reveals bilaterally enlarged kidneys with patchy areas of increased density. The renal veins are patent. Kidney biopsy is performed, and results are pending.

Which of the following is the most likely diagnosis?

(A) Collapsing focal segmental glomerulosclerosis
(B) IgA nephropathy
(C) Membranous nephropathy
(D) Postinfectious glomerulonephritis

Item 5

A 50-year-old woman is evaluated during a routine office visit. She is asymptomatic and takes no medications. Her father and sister have essential hypertension.

On physical examination, vital signs are normal except for a blood pressure of 136/86 mm Hg. BMI is 24. The remainder of the physical examination, including cardiopulmonary and funduscopic examinations, is normal.

Laboratory studies, including levels of plasma fasting glucose, blood urea nitrogen, and serum creatinine levels and a urinalysis, are normal. Radiograph of the chest and an electrocardiogram are normal.

Which of the following is the most appropriate next step in this patient's management?

(A) Ambulatory blood pressure monitoring
(B) Follow-up in 1 month
(C) Hydrochlorothiazide
(D) Lifestyle modification

Item 6

A 19-year-old woman is evaluated for a 3-month history of periorbital edema, ankle edema that worsens towards the end of the day, and foamy urine. Medical history is unremarkable, and she takes no medications.

On physical examination, temperature is normal, blood pressure is 112/70 mm Hg, pulse rate is 60/min, and respiration rate is 12/min. BMI is 24. Funduscopic examination is normal. There is 2+ bilateral pedal edema.

Laboratory studies:

Serum creatinine	0.8 mg/dL (70.7 μmol/L)
Urinalysis	4+ protein; no blood; no bacteria
Urine protein-creatinine ratio	10 mg/mg

Kidney biopsy is performed. Electron microscopy of the specimen reveals diffuse foot process effacement. Light microscopy is normal. Immunofluorescence testing shows no immune complex deposits.

Which of the following is the most appropriate treatment for this patient?

(A) Cyclophosphamide
(B) Cyclosporine
(C) Prednisone
(D) Tacrolimus

Item 7

A 64-year-old man comes for a routine physical examination. During the past year, his urine output has increased and he urinates approximately two to three times nightly. He does not have daytime urinary frequency, urinary hesitancy, or a decreased urinary stream. He also has had increased thirst and has been drinking more water than usual. His weight has been stable. He has bipolar disorder that was treated with lithium for 20 years; 10 years ago, he was switched to divalproex sodium. His brother has sickle cell trait.

On physical examination, he is afebrile, blood pressure is 148/88 mm Hg, pulse rate is 78/min, and respiration rate is 18/min. BMI is 20. The remainder of the physical examination is normal.

Laboratory studies:

Glucose (nonfasting)	133 mg/dL (7.4 mmol/L)
Sodium	146 meq/L (146 mmol/L)
Potassium	3.6 meq/L (3.6 mmol/L)
Chloride	107 meq/L (107 mmol/L)
Bicarbonate	26 meq/L (26 mmol/L)
Blood urea nitrogen	34 mg/dL (12.1 mmol/L)
Serum creatinine	2.1 mg/dL (185.6 μmol/L)
Urinalysis	pH 7.0; specific gravity 1.005; trace protein; no blood
Urine osmolality	150 mosm/kg H$_2$O (150 mmol/kg H$_2$O) (normal 300-900 mosm/kg H$_2$O [300-900 mmol/kg H$_2$O])
Urine protein-creatinine ratio	0.3 mg/mg

On abdominal ultrasound, the right kidney is 8.6 cm and the left kidney is 9.3 cm. There is no hydronephrosis.

Which of the following is the most likely diagnosis?

(A) Diabetic nephropathy
(B) Lithium-induced nephrotoxicity
(C) Obstructive uropathy
(D) Sickle cell nephropathy

Item 8

A 32-year-old man is brought to the emergency department after becoming disoriented, combative, and agitated earlier that day. He is accompanied by a friend, who states that the patient has a history of alcohol and drug abuse, including inhalants.

On physical examination, the patient is uncooperative and slightly disoriented. Temperature is normal, blood pressure is 140/88 mm Hg, and pulse rate is 98/min. The remainder of the examination is normal.

Laboratory studies:

Fasting glucose	110 mg/dL (6.1 mmol/L)
Sodium	142 meq/L (142 mmol/L)
Potassium	4.1 meq/L (4.1 mmol/L)
Chloride	109 meq/L (109 mmol/L)
Bicarbonate	23 meq/L (23 mmol/L)
Blood urea nitrogen	18 mg/dL (6.4 mmol/L)

Plasma osmolality	320 mosm/kg H_2O (320 mmol/kg H_2O)
Serum creatinine	1.1 mg/dL (97.2 µmol/L)
Serum ketones	Positive
Urinalysis	Trace glucose; 4+ ketones

Arterial blood gas studies (with the patient breathing ambient air):

pH	7.4
Pco_2	44 mm Hg
Po_2	92 mm Hg

Which of the following is the most likely cause of this patient's clinical presentation?

(A) Alcoholic ketoacidosis

(B) Diabetic ketoacidosis

(C) Ethylene glycol

(D) Isopropyl alcohol

(E) Toluene

Item 9

A 45-year-old woman is evaluated during a follow-up office visit. At a new patient office visit 3 weeks ago, her blood pressure was 150/95 mm Hg. During a routine visit to the gynecologist last month, her blood pressure was normal. Her blood pressure also was normal when she donated blood 3 months ago. Medical history is unremarkable, and she takes no medications. Her father has high blood pressure.

On physical examination, she appears nervous. Vital signs are normal except for a blood pressure of 150/90 mm Hg. BMI is 26. The remainder of the examination, including funduscopic examination, is normal. Laboratory studies, including plasma fasting glucose, serum electrolyte, blood urea nitrogen, and serum creatinine levels and a urinalysis, are normal. An electrocardiogram is normal with no evidence of left ventricular hypertrophy.

Which of the following is the most appropriate next step in this patient's management?

(A) Ambulatory blood pressure monitoring

(B) Echocardiography

(C) Follow-up office visit in 1 year

(D) Hydrochlorothiazide

Item 10

A 45-year-old man comes for a follow-up evaluation for chronic kidney disease. He was diagnosed with chronic kidney disease 5 years ago, and his condition has progressively worsened. Current medications are lisinopril, furosemide, lovastatin calcium acetate with meals, calcitriol, ferrous sulfate, and epoetin alfa.

On physical examination, temperature is normal, blood pressure is 128/68 mm Hg, pulse rate is 80/min, and respiration rate is 15/min. BMI is 29. Cardiopulmonary examination is normal. There is no asterixis. There is no peripheral edema.

On laboratory studies, the estimated glomerular filtration rate is 29 mL/min/1.73 m². Urinalysis reveals trace protein and no hematuria or pyuria.

In addition to discussing this patient's clinical situation and worsening kidney function, which of the following is the most appropriate next step in management?

(A) Contrast-enhanced abdominal CT

(B) Discussion of options for kidney replacement therapy

(C) ^{125}I-iothalamate kidney scanning

(D) Kidney biopsy

Item 11

A 65-year-old man is evaluated for a 3-month history of progressive malaise, fatigue, and weakness. He has a 10-year history of hypertension treated with hydrochlorothiazide and atenolol.

On physical examination, vital signs including blood pressure are normal. The remainder of the physical examination is unremarkable.

Laboratory studies:

Hematocrit	25%
Leukocyte count	5600/µL (5.6×10^9/L)
Platelet count	340,000/µL (340×10^9/L)
Glucose (fasting)	110 mg/dL (6.1 mmol/L)
Sodium	135 meq/L (135 mmol/L)
Potassium	3.0 meq/L (3.0 mmol/L)
Chloride	105 meq/L (105 mmol/L)
Bicarbonate	18 meq/L (18 mmol/L)
Blood urea nitrogen	22 mg/dL (7.8 mmol/L)
Serum creatinine	1.8 mg/dL (159.1 µmol/L)
Urinalysis	pH 5.5; trace protein; 1+ glucose
Urine protein-creatinine ratio	4.8 mg/mg

Arterial blood gas studies (with the patient breathing ambient air):

pH	7.33
Pco_2	28 mm Hg

Polarized light microscopy of the urine sediment is normal.

Which of the following is the most likely diagnosis?

(A) Diabetic nephropathy

(B) Distal (type 1) renal tubular acidosis

(C) Hypertensive nephrosclerosis

(D) Proximal (type 2) renal tubular acidosis

Item 12

A 48-year-old man with end-stage kidney disease believed to be caused by hypertension and known kidney cysts is evaluated during a routine follow-up visit. He has been on hemodialysis for the past 12 months and is planning to undergo cadaveric kidney transplantation. Medications are lisinopril, metoprolol, nifedipine, sevelamer, and daily aspirin.

On physical examination, temperature is normal, blood pressure is 142/78 mm Hg, pulse rate is 68/min, and respiration rate is 18/min. Cardiac examination is normal. Abdominal examination reveals palpable kidneys. There is 1+ bilateral peripheral edema.

Laboratory studies:

Blood urea nitrogen	64 mg/dL (22.8 mmol/L)
Serum creatinine	8.0 mg/dL (707.2 µmol/L)
Urinalysis	2+ blood; 1+ protein; 5-10 erythrocytes/hpf

Abdominal ultrasound reveals bilateral 9-cm kidneys with several simple-appearing cysts and a 4.5-cm complex cyst or mass lesion in the right upper pole.

Which of the following diagnostic studies of the kidneys is the most appropriate next step in this patient's management?

(A) Abdominal CT with iodinated contrast
(B) Kidney biopsy
(C) MRI with gadolinium
(D) Repeat ultrasonography in 6 months

Item 13

A 38-year-old woman comes for a new patient evaluation. A blood pressure measurement obtained at a health fair last month was elevated. Approximately 1 year ago, she had an episode of hematuria. She also has occasional flank pain and has had two episodes of pyelonephritis. Her mother has hypertension and "kidney problems," and her uncle is on dialysis. Her paternal grandfather died of a stroke at age 62 years.

On physical examination, vital signs are normal except for a blood pressure of 160/110 mm Hg. BMI is 24. Cardiac examination reveals a slightly displaced point of maximal impulse. Abdominal examination reveals moderate fullness and mild tenderness that is greater on the left side.

Laboratory studies:

Sodium	140 meq/L (140 mmol/L)
Potassium	4.4 meq/L (4.4 mmol/L)
Chloride	100 meq/L (100 mmol/L)
Bicarbonate	24 meq/L (24 mmol/L)
Blood urea nitrogen	15 mg/dL (5.4 mmol/L)
Serum creatinine	1.0 mg/dL (88.4 µmol/L)
Urinalysis	3-5 erythrocytes/hpf
Urine albumin-creatinine ratio	75 mg/g

Which of the following diagnostic studies should be performed next?

(A) Kidney angiography
(B) Kidney biopsy
(C) Kidney ultrasonography
(D) Plasma aldosterone-plasma renin activity ratio

Item 14

A 27-year-old woman comes for a routine evaluation. She was diagnosed with autosomal-dominant polycystic kidney disease during a family screening program 2 years ago. She is asymptomatic and has no history of hematuria, kidney stones, or hypertension. She does not smoke cigarettes. Her mother also has autosomal-dominant polycystic kidney disease and recently experienced a ruptured cerebral aneurysm.

On physical examination, temperature is normal, blood pressure is 115/65 mm Hg, pulse rate is 62/min, and respiration rate is 10/min. BMI is 26. The kidneys are palpable. Neurologic examination is normal.

The serum creatinine level is 0.9 mg/dL (79.6 µmol/L).

Which of the following is the most appropriate next step in this patient's management?

(A) Four-vessel cerebral angiography
(B) Magnetic resonance cerebral angiography
(C) MRI of the brain
(D) No additional management

Item 15

A 42-year-old woman is evaluated for a 3-month history of progressive cervical lymphadenopathy, fatigue, night sweats, bilateral lower-extremity and abdominal wall edema, and a 4.5-kg (10.0-lb) weight gain. History is significant for three episodes of weight gain and facial and lower-extremity edema lasting 4 weeks in her 20s and 30s. Her only current medication is a multivitamin.

After an evaluation and lymph node biopsy, she is diagnosed with stage IIIB Hodgkin lymphoma.

Laboratory studies:

Serum creatinine	1.3 mg/dL (114.9 µmol/L)
Urinalysis	2+ blood; 4+ protein; dysmorphic erythrocytes and occasional granular casts
Urine protein-creatinine ratio	9.25 mg/mg

On kidney ultrasound, the kidneys are 13.5 cm bilaterally and edematous. The corticomedullary junction is apparent, and there is no hydronephrosis.

Which of the following is the most likely cause of this patient's nephrotic syndrome?

(A) Focal segmental glomerulosclerosis
(B) IgA nephropathy
(C) Membranous glomerular nephropathy
(D) Minimal change disease

Item 16

A 19-year-old woman comes for a new patient evaluation. She was previously diagnosed with hypertension and abnormal results on urinalysis. She is 14 weeks pregnant, and this is her first pregnancy. She has type 1 diabetes mellitus. Family history is positive for hypertension and type 2 diabetes mellitus. She uses insulin glargine and insulin lispro and a prenatal vitamin.

On physical examination, blood pressure is 150/90 mm Hg. BMI is 22. The remainder of the examination is unremarkable.

Laboratory studies:

Blood urea nitrogen	16 mg/dL (5.7 mmol/L)
Serum creatinine	1.5 mg/dL (132.6 µmol/L)
Sodium	136 meq/L (136 mmol/L)
Potassium	3.8 meq/L (3.8 mmol/L)
Chloride	100 meq/L (100 mmol/L)
Bicarbonate	24 meq/L (24 mmol/L)
Urinalysis	2+ protein; no leukocytes or erythrocytes

Which of the following is the most likely diagnosis?

(A) Chronic essential hypertension
(B) Chronic kidney disease
(C) Gestational hypertension
(D) Normal physiologic changes of pregnancy
(E) Preeclampsia

Item 17

A 25-year-old woman is evaluated in the urgent care department because of the recent onset of heel pain that is especially severe when jogging. She has been taking ibuprofen for the past 7 days. Her only additional medications are a low-dose oral contraceptive that she has been taking for the past 5 years and a multivitamin. She does not smoke cigarettes. She is otherwise healthy and has no history of hypertension.

On physical examination, blood pressure is 162/102 mm Hg and pulse rate is 90/min. BMI is 24. The remainder of the examination, including cardiopulmonary, funduscopic, and neurologic examinations, is normal.

Laboratory studies, including blood urea nitrogen, serum creatinine, and urinalysis, are normal.

Which of the following is the most appropriate management of this patient's hypertension?

(A) Begin captopril
(B) Begin hydrochlorothiazide
(C) Begin labetalol
(D) Discontinue ibuprofen

Item 18

A 45-year-old man with a 10-year history of HIV infection is evaluated in the hospital for an elevated serum creatinine level and abnormal urinalysis 5 days after admission for cytomegalovirus retinitis and latent syphilis. He has previously refused treatment with highly active antiretroviral therapy. Medications are ganciclovir, trimethoprim-sulfamethoxazole, metoprolol, intramuscular penicillin G benzathine, and low-molecular-weight heparin.

On physical examination, temperature is normal, blood pressure is 150/88 mm Hg, pulse rate is 88/min, and respiration rate is 16/min. BMI is 22. Funduscopic examination reveals yellow-white, fluffy retinal lesions adjacent to retinal vessels. Cardiopulmonary examination is normal.

Cutaneous and neurologic examinations are normal. There is trace bilateral lower-extremity edema.

Laboratory studies:

Hemoglobin	8.6 g/dL (86 g/L)
Leukocyte count	4800/µL (4.8 × 10⁹/L)
Platelet count	168,000/µL (168 × 10⁹/L)
CD4 cell count	60/µL
HIV RNA viral load	147,300 copies/mL
VDRL	Positive
Antibodies to hepatitis C virus (anti-HCV)	Positive
C3	71 mg/dL (710 mg/L)
C4	7 mg/dL (70 mg/L) (normal 13-38 mg/dL [130-380 mg/dL])
Serum creatinine	1.9 mg/dL (168 µmol/L)
Urinalysis	3+ protein; 1+ blood; 15 dysmorphic erythrocytes/hpf; 2-5 leukocytes/hpf; occasional erythrocyte casts
Urine protein-creatinine ratio	2.3 mg/mg

On kidney ultrasound, the right kidney is 11.6 cm and the left kidney is 11.8 cm. The echotexture of the renal parenchyma is diffusely increased. There is no hydronephrosis, and no calculi or solid masses are seen.

Which of the following is the most likely diagnosis?

(A) Acute interstitial nephritis
(B) Collapsing focal segmental glomerulosclerosis
(C) Immune complex–mediated glomerular nephritis
(D) Pigment nephropathy

Item 19

A 59-year-old woman is evaluated for a 2-week history of right hip pain. She has chronic kidney disease treated with peritoneal dialysis. Medications are epoetin alfa, calcium acetate, calcitriol, and a multivitamin. She has no history of exposure to aluminum-containing medications.

On physical examination, vital signs are normal. There is tenderness over the right lateral trochanter. Internal and external rotation of the hip elicit pain.

Laboratory studies:

Phosphorus	5.6 mg/dL (1.8 mmol/L)
Calcium	10.2 mg/dL (2.5 mmol/L)
Alkaline phosphatase	86 U/L
Intact parathyroid hormone	21 pg/mL (21 ng/L)
1,25-dihydroxyvitamin D	52 pg/mL (124.8 pmol/L)
25-hydroxyvitamin D	15 ng/mL (37.4 nmol/L)

Plain radiograph of the right hip shows diffuse osteopenia. An area of lucency is seen along the medial aspect of the femoral neck on the right side consistent with a stress fracture.

Which of the following is the most likely cause of this patient's bone disease?

(A) Adynamic bone disease
(B) β₂-Microglobulin–associated amyloidosis

(C) Osteitis fibrosa cystica

(D) Osteomalacia

Item 20

A 48-year-old man is evaluated for an abnormal urinalysis discovered last week during an examination for a worker's compensation claim. Four months ago, he injured his back lifting a box at work. Since then, he has had chronic low back pain for which he takes acetaminophen daily. He has not worked for 3 months. He has no other symptoms or medical problems and takes no additional medications.

On physical examination, temperature is normal, blood pressure is 145/88 mm Hg, pulse rate is 92/min, and respiration rate is 12/min. BMI is 33. The chest is clear to auscultation. He has full range of motion of the back without evidence of point tenderness. Neurologic examination is normal. There is 1+ bilateral peripheral edema.

Imaging studies of the lumbosacral spine and pelvis obtained last week are normal.

Laboratory studies:

Serum total cholesterol	220 mg/dL (5.7 mmol/L)
Serum creatinine	1.0 mg/dL (88.4 µmol/L)
Urinalysis	4+ protein; no leukocytes or erythrocytes
Urine protein-creatinine ratio	4.5 mg/mg

Kidney biopsy is performed. Electron microscopy of a kidney biopsy specimen reveals subepithelial deposition of immune complexes.

In addition to adding a statin agent, which of the following is the most appropriate management for this patient?

(A) Lisinopril

(B) Mycophenolate mofetil

(C) Plasmapheresis

(D) Prednisone and cyclophosphamide

Item 21

A 44-year-old woman is evaluated for worsening fatigue. She has chronic headache for which she has taken acetaminophen and aspirin two to three times daily for the past 12 years. She also has hypertension treated with hydrochlorothiazide.

On physical examination, she is afebrile, blood pressure is 148/88 mm Hg, pulse rate is 60/min, and respiration rate is 18/min. BMI is 33. The remainder of the examination is normal.

Laboratory studies:

Hemoglobin	10.5 g/dL (105 g/L) (12.2 g/dL [122 g/L] 6 months ago)
Sodium	139 meq/L (139 mmol/L)
Potassium	5 meq/L (5 mmol/L)
Chloride	108 meq/L (108 mmol/L)
Bicarbonate	22 meq/L (22 mmol/L)
Ferritin	15 ng/mL (15 µg/L)
Transferrin saturation	11%

Albumin	3.8 g/dL (38 g/L)
Calcium	8.8 mg/dL (2.2 mmol/L)
Blood urea nitrogen	24 mg/dL (8.6 mmol/L)
Serum creatinine	1.7 mg/dL (150.3 µmol/L) (1.5 mg/dL [132.6 µmol/L] 6 months ago)
Urinalysis	1+ protein; no blood; 1+ glucose; 5-10 leukocytes/hpf; no bacteria
Urine protein-creatinine ratio	0.7 mg/mg

On kidney ultrasound, the left kidney is 8.7 cm with a small simple cyst, and the right kidney is 9.5 cm. There is no hydronephrosis.

Which of the following is the most appropriate next step in this patient's management?

(A) Abdominal CT without radiocontrast

(B) Discontinuation of analgesics

(C) Kidney biopsy

(D) Serum protein electrophoresis

Item 22

A 35-year-old man comes for a new patient evaluation. He takes no medications. His parents both have diabetes mellitus.

On physical examination, blood pressure is 160/100 mm Hg. BMI is 31. The remainder of the examination is unremarkable.

Laboratory studies, including serum electrolyte, blood urea nitrogen, and creatinine levels and urinalysis, are normal.

In addition to lifestyle modification, which of the following is the most appropriate next step in this patient's management?

(A) Lisinopril and hydrochlorothiazide

(B) Metoprolol and hydrochlorothiazide

(C) Terazosin

(D) No therapy

Item 23

A 22-year-old woman is evaluated for a 3-week history of increasing lower-extremity edema that worsens at the end of the day. She has periorbital edema when she awakens and has gained 6.8 kg (15.0 lb). She has had headaches for the past 3 days for which she has been taking ibuprofen.

On physical examination, temperature is normal, blood pressure is 162/88 mm Hg, pulse rate is 78/min, and respiration rate is 18/min. BMI is 28. There is periorbital and facial edema. Cardiopulmonary, funduscopic, and musculoskeletal examinations are normal. There is 2+ bilateral edema of the lower extremities.

Laboratory studies:

Hemoglobin	12.8 g/dL (128 g/L)
Glucose (fasting)	97 mg/dL (5.4 mmol/L)
Total cholesterol	420 mg/dL (10.9 mmol/L)

Albumin	2.4 g/dL (24 g/L)
Blood urea nitrogen	20 mg/dL (7.1 mmol/L)
Serum creatinine	1.1 mg/dL (97.2 μmol/L)
Urinalysis	Specific gravity 1.015; 1+ blood; 3+ protein; 5-10 dysmorphic erythrocytes/hpf; oval fat bodies; no casts
Urine protein-creatinine ratio	10 mg/mg

Which of the following is most likely to establish a diagnosis?

(A) ANCA assay

(B) Kidney biopsy

(C) Kidney ultrasonography

(D) Measurement of urine eosinophils

Item 24

A 56-year-old man comes for a follow-up examination. Two weeks ago, he was evaluated in the emergency department for acute flank pain caused by a passed uric acid stone; since then, he has been asymptomatic and has felt well. He believes he had a kidney stone 5 years ago but did not seek medical attention at that time. He has hypertension and a 3-year history of infrequent gouty attacks. His only medication is lisinopril.

On physical examination, temperature is normal, blood pressure is 132/80 mm Hg, pulse rate is 70/min, and respiration rate is 18/min. BMI is 21. The remainder of the examination is unremarkable.

Laboratory studies:

Sodium	138 meq/L (138 mmol/L)
Potassium	4.5 meq/L (4.5 mmol/L)
Chloride	100 meq/L (100 mmol/L)
Bicarbonate	24 meq/L (24 mmol/L)
Blood urea nitrogen	12 mg/dL (4.3 mmol/L)
Serum uric acid	7 mg/dL (0.4 mmol/L)
Serum creatinine	1.1 mg/dL (97.2 μmol/L)
Urinalysis	pH 5.5; no protein or blood

Kidney ultrasound is normal.

In addition to ingesting more fluid daily and restricting sodium intake, which of the following is the most appropriate next step in this patient's management?

(A) Allopurinol

(B) Hydrochlorothiazide

(C) Potassium citrate

(D) Probenecid

Item 25

A 44-year-old man is evaluated in the hospital because of disorientation and hallucinations. He was admitted to the hospital 4 days ago for a subarachnoid hemorrhage that was repaired with surgical clipping. His medical history is otherwise unremarkable; before he was admitted to the hospital, he took no medications.

On physical examination, he is disoriented, confused, and hallucinating. Temperature is normal, blood pressure is 140/80 mm Hg, pulse rate is 90/min, and respiration rate is 16/min. Upon standing, his blood pressure is 120/60 mm Hg and pulse rate is 110/min. The remainder of the physical examination is normal.

Laboratory values were normal on admission.

Current laboratory studies:

Sodium	118 meq/L (118 mmol/L)
Potassium	4.1 meq/L (4.1 mmol/L)
Chloride	85 meq/L (85 mmol/L)
Bicarbonate	23 meq/L (23 mmol/L)
Serum osmolality	248 mosm/kg H$_2$O (248 mmol/kg H$_2$O)
Serum uric acid	6.8 mg/dL (0.4 mmol/L)
Spot urine sodium	105 meq/L (105 mmol/L)
Spot urine potassium	20 meq/L (20 mmol/L)
Spot urine chloride	90 meq/L (90 mmol/L)
Urine osmolality	633 mosm/kg H$_2$O (633 mmol/kg H$_2$O)

Which of the following is the most likely cause of this patient's hyponatremia?

(A) Adrenal insufficiency

(B) Cerebral salt wasting

(C) Hypothyroidism

(D) Syndrome of inappropriate antidiuretic hormone secretion

Item 26

A 35-year-old woman is evaluated for persistent fatigue. She does not have headaches or palpitations. She has a 10-year history of difficult-to-control hypertension currently being treated with ramipril. Family history is significant for essential hypertension.

On physical examination, blood pressure is 168/110 mm Hg without orthostatic changes. BMI is 24. Cardiac examination reveals a prominent precordial cardiac impulse. There is no edema.

Laboratory studies:

Glucose (fasting)	80 mg/dL (4.4 mmol/L)
Sodium	143 meq/L (143 mmol/L)
Potassium	3.2 meq/L (3.2 mmol/L)
Chloride	102 meq/L (102 mmol/L)
Bicarbonate	28 meq/L (28 mmol/L)
Blood urea nitrogen	18 mg/dL (6.4 mmol/L)
Serum creatinine	1.0 mg/dL (88.4 μmol/L)
Plasma renin activity	0.2 ng/mL/h (normal 0.6-4.3 ng/mL/h)
Urinalysis	Normal

Which of the following is the most likely diagnosis?

(A) Essential hypertension

(B) Pheochromocytoma

(C) Primary aldosteronism

(D) Renovascular hypertension

Item 27

A 33-year-old man comes for a follow-up evaluation for persistent microscopic hematuria and proteinuria. He feels well and is otherwise asymptomatic. He has no history of edema or gross hematuria. There is no family history of kidney disease.

On physical examination, temperature is normal, blood pressure is 142/96 mm Hg, pulse rate is 72/min, and respiration rate is 14/min. BMI is 29. The remainder of the examination, including cutaneous and neurologic examinations, is normal.

Laboratory studies:

Complete blood count	Normal
Albumin	3.2 g/dL (32 g/L)
Liver chemistry studies	Normal
Blood urea nitrogen	17 mg/dL (6.0 mmol/L)
Urinalysis	2+ blood; 2+ protein; 15-20 dysmorphic erythrocytes/hpf with hyaline casts
Urine protein-creatinine ratio	5.2 mg/mg

Kidney biopsy reveals diffuse mesangioproliferative lesions throughout all glomeruli with cellular proliferation. Immunofluorescence testing reveals significant IgA deposition and IgG, C3, and C4 deposition.

In addition to enalapril, which of the following is the most appropriate next step in this patient's management?

(A) Azathioprine
(B) Cyclophosphamide
(C) Methylprednisolone
(D) Mycophenolate mofetil

Item 28

A 22-year-old man comes for a routine evaluation. He has a history of type 1 diabetes mellitus and began taking insulin glargine and insulin lispro 8 years ago. Two days ago, he participated in a marathon race.

On physical examination, temperature is 36.4 °C (97.5 °F), blood pressure is 112/70 mm Hg, pulse rate is 60/min, and respiration rate is 15/min. BMI is 24. Funduscopic examination is normal. There is normal sensation in the extremities.

Laboratory studies:

Hemoglobin A_{1c}	5.8%
Urinalysis	Normal
Urine albumin-creatinine ratio	100 mg/g

In addition to refraining from heavy exercise, which of the following is the most appropriate next step in this patient's management?

(A) Begin losartan
(B) Perform kidney biopsy
(C) Repeat urine albumin-creatinine ratio in 1 year
(D) Repeat urine albumin-creatinine ratio in 2 weeks

Item 29

A 19-year-old man is evaluated in the emergency department for altered mental status. He is accompanied by a friend, who states that the patient was asymptomatic 12 hours ago. Medical history is noncontributory, and he takes no medications. He does not drink alcoholic beverages or use illicit drugs.

On physical examination, the patient is comatose. He is afebrile, blood pressure is 90/60 mm Hg, pulse rate is 110/min, and respiration rate is 28/min. Cardiopulmonary examination is normal. Arterial oxygen saturation is 96% by pulse oximetry with the patient breathing ambient air. There are no localized findings on neurologic examination.

Laboratory studies:

Glucose (fasting)	114 mg/dL (6.3 mmol/L)
Sodium	142 meq/L (142 mmol/L)
Potassium	3.6 meq/L (3.6 mmol/L)
Chloride	108 meq/L (108 mmol/L)
Bicarbonate	14 meq/L (14 mmol/L)
Blood urea nitrogen	14 mg/dL (5.0 mmol/L)
Plasma osmolality	290 mosm/kg H_2O (290 mmol/kg H_2O)
Urinalysis	1+ ketones; no glucose

Arterial blood gas studies (with the patient breathing ambient air):

pH	7.42
P_{CO_2}	20 mm Hg
P_{O_2}	94 mm Hg

Which of the following is the most likely cause of this patient's acid-base disorder?

(A) Alcoholic ketoacidosis
(B) Ethylene glycol toxicity
(C) Methanol toxicity
(D) Salicylate toxicity

Item 30

A 25-year-old woman comes for an evaluation before undergoing nephrectomy for a living related donor kidney transplantation to her brother. Her medical history is unremarkable.

On physical examination, temperature is normal, blood pressure is 116/68 mm Hg, pulse rate is 72/min, and respiration rate is 18/min. Weight is 61 kg (135 lb), and BMI is 23.

The following laboratory studies were obtained 1 week ago:

Serum creatinine	0.8 mg/dL (70.7 µmol/L)
Urine creatinine	47 mg/dL
Creatinine clearance	26 mL/min

24-Hour urine collection:

Urine volume	650 mL/24 h (650 mL/d)
Total protein excretion	50 mg/24 h (50 mg/d)
Total creatinine excretion	475 mg/24 h

CT of the abdomen obtained last week is normal and reveals single renal arteries bilaterally.

Which of the following is the most appropriate next step in this patient's evaluation?

(A) Measure cystatin C
(B) Reject as a potential donor
(C) Repeat timed urine collection
(D) Use the Modified Diet in Renal Disease Study equation

Item 31

A 25-year-old woman is evaluated for a 5-year history of difficult-to-treat hypertension. Medical history is unremarkable. Her only medication is diltiazem. There is no family history of hypertension.

On physical examination, blood pressure is 180/115 mm Hg, pulse rate is 88/min, and respiration rate is 16/min. Cardiopulmonary examination reveals a prominent precordial heave and an abdominal bruit. Funduscopic examination reveals grade 2 hypertensive retinopathy.

Laboratory studies:

Sodium	140 meq/L (140 mmol/L)
Potassium	3.7 meq/L (3.7 mmol/L)
Chloride	100 meq/L (100 mmol/L)
Bicarbonate	28 meq/L (28 mmol/L)
Blood urea nitrogen	18 mg/dL (6.4 mmol/L)
Serum creatinine	1.0 mg/dL (88.4 μmol/L)
Plasma renin activity	10 ng/mL/h (normal 0.6-4.3 ng/mL/h)

Which of the following diagnostic studies of the renal arteries should be performed next?

(A) CT angiography
(B) Duplex Doppler ultrasonography
(C) Intra-arterial digital subtraction angiography
(D) Magnetic resonance angiography

Item 32

A 52-year-old woman comes for a routine evaluation. She was diagnosed with autosomal-dominant polycystic kidney disease (ADPKD) at 25 years of age. She is asymptomatic and has no history of hypertension, hematuria, or infection. Screening tests for cerebral aneurysms have been negative. Two siblings have ADPKD. Her father also had ADPKD and died of a ruptured cerebral aneurysm at 42 years of age. She takes no medications and does not follow a restricted diet.

On physical examination, temperature is normal, blood pressure is 110/72 mm Hg, pulse rate is 72/min, and respiration rate is 16/min. BMI is 28. Cardiopulmonary examination is normal. Abdominal examination reveals no organomegaly.

Laboratory studies:

Complete blood count	Normal
Liver chemistry studies	Normal
Blood urea nitrogen	11 mg/dL (3.9 mmol/L)
Serum creatinine	1.0 mg/dL (88.4 μmol/L)
Urinalysis	Normal
Urine protein-creatinine ratio	0.1 mg/mg

On abdominal ultrasound, the kidneys are 14.5 cm bilaterally. Multiple cysts are seen on the liver. Estimated total kidney volume is 550 cm³ (normal total kidney volume 230 cm³).

Which of the following is the most appropriate next step in this patient's management?

(A) Enalapril
(B) Enalapril and low-protein diet
(C) Sirolimus
(D) No change in management

Item 33

A 72-year-old man is admitted to the hospital with a 3-month history of progressive dyspnea, bilateral lower-extremity edema, and nonradiating pain in the right flank. He has gained 3.2 kg (7 lb). He was diagnosed with benign prostatic hyperplasia 3 years ago. He has a 30-year history of hypertension. Medications are lisinopril and terazosin.

On physical examination, temperature is 36.5 °C (97.8 °F), blood pressure is 158/92 mm Hg, pulse rate is 82/min, and respiration rate is 12/min. BMI is 31. Jugular venous pressure is normal. Cardiopulmonary examination reveals decreased breath sounds at both lung bases. Abdominal and neurologic examinations are normal.

Laboratory studies:

Hemoglobin	14.3 g/dL (143 g/L)
Glucose (fasting)	85 mg/dL (4.7 mmol/L)
Serum total cholesterol	320 mg/dL (8.3 mmol/L)
Blood urea nitrogen	32 mg/dL (11.4 mmol/L)
Serum creatinine	2.1 mg/dL (185.6 μmol/L)
Urinalysis	3+ protein; occasional hyaline casts
Urine protein-creatinine ratio	8 mg/mg

Serum and urine protein electrophoreses are normal. A chest radiograph shows normal heart size and bilateral pleural effusions. On kidney ultrasound, the right kidney is 13.5 cm and the left kidney is 12.0 cm. There is increased echogenicity and no hydronephrosis. Doppler ultrasound shows possible right renal vein thrombosis.

Which of the following is the most likely diagnosis?

(A) IgA nephropathy
(B) Membranous nephropathy
(C) Multiple myeloma
(D) Obstructive nephropathy

Item 34

A 45-year-old woman comes for an office visit after blood pressure measurements obtained during two gynecologist visits over the past year were elevated. She has hypothyroidism. She does not smoke cigarettes, drink alcoholic beverages, or use table salt. She walks 30 minutes each day. Her only medication is levothyroxine. Her mother has hypertension, and her father died of prostate cancer.

On physical examination, blood pressure is 155/95 mm Hg, pulse rate is 72/min, and respiration rate is 14/min. BMI is 25. The remainder of the examination, including cardiopulmonary examination, is normal.

Laboratory studies, including hematocrit, serum potassium, and serum creatinine levels and urinalysis, are normal. An electrocardiogram is normal.

Which of the following diagnostic studies is indicated for this patient?

(A) 24-Hour urine protein collection and urine free cortisol

(B) Exercise stress test, echocardiography, and kidney ultrasonography

(C) Fasting glucose, lipid profile, and serum calcium

(D) Plasma aldosterone-plasma renin activity ratio and plasma metanephrines

Item 35

A 70-year-old woman comes for a follow-up office visit. Six weeks ago, she was diagnosed with dyspepsia and began taking omeprazole. She has stage 3 chronic kidney disease, hypertension, and osteoarthritis. Two months ago, her serum creatinine level was 1.5 mg/dL (132.6 µmol/L). Additional medications are atenolol, enalapril, hydrochlorothiazide, acetaminophen, and low-dose aspirin; her dosages of these agents have not changed in more than 1 year.

On physical examination, temperature is normal, blood pressure is 150/80 mm Hg, and pulse rate is 60/min without orthostatic changes. Respiration rate is 16/min. The remainder of the examination is normal.

Laboratory studies:

Sodium	140 meq/L (140 mmol/L)
Potassium	5.5 meq/L (5.5 mmol/L)
Chloride	109 meq/L (109 mmol/L)
Bicarbonate	18 meq/L (18 mmol/L)
Serum creatinine	3.5 mg/dL (309.4 µmol/L)
Urinalysis	Specific gravity 1.009; pH 5.0; 1+ protein; trace blood; 5-10 leukocytes/hpf; Hansel stain shows <1 eosinophil/mL
Urine protein-creatinine ratio	0.638 mg/mg

Which of the following is the most likely diagnosis?

(A) Acute tubular necrosis

(B) Angiotensin-converting enzyme inhibitor–induced acute kidney injury

(C) Focal segmental glomerulosclerosis

(D) Interstitial nephritis

Item 36

A 55-year-old man comes for a new patient evaluation. He was diagnosed with type 2 diabetes mellitus 15 years ago. He also has hypertension and a 1-year history of right knee osteoarthritis that is well controlled with maximal-dose ibuprofen. He has not been evaluated by a physician in 3 years, and his last 90-day prescription refills were filled at that time. The patient brings empty medicine bottles for hydrochlorothiazide, losartan, metformin, and pravastatin. His only symptoms are fatigue, recent loss of appetite, and ankle swelling.

On physical examination, temperature is 37.2 °C (98.9 °F), blood pressure is 146/92 mm Hg, pulse rate is 70/min, and respiration rate is 14/min. BMI is 31. There is no jugular venous distention. Cardiac examination reveals distant heart sounds with no murmur. The lungs are clear to auscultation. There is bilateral lower-extremity edema to the mid shin. There are normal pedal pulses, and sensation is intact.

Laboratory studies:

Glucose (nonfasting)	230 mg/dL (12.8 mmol/L)
Sodium	142 meq/L (142 mmol/L)
Potassium	5.7 meq/L (5.7 mmol/L)
Chloride	108 meq/L (108 mmol/L)
Bicarbonate	18 meq/L (18 mmol/L)
Serum creatinine	2.5 mg/dL (221 µmol/L)
Urine protein-creatinine ratio	0.46 mg/mg
Urinalysis	Specific gravity 1.015; 3+ protein; 2+ glucose; no casts

In addition to initiating furosemide, which of the following is the most appropriate initial step in managing this patient's chronic kidney disease?

(A) Begin hydrochlorothiazide

(B) Begin losartan

(C) Begin spironolactone

(D) Discontinue ibuprofen

Item 37

A 35-year-old man comes for a follow-up evaluation for recurrent symptomatic calcium oxalate kidney stones. His episodes of nephrolithiasis are associated with significant pain and are disabling. His last attack was 1 month ago. He first developed kidney stones 5 years ago and typically has one to two episodes each year. He has been adherent to recommendations to increase his fluid intake and maintain a low-sodium diet.

On physical examination, vital signs are normal. BMI is 26. The remainder of the examination is unremarkable.

Laboratory studies:

Urinalysis	pH 5.0; 1+ blood; no protein; 0-3 erythrocytes/hpf; no bacteria; no glucose
Urine calcium excretion	230 mg/24 h (5.8 mmol/d)
Urine uric acid excretion	300 mg/24 h (1.7 mmol/d)
Urine citric acid excretion	350 mg/24 h (350 mg/d) (normal range, 320-1240 mg/24 h [320-1240 mg/d])
Urine oxalate excretion	140 mg/24 h (1596 µmol/d) (normal range, 9.7 to 40.5 mg/24 h [110.6 to 461.7 µmol/d])
Urine volume	2500 mL/24 h (2500 mL/d)

Radiograph of the kidneys, ureters, and bladder reveals a 3-mm calculus in the right upper pole.

In addition to avoiding foods high in oxalate and adhering to a low-protein diet, which of the following is the most appropriate next step in this patient's management?

(A) Begin allopurinol

(B) Begin hydrochlorothiazide

(C) Begin sodium citrate

(D) Increase dietary calcium intake

Item 38

A 65-year-old man comes for a follow-up office visit. Three weeks ago, he was admitted to the hospital for deep venous thrombosis of the left leg. He was treated with low-molecular-weight heparin followed by warfarin. He takes no other medications. He has a 30-pack-year history of cigarette smoking and currently smokes 2 packs of cigarettes daily.

Vital signs and physical examination are normal.

Urinalysis 6 months ago revealed trace protein and 1+ blood.

Laboratory studies obtained today:

INR	3.8
Serum creatinine	1.4 mg/dL (123.7 µmol/L)
Urinalysis	Specific gravity 1.015; no protein; 1+ blood; 5-10 erythrocytes/hpf; no casts

On kidney ultrasound, the right kidney is 10.4 cm with a 3-mm nonobstructing stone in the right lower pole. The left kidney is 9.0 cm.

In addition to counseling about smoking cessation, which of the following is the most appropriate next step in this patient's management?

(A) Cystoscopy

(B) Discontinuation of warfarin

(C) Kidney biopsy

(D) Metabolic stone evaluation

Item 39

A 68-year-old man is evaluated for a 3-month history of peripheral edema. He has recently noticed exertional dyspnea but has not had chest pain. He has no history of liver or kidney disease or deep venous thrombosis. He does not drink alcoholic beverages or smoke cigarettes. His only medication is a multivitamin.

On physical examination, temperature is normal, blood pressure is 132/77 mm Hg, pulse rate is 80/min, and respiration rate is 18/min. BMI is 29. Funduscopic examination is normal. Cardiac examination reveals an S_3 and a grade 2/6 holosystolic murmur at the left sternal border that radiates to the cardiac apex. Pulmonary examination reveals bilateral basilar crackles. The appearance of the tongue is shown in the next column. There are ecchymoses on the arms and legs. Hepatomegaly is present. There is 2+ bilateral peripheral edema and normal sensation in the extremities.

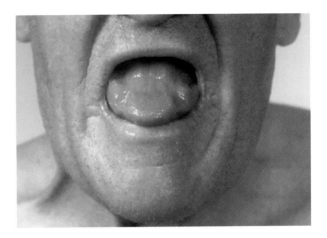

Laboratory studies:

Hemoglobin	11.0 g/dL (110 g/L)
Prothrombin time	15 s
INR	3.5
Serum creatinine	2.3 mg/dL (203.3 µmol/L)
Urinalysis	Normal
Urine protein-creatinine ratio	5 mg/mg

Urine immunoelectrophoresis shows a paraprotein λ spike. Chest radiograph shows an enlarged cardiac silhouette. On kidney ultrasound, the kidneys are 12.5 cm bilaterally.

Which of the following diagnostic studies should be performed next?

(A) Abdominal fat pad biopsy

(B) Bone marrow biopsy

(C) Kidney biopsy

(D) Liver biopsy

Item 40

A 59-year-old woman with a history of coronary artery disease comes for a routine physical examination. She is asymptomatic. One year ago, she underwent placement of a drug-eluting stent in the right coronary artery. She also has hypertension and dyslipidemia. Average home blood pressure measurement is 125/80 mm Hg. Medications are clopidogrel, metoprolol, simvastatin, and low-dose aspirin.

On physical examination, vital signs are normal except for a blood pressure of 135/82 mm Hg in both arms. BMI is 32. The remainder of the physical examination is normal.

Laboratory studies:

Glucose (fasting)	98 mg/dL (5.4 mmol/L)
Total cholesterol	190 mg/dL (4.9 mmol/L)
High-density lipoprotein cholesterol	45 mg/dL (1.2 mmol/L)
Low-density lipoprotein cholesterol	100 mg/dL (2.6 mmol/L)
Triglycerides	225 mg/dL (2.5 mmol/L)
Serum creatinine	1.4 mg/dL (123.8 µmol/L)
Urinalysis	Normal

Which of the following diagnostic studies should be performed next in this patient?

(A) 24-Hour urine collection for protein
(B) Kidney ultrasonography
(C) Spot urine albumin-creatinine ratio
(D) No further studies at this time

Item 41

A 76-year-old man with acute coronary syndrome is evaluated in the hospital after undergoing dilatation and stenting for right coronary artery stenosis. Because he has a 30-year history of hypertension, kidney angiography was performed during coronary angiography and revealed left renal artery stenosis with 60% to 70% luminal narrowing.

Two years ago, he underwent carotid endarterectomy; he recalls being told at that time that he had a "kidney problem." His hypertension is well controlled with hydrochlorothiazide and lisinopril. He also takes metoprolol, atorvastatin, clopidogrel, and low-dose aspirin. His mother had hypertension and died of a stroke at age 85 years.

On physical examination, blood pressure is 140/70 mm Hg, pulse rate is 60/min, and respiration rate is 12/min. BMI is 25. Cardiopulmonary examination reveals carotid, abdominal, and femoral artery bruits.

Laboratory studies:

Sodium	141 meq/L (141 mmol/L)
Potassium	3.7 meq/L (3.7 mmol/L)
Chloride	100 meq/L (100 mmol/L)
Bicarbonate	28 meq/L (28 mmol/L)
Blood urea nitrogen	40 mg/dL (14.3 mmol/L) (unchanged for the past 2 years)
Serum creatinine	2.0 mg/dL (176.8 µmol/L) (unchanged for the past 2 years)
Plasma renin activity	2.0 ng/mL/h (normal range, 0.6-3.0 ng/mL/h)
Estimated glomerular filtration rate	40 mL/min/1.73 m^2

Which of the following is the most appropriate next step in the management of this patient's hypertension?

(A) Kidney angioplasty
(B) Referral to a nephrologist
(C) Surgical renal revascularization
(D) No change in management

Item 42

A 23-year-old man with HIV infection is evaluated in the hospital for the recent onset of hyperkalemia. He was admitted to the hospital 1 week ago for severe *Pneumocystis jirovecii* pneumonia; intravenous pentamidine and corticosteroids were begun at that time. For the past 2 months, he has been taking highly active antiretroviral therapy. He has a sulfa allergy.

Physical examination is unremarkable, and there is no evidence of hypovolemia or edema.

Laboratory studies:

	On admission	Today
Sodium	131 meq/L (131 mmol/L)	132 meq/L (132 mmol/L)
Potassium	4.8 meq/L (4.8 mmol/L)	6.2 meq/L (6.2 mmol/L)
Chloride	95 meq/L (95 mmol/L)	104 meq/L (104 mmol/L)
Bicarbonate	22 meq/L (22 mmol/L)	18 meq/L (18 mmol/L)
Blood urea nitrogen	20 mg/dL (7.1 mmol/L)	21 mg/dL (7.5 mmol/L)
Serum creatinine	1.3 mg/dL (114.9 µmol/L)	1.4 mg/dL (123.8 µmol/L)
Urinalysis	Normal	Normal

Which of the following is the most likely cause of this patient's hyperkalemia?

(A) Adrenal insufficiency
(B) Impaired kidney potassium excretion
(C) Lactic acidosis
(D) Proximal renal tubular acidosis
(E) Rhabdomyolysis

Item 43

A 35-year-old woman with a history of stage 4 chronic kidney disease and hypertension caused by focal segmental glomerulosclerosis is evaluated for a 2-month history of fatigue. She has no shortness of breath, melena, or menorrhagia. Medications are lisinopril, low-dose aspirin, sevelamer, and furosemide. Family history is negative for anemia.

On physical examination, vital signs are normal. There is conjunctival pallor. Abdominal examination is normal. A stool specimen is negative for occult blood.

Laboratory studies:

Hemoglobin	8.6 g/dL (86 g/L)
Leukocyte count	5600/µL (5.6 × 10^9/L)
Mean corpuscular volume	82 fL
Reticulocyte count	0.5% of erythrocytes
Mean corpuscular hemoglobin	28 pg
Ferritin	25 ng/mL (25 mg/L)
Transferrin saturation	8%
Vitamin B$_{12}$	600 pg/mL (442.8 pmol/L)
Serum folate	15 ng/mL (33.9 nmol/L)
Serum creatinine	3.8 mg/dL (335.9 µmol/L)

Which of the following is the most appropriate next step in this patient's management?

(A) Begin epoetin alfa
(B) Begin iron
(C) Measure serum erythropoietin
(D) Schedule bone marrow examination

Item 44

A 62-year-old man is evaluated for a 2-month history of progressive fatigue, dyspnea on exertion, anorexia, and nausea. He has no other medical problems and takes no medications.

On physical examination, temperature is normal, blood pressure is 157/88 mm Hg, pulse rate is 86/min, and respiration rate is 22/min. BMI is 31. The conjunctivae are pale. On cardiopulmonary examination, the point of maximal impulse is displaced laterally. There is dullness to percussion at both lung bases. Abdominal examination reveals no organomegaly. There is bilateral lower-extremity edema. Neurologic examination reveals mild asterixis.

Laboratory studies:

Hemoglobin	7.2 g/dL (72 g/L)
Total protein	9.8 g/dL (98 g/L)
Calcium	10.2 mg/dL (2.5 mmol/L)
Phosphorus	6.8 mg/dL (2.2 mmol/L)
Serum parathyroid hormone	92 pg/mL (92 ng/L)
Blood urea nitrogen	98 mg/dL (35.0 mmol/L)
Serum creatinine	9.8 mg/dL (866.3 µmol/L)
Urinalysis	2+ protein
Urine protein-creatinine ratio	5 mg/mg

Serum and urine protein electrophoreses are positive for a monoclonal IgG K spike. On kidney ultrasound, both kidneys are 13.5 cm and there is increased bilateral echogenicity. There is no evidence of obstruction. Chest radiograph shows cardiomegaly and bilateral pleural effusions.

Which of the following is the most appropriate next step in this patient's management?

(A) Chemotherapy
(B) Hemodialysis and plasmapheresis
(C) Hemodialysis, plasmapheresis, and chemotherapy
(D) Plasma exchange and chemotherapy

Item 45

A 35-year-old woman is contemplating pregnancy and comes for a preconception evaluation. She has a 4-year history of essential hypertension. She has discontinued lisinopril and feels well, and a review of her medical records shows no evidence of hypertensive complications or other medical conditions.

On physical examination, blood pressure is 160/98 mm Hg and pulse rate is 90/min. Funduscopic, cardiac, and pulmonary examinations are normal. There is trace bilateral ankle edema.

Serum creatinine is 0.6 mg/dL (53.0 µmol/L). Urinalysis is normal.

Treatment with which of the following agents is most appropriate for this patient?

(A) Atenolol
(B) Hydrochlorothiazide
(C) Labetalol
(D) Lisinopril
(E) Losartan

Item 46

A 28-year-old female graduate student with progressive chronic kidney disease due to IgA nephropathy and hypertension is evaluated in the office. She has fistulous Crohn disease for which she has undergone multiple abdominal surgeries, including distal ileum and proximal colon resection as well as a temporary ileostomy and subsequent ileocolic anastomosis. She has been referred to a nephrologist, nutritionist, and social worker and has discussed various methods of kidney replacement therapy, including the risks and benefits. She would prefer kidney transplantation. Medications are lisinopril, calcium acetate, and epoetin alfa. There is no family history of kidney disease. She has type O blood, and her mother and father have blood types B and A, respectively. She has no siblings.

On physical examination, temperature is 36.8 °C (98.2 °F), blood pressure is 130/78 mm Hg, pulse rate is 62/min, and respiration rate is 14/min. BMI is 24. Cardiopulmonary examination is normal.

Estimated glomerular filtration rate is 23 mL/min/ 1.73 m^2.

Which of the following is the most appropriate next step in this patient's management?

(A) Begin training for peritoneal dialysis
(B) Evaluate her father as a potential kidney donor
(C) Evaluate her mother as a potential kidney donor
(D) Plan placement of an arteriovenous fistula

Item 47

A 68-year-old man is evaluated for a 6-month history of increasing fatigue and back pain. He also has a 3-week history of anorexia, occasional nausea, and increased urination. His only medications are ibuprofen and acetaminophen as needed to relieve his pain.

On physical examination, temperature is normal, blood pressure is 120/70 mm Hg, pulse rate is 100/min, and respiration rate is 12/min. BMI is 32.

Laboratory studies:

Hematocrit	30%
Serum glucose (fasting)	96 mg/dL (5.3 mmol/L)
Bicarbonate	14 meq/L (14 mmol/L)
Total protein	9.2 g/dL (92 g/L)
Albumin	4.0 g/dL (40 g/L)
Calcium	11.3 mg/dL (2.8 mmol/L)
Phosphorus	1.8 mg/dL (0.6 mmol/L)
Serum creatinine	1.4 mg/dL (123.8 µmol/L)
Urinalysis	2+ glucose; no protein

Which of the following diagnostic studies is indicated for this patient?

(A) Glucose tolerance testing
(B) Parathyroid hormone level
(C) Urine immunoelectrophoresis
(D) Urine pH testing

Item 48

A 45-year-old black woman is evaluated for a 2-month history of fatigue, nonproductive cough, decreased appetite, intermittent fever, right upper-quadrant abdominal pain, and a 4.5-kg (10.0-lb) weight loss.

On physical examination, temperature is 37.8 °C (100.0 °F), blood pressure is 104/68 mm Hg, pulse rate is 100/min, and respiration rate is 16/min. BMI is 28. There are several erythematous 5- to 10-mm maculopapular lesions on the forehead. Cardiopulmonary examination is normal. Abdominal examination reveals hepatomegaly. There is bilateral inguinal lymphadenopathy. There is no edema.

Laboratory studies:

Hemoglobin	12.2 g/dL (122 g/L)
Albumin	4.0 g/dL (40 g/L)
Phosphorus	4.0 mg/dL (1.3 mmol/L)
Calcium	11.2 mg/dL (2.8 mmol/L)
Serum creatinine	2.0 mg/dL (176.8 µmol/L)
Urinalysis	1+ protein; 20 leukocytes/hpf; occasional leukocyte casts
Urine protein-creatinine ratio	0.914 mg/mg

Tuberculin skin testing is negative. Urine culture is negative. Chest radiograph shows bilateral hilar lymphadenopathy. On kidney ultrasound, the right kidney is 13.7 cm and the left kidney is 15.4 cm. There is no hydronephrosis, and no kidney calculi are seen.

Which of the following is the most likely diagnosis?

(A) Amyloidosis
(B) Sarcoidosis
(C) Sjögren syndrome
(D) Systemic lupus erythematosus

Item 49

A 55-year-old woman is evaluated for a possible endocrine tumor. Her sister was recently diagnosed with a pheochromocytoma.

On physical examination, blood pressure is 140/95 mm Hg, pulse rate is 90/min, and respiration rate is 18/min. BMI is 24. The thyroid is normal to palpation. The remainder of the examination, including cardiopulmonary examination, is normal.

Laboratory studies reveal normal serum calcium and calcitonin levels and elevated plasma metanephrine levels. A subsequent abdominal MRI reveals a solitary right adrenal mass.

In addition to referral for genetic counseling, which of the following is the most appropriate long-term management for this patient?

(A) Hydrochlorothiazide
(B) Labetalol
(C) Lisinopril
(D) Right adrenalectomy

Item 50

A 65-year-old man with a history of stage 4 chronic kidney disease and hypertension comes for a follow-up examination. Two days ago, he was discharged from the hospital after being admitted for 4 days for pneumonia. During his hospitalization, his blood pressure averaged 130/70 mm Hg and he was not exposed to radiocontrast agents. He was treated with ceftriaxone and azithromycin; on discharge, these agents were discontinued and he began oral levofloxacin. Since his discharge, he has had nausea, vomiting, and anorexia. He believes that his urine output over the past day has been less than 500 mL. Additional medications are lisinopril, calcium carbonate, and low-dose aspirin.

On physical examination, temperature is 35.8 °C (96.4 °F), blood pressure is 110/50 mm Hg standing and 110/80 mm Hg supine, pulse rate is 100/min standing and 96/min supine, and respiration rate is 16/min. The remainder of the examination is normal except for crackles heard at the base of the lungs bilaterally.

Laboratory studies:

Serum creatinine	6.0 mg/dL (530.4 µmol/L) (4.5 mg/dL [397.8 µmol/L] in the hospital)
Urinalysis	Specific gravity 1.016; no protein or blood; occasional hyaline casts
Fractional excretion of sodium	4%

Which of the following is the most likely cause of this patient's acute kidney injury?

(A) Acute interstitial nephritis
(B) Acute tubular necrosis
(C) Prerenal azotemia
(D) Renal vein thrombosis

Item 51

An 85-year-old man is evaluated in the emergency department for a 1-week history of progressive weakness, lethargy, and diffuse back and abdominal pain. He has not had fever, chills, dyspnea, or gross hematuria. His weight has been stable. He underwent right nephrectomy for renal-cell carcinoma 5 years ago. Surveillance kidney ultrasound 6 months ago showed no evidence for a solid mass and no hydronephrosis.

On physical examination, vital signs are normal. He appears lethargic. There is no pericardial rub. The lungs are clear to auscultation. The abdomen is soft and nontender. There is trace bilateral pretibial edema. The prostate is enlarged and symmetric without nodules.

Laboratory studies:

Hemoglobin	9.4 g/dL (94 g/L)
Leukocyte count	18,000/µL (18 × 10⁹/L)
Blood urea nitrogen	107 mg/dL (38.2 mmol/L)
Serum creatinine	8.4 mg/dL (742.6 µmol/L) (1.3 mg/dL [114.9 µmol/L] 2 months ago)
Urinalysis	Specific gravity 1.010; pH 5.0; trace blood; 3 erythrocytes/hpf; no protein, glucose, leukocyte esterase, ketones, or casts

Kidney ultrasound shows moderate to severe left hydronephrosis and a dilated proximal left ureter. A Foley catheter is placed with drainage of 30 mL of urine.

Which of the following is the next best step in this patient's management?

(A) Furosemide
(B) Hemodialysis
(C) Magnetic resonance urography
(D) Nephrostomy tube placement
(E) Observation

Item 52

A 22-year-old woman is evaluated at an on-site medical center after collapsing while running a marathon. She is disoriented. During the evaluation, she experiences a generalized tonic-clonic seizure lasting 3 minutes. A wristband indicates that she has diabetes mellitus.

On physical examination, temperature is normal, blood pressure is 120/60 mm Hg, pulse rate is 100/min, and respiration rate is 28/min. There is no evidence of hypovolemia or edema. Cardiopulmonary examination is normal. On neurologic examination, she is confused but has no evidence of a focal neurologic deficit.

On laboratory studies, the glucose level is 120 mg/dL (120 mmol/L) and the sodium level is 118 meq/L (118 mmol/L).

Which of the following is the most appropriate next step in this patient's management?

(A) 3% saline infusion
(B) 50% glucose by intravenous bolus
(C) Intravenous furosemide
(D) Normal saline infusion

Item 53

An 85-year-old woman comes for a follow-up evaluation for hypertension. She has not had lightheadedness, exertional chest pain, shortness of breath, or edema. She does not smoke and adheres to a Dietary Approaches to Stop Hypertension (DASH) diet. At an office visit 1 month ago, her blood pressure was 170/70 mm Hg. She was diagnosed with hypertension and chronic stable angina 7 years ago and currently takes metoprolol, sublingual nitroglycerin as needed, and aspirin.

On physical examination, blood pressure is 186/70 mm Hg, pulse rate is 60/min, and respiration rate is 12/min. BMI is 22. Cardiopulmonary examination reveals no jugular venous distention, carotid bruits, murmur, extra cardiac sounds, or pulmonary crackles. The abdomen is soft without masses or bruits. Neurologic examination is normal.

Laboratory studies:

Serum electrolytes	Normal
Blood urea nitrogen	20 mg/dL (7.1 mmol/L)
Serum creatinine	1.2 mg/dL (106.0 μmol/L)
Urinalysis	Normal

An electrocardiogram demonstrates increased voltage in the precordial leads. Ultrasonography of the kidneys is normal.

In addition to reinforcing lifestyle modifications, which of the following is the most appropriate next step in this patient's management?

(A) Follow-up in 3 to 6 months
(B) Hydrochlorothiazide
(C) Lisinopril
(D) Losartan

Item 54

A 33-year-old woman comes for follow-up examination for a left fibula fracture due to a fall 1 week ago. She has hypertension and stage 5 chronic kidney disease treated with home hemodialysis. Medications are lisinopril, sevelamer, epoetin alfa, paricalcitol, and kidney vitamins.

On physical examination, temperature is normal, blood pressure is 130/70 mm Hg, pulse rate is 88/min, and respiration rate is 12/min. BMI is 29. Cardiopulmonary examination is normal. An arteriovenous fistula is present in the left forearm. Except for a cast on her left leg, musculoskeletal examination is normal and reveals no bone pain.

Laboratory studies:

Hemoglobin	10.3 g/dL (103 g/L)
Albumin	3.5 g/dL (35 g/L)
Phosphorus	5.8 mg/dL (1.9 mmol/L)
Calcium	8.4 mg/dL (2.1 mmol/L)
Parathyroid hormone	700 pg/mL (700 ng/L)
Alkaline phosphatase	330 U/L

Which of the following is the most likely cause of this patient's bone disease?

(A) Adynamic bone disease
(B) Avascular necrosis
(C) Osteoporosis
(D) Secondary hyperparathyroidism

Item 55

A 29-year-old woman comes for a follow-up office visit. Six months ago, she underwent double-lung transplantation for cystic fibrosis. She was diagnosed with *Pseudomonas* bronchitis 14 days ago and began oral ciprofloxacin and intravenous tobramycin at that time. Today, she states that her cough has resolved, she has not had fever, and she feels well. Additional medications are acyclovir, mycophenolate mofetil, prednisone, tacrolimus, and trimethoprim-sulfamethoxazole.

On physical examination, temperature is 36.6 °C (97.8 °F), blood pressure is 132/80 mm Hg, pulse rate is 90/min, and respiration rate is 18/min. Cardiopulmonary examination is normal. Cutaneous examination is normal. There is no asterixis. There is no edema.

Laboratory studies:

Hemoglobin	12.0 g/dL (120 g/L)
Leukocyte count	8400/µL (8.4 × 10⁹/L) (83% neutrophils, 12% lymphocytes, no eosinophils)
Platelet count	335,000/µL (335 × 10⁹/L)
Serum creatinine	2.3 mg/dL (203.2 µmol/L) (1.2 mg/dL [106.0 µmol/L] 6 weeks ago)
Urinalysis	Specific gravity 1.011; pH 5.5; 1+ protein; no blood; 2-5 erythrocytes/hpf; no leukocyte esterase

Urine sediment findings are shown.

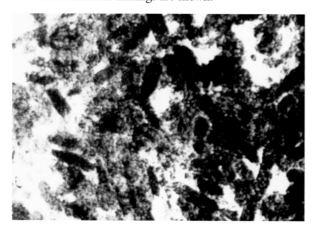

Kidney ultrasound shows normal-sized kidneys and no hydronephrosis.

Which of the following is the most likely cause of this patient's findings?

(A) Acute interstitial nephritis
(B) Acute tubular necrosis
(C) Tacrolimus
(D) Trimethoprim

Item 56

A 20-year-old woman is evaluated in the emergency department for a generalized tonic-clonic seizure. She is accompanied by a friend, who states that the patient took 3,4-methylenedioxymethamphetamine (ecstasy) several hours earlier.

On physical examination, temperature is 37.8 °C (100.0 °F), blood pressure is 90/50 mm Hg, and respiration rate is 24/min. On neurologic examination, she is unresponsive to painful stimuli, but there are no localizing neurologic findings. The remainder of the physical examination is unremarkable.

Laboratory studies:

Sodium	118 meq/L (118 mmol/L)
Potassium	4.1 meq/L (4.1 mmol/L)
Chloride	90 meq/L (90 mmol/L)
Bicarbonate	19 meq/L (19 mmol/L)
Blood urea nitrogen	18 mg/dL (6.4 mmol/L)
Serum creatinine	0.9 mg/dL (79.6 µmol/L)

Which of the following is the most appropriate next step in this patient's management?

(A) 3% saline infusion
(B) Intravenous conivaptan
(C) Intravenous desmopressin
(D) Intravenous furosemide

Item 57

A 22-year-old woman comes for a routine office visit. Medical history is insignificant, and she takes no medications. Her father and brother have kidney stones caused by high levels of urine calcium. She has increased her fluid intake.

On physical examination, vital signs are normal. BMI is 27.

Laboratory studies:

Blood urea nitrogen	10 mg/dL (3.6 mmol/L)
Serum creatinine	0.7 mg/dL (61.9 µmol/L)
Urinalysis	pH 5.0; no protein or blood

Which of the following is the most appropriate next step in this patient's management?

(A) Add a calcium supplement
(B) Decrease dietary animal protein intake
(C) Increase dietary calcium intake
(D) Increase dietary sucrose intake

Item 58

A 22-year-old man comes for a routine evaluation. He feels well but has gained 6.8 kg (15 lb) during the past 4 years. He has a 3-pack-year history of cigarette smoking. He has a sedentary job as a software engineer and consumes two beers on most nights. His parents both have hypertension, and his mother has type 2 diabetes mellitus.

On physical examination, blood pressure is 140/95 mm Hg, pulse rate is 90/min, and respiration rate is 12/min. BMI is 29. There is no evidence of edema.

Laboratory studies, including plasma fasting glucose, a fasting lipid panel, serum electrolytes, serum creatinine, and urinalysis, are normal.

Which of the following is the most appropriate next step in this patient's management?

(A) Atenolol
(B) Diltiazem
(C) Hydrochlorothiazide
(D) Lifestyle modifications
(E) Lisinopril

Item 59

A 75-year-old woman is evaluated for a progressively increasing serum creatinine level. She was admitted to the hospital 3 days ago for crampy abdominal pain; low-grade fever; and loose, mucus-streaked stools. She has a history of hypertension and chronic kidney disease; her serum creatinine level was 1.2 mg/dL (106.0 µmol/L) 1 month ago.

Medications are enalapril, hydrochlorothiazide, and low-dose aspirin.

Colonoscopy showed areas of erythematous, eroded, friable, hemorrhagic, ulcerated mucosa with a decreased vascular pattern in the descending colon. Intravenous hydration is maintained and supplemented with oral intake.

On physical examination today, temperature is normal, blood pressure is 142/88 mm Hg, and pulse rate is 80/min without orthostatic changes. Respiration rate is 14/min. Skin turgor is normal. There is no rash or lymphadenopathy. Cardiopulmonary examination is normal. The abdomen is tender to palpation in the upper- and lower-left quadrants. There is trace bilateral pretibial edema.

Laboratory studies:

Hemoglobin	12.2 g/dL (122 g/L)
Leukocyte count	18,200/µL (18.2 × 10⁹/L)
Platelet count	150,000/µL (150 × 10⁹/L)
Phosphorus	18.7 mg/dL (6.0 mmol/L)
Calcium	8.3 mg/dL (2.0 mmol/L)
Serum creatinine	2.3 mg/dL (203.3 µmol/L) (1.3 mg/dL [114.9 µmol/L] 3 days ago)
Serum uric acid	6 mg/dL (0.35 mmol/L)
Urinalysis	Specific gravity 1.011; pH 5.0; no blood, protein, or casts

Peripheral blood smear shows no schistocytes. On kidney ultrasound, the right kidney is 11.6 cm and the left kidney is 11.8 cm. There is no hydronephrosis.

Which of the following is the most likely diagnosis?

(A) Acute phosphate nephropathy
(B) Acute urate nephropathy
(C) Hemolytic uremic syndrome
(D) Prerenal azotemia

Item 60

An 18-year-old woman is evaluated for a 3-month history of foamy urine and swelling of the feet. Three years ago, she was diagnosed with type 1 diabetes mellitus. Medications are insulin glargine and insulin lispro.

On physical examination, temperature is 36.6 °C (97.8 °F), blood pressure is 100/70 mm Hg, pulse rate is 80/min, and respiration rate is 15/min. BMI is 22. There is periorbital edema. Funduscopic examination is normal. There is no jugular venous distention, cardiac examination is normal without murmurs or extra sounds, and the lungs are clear. There is 1+ bilateral pitting edema of the lower extremities.

Laboratory studies:

Hemoglobin A₁c	7.7%
Serum creatinine	0.6 mg/dL (53.0 µmol/L)
Total cholesterol	220 mg/dL (5.7 mmol/L)
Urinalysis	4+ protein; no blood; several oval fat bodies; no bacteria
Urine protein-creatinine ratio	4 mg/mg

In addition to initiating therapy with an angiotensin-converting enzyme inhibitor, which of the following is the most appropriate next step in this patient's management?

(A) Cyclosporine
(B) Kidney biopsy
(C) Prednisone
(D) Repeat urinalysis in 3 months

Item 61

A 55-year-old woman is admitted to the hospital with a 3-week history of nausea, vomiting, and decreased oral intake. She was diagnosed with stage IIB cervical cancer 3 months ago. Six weeks ago, she completed primary radiotherapy with adjuvant weekly cisplatin. During a follow-up office visit 1 week ago, her serum creatinine level was 1.3 mg/dL (114.9 µmol/L) (baseline 0.8 mg/dL [70.7 µmol/L]). Intravenous saline was administered, but her symptoms did not improve. Her only current medication is ondansetron as needed.

On physical examination, she appears cachectic. She is afebrile, blood pressure is 118/68 mm Hg without orthostatic changes, pulse rate is 90/min, and respiration rate is 18/min. BMI is 19.5. The bladder dome is not palpable. The remainder of the physical examination is normal.

Laboratory studies:

Hemoglobin	10.2 g/dL (102 g/L)
Platelet count	165,000/µL (165 × 10⁹/L)
Sodium	140 meq/L (140 mmol/L)
Potassium	5.3 meq/L (5.3 mmol/L)
Chloride	112 meq/L (112 mmol/L)
Bicarbonate	18 meq/L (18 mmol/L)
Blood urea nitrogen	122 mg/dL (43.5 mmol/L)
Serum creatinine	5.1 mg/dL (450.8 µmol/L)
Urinalysis	pH 5.0; 1+ protein; 1+ blood; 0-5 erythrocytes/hpf; no bacteria; no glucose

Which of the following is the most likely diagnosis?

(A) Cisplatin nephrotoxicity
(B) Hypovolemia
(C) Membranous nephropathy
(D) Obstructive nephropathy

Item 62

A 55-year-old man comes for a follow-up office visit after laboratory studies reveal a diagnosis of type 2 diabetes mellitus. He was diagnosed with hypertension 5 years ago; since then, his systolic blood pressure has ranged from 136 to 142 mm Hg and his diastolic blood pressure has ranged from 85 to 92 mm Hg. He has no history of heart or kidney disease. He currently takes hydrochlorothiazide, 12.5 mg/d, and lisinopril, 10 mg/d. His parents both have hypertension and diabetes.

On physical examination, he is afebrile, blood pressure is 138/84 mm Hg, pulse rate is 78/min, and respiration rate is 16/min. BMI is 28. The remainder of the examination is normal.

On laboratory studies, serum electrolyte, blood urea nitrogen, and serum creatinine levels are normal and the urine albumin-creatinine ratio is 20 mg/g.

Which of the following is the maximal allowable target blood pressure for this patient?

(A) Less than 115/75 mm Hg
(B) Less than 125/75 mm Hg
(C) Less than 130/80 mm Hg
(D) Less than 140/90 mm Hg

Item 63

A 45-year-old woman comes for follow-up evaluation for persistent nonproductive cough, facial pain, and fever and is diagnosed with acute sinusitis. Five years ago, she underwent living related donor kidney transplantation for end-stage kidney disease. Medications are tacrolimus, mycophenolate mofetil, prednisone, and hydrochlorothiazide.

On physical examination, temperature is normal, blood pressure is 128/78 mm Hg, pulse rate is 64/min, and respiration rate is 14/min. BMI is 27. The chest is clear to auscultation, and the remainder of the examination is normal.

Which of the following agents is contraindicated in this patient?

(A) Cephalexin
(B) Ciprofloxacin
(C) Erythromycin
(D) Trimethoprim-sulfamethoxazole

Item 64

A 62-year-old man comes for a follow-up office visit for persistent hematuria. He feels well, and his weight has been stable. He has worked his entire life as an accountant, does not smoke cigarettes or use tobacco products, and has no other medical problems.

On physical examination, temperature is normal, blood pressure is 132/76 mm Hg, pulse rate is 64/min, and respiration rate is 18/min. BMI is 26. The remainder of the physical examination is unremarkable.

On laboratory studies, the serum creatinine level is 1.1 mg/dL (97.2 µmol/L) and microscopic urinalysis reveals 10 erythrocytes/hpf.

Abdominal CT with iodinated contrast reveals a 3-cm Bosniak category III complex kidney cyst in the left upper pole of the left kidney. On kidney ultrasound, the left kidney is 11.5 cm with a 3.2-cm complex cyst in the left upper pole.

Which of the following is the most appropriate next step in this patient's management?

(A) Kidney biopsy
(B) Repeat abdominal CT in 6 months
(C) Surgical resection
(D) No further evaluation

Item 65

A 68-year-old man comes for a routine evaluation. He has a 20-year history of difficult-to-treat hypertension. He has gained over 9.1 kg (20 lb) in the last 15 years. He does not smoke cigarettes and consumes less than 2 oz of alcohol daily and less than 8 oz weekly. He tries to walk 6 blocks every day. Medications are lisinopril, 20 mg/d; amlodipine, 10 mg/d; and hydrochlorothiazide, 25 mg/d. He adheres to his medication regimen and takes no over-the-counter medications.

On physical examination, blood pressure is 160/95 mm Hg. BMI is 32. He has generalized obesity without skin changes. There is generalized abdominal obesity but no tenderness or organomegaly. The remainder of the examination is normal.

Laboratory studies reveal normal serum electrolyte, blood urea nitrogen, and serum creatinine levels and a urine albumin-creatinine ratio of 50 mg/g. A work-up for secondary hypertension is negative.

Therapeutic lifestyle changes are reinforced.

Which of the following is the most appropriate next step in this patient's management?

(A) Atenolol
(B) Clonidine
(C) Doxazosin
(D) Spironolactone

Item 66

A 69-year-old woman is evaluated for a progressive 6-month history of fatigue and weakness. She has had painful paresthesias on the dorsum of the right foot for the past 10 days and weakness in the right wrist for the past 2 days. She also has had fever and night sweats accompanied by arthralgia and myalgia. She has had a 4.1-kg (9-lb) weight loss during this time and over the past month has developed anorexia and nausea. Colonoscopy, mammography, and Pap smear performed 2 months ago were normal. Her medical history is otherwise unremarkable, and she takes no medications.

On physical examination, temperature is normal, blood pressure is 155/115 mm Hg, pulse rate is 102/min, and respiration rate is 18/min. BMI is 28. There is jugular venous distention. Cardiac examination reveals a summation gallop. Left and right renal bruits are heard during systole and diastole. The lungs are clear to auscultation. She is unable to dorsiflex the right foot, and extension of the right wrist is weak. There is 2+ ankle edema bilaterally. There are no skin lesions and no evidence of synovitis.

Laboratory studies:

Hemoglobin	10 g/dL (100 g/L)
Erythrocyte sedimentation rate	98 mm/h
Blood urea nitrogen	30 mg/dL (10.7 mmol/L)
Serum creatinine	1.2 mg/dL (106.0 µmol/L)
Antinuclear antibodies	Negative
Rheumatoid factor	Negative
c-ANCA	Negative
p-ANCA	Negative

C3 and C4   Normal
Urinalysis   2+ protein; no casts
Urine protein-
    creatinine ratio   0.36 mg/mg

Serum and urine electrophoreses are negative. Blood cultures are pending. Echocardiography is negative for valvular disease, valvular vegetation, or tumor. On kidney ultrasound, the kidneys are 11 cm bilaterally. There is no hydronephrosis.

Which of the following studies is most likely to yield a definitive diagnosis?

(A) Abdominal fat pad aspiration

(B) Angiography of the renal arteries

(C) Kidney biopsy

(D) Skin biopsy

Item 67

A 52-year-old woman is evaluated for dysuria, urinary frequency, and lower abdominal pain of 2 days' duration. Medical history is significant for urinary tract infection that occurs three to four times yearly. She also has hypertension treated with amlodipine.

On physical examination, temperature is 37.4 °C (99.3 °F), blood pressure is 152/96 mm Hg, pulse rate is 80/min, and respiration rate is 18/min. BMI is 41. The remainder of the examination is normal except for mild suprapubic tenderness.

Laboratory studies:

Leukocyte count   7000/μL (7×10^9/L)
Blood urea nitrogen   12 mg/dL (4.3 mmol/L)
Serum creatinine   1.0 mg/dL (88.4 μmol/L)
Urinalysis   pH 8.0; 1+ blood; no protein; 3-5 erythrocytes/hpf; leukocyte esterase; leukocyte clumps; nitrites

Abdominal CT reveals a 4-cm staghorn calculus on the right kidney.

Which of the following is the most appropriate next step in this patient's management?

(A) Extracorporeal shock-wave lithotripsy

(B) Intravenous cephalexin

(C) Percutaneous nephrolithotomy

(D) Start potassium citrate

Item 68

A 56-year old man with a history of alcoholism is found lying on the street. On arrival at the emergency department, he is confused.

On physical examination, temperature is 36.1 °C (97.0 °F), blood pressure is 126/80 mm Hg, and pulse rate is 70/min. Funduscopic examination shows no papilledema. Cardiac, pulmonary, and abdominal examinations are normal.

Laboratory studies:

Glucose (fasting)   86 mg/dL (4.8 mmol/L)
Blood urea nitrogen   45 mg/dL (16.0 mmol/L)
Serum creatinine   2.8 mg/dL (247.5 μmol/L)
Sodium   138 meq/L (138 mmol/L)
Potassium   5.4 meq/L (5.4 mmol/L)
Chloride   98 meq/L (98 mmol/L)
Bicarbonate   14 meq/L (14 mmol/L)
Plasma osmolality   316 mosm/kg H_2O (316 mmol/kg H_2O)
Urinalysis   Calcium oxalate crystals

Arterial blood gas studies (with the patient breathing ambient air):

pH   7.28
P_{CO_2} 29 mm Hg
P_{O_2} 80 mm Hg

Which of the following is the most likely diagnosis?

(A) Alcoholic ketoacidosis

(B) Diabetic ketoacidosis

(C) Ethylene glycol poisoning

(D) Lactic acidosis

Item 69

A 28-year-old woman comes for a routine evaluation. She would like to conceive a child within the next 3 months. She was diagnosed with type 1 diabetes mellitus at age 9 years. She also has a history of hypertension. Medications are lisinopril, hydrochlorothiazide, and insulin glargine and insulin lispro.

On physical examination, blood pressure is 110/70 mm Hg. BMI is 23.

Laboratory studies, including serum creatinine, are normal except for a urine albumin-creatinine ratio of 400 mg/g.

Which of the following is the most appropriate next step in this patient's management?

(A) Discontinue hydrochlorothiazide

(B) Discontinue lisinopril

(C) Switch lisinopril to losartan

(D) No change in therapy at this time

Item 70

A 47-year-old man with a long-standing history of alcoholism is hospitalized for abdominal pain, nausea, and vomiting of 7 days' duration. His last drink was 6 days ago. He has lost approximately 10% of his body weight over the past 4 months; he states that his weight loss was caused by drinking alcohol and not eating.

On physical examination, he appears cachectic. Temperature is 37.1 °C (98.8 °F), blood pressure is 100/70 mm Hg, pulse rate is 110/min, and respiration rate is 18/min. BMI is 17. He is not confused or tremulous. There is midepigastric tenderness without rebound. Bowel sounds are present. Neurologic examination is normal.

Laboratory studies:

Amylase	300 U/L
Lipase	150 U/L
Sodium	130 meq/L (130 mmol/L)
Potassium	3.4 meq/L (3.4 mmol/L)
Chloride	90 meq/L (90 mmol/L)
Bicarbonate	20 meq/L (20 mmol/L)
Phosphorus	3.5 mg/dL (1.1 mmol/L)
Calcium	9.0 mg/dL (2.2 mmol/L)
Urinalysis	Positive for ketones

The patient receives immediate thiamine replacement, folic acid supplementation, and a multivitamin followed by vigorous intravenous fluid replacement with 5% dextrose and normal saline with aggressive potassium replacement. Morphine is used to control pain.

Eighteen hours later, the patient's abdominal pain has improved but he becomes restless, agitated, and extremely weak and is barely able to raise his extremities against gravity.

Which of the following is the most likely cause of this patient's new findings?

(A) Hypercalcemia

(B) Hypokalemia

(C) Hyponatremia

(D) Hypophosphatemia

Item 71

A 33-year-old man comes for a follow-up evaluation. Two weeks ago, he underwent living unrelated kidney transplantation for end-stage kidney disease secondary to focal segmental glomerulosclerosis. Before kidney transplantation, he had been anuric and underwent dialysis. Current medications are tacrolimus, mycophenolate mofetil, prednisone, fluconazole, valganciclovir, and trimethoprim-sulfamethoxazole.

On physical examination, temperature is normal, blood pressure is 138/98 mm Hg, pulse rate is 80/min, and respiration rate is 15/min. BMI is 29. Cardiopulmonary and funduscopic examinations are normal. There are staples at the kidney transplantation incision site in the lower right quadrant of the abdomen. There is 1+ bilateral peripheral edema.

Laboratory studies:

Glucose (nonfasting)	130 mg/dL (7.2 mmol/L)
Serum creatinine	1.7 mg/dL (150.3 µmol/L)
Urinalysis	4+ protein; 5-10 erythrocytes/hpf

Which of the following is the most likely diagnosis?

(A) Diabetic nephropathy

(B) IgA nephropathy

(C) Membranous nephropathy

(D) Recurrent focal segmental glomerulosclerosis

Item 72

A 70-year-old woman comes for routine follow-up evaluation for recently diagnosed chronic kidney disease and hypertension. She is asymptomatic. Her only medication is lisinopril, which was titrated up to the maximal dosage over the past 3 months; she is adherent to this therapy and to a sodium-restricted diet.

On physical examination, vital signs are normal except for a blood pressure of 160/90 mm Hg. The remainder of the examination is normal except for trace bilateral pedal edema.

Laboratory studies:

Potassium	5.0 meq/L (5.0 mmol/L)
Serum creatinine	1.3 mg/dL (114.9 µmol/L)
Urine protein-creatinine ratio	2.1 mg/mg

Which of the following is the most appropriate treatment for this patient?

(A) Chlorthalidone

(B) Losartan

(C) Metoprolol

(D) Verapamil

Answers and Critiques

Item 1   Answer: B

Educational Objective: Evaluate a patient with diabetes mellitus and chronic kidney disease.

Kidney biopsy would be appropriate for this patient. This study is recommended in patients with diabetes mellitus who have features of kidney disease that are not consistent with diabetic nephropathy in order to establish a diagnosis and determine the most appropriate treatment. Diabetic nephropathy is characterized by proteinuria, hypertension, and a decline in the glomerular filtration rate in patients with a long-standing history of type 1 diabetes or a 5- to 10-year history of type 2 diabetes. This condition usually progresses from microalbuminuria to macroalbuminuria to an elevated serum creatinine level over a number of years.

This patient's long-standing history of diabetes and proteinuria is suggestive of diabetic nephropathy; however, hematuria and the rapid onset of symptomatic nephrotic syndrome are not consistent with this condition and raise suspicion for primary glomerular disease. Furthermore, patients with diabetic nephropathy often have diabetic retinopathy.

Cystoscopy would be considered in an adult with hematuria of uncertain origin in order to exclude bladder cancer. Similarly, imaging studies may help to evaluate urinary tract obstruction, kidney stones, kidney cysts or masses, renal vascular diseases, and vesicoureteral reflux. However, cystoscopy or a spiral CT would not be warranted in a patient with erythrocyte casts seen on urinalysis, which suggests glomerular hematuria.

Observation alone would place this patient at risk for progressive kidney injury if her condition remains untreated.

KEY POINT

- Kidney biopsy is recommended in patients with diabetes mellitus and the nephrotic syndrome who have features of kidney disease that are not consistent with diabetic nephropathy.

Bibliography

Lin YL, Peng SJ, Ferng SH, Tzen CY, Yang CS. Clinical indicators which necessitate renal biopsy in type 2 diabetes mellitus patients with renal disease. Int J Clin Pract. 2009;63(8):1167-1176. [PMID: 18422591]

Item 2   Answer: C

Educational Objective: Manage a patient with an acute attack of nephrolithiasis.

Intravenous saline is appropriate for this patient. This patient's nausea, vomiting, flank pain that radiates to the groin, and abnormal urinalysis findings are consistent with acute nephrolithiasis. The presence of a kidney calculus on CT of the abdomen confirms this diagnosis. Kidney stones less than 5 mm in diameter are likely to pass spontaneously with hydration and analgesics.

Kidney stones may take several days to weeks to pass spontaneously. If a stone does not pass within 2 to 4 weeks, rapid stone removal is indicated. This intervention also is recommended for patients with infection, intractable nausea and vomiting, complete obstruction or anuria, and stones greater than 1 cm in diameter. Extracorporeal shock-wave lithotripsy would be warranted in these settings or in a patient with a stone that is less than 1 cm in diameter located within the kidney or higher than mid ureter, which is not consistent with this patient's presentation. Furthermore, even if stone removal were indicated for this patient, flexible ureteroscopy would be a more appropriate method than extracorporeal shock-wave lithotripsy to remove a stone located in the distal ureter.

Percutaneous nephrostomy would be indicated in a patient with a staghorn calculus, to relieve an obstructed urinary collecting system if retrograde nephrostomy cannot be performed, or to obtain anatomic access in conjunction with extracorporeal shock-wave lithotripsy. This intervention would not be warranted at this time in a patient with only mild hydronephrosis with a stone that is likely to pass spontaneously.

Intravenous antibiotic therapy would be indicated to treat an infected kidney stone or infection due to a dilated collecting system. However, infection is unlikely in the absence of fever, pyuria, or bacteria on urinalysis.

KEY POINT

- Kidney stones less than 5 mm in diameter are likely to pass spontaneously with hydration and analgesics.

Bibliography

Miller N, Lingeman J. Management of kidney stones. BMJ. 2007;334(7591):468-472. [PMID: 17332586]

Item 3   Answer: B

Educational Objective: Manage a patient at risk for contrast-induced nephropathy.

This patient is at risk for contrast-induced nephropathy, and the most appropriate next step in management is intravenous furosemide. Contrast-induced nephropathy is characterized by an increase in the serum creatinine level 24 to 48 hours after contrast administration. Risk factors for this condition include age greater than 75 years, heart failure, hypertension, diabetes mellitus, and chronic kidney disease.

Diuretics are associated with an increased risk of acute kidney injury and should be withheld before contrast administration in patients with normal or near-normal volume status. However, withholding diuretics would not be appropriate for a patient with heart failure. When cardiac catheterization can be safely delayed, use of diuretics to correct significant hypervolemia before contrast administration helps to optimize cardiac output and thus kidney perfusion and decreases the risk of contrast-induced nephropathy. Serum electrolyte levels, kidney function, and volume status also should be closely monitored to avoid overdiuresis.

Discontinuation of NSAIDs and metformin also is indicated in patients undergoing procedures that involve contrast administration. These agents can be reinitiated once kidney function has been shown to be stable for several days after contrast exposure.

Two well-designed randomized controlled trials have demonstrated that fenoldopam does not reduce the risk of contrast-associated acute kidney injury. Therefore, this agent is not recommended to prevent contrast-induced nephropathy.

Before contrast administration, angiotensin-converting enzyme inhibitors should be discontinued in most patients with acute kidney injury but can be continued in those with stable kidney function. In this patient, enalapril is likely to promote improved cardiac output and kidney perfusion and should be continued.

Isotonic bicarbonate or saline administered both before and after contrast administration helps to prevent contrast-induced nephropathy but would not be initially appropriate in this patient with heart failure. Isotonic saline may have equal efficacy to isotonic bicarbonate in the prevention of contrast-induced nephropathy.

KEY POINT

- **Before radiocontrast is used, the cardiac output and kidney perfusion should be optimized when possible to decrease the risk of contrast-induced nephropathy.**

Bibliography

McCullough PA. Contrast-induced acute kidney injury [erratum in: J Am Coll Cardiol. 2008;51(22):2197]. J Am Coll Cardiol. 2008;51(15):1419-1428. [PMID: 18402894]

Item 4   Answer: A

Educational Objective: Diagnose HIV-associated nephropathy.

This patient most likely has HIV-associated nephropathy (HIVAN) caused by collapsing focal segmental glomerulosclerosis (FSGS). Collapsing FSGS is the most common kidney disease associated with HIV infection and predominantly affects black patients. HIVAN is classically associated with a low CD4 cell count and high HIV RNA viral load but may manifest differently in patients whose HIV infection is well controlled with highly active antiretroviral therapy (HAART) or who have an acute retroviral syndrome. Collapsing FSGS is characterized by hypoalbuminemia, edema, heavy proteinuria, and minimal erythrocytes and leukocytes in the urine. Most patients have a normal blood pressure.

HAART is considered the treatment of choice in patients with HIVAN, and protease inhibitor–based HAART regimens have been shown to reduce the progression of kidney disease in this setting; adding corticosteroids to this therapy may provide further benefit. In addition, treatment with an angiotensin-converting enzyme inhibitor or an angiotensin receptor blocker helps to decrease urine protein excretion.

Postinfectious glomerulonephritis and IgA nephropathy are possible kidney complications of HIV infection. Postinfectious glomerulonephritis can potentially develop after numerous bacterial infections, which frequently occur in patients with HIV infection. IgA nephropathy may be the result of IgA interaction with HIV antigens but would manifest as minimal proteinuria and an active urine sediment, which is not compatible with this patient's presentation.

Membranous nephropathy can cause the nephrotic syndrome in patients with HIV infection. Membranous nephropathy is most commonly associated with HIV infection–related complications such as hepatitis B or C virus infection or syphilis and may be associated with renal vein thrombosis, which are absent in this patient. This condition also is associated with systemic lupus erythematosus and the use of certain drugs, but these circumstances are unlikely in a patient who takes no medications and has a negative antinuclear antibody assay.

KEY POINT

- **The most common cause of HIV-associated nephropathy is collapsing focal segmental glomerulosclerosis, which is characterized by massive proteinuria.**

Bibliography

de Silva Ti, Post FA, Griffin MD, Dockrell DH. HIV-1 infection and the kidney: an evolving challenge in HIV medicine. Mayo Clin Proc. 2007;82(9):1103-1116. [PMID: 17803878]

Item 5   Answer: D

Educational Objective: Manage a patient with prehypertension.

This patient has prehypertension, defined by the Seventh Report of the Joint National Committee on Prevention, Detection, Evaluation and Treatment of High Blood Pressure (JNC 7) guidelines as a blood pressure between 120 to 139/80 to 89 mm Hg. The most appropriate next step in this patient's management is lifestyle modification, defined by JNC 7 as maintaining a normal body weight, regular aerobic physical activity, adhering to a Dietary Approaches to Stop Hypertension (DASH) diet, reducing sodium intake, and moderating alcohol intake.

The relationship between blood pressure and cardiovascular morbidity and mortality is linear, and the risk for ischemic heart disease and stroke progressively increases in patients with a blood pressure higher than 115/75 mm Hg. Lifestyle modifications help to lower blood pressure, modify additional cardiovascular risk factors, and can decrease the incidence of overt hypertension in patients with prehypertension.

Ambulatory blood pressure monitoring is primarily indicated for patients with white coat hypertension, characterized by at least three separate office blood pressure measurements above 140/90 mm Hg with at least two sets of measurements below 140/90 mm Hg obtained in nonoffice settings.

The 2007 United States Preventive Services Task Force guidelines recommend screening every 2 years for persons with blood pressure less than 120/80 mm Hg and annual assessment for patients with blood pressure less than 120 to 139/80 to 89 mm Hg. The JNC 7 recommends that patients beginning a new antihypertensive drug should be reevaluated in 1 month. Because this patient is not starting a new drug, a return visit in 1 month is not necessary.

JNC 7 recommends a thiazide diuretic as initial therapy in patients with uncomplicated hypertension. However, current data do not support pharmacologic treatment in patients with prehypertension with no other major risk factors for hypertension, such as diabetes mellitus, kidney disease, or evidence of target organ damage.

KEY POINT

- Lifestyle modifications such as maintaining a normal body weight, regular aerobic physical activity, adhering to a Dietary Approaches to Stop Hypertension (DASH) diet, reducing sodium intake, and moderating alcohol intake are indicated for patients with prehypertension who do not have other major risk factors for hypertension.

Bibliography

Chobanian AV, Bakris GL, Black HR, et al; National Heart, Lung, and Blood Institute Joint National Committee on Prevention, Detection, Evaluation, and Treatment of High Blood Pressure; National High Blood Pressure Education Program Coordinating Committee. The Seventh Report of the Joint National Committee on Prevention, Detection, Evaluation, and Treatment of High Blood Pressure: the JNC 7 report [erratum in: JAMA. 2003;290(2):197]. JAMA. 2003;289(19):2560-2572. [PMID: 12748199]

Item 6　　Answer:　C

Educational Objective:　Treat minimal change disease.

This patient most likely has minimal change disease (MCD), and the most appropriate treatment is prednisone. MCD is the most common cause of the nephrotic syndrome in children and commonly causes this syndrome in young adults. MCD is characterized by the sudden development of an elevated urine protein-creatinine ratio that may exceed 9 mg/mg; this patient's foamy urine is most likely caused by her proteinuria. Additional manifestations of the nephrotic syndrome include edema, hypoalbuminemia, and hyperlipidemia.

The serum creatinine level in patients with MCD may be normal or slightly elevated, light microscopy reveals no discernible abnormalities, and immunofluorescence microscopy shows no immunoreactants. Effacement or flattening of glomerular epithelial cells seen on electron microscopy is diagnostic of this condition. Approximately 33% of patients with MCD have a single episode of the nephrotic syndrome followed by long-term remission, but most patients have relapsing disease.

Few trials have been performed in adults with MCD, and treatment in affected adults mirrors that used in children. Corticosteroid therapy is the initial treatment of choice in this condition.

Approximately 25% of patients with MCD are resistant to corticosteroid therapy.

Cyclophosphamide, cyclosporine, or tacrolimus would be indicated for patients with this condition who are corticosteroid resistant, become corticosteroid dependent, or have frequent relapses. However, none of these agents would be warranted in this patient until prednisone therapy is tried.

KEY POINT

- Corticosteroid therapy is the initial treatment of choice in patients with minimal change disease, which is characterized by the sudden development of an elevated urine protein-creatinine ratio that may exceed 9 mg/mg.

Bibliography

Palmer S, Nand K, Strippoli G. Interventions for minimal change disease in adults with nephrotic syndrome. Cochrane Database Syst Rev. 2008;(1):CD001537. [PMID: 18253993]

Item 7　　Answer:　B

Educational Objective:　Diagnose lithium-induced nephrotoxicity.

This patient most likely has lithium-induced nephrotoxicity. This condition is associated with chronic tubulointerstitial disease. The dose and duration of treatment with lithium are the most important predictors of the development of nephrotoxicity. Kidney function in patients with lithium nephrotoxicity may decline slowly, and a period of 20 years typically passes between the initiation of lithium therapy and end-stage kidney disease. Nephrotoxicity may be irreversible even after discontinuation of this agent. This patient's polyuria, nocturia, mild hypernatremia, and dilute urine are most likely caused by nephrogenic diabetes insipidus, which is characteristic of lithium-induced nephrotoxicity.

Diabetic nephropathy manifests as microalbuminuria or albuminuria and a reduced estimated glomerular filtration rate. This patient's polyuria and nocturia also are consistent with diabetes mellitus. However, this patient's plasma glucose level is not sufficiently high to confirm a diagnosis of diabetes. Furthermore, patients with diabetes who have nocturia and mild hypernatremia also usually have glycosuria.

Obstructive uropathy is a common cause of kidney disease in men and is associated with lower urinary tract symptoms, such as nocturia. However, obstructive uropathy sufficient to cause this patient's kidney disease is unlikely in the presence of kidney ultrasound findings that exclude an obstruction.

Sickle cell nephropathy is associated with kidney diseases such as papillary necrosis, rhabdomyolysis, kidney infarction, and secondary focal segmental glomerulosclerosis. This condition also commonly causes flank pain, hematuria, and nephrotic-range proteinuria, which are absent in this patient.

KEY POINT

- Lithium-induced nephrotoxicity may manifest as nephrogenic diabetes insipidus and typically progresses slowly.

Bibliography

Garofeanu C, Weir M, Rosas-Arellano P, Henson G, Garg A, Clark W. Causes of reversible nephrogenic diabetes insipidus: a systemic review. Am J Kidney Dis. 2005;45(4):626-637. [PMID: 15806465]

Item 8 Answer: D

Educational Objective: Diagnose isopropyl alcohol poisoning.

This patient most likely has isopropyl alcohol poisoning. Manifestations of this condition resemble those in ethanol intoxication and include inebriation and a depressed mental status. Isopropyl alcohol ingestion causes acetone production, which results in ketones in the blood and urine. However, because bicarbonate is not consumed during acetone production, metabolic acidosis is absent in this setting. Isopropyl alcohol poisoning is characterized by an increased osmolal gap in the setting of positive serum and urine ketones. The osmolal gap is the difference between the measured and calculated osmolality, with the calculated osmolality obtained using the following formula:

Plasma Osmolality (mosm/kg H_2O) = 2 × Serum Sodium (meq/L) + Blood Urea Nitrogen (mg/dL)/2.8 + Glucose (mg/dL)/18

This patient's calculated plasma osmolality is 296 mosm/kg H_2O (296 mmol/kg H_2O) and the calculated osmolal gap is 24 mosm/kg H_2O (24 mmol/kg H_2O), whereas the normal osmolal gap is approximately 10 mosm/kg H_2O (10 mmol/kg H_2O). An elevated osmolal gap suggests the presence of an unmeasured osmole and is most commonly caused by ethanol. The osmolal gap is also elevated in the presence of ethylene glycol, methanol, and isopropyl alcohol. However, isopropyl alcohol does not cause an elevated anion gap metabolic acidosis (methanol and ethylene glycol poisoning) and is not associated with retinal abnormalities (methanol poisoning) or kidney failure (ethylene glycol poisoning).

This patient's confusion and disorientation are consistent with ethylene glycol poisoning, diabetic ketoacidosis, and alcoholic ketoacidosis; however, these conditions would be associated with an anion gap metabolic acidosis. Toluene, an industrial solvent that can be abused as an inhalant, may cause confusion and disorientation in addition to metabolic acidosis, hypokalemia, hypophosphatemia, rhabdomyolysis, and elevated creatine kinase level. The absence of metabolic acidosis and hypokalemia makes toluene poisoning unlikely.

KEY POINT

- Isopropyl alcohol poisoning is characterized by an increased osmolal gap in the setting of positive serum and urine ketones and does not cause metabolic acidosis.

Bibliography

Zaman F, Pervez A, Abreo K. Isopropyl alcohol intoxication: a diagnostic challenge. Am J Kidney Dis. 2002;40(3):E12. [PMID: 12200829]

Item 9 Answer: A

Educational Objective: Diagnose white coat hypertension.

This patient most likely has white coat hypertension. This condition is characterized by at least three separate office blood pressure measurements above 140/90 mm Hg with at least two sets of measurements below 140/90 mm Hg obtained in nonoffice settings, accompanied by the absence of target organ damage. Ambulatory blood pressure monitoring is considered the gold standard for diagnosing white coat hypertension. This technique provides multiple blood pressure measurements in the nonoffice setting over a prolonged period of time and evaluates mean 24-hour blood pressure, mean daytime blood pressure, mean nighttime blood pressure, the average difference between waking and sleeping blood pressure, and blood pressure variability.

Home blood pressure monitoring is helpful for managing white coat hypertension but may be less accurate than ambulatory blood pressure monitoring for diagnosing this condition.

Compared with electrocardiography, echocardiography is more sensitive for detecting manifestations of hypertensive heart disease, such as left ventricular hypertrophy or diastolic dysfunction. Echocardiography would be reasonable if ambulatory blood pressure monitoring reveals an average 24-hour blood pressure measurement close to 130/80 mm Hg, which is the threshold for initiating treatment but is not warranted at this time.

Follow-up evaluation should occur sooner than 1 year until the diagnosis of either hypertension or prehypertension is excluded.

A thiazide diuretic is the most appropriate initial therapy in patients with uncomplicated hypertension. However, a diagnosis of hypertension has not been established in this patient, and unnecessarily initiating treatment with an agent with potential adverse effects would be inappropriate. Patients with white coat hypertension are at lower risk for cardiovascular events than those with sustained hypertension, and drug treatment of white coat hypertension has not been shown to reduce morbid events.

KEY POINT

- Ambulatory blood pressure monitoring is the gold standard for diagnosing white coat hypertension.

Bibliography

Pickering TG, Shimbo D, Haas D. Ambulatory blood-pressure monitoring. N Engl J Med. 2006;354(22):2368-2374. [PMID: 16738273]

Item 10   Answer: B

Educational Objective: Manage stage 4 chronic kidney disease.

This patient has an estimated glomerular filtration rate (eGFR) of 24 mL/min/1.73 m² according to the estimated Modification of Diet in Renal Disease Study equation, which is consistent with stage 4 chronic kidney disease (CKD). In patients with CKD, early referral to a nephrologist, nutritionist, and social worker is indicated, usually before the eGFR is below 30 mL/min/1.73 m². The National Kidney Foundation's Kidney Disease Outcomes Quality Initiative (NKF K/DOQI) practice guidelines also recommend that discussion of options for kidney replacement therapy begin when patients reach stage 4 CKD (eGFR <30 mL/min/1.73 m²).

Contrast-enhanced CT of the abdomen can differentiate neoplastic lesions from benign cystic structures in the kidney but is contraindicated in patients with CKD, who are at risk for contrast-associated acute kidney injury. Furthermore, this patient's 5-year history of steadily progressive kidney failure and urinalysis results do not suggest malignancy.

Kidney biopsies are commonly performed in adults with the nephrotic syndrome or glomerulonephritis with no obvious postinfectious glomerular disease, children with corticosteroid-resistant nephrotic syndrome, and all patients with acute kidney injury of unclear cause. In patients with stage 4 CKD and a bland urinalysis, kidney biopsy is unlikely to clarify the diagnosis, provide prognostic information, or assist in management.

¹²⁵I-iothalamate scanning provides estimates of glomerular filtration that are nearly identical to those using measurement of inulin clearance, which is the gold standard for estimation of the GFR. However, radionuclide scanning is of limited use in evaluating kidney function and is therefore not commonly used for this purpose. In addition, an accurate estimation of the GFR would not help to guide this patient's management.

KEY POINT

- Discussion of options for kidney replacement therapy should begin when patients reach stage 4 chronic kidney disease.

Bibliography

Hemodialysis Adequacy 2006 Work Group. Clinical practice guidelines for hemodialysis adequacy, update 2006. Am J Kidney Dis. 2006;48(Suppl 1):S2-S90. [PMID: 16813990]

Item 11   Answer: D

Educational Objective: Diagnose proximal (type 2) renal tubular acidosis.

This patient most likely has proximal (type 2) renal tubular acidosis (RTA) secondary to multiple myeloma. Multiple myeloma is one of many diseases that can cause the combination of RTA and proximal tubule dysfunction known as Fanconi syndrome. Multiple myeloma is consistent with this patient's anemia; mildly elevated serum creatinine level; and significant proteinuria despite only trace protein detected on dipstick urinalysis, which suggests the excretion of a cationic protein compatible with the immunoglobulin secretion associated with multiple myeloma. RTA is characterized by a normal anion gap metabolic acidosis, hypokalemia, and an intact ability to lower the urine pH.

Diabetic nephropathy may account for this patient's glycosuria and proteinuria but would not explain his normal anion gap acidosis and hypokalemia or the discrepancy between the urine dipstick protein level and the urine protein-creatinine ratio. Furthermore, diabetic nephropathy is typically associated with a type 4 RTA due to hyporeninemic hypoaldosteronism and hyperkalemia.

Hypokalemia and normal anion gap acidosis are consistent with hypokalemic distal RTA, which commonly is associated with nephrocalcinosis. This condition manifests as a persistently alkaline urine pH, whereas the urine pH in patients with proximal RTA is initially alkaline but may acidify once the serum bicarbonate level decreases. Hypokalemic distal RTA also is usually associated with a significantly decreased serum bicarbonate level and severe muscle weakness and would not explain this patient's glycosuria or proteinuria.

Hypertensive nephrosclerosis is a common cause of chronic kidney disease and typically develops in patients with a long-standing history of hypertension and slowly progressive chronic kidney disease. Hypertensive nephrosclerosis would not explain this patient's normal anion gap acidosis, hypokalemia, or significant proteinuria.

KEY POINT

- Proximal (type 2) renal tubular acidosis secondary to multiple myeloma is characterized by a normal anion gap metabolic acidosis, hypokalemia, and an intact ability to lower the urine pH.

Bibliography

Batuman V. Proximal tubular injury in myeloma. Contrib Nephrol. 2007;153:87-104. [PMID: 17075225]

Item 12   Answer: A
Educational Objective: Diagnose complex kidney cysts in a patient with end-stage kidney disease.

Abdominal CT with iodinated contrast is the imaging test of choice for further characterizing complex kidney cysts or mass lesions in patients with end-stage kidney disease (ESKD) requiring dialysis therapy. Iodinated contrast–enhanced imaging studies are more likely to reveal a malignancy compared with studies that do not use iodinated contrast.

Kidney biopsy is indicated to help diagnose glomerular diseases or unexplained kidney dysfunction but places patients with renal cell carcinoma at significant risk for bleeding and possible tumor spread. Therefore, this study typically is not recommended for the diagnosis of this condition. In addition, biopsy is contraindicated in patients with ESKD who also have an increased risk for bleeding because of a platelet dysfunction.

In patients with kidney disease, use of MRI with gadolinium-containing contrast agents may be a significant risk factor for nephrogenic systemic fibrosis (NSF), a recently recognized condition that manifests as thickening and woody edema of the skin primarily involving the hands and feet. Patients with an estimated glomerular filtration rate of less than 40 mL/min/1.73 m^2 are believed to be at the greatest risk for developing NSF after administration of gadolinium, and use of this agent should be avoided in this population group.

Repeat ultrasonography in 6 months would not be recommended in patients with ESKD, who have an increased risk for renal cell carcinoma. Furthermore, this patient is actively being evaluated for kidney transplantation, and prompt diagnosis of a malignant neoplasm would prevent his ability to undergo transplantation at this time.

KEY POINT

- Abdominal CT with iodinated contrast is the imaging test of choice for further characterizing complex kidney cysts or mass lesions in patients with end-stage kidney disease requiring dialysis therapy.

Bibliography

Deo A, Fogel M, Cowper SE. Nephrogenic systemic fibrosis: A population study examining the relationship of disease development to gadolinium exposure. Clin J Am Soc Nephrol. 2007;2(2):264-267. [PMID: 17699423]

Item 13   Answer: C
Educational Objective: Diagnose secondary hypertension due to polycystic kidney disease.

This patient's significant hypertension, normal kidney function, microalbuminuria, and family history of kidney disease and hypertension are consistent with autosomal-dominant polycystic kidney disease (ADPKD). Her mild fullness and tenderness of the abdomen and history of upper urinary tract infections are further suggestive of this condition. ADPKD is also associated with cerebral aneurysms, hepatic cysts, mitral and aortic valve prolapse, colonic diverticular disease, pancreatic cysts, and thoracic and abdominal aortic aneurysms. The presence of at least two cysts in each kidney visualized on kidney ultrasonography in a patient with a family history of polycystic kidney disease would confirm the diagnosis of this condition.

Renal artery stenosis caused by fibromuscular dysplasia of the renal artery may cause hypertension in a young woman. The gold standard for diagnosing renal artery stenosis is kidney angiography, but this patient's clinical presentation is more compatible with ADPKD.

Kidney biopsy is indicated for patients with kidney disease when less invasive diagnostic studies cannot determine a diagnosis and a pathologic evaluation would be helpful. Kidney biopsy is commonly performed in adults with the nephrotic syndrome or glomerulonephritis with no obvious postinfectious glomerular disease and all patients with acute kidney injury of unclear cause. This patient does not fulfill any of these indications for a kidney biopsy.

A plasma aldosterone-plasma renin activity ratio would help to diagnose primary aldosteronism. However, this condition is unlikely in a patient with normal serum electrolyte levels. Primary aldosteronism also would not explain this patient's abdominal examination findings, microalbuminuria, or hematuria and is not compatible with this patient's family history.

KEY POINT

- The diagnosis of polycystic kidney disease can be confirmed by the presence of at least two cysts in each kidney on kidney ultrasonography in a patient with a family history of this condition.

Bibliography

Chapman AB. Approaches to testing new treatments in autosomal dominant polycystic kidney disease: insights from the CRISP and HALT-PKD studies. Clin J Am Soc Nephrol. 2008;3(4):1197-1204. [PMID: 18579674]

Item 14　　Answer:　B

Educational Objective: Manage a patient with polycystic kidney disease with risk factors for intracranial aneurysm.

The most appropriate next step in this patient's management is to schedule magnetic resonance angiography of the cerebral arteries. Intracranial aneurysm occurs in 5% of patients with autosomal-dominant polycystic kidney disease (ADPKD). The most important risk factor for intracranial aneurysm in patients with ADPKD is a family member with an intracranial aneurysm. The risk for developing an aneurysm in this setting increases to 20% in patients with a family member who has had a ruptured aneurysm and is highest in those with a first-degree relative who has had a ruptured aneurysm. All patients with a family history of intracranial aneurysm, particularly ruptured aneurysm, should undergo screening for an intracranial aneurysm.

Experts also recommend screening for intracranial aneurysm for patients with ADPKD who work in professions associated with an increased risk for rupture (such as scuba divers, weightlifters, and those who engage in the Valsalva maneuver) or where others would be at risk in the event of a rupture (such as airline pilots). This screening is recommended even in the absence of a family history of a ruptured cerebral aneurysm.

Either contrast-enhanced magnetic resonance or CT angiography is adequate to identify most aneurysms that are 3 mm or larger and is considered the initial screening test of choice for an intracranial aneurysm. Depending on vessel visualization, further imaging may be needed.

KEY POINT

- **The most important risk factor for intracranial aneurysm in patients with autosomal-dominant polycystic kidney disease is a family member with an intracranial aneurysm.**

Bibliography

Ring T, Spiegelhalter D. Risk of intracranial aneurysm bleeding in autosomal-dominant polycystic kidney disease. Kidney Int. 2007; 72(11):1400-1402. [PMID: 17882153]

Item 15　　Answer:　D

Educational Objective: Diagnose minimal change disease secondary to Hodgkin lymphoma.

This patient has minimal change disease secondary to Hodgkin lymphoma. Minimal change disease is a relapsing-remitting condition that may occur secondary to NSAID or lithium use, mononucleosis, or malignancy and may be the presenting symptom of Hodgkin lymphoma. Minimal change disease is characterized by sudden, massive proteinuria associated with a urine protein-creatinine ratio that may exceed 9 mg/mg. This condition also may cause mildly elevated blood pressure, hypoalbuminemia, and anasarca.

Proteinuria that develops after remission of Hodgkin lymphoma often indicates disease relapse. Therefore, close monitoring of the protein-creatinine ratio is indicated once remission is achieved to evaluate whether additional therapy is needed after chemotherapy and radiation therapy are completed.

In patients with solid tumors, the nephrotic syndrome is usually associated with membranous glomerular nephropathy; however, minimal change disease predominates in those with hematologic malignancies, particularly Hodgkin lymphoma.

Focal segmental glomerulosclerosis is the least frequently reported cause of the nephrotic syndrome in patients with hematologic malignancies and most often develops after transplantation or intense chemotherapy.

IgA nephropathy is not commonly associated with lymphoma or myeloproliferative disorders.

KEY POINT

- **Minimal change disease may be the presenting symptom of Hodgkin lymphoma and is characterized by sudden, massive proteinuria.**

Bibliography

Mallouk A, Pham PT, Pham PC. Concurrent FSGS and Hodgkin's lymphomas: case report and literature review on the link between nephrotic glomerulopathies and hematological malignancies. Clin Exp Nephrol. 2006;10(4):284-289. [PMID: 17186334]

Item 16　　Answer:　B

Educational Objective: Diagnose chronic kidney disease in a pregnant patient.

This patient most likely has chronic kidney disease. This condition is the most likely diagnosis in patients with elevated serum creatinine levels and proteinuria early in pregnancy. This patient's elevated blood pressure also is suggestive of chronic kidney disease.

Proteinuria and an elevated serum creatinine level indicate the presence of kidney disease, which is not consistent with chronic essential hypertension. Proteinuria also is unlikely in a young patient with essential hypertension.

Gestational hypertension is characterized by normal blood pressure measurements in early pregnancy and hypertension that develops during the latter part of pregnancy. Unlike preeclampsia, this condition is not associated with proteinuria, elevated serum creatinine levels, or hyperuricemia. Hypertension that presents in patients who are pregnant for less than 20 weeks is most likely caused by a chronic condition that preceded pregnancy.

Hypertension, an elevated serum creatinine level, and proteinuria are not normal physiologic changes during pregnancy. Pregnancy is characterized by marked vasodilatation that is detectable in the first trimester and causes a lower blood pressure and higher pulse rate. Throughout gestation, blood pressure and renal vascular resistance are decreased, the renal plasma flow and glomerular filtration rate are increased, and creatinine production remains unchanged.

Preeclampsia would not develop before 20 weeks of pregnancy in the absence of a molar pregnancy.

KEY POINT

- Chronic kidney disease is the most likely diagnosis in patients with elevated serum creatinine levels and proteinuria early in pregnancy.

Bibliography

Frishman WH, Veresh M, Schlocker SJ, Tejani N. Pathophysiology and medical management of systemic hypertension in preeclampsia. Curr Hypertens Rep. 2006;8(6):502-511. [PMID: 17087860]

Item 17   Answer: D

Educational Objective: Evaluate hypertension in a patient using an oral contraceptive and an NSAID.

NSAIDs such as ibuprofen can cause significant hypertension in some individuals, and this agent is the most likely cause of this patient's condition. Therefore, the most appropriate next step in this patient's management is to discontinue ibuprofen. Some women may develop high blood pressure when using oral contraceptives, but the incidence of hypertension attributable to these agents has decreased since the dosage of ethinyl estradiol has been lowered. Furthermore, this patient has been normotensive despite using an oral contraceptive for the past 5 years, which makes this medication an unlikely cause of her hypertension.

Urgent antihypertensive therapy is warranted in patients with a hypertensive emergency such as hypertensive encephalopathy (which manifests as focal neurologic signs and altered mental status), heart failure, acute coronary syndrome, or a cerebrovascular accident. However, this patient's clinical presentation is not consistent with these conditions, and urgent treatment of her blood pressure is not needed.

KEY POINT

- Oral contraceptives and NSAIDs can cause hypertension.

Bibliography

Ashraf MS, Vongpatanasin W. Estrogen and hypertension. Curr Hypertens Rep. 2006;8(5):368-376. [PMID: 16965722]

Item 18   Answer: C

Educational Objective: Diagnose immune complex–mediated glomerular nephritis in a patient with HIV infection.

Patients with HIV infection are at risk for numerous kidney-related diseases that often manifest as glomerular hematuria, proteinuria, and an elevated serum creatinine level. This patient's increased serum creatinine level accompanied by hypocomplementemia and dysmorphic erythrocytes and erythrocyte casts seen on urinalysis is most consistent with immune complex–mediated glomerular nephritis. Syphilis and hepatitis C virus infection also may be associated with this condition.

Acute interstitial nephritis may be associated with cytomegalovirus infection or use of trimethoprim-sulfamethoxazole. However, this condition is usually associated with leukocyte casts seen on urinalysis and may be accompanied by fever, rash, or eosinophilia.

HIV nephropathy is a form of collapsing focal segmental glomerulosclerosis (FSGS) that is found in 60% of kidney biopsies in patients with HIV infection and kidney disease. This condition typically develops in black patients with high HIV RNA viral loads and manifests as the nephrotic syndrome with normal serum complement levels and fatty casts and oval fat bodies in the urine sediment. This patient's hypocomplementemia and urinalysis findings are more consistent with immune complex–mediated glomerular nephritis than with collapsing FSGS.

Rhabdomyolysis and pigment nephropathy may occur in association with HIV infection. In this setting, the urine dipstick indicator for blood would be falsely positive because of the presence of myoglobin. The absence of pigmented or muddy brown casts on urinalysis also argues against a diagnosis of pigment nephropathy.

KEY POINT

- Immune complex–mediated glomerular nephritis is characterized by hypocomplementemia and dysmorphic erythrocytes and erythrocyte casts seen on urinalysis.

Bibliography

Titan SM, Testagrossa L, Saldanha LB, Barros RT, Woronik V. HIV infection and acute glomerulonephritis. Clinics (Sao Paulo). 2007;62(5):653-656. [PMID: 17952332]

Item 19   Answer: A

Educational Objective: Diagnose adynamic bone disease in a patient with chronic kidney disease.

This patient most likely has adynamic bone disease caused by progressive changes in mineral and bone metabolism associated with chronic kidney disease (CKD). This patient's osteopenia, fracture, and bone pain accompanied by a serum parathyroid hormone level below 100 pg/mL (100 ng/L) and a normal alkaline phosphatase level are consistent with this condition. Adynamic bone disease is a leading cause of bone disorders in patients with stage 5 CKD. Risk factors for this condition include advanced age, diabetes mellitus, poor nutrition, and oversuppression of parathyroid hormone with therapeutic agents.

This patient's 1,25-dihydroxyvitamin D level above 30 pg/mL (72 pmol/L) is consistent with repletion of vitamin D stores with calcitriol. The relatively low 25-hydroxyvitamin D level may be caused by reduced cutaneous synthesis and decreased dietary intake. Decreased hepatic 25-hydroxylation also may occur in patients with CKD.

Patients with CKD may develop β_2-microglobulin–associated amyloidosis, osteitis fibrosa cystica, and osteomalacia. Bone disease in patients with β_2-microglobulin–associated amyloidosis is characterized by cystic bone lesions at the end of long bones that can enlarge over time, resulting in pathologic fractures. This patient's radiographs do not reveal these lesions.

Osteitis fibrosa cystica manifests as hyperphosphatemia, hypocalcemia, and 1,25-dihydroxyvitamin D deficiency, which stimulate parathyroid hormone secretion and lead to increased bone turnover. Affected patients usually have radiographic evidence of sclerosis and subperiosteal bone resorption as well as elevated serum parathyroid hormone and alkaline phosphatase levels.

Osteomalacia is relatively uncommon and usually develops after exposure to aluminum-containing phosphate binders. Patients with osteomalacic renal osteodystrophy also usually have elevated serum parathyroid hormone levels.

KEY POINT

- **Adynamic bone disease is a major cause of bone disease in patients with stage 5 chronic kidney disease and usually manifests as osteopenia, fractures, and bone pain accompanied by a serum parathyroid hormone level below 100 pg/mL (100 ng/L) and a normal alkaline phosphatase level.**

Bibliography
National Kidney Foundation. K/DOQI clinical practice guidelines for bone metabolism and disease in chronic kidney disease. Am J Kidney Dis. 2003;42(4 Suppl 3):S12–S28. [PMID: 14520607]

Item 20   Answer: A

Educational Objective: Treat membranous nephropathy.

This patient has membranous nephropathy, and lisinopril is the most appropriate treatment. Membranous nephropathy is a common cause of the nephrotic syndrome, which may manifest as edema, nephrotic-range proteinuria, and hyperlipidemia. Membranous nephropathy is characterized by subepithelial deposition of immune complexes on electron microscopy of a kidney biopsy specimen.

This patient's normal kidney function and urine protein-creatinine ratio between 4 and 8 mg/mg place him at medium risk for disease progression; however, aggressive therapy is still warranted to reduce the rate of progression. In this population group, dietary protein restriction should be initiated, and an angiotensin-converting enzyme inhibitor or angiotensin receptor blocker should be used to control blood pressure and reduce proteinuria to at least 60% of the baseline excretion with an ideal protein-creatinine ratio between 0.5

and 1.0 mg/mg. A statin agent also is indicated to help manage this patient's hyperlipidemia.

The clinical outcome of membranous nephropathy may improve without immunosuppressive therapy. Therefore, supportive therapy can be tried for 6 months even in medium-risk patients. In this population group, immunosuppressive treatment would be warranted only if the proteinuria persists or the clinical presentation deteriorates after this time.

Plasmapheresis is considered standard therapy for anti–glomerular basement membrane antibody disease (Goodpasture syndrome). This intervention also helps manage acute kidney injury due to multiple myeloma, rapidly progressive glomerulonephritis, and cryoglobulinemia. However, plasmapheresis is not indicated for patients with membranous nephropathy.

KEY POINT

- **Dietary protein restriction and an angiotensin-converting enzyme inhibitor or angiotensin receptor blocker can be tried for 6 months in patients with membranous nephropathy who have a urine protein-creatinine ratio of 4 to 8 mg/mg and normal kidney function.**

Bibliography
Lai KN. Membranous nephropathy: when and how to treat. Kidney Int. 2007;71(9):841-843. [PMID: 17457329]

Item 21   Answer: B

Educational Objective: Diagnose analgesic nephropathy.

This patient most likely has analgesic nephropathy, and discontinuation of analgesics is indicated. Analgesic nephropathy manifests as chronic tubulointerstitial nephritis characterized by a slow, progressive increase in the serum creatinine level; a bland urine sediment; non–nephrotic-range proteinuria; and sterile pyuria. Discontinuation of the inciting agent(s) in patients with analgesic nephropathy has been shown to stabilize kidney function but does not reverse damage.

Use of combination analgesics such as acetaminophen and aspirin with caffeine or codeine may increase the risk of analgesic nephropathy. Additional risk factors include use of more than 0.3 kg of analgesics yearly and prolonged use of these agents.

Previously, the presence of small, indented, calcified kidneys (SICK) on non–radiocontrast-enhanced abdominal CT was believed to be sensitive for the diagnosis of chronic tubulointerstitial disease associated with analgesic use. However, results from the National Analgesic Nephropathy Study published in 2003 showed that these findings had a sensitivity of only 5% to 26% for this condition. Non–radiocontrast-enhanced abdominal CT is therefore no longer indicated in the evaluation of patients whose clinical presentation is suspicious for analgesic nephropathy.

Kidney biopsy would be indicated to evaluate a patient with unexplained acute kidney injury, the nephrotic syndrome, or suspected glomerulonephritis. However, kidney biopsy results rarely alter the disease outcome in patients with suspected chronic tubulointerstitial disease because specific therapy is lacking for chronic tubulointerstitial diseases other than sarcoidosis and multiple myeloma.

Serum protein electrophoresis would be warranted to screen for multiple myeloma in patients older than 50 years of age and in those who have anemia out of proportion to the degree of kidney failure. However, this patient is younger than 50 years of age, and her low serum ferritin level and transferrin saturation suggest that her anemia is caused by chronic NSAID-induced gastrointestinal hemorrhage. Furthermore, multiple myeloma is usually associated with hypercalcemia.

KEY POINT

- **Discontinuation of the inciting agent(s) in patients with analgesic nephropathy has been shown to stabilize kidney function but does not reverse damage.**

Bibliography

Henrich W, Clark R, Kelly J, et al. Non–contrast-enhanced computerized tomography and analgesic-related kidney disease: report of the National Analgesic Nephropathy Study. J Am Soc Nephrol. 2006;17(5):1472-1480. [PMID: 16611714]

Item 22   Answer: A

Educational Objective: **Manage hypertension in a patient with risk factors for diabetes mellitus.**

This patient has stage 2 hypertension (systolic blood pressure ≥160 mm Hg or diastolic blood pressure ≥100 mm Hg), and both lifestyle modifications and antihypertensive therapy are indicated. The Seventh Report of the Joint National Committee on Prevention, Detection, Evaluation and Treatment of High Blood Pressure (JNC 7) guidelines recommend initiating treatment with two medications in patients with stage 2 hypertension or those whose blood pressure is greater than 20 mm Hg systolic or 10 mm Hg diastolic above target. Low-dose hydrochlorothiazide and an angiotensin-converting enzyme (ACE) inhibitor would be reasonable in this patient to ensure adequate blood pressure control. Careful follow-up and monitoring for signs of impaired fasting glucose or glucose intolerance also are recommended.

A recent study in older patients with preexisting heart disease and/or diabetes mellitus demonstrated favorable outcomes with a combination of an ACE inhibitor and calcium channel blocker. This strategy also would be acceptable, especially in patients with an elevated fasting glucose or hemoglobin A_{1c} level.

Lifestyle modifications alone or monotherapy with terazosin would not be appropriate in a patient with stage 2 hypertension. Combination therapy with metoprolol and hydrochlorothiazide may pose an increased risk of worsening insulin resistance in a patient who already has several risk factors for type 2 diabetes mellitus, including obesity and a family history of diabetes. Generally, renin-angiotensin system inhibitors are associated with a lower incidence of diabetes compared with diuretics and β-blockers.

KEY POINT

- **Generally, angiotensin-converting enzyme inhibitors and angiotensin receptor blockers are associated with a lower incidence of new-onset diabetes mellitus compared with diuretics and β-blockers.**

Bibliography

Elliott WJ, PM Meyer. Incident diabetes in clinical trials of antihypertensive drugs: a network meta-analysis [erratum in: Lancet. 2007; 369(9572):1518]. Lancet. 2007;369(9557):201-207. [PMID: 17240286]

Item 23   Answer: B

Educational Objective: **Diagnose the nephrotic syndrome.**

This patient's facial and lower-extremity edema, hypertension, hypoalbuminemia, and proteinuria associated with a urine protein-creatinine ratio above 3 mg/mg are suggestive of the nephrotic syndrome. Additional manifestations of the nephrotic syndrome include hypercholesterolemia and hypocalcemia.

In patients with a glomerular injury, kidney biopsy frequently is needed to determine the diagnosis, indicate the cause, predict the natural history and prognosis of the injury, and guide treatment. Kidney biopsy is the study of choice in adults when the nephrotic syndrome is suspected and can differentiate among the causes of this condition, which include focal segmental glomerulosclerosis, membranous glomerulopathy, minimal change disease, and amyloidosis.

The presence of ANCAs would help to confirm the underlying cause of this patient's glomerular disease. However, in this patient, these findings alone would not establish the cause of the nephrotic syndrome because these results may be falsely positive and may not correlate with the disease process ongoing in the kidneys.

Kidney ultrasonography would evaluate kidney size and echogenicity and identify obstruction, mass lesions, or stones. This study is recommended for all patients with kidney disease but is unlikely to contribute to the diagnosis of the nephrotic syndrome in this patient.

Urine eosinophils typically are associated with inflammatory states in the kidney such as acute interstitial nephritis and vasculitis. In this patient, NSAID use may cause acute interstitial nephritis that manifests as pyuria, hematuria, and eosinophiluria; however, this clinical presentation would be unlikely in a patient using ibuprofen for a short amount of time. NSAIDs also may cause membranous nephropathy or minimal change disease associated with the nephrotic syndrome, but diagnosis of these conditions would require kidney biopsy.

KEY POINT

- Kidney biopsy is the study of choice in adults when the nephrotic syndrome is suspected and helps to differentiate among the causes of this condition.

Bibliography

Fuiano G, Mazza G, Comi N, et al. Current indications for renal biopsy: A questionnaire based survey. Amer J Kidney Dis. 2000; 35(3):448-457. [PMID: 10692270]

Item 24   Answer: C

Educational Objective: Manage recurrent uric acid nephrolithiasis.

The most appropriate next step in management is potassium citrate. This patient has a history of gout, recurrent uric acid stones, and an acidic urine. Consumption of more than 2 L of fluid daily and restriction of sodium intake are recommended for all patients with a history of nephrolithiasis, and targeted therapy is recommended for patients with a metabolic abnormality that favors stone formation. Because the solubility of uric acid increases in alkaline urine, use of potassium citrate to obtain a urine pH above 6.0 would decrease this patient's risk for recurrent uric acid stones.

Most experts only use allopurinol to reduce urine uric acid excretion in patients with hyperuricosuria in whom alkalinization is difficult, poorly tolerated, or not completely effective. In addition, reducing urine uric acid excretion with allopurinol would be relatively ineffective in patients with a low pH. Furthermore, this patient has borderline hyperuricemia and infrequent gouty attacks and may not need prophylactic allopurinol, which is typically used in patients with one to two acute gouty attacks per year.

Thiazide diuretics reduce urine calcium by stimulating kidney calcium absorption and may help to prevent recurrent calcium-containing stones, but mild volume depletion and decreased uric acid secretion associated with use of these agents may cause hyperuricemia. Thiazide diuretics also may increase the frequency of gouty attacks and are therefore not indicated in this patient.

Probenecid prevents proximal tubular reabsorption of uric acid, which may lead to hyperuricosuria and recurrent uric acid stone formation. Therefore, this agent is contraindicated in patients with a history of uric acid stones.

KEY POINT

- Alkalinization of the urine with potassium citrate therapy to obtain a urine pH above 6.0 decreases the risk of recurrent uric acid stones.

Bibliography

Goldfarb DS. In the clinic. Nephrolithiasis. Ann Intern Med. 2009;151:ITC2. [PMID: 19652185]

Item 25   Answer: B

Educational Objective: Diagnose cerebral salt wasting.

Cerebral salt wasting (CSW) is a rare cause of hyponatremia. This condition typically occurs within a few days of a neurosurgical procedure or subarachnoid hemorrhage and is characterized by kidney salt wasting, hyponatremia, and hypotension. Laboratory findings may include a serum sodium level less than 135 meq/L (135 mmol/L), low or low-normal plasma osmolality, elevated urine osmolality, and an elevated spot urine sodium level relative to the hyponatremia. CSW is distinguished from the syndrome of inappropriate antidiuretic hormone secretion (SIADH) by the presence of hypotension, which reflects the decreased intravascular volume associated with kidney salt wasting. The treatment of CSW is intravenous normal saline.

This patient's kidney salt wasting and volume depletion are consistent with adrenal insufficiency. However, this patient has no predisposing factors for hypoadrenalism, such as discontinuation of long-term corticosteroid therapy, sepsis, or autoimmune disease. Furthermore, hyperkalemia and a mild, non–anion gap metabolic acidosis are found in over 60% of patients with adrenal insufficiency but are absent in this patient.

Hypothyroidism can lead to hyponatremia but would not explain this patient's volume-depleted state. Furthermore, thyroid hormone deficiency leads to increased central release of antidiuretic hormone, and hypothyroidism-associated hyponatremia usually resembles SIADH and not CSW.

Patients with SIADH are euvolemic or slightly volume expanded, which is not consistent with this patient's presentation. In addition, patients with SIADH usually have extremely decreased serum uric acid levels, because volume expansion in this setting causes decreased uric acid absorption in the proximal nephron.

KEY POINT

- Cerebral salt wasting may affect patients undergoing neurosurgery, particularly those with subarachnoid hemorrhage, and manifests as hyponatremia, increased urine sodium excretion, concentrated urine, and evidence of hypovolemia.

Bibliography

Palmer BF. Hyponatremia in patients with central nervous system disease: SIADH or CSW. Trends Endocrinol Metab. 2003;14(4):182-187. [PMID: 12714279]

Item 26   Answer: C

Educational Objective: Diagnose primary aldosteronism.

This patient most likely has primary aldosteronism, which most commonly manifests as hypertension. Primary aldosteronism frequently causes stage 2 hypertension (systolic blood pressure ≥160 mm Hg or diastolic blood pressure ≥100 mm Hg) that is resistant to numerous antihypertensive agents, particularly those that primarily function as inhibitors of the renin-angiotensin system. Other manifestations of mineralocorticoid excess include hypernatremia (serum sodium level typically between 143 and 147 meq/L [143-147 mmol/L]) and mild metabolic alkalosis. This condition also may cause unprovoked hypokalemia, and this patient's low serum potassium level despite ramipril therapy is consistent with primary aldosteronism.

The severity of this patient's hypertension and her young age of onset of this condition are unusual for essential hypertension and are more consistent with secondary hypertension. In addition, essential hypertension is not associated with hypokalemia and metabolic alkalosis.

Patients with pheochromocytoma may have stage 2 hypertension but are usually slightly volume depleted and have normal or elevated plasma renin activity. Orthostatic hypotension caused by hypovolemia and impaired vasoconstrictive responses occurs in 40% of patients. Patients also may have tremor, anxiety, and pallor; however, flushing is uncommon. Hypokalemia and metabolic alkalosis are not associated with pheochromocytoma.

The onset of severe hypertension at a young age is suggestive of renovascular hypertension due to fibromuscular dysplasia. However, the plasma renin activity in patients with this condition is usually elevated. Furthermore, patients with renal artery stenosis treated with an angiotensin-converting enzyme inhibitor such as ramipril often experience an increase in the serum creatinine level without a clinically significant reduction in blood pressure.

KEY POINT

- **Manifestations of primary aldosteronism include hypernatremia, hypokalemia, mild metabolic alkalosis, suppressed plasma renin activity, and stage 2 hypertension.**

Bibliography

Funder JW, Carey RM, Fardella C, et al; Endocrine Society. Case detection, diagnosis, and treatment of patients with primary aldosteronism: an endocrine society clinical practice guideline. J Clin Endocrinol Metab. 2008;93(9):3266-3281. [PMID: 18552288]

Item 27   Answer: C

Educational Objective: Manage a patient with IgA nephropathy at risk for progression to kidney failure.

This patient most likely has IgA nephropathy, and the most appropriate next step is pulse methylprednisolone. This condition is a consequence of defective mucosal immunity in which IgA molecules react to as-yet unidentified antigens. Once deposited in the glomeruli, these immune complexes incite an inflammatory response. On kidney biopsy, IgA is the dominant type of immunoglobulin observed by immunofluorescence microscopy.

IgA nephropathy may manifest as gross hematuria usually associated with a pharyngitic or gastrointestinal infection; persistent asymptomatic microscopic hematuria and proteinuria; or the nephrotic syndrome. Approximately 5% to 10% of affected patients present with rapidly progressive glomerulonephritis caused by diffuse proliferative glomerulonephritis or, rarely, a concomitant unrelated glomerulopathy.

Although IgA nephropathy usually is a benign condition, approximately 15% of patients develop end-stage kidney disease within 10 years of diagnosis. This patient also has several poor prognostic factors for this condition, which include male sex, urine protein excretion greater than 1 mg/mg, hypoalbuminemia, hypertension, and histologic evidence of diffuse disease with interstitial fibrosis.

Because proteinuria is a significant risk factor for the progression of kidney disease, use of an angiotensin-converting enzyme inhibitor and/or an angiotensin receptor blocker is indicated to decrease urine protein excretion in patients with IgA nephropathy. Use of an immunosuppressive agent is warranted to further decrease proteinuria and slow the progression of kidney insufficiency in patients with aggressive IgA nephropathy and poor prognostic factors who do not yet have a significant loss of kidney function.

Azathioprine and cyclophosphamide have demonstrated efficacy in small numbers of patients with IgA nephropathy but have not yet definitively been proved to be beneficial.

Controlled trials evaluating the role of mycophenolate mofetil in the treatment of IgA nephropathy have yielded conflicting results. Sufficient evidence for the use of this agent in patients with this condition is lacking.

KEY POINT

- **In addition to therapy to inhibit the renin-angiotensin system, immunosuppressive therapy is indicated in patients with IgA nephropathy at risk for progression to kidney failure who do not yet have significant loss of kidney function.**

Bibliography

Donadio JV, Grande JP. IgA nephropathy. N Engl J Med. 2002; 347(10):738-748. [PMID: 12213946]

Item 28   Answer: D

Educational Objective: Manage new-onset microalbuminuria in a patient with type 1 diabetes mellitus.

Annual measurement of the urine albumin excretion is indicated for patients with type 1 diabetes mellitus. However, because this patient's albumin excretion was abnormal, repeat testing in less than 1 year is warranted in order to determine whether his proteinuria is transient or persistent. Fever and exercise can cause a transient increase in protein excretion, and this patient's participation in a marathon 2 days ago may explain his proteinuria. Repeat urinalyses should be performed twice within the next 6 months, and the presence of microalbuminuria (defined as a urine albumin-creatinine ratio between 30 and 300 mg/g) would be confirmed if two of the three urine samples are positive. Therefore, in this patient, repeat urinalysis in 2 weeks is reasonable.

Kidney biopsy is not indicated unless the presence of proteinuria has been established.

Microalbuminuria is the first detectable manifestation of diabetic nephropathy and typically occurs 5 to 15 years after the diagnosis of type 1 diabetes mellitus, but a diagnosis of microalbuminuria has not yet been confirmed in this patient. Diabetic nephropathy also is typically associated with hypertension and diabetic retinopathy, which are absent in this patient. Treatment for diabetic nephropathy with an angiotensin-converting enzyme inhibitor or an angiotensin receptor blocker is not appropriate at this time.

KEY POINT

- **Because factors such as fever and exercise can cause a transient increase in protein excretion, patients with type 1 diabetes mellitus who have abnormal findings on annual measurement of the urine albumin excretion should undergo repeat urinalyses twice within the next 6 months; positive findings on two of the three urine samples would confirm a diagnosis of microalbuminuria (defined as a urine albumin-creatinine ratio between 30 and 300 mg/g).**

Bibliography

Smellie WS, Forth J, Bareford D, et al. Best practice in primary care pathology: review 3 [erratum in: J Clin Pathol. 2006;59(10):1116]. J Clin Pathol. 2006;59(8):781-789. [PMID: 16873560]

Item 29   Answer: D

Educational Objective: Diagnose salicylate toxicity.

This patient most likely has salicylate toxicity, which is characterized by the presence of an anion gap metabolic acidosis and respiratory alkalosis. An anion gap metabolic acidosis is indicated by this patient's low serum bicarbonate level and anion gap of 20. This patient's predicted P_{CO_2} is 29 ± 2 mm Hg, which can be calculated using Winter's formula:

$$\text{Expected } P_{CO_2} = 1.5 \times [\text{Bicarbonate}] + 8 \pm 2 \text{ mm Hg}$$

The measured P_{CO_2} of 20 mm Hg is lower than expected for the degree of metabolic acidosis present, which confirms the presence of a concurrent respiratory alkalosis. A common cause of mixed anion gap metabolic acidosis and respiratory alkalosis is salicylate toxicity, which can be diagnosed by measuring the serum salicylate level. Increased ketogenesis is another feature of salicylate overdose.

Alcoholic ketoacidosis, ethylene glycol toxicity, and methanol toxicity can cause anion gap metabolic acidosis but not respiratory alkalosis. In addition, alcohol poisoning would be accompanied by an increased osmolal gap. The osmolal gap is obtained by calculating the difference between the calculated and measured plasma osmolality. This patient's calculated plasma osmolality of 295 mosm/kg H_2O (295 mmol/kg H_2O) can be obtained using the following formula:

Plasma Osmolality (mosm/kg H_2O) = 2 × [Serum Sodium] + [Blood Urea Nitrogen]/2.8 + [Plasma Glucose]/18

The measured osmolality is 290 mosm/kg H_2O (290 mmol/kg H_2O). The osmolal gap is therefore 5 mosm/kg H_2O (5 mmol/kg H_2O) (normal <10 mosm/kg H_2O [<10 mmol/kg H_2O]), which excludes alcohol poisoning.

KEY POINT

- **Salicylate toxicity is a common cause of mixed anion gap metabolic acidosis and respiratory alkalosis.**

Bibliography

Kamel KS, Halperin ML. An improved approach to the patient with metabolic acidosis: a need for four amendments. J Nephrol. 2006;9(19 Suppl 9):S76-85. [PMID: 16736445]

Item 30   Answer: C

Educational Objective: Evaluate kidney function in a healthy adult.

The most appropriate next step is to repeat the timed urine collection for creatinine clearance. Over- or undercollection of a sample obtained for 24-hour urine collection may result in an inaccurate estimated glomerular filtration rate (eGFR), but the accuracy of this study can be assessed by comparing the total urine creatinine excretion with the expected value of creatinine excretion (20 to 25 mg/kg/24 h (20 to 25 mg/kg/d) in men, 15 to 20 mg/kg/24 h in women (15 to 20 mg/kg/d). In this patient, who weighs 61 kg, the complete 24-hour urine collection should yield a total creatinine excretion between 915 and 1220 mg/24 h (915 and 1220 mg/d); her reported total creatinine excretion of 475 mg/24 h (475 mg/d) indicates that the sample was undercollected and that her creatinine clearance of 26 mL/min is inappropriately low. Repeat 24-hour urine collection is indicated before deciding whether this patient is an appropriate donor.

Rejection of this patient as a kidney donor would be premature without repeating the timed urine collection and creatinine clearance measurement.

Cystatin C measurement has been shown to be more effective than serum creatinine measurement as a marker for estimating the GFR in some populations, such as the elderly, patients with reduced muscle mass, or patients with cancer. However, this study is not widely available, and there is no evidence that estimating kidney function using cystatin C measurements results in better outcomes compared with measuring creatinine clearance using a timed urine collection.

Use of mathematical formulas for estimating the glomerular filtration rate should be limited to patients with stages 3 to 5 chronic kidney disease or those with an eGFR of 59 mL/min/1.73 m^2 or less. In healthy persons, these formulas have been shown to underestimate the eGFR compared with radionuclide kidney scanning using iothalamate, which is the gold standard for estimating the GFR in this population group; however, the cost and limited availability of iothalamate preclude the routine use of this study. Timed urine collection, including an estimation of the creatinine clearance and quantification of proteinuria, is therefore often used as an alternative to kidney scanning.

KEY POINT

- **The accuracy of timed urine collection can be assessed by comparing the total urine creatinine excretion with the expected value of creatinine excretion.**

Bibliography

Kasiske B, Ravenscraft M, Ramos E, Gaston R, Bia M, Danovitch G. The evaluation of living renal transplant donors: clinical practice guidelines. Ad Hoc Clinical Practice Guidelines Subcommittee of the Patient Care and Education Committee of the American Society of Transplant Physicians. J Am Soc Neph. 1996;7(11):2288-2313. [PMID: 8959619]

Item 31   Answer: C

Educational Objective: Diagnose renovascular hypertension due to fibromuscular dysplasia.

This patient's stage 2 hypertension (systolic blood pressure ≥160 mm Hg and diastolic blood pressure ≥100 mm Hg), evidence of target organ damage (funduscopic changes and enlarged heart), and abdominal bruit are strongly suggestive of secondary hypertension caused by renovascular disease. Her mild hypokalemic metabolic alkalosis and elevated plasma renin activity also are consistent with this condition. Renovascular hypertension is defined as hypertension caused by narrowing of one or more of the renal arteries. In this setting, underperfusion and ischemia of the kidneys lead to stimulation of the renin-angiotensin system. Sodium retention and increased volume may contribute to hypertension in patients with bilateral disease and/or renal parenchymal disease.

The most likely cause of renovascular hypertension in a young patient is fibromuscular dysplasia. The gold standard for diagnosing this condition is visualization of renal artery stenosis via intra-arterial digital subtraction angiography. Intra-arterial digital subtraction angiography is particularly indicated in patients with normal or near-normal kidney function and a high pretest probability of renal artery stenosis, such as this patient. If a diagnosis of renovascular hypertension is confirmed, angioplasty of the renal artery may be performed during this procedure.

Magnetic resonance angiography and CT angiography of the renal arteries also may confirm a diagnosis of renovascular hypertension but are less sensitive and specific for renal artery stenosis than intra-arterial digital subtraction angiography. Furthermore, in a young, otherwise healthy patient with normal kidney function who has severe hypertension, the risk of misdiagnosis of renovascular hypertension due to a false-negative result far outweighs the risk of intra-arterial digital subtraction kidney angiography.

Duplex Doppler ultrasonography of the renal arteries may help to identify renal artery stenosis and assess blood flow, but this procedure takes more than 2 hours to perform and is dependent on the skills of the operator. This indirect measurement of renal vascular flow is not the first test of choice in a patient with a very high pretest probability of renal artery stenosis.

KEY POINT

- **The gold standard for diagnosing renovascular hypertension is intra-arterial digital subtraction angiography.**

Bibliography

Bloch, MJ, Basile J. Diagnosis and management of renovascular disease and renovascular hypertension. J Clin Hypertens (Greenwich). 2007;9(5):381-389. [PMID: 17485974]

Item 32   Answer: D

Educational Objective: Manage autosomal-dominant polycystic kidney disease.

No change in this patient's management is warranted at this time. Autosomal-dominant polycystic kidney disease (ADPKD) is a slowly progressive disease characterized by cyst expansion and kidney enlargement that can cause kidney failure. Complications such as gross hematuria, hypertension, and progressive kidney injury also may develop.

Mutations on the genes *PKD1* and *PKD2* are responsible for ADPKD. Patients with milder disease and a later onset of hypertension and kidney failure typically have mutations on *PKD2*. This patient's relatively small kidney size and absence of hypertension or proteinuria also place her at low risk for disease progression. Therefore, home blood pressure measurement every month and urinalysis every 6 months is sufficient at this time. Further evaluation may be warranted if the blood pressure or urine protein excretion increases.

In animal studies, low-dose therapy with the mammalian target of rapamycin (mTOR) inhibitor sirolimus has been shown to be extremely effective in slowing the progression of kidney cystic disease. However, testing in humans has not yet substantiated the potential benefits of this agent. Furthermore, *PKD2* mutations may not directly affect mTOR activity, and disease associated with this mutation may not respond to sirolimus therapy.

Angiotensin-converting enzyme (ACE) inhibitors can effectively reduce blood pressure in hypertensive patients with polycystic kidney disease and may slow the progression of secondary glomerulosclerosis that contributes to kidney failure in these patients. Combination therapy with an ACE inhibitor and angiotensin receptor blocker may reduce the production of cytokines responsible for kidney fibrosis associated with progressive kidney injury in these patients and is currently under investigation. Recommending an ACE inhibitor or an angiotensin receptor blocker in an asymptomatic, normotensive patient would be premature.

Because polycystic kidney disease is not a glomerular disease, a low-protein diet is unlikely to help prevent progressive kidney disease in this patient. In addition, clinical trials of protein excretion have yielded mixed results with this intervention.

KEY POINT

- Small kidney size and the absence of hypertension or proteinuria are associated with a low risk for disease progression in patients with autosomal-dominant polycystic kidney disease.

Bibliography

Granthamm JJ, Chapman AB, Torres VE. Volume progression in autosomal dominant polycystic kidney disease is the major factor determining clinical outcomes. Clin J Am Soc Nephrol. 2006;1(1): 148-157. [PMID: 17699202]

Item 33   Answer: B

Educational Objective: Diagnose membranous glomerular nephropathy.

This patient most likely has membranous nephropathy, which may occur secondary to infection, autoimmune diseases, malignancies, and use of drugs such as NSAIDs. In most patients with malignancy-associated membranous nephropathy, malignancy is already diagnosed or suspected by the time proteinuria is discovered. Patients recently diagnosed with membranous nephropathy should undergo age- and sex-appropriate screening for malignancies; additional screening tests should be guided by the patient's clinical presentation. Many experts also recommend serologic screening for hepatitis B and C virus and syphilis and an antinuclear antibody assay in these patients.

Membranous nephropathy is the most common cause of primary nephrotic syndrome in patients older than 70 years of age. This syndrome may manifest as a urine protein excretion above 3.5 g/24 h (3.5 g/d), edema, hypoalbuminemia, hyperlipidemia, and lipiduria.

Membranous nephropathy is often associated with microscopic hematuria and an increased risk for large-vein thromboses. Renal vein thrombosis in particular may develop in these patients and frequently manifests as flank pain and worsening proteinuria and kidney insufficiency.

Renal vein thrombosis also may be associated with pulmonary emboli.

Patients with IgA nephropathy typically have an active nephritic urine sediment and often have gross hematuria; progressive kidney failure is rare in these patients. IgA nephropathy also does not commonly cause renal vein thrombosis.

Multiple myeloma may manifest as kidney insufficiency and proteinuria but is unlikely in a patient with normal results on serum and urine protein electrophoreses.

Patients with benign prostatic hyperplasia have an increased risk for obstructive nephropathy, but the absence of hydronephrosis or an increased postvoid residual volume argues against this diagnosis. Furthermore, obstructive nephropathy secondary to prostatic hyperplasia is not associated with the nephrotic syndrome or renal vein thrombosis.

KEY POINT

- Membranous nephropathy may occur secondary to malignancy and is associated with renal vein thrombosis.

Bibliography

Deegens JK, Wetzels JF. Membranous nephropathy in the older adult: epidemiology, diagnosis and management. Drugs Aging. 2007; 24(9):717-732. [PMID 17727303]

Item 34   Answer: C

Educational Objective: Evaluate a patient with newly diagnosed hypertension.

Routine laboratory tests recommended by the Seventh Report of the Joint National Committee on Prevention, Detection, Evaluation, and Treatment of High Blood Pressure (JNC 7) include electrocardiography; urinalysis; and measurement of the plasma glucose, hematocrit, serum potassium, serum creatinine (or estimated glomerular filtration rate), serum calcium, and lipid profile. These tests help suggest causes of secondary hypertension, metabolic abnormalities that often accompany hypertension and influence treatment, and evidence of end-organ disease. More extensive testing to identify secondary causes of hypertension is not warranted unless the blood pressure cannot be controlled with medical therapy. A urine albumin-creatinine ratio is optional in some patients, but a 24-hour urine protein excretion is not recommended in the absence of other evidence of glomerular disease.

A 24-hour urine cortisol measurement to exclude Cushing disease would be recommended only in patients with features suggestive of cortisol excess. Similarly, a plasma aldosterone-plasma renin activity ratio to screen for primary aldosteronism is not indicated in the absence of hypokalemia, hypernatremia, resistant hypertension, and other features consistent with mineralocorticoid hypertension.

Plasma metanephrine measurement helps to screen for pheochromocytoma, but this condition is unlikely in a patient without labile hypertension, palpitations, excessive sweating, or flushing.

Echocardiography is not warranted in a patient without features of valvular dysfunction or heart failure, and an exercise stress test is not indicated in patients without chest pain or chest pain–equivalent symptoms.

Kidney ultrasonography would be indicated only if initial testing reveals kidney abnormalities such as an elevated serum creatinine level or abnormal urinalysis results, or if the family history is suggestive of autosomal-dominant polycystic kidney disease.

KEY POINT

- Recommended evaluation of patients with newly diagnosed hypertension includes electrocardiography; urinalysis; and measurement of the plasma glucose, hematocrit, serum potassium, serum creatinine (or estimated glomerular filtration rate), serum calcium, and lipid profile.

Bibliography

Lenfant C, Chobanian AV, Jones DW, Roccella EJ; Joint National Committee on the Prevention, Detection, Evaluation, and Treatment of High Blood Pressure. Seventh report of the Joint National Committee on the Prevention, Detection, Evaluation, and Treatment of High Blood Pressure (JNC 7): resetting the hypertension sails. Hypertension. 2003;41(6):1178-1179. [PMID: 12756222]

Item 35   Answer: D
Educational Objective: Diagnose proton pump inhibitor–induced interstitial nephritis.

This patient most likely has interstitial nephritis caused by proton pump inhibitor (PPI) use. Classic drug-induced interstitial nephritis may manifest as fever, rash, pruritus, eosinophilia, and fever and results in kidney failure within days. However, patients with interstitial nephritis induced by PPIs and NSAIDs usually do not have rash or fever and typically develop kidney failure over weeks to months. Only one third of patients with PPI-related interstitial nephritis have eosinophilia.

This patient's pyuria, tubular-range proteinuria, hyperkalemia, and metabolic acidosis suggestive of distal tubular dysfunction also are consistent with PPI-induced interstitial nephritis. Corticosteroid therapy and discontinuation of the inciting agent often help to improve kidney function in patients with PPI-induced interstitial nephritis.

Acute tubular necrosis is the most common cause of acute kidney injury in the hospital setting but is unlikely in the absence of a preceding kidney ischemic event such as hypotension, volume depletion, or use of nephrotoxic medications or radiocontrast agents. Acute tubular necrosis also is usually associated with muddy brown casts seen on urinalysis.

Use of angiotensin-converting enzyme inhibitors and angiotensin receptor blockers reduces intraglomerular capillary pressure through efferent arteriolar vasodilation and may therefore cause acute kidney dysfunction known as "functional prerenal azotemia." However, patients with this form of acute kidney disease would have a bland urine sediment.

Focal segmental glomerulosclerosis typically manifests as the acute or insidious onset of the nephrotic syndrome, and many patients have hypertension and kidney insufficiency. This patient's non–nephrotic-range proteinuria argues against this condition.

KEY POINT

- Patients with interstitial nephritis induced by proton pump inhibitors and NSAIDs usually do not have rash or fever and typically develop kidney failure over weeks to months.

Bibliography

Brewster UC, Perazella MA. Acute kidney injury following proton pump inhibitor therapy. Kidney Int. 2007;71(6):589-593. [PMID: 17164832]

Item 36   Answer: D
Educational Objective: Manage chronic kidney disease in a patient with hyperkalemia.

Discontinuation of ibuprofen and initiation of furosemide are the most appropriate next steps in the initial management of this patient's chronic kidney disease. This patient's long-standing history of inadequately controlled diabetes mellitus, hypertension, proteinuria, and elevated serum creatinine level are consistent with diabetic nephropathy. Aggressive blood pressure control, particularly with pharmacologic modulators of the renin-angiotensin-aldosterone system, would help to slow the progression of this patient's disease but will likely worsen his hyperkalemia.

Until the glomerular filtration rate decreases to less than 15 mL/min/1.73 m^2, chronic kidney disease usually does not cause hyperkalemia without other mitigating factors. These factors include use of medications that interfere with the renin-angiotensin-aldosterone system and NSAIDs. Use of the NSAID ibuprofen is most likely contributing to this patient's hyperkalemia and reduced glomerular filtration rate and should be discontinued.

However, discontinuing ibuprofen alone would most likely not help to lower this patient's blood pressure, control volume overload, or fully correct his hyperkalemia; the addition of a loop diuretic is therefore warranted. If needed, additional interventions to help decrease the risk of hyperkalemia include adherence to a low-potassium diet and use of sodium bicarbonate.

Thiazide diuretics are largely ineffective in individuals with an estimated glomerular filtration rate below 30 mL/min/1.73 m^2.

The addition of losartan would worsen this patient's hyperkalemia and would not be recommended.

Spironolactone has been shown to further decrease urine protein excretion when added to either angiotensin-converting enzyme inhibitors or angiotensin receptor blockers in patients with diabetic nephropathy. However, this agent impairs kidney potassium excretion and also would further exacerbate this patient's hyperkalemia.

- Discontinuation of medications that interfere with the renin-angiotensin-aldosterone system, including angiotensin-converting enzyme inhibitors, angiotensin receptor blockers, and NSAIDs, is warranted to help correct hyperkalemia in the setting of renin-angiotensin inhibition.

Bibliography

Palmer BF. Managing hyperkalemia caused by inhibitors of the renin-angiotensin-aldosterone system. N Engl J Med. 2004;351(6):585-592. [PMID: 15295051]

Item 37   Answer: D

Educational Objective: Manage a patient with recurrent calcium oxalate stone formation.

An increase in dietary calcium intake and initiation of a low-protein diet are indicated for this patient. This patient most likely has recurrent calcium oxalate stones due to secondary hyperoxaluria. Hyperoxaluria is caused by increased gastrointestinal absorption of oxalate, whereas secondary hyperoxaluria is usually caused by increased intake of oxalate-rich foods such as rhubarb, peanuts, spinach, beets, and chocolate. Therefore, dietary restriction of oxalate-rich foods would decrease this patient's risk of recurrent calcium oxalate stones. Furthermore, oxalate binds to urine calcium as it is eliminated by the kidneys, which results in calcium oxalate stone formation. With a high-calcium diet, the calcium binds to oxalate in the gut and prevents its absorption and ultimate filtration at the level of the kidneys.

Allopurinol decreases the production of uric acid available for stone formation and is indicated to treat recurrent uric acid stones. This agent would not affect this patient's calcium oxalate stone formation.

In patients with calcium-containing stones and hypercalciuria, hydrochlorothiazide is recommended to treat hypercalciuria, increase calcium reabsorption in the kidney, and therefore reduce the amount of calcium available in the urine to form stones. However, this patient's 24-hour urine collection findings suggest that hyperoxaluria is the causative factor for stone formation, not hypercalciuria.

Alkalinization of the urine with citrate decreases the solubility of calcium oxalate and may help to prevent recurrent kidney stones, but potassium citrate would be more appropriate than sodium citrate in this patient. Sodium increases calcium excretion in the urine and may exacerbate hypercalciuria and calcium-containing stone formation. The use of citrate to alkalinize the urine also may cause calcium phosphate stone formation.

- In patients with recurrent calcium oxalate stones and hyperoxaluria, increased dietary calcium intake and avoidance of oxalate-rich foods such as rhubarb, peanuts, spinach, beets, and chocolate are recommended to decrease the risk of stone formation.

Bibliography

Goldfarb DS. In the clinic. Nephrolithiasis. Ann Intern Med. 2009;151:ITC2. [PMID: 19652185]

Item 38   Answer: A

Educational Objective: Manage persistent hematuria.

The most appropriate next step is cystoscopy. This patient has persistent hematuria, defined as the presence of 3 or more erythrocytes/hpf in the urine detected on two or more samples. Bleeding in patients with persistent hematuria may originate anywhere along the genitourinary tract, and differentiating between glomerular and nonglomerular hematuria helps to guide management. This patient's normal-appearing erythrocytes revealed on urine microscopy and absence of erythrocyte casts and protein in the urine are consistent with nonglomerular hematuria.

One possible cause of persistent nonglomerular hematuria is genitourinary tract malignancy. Risk factors for these malignancies include male sex, age greater than 50 years, tobacco use, and exposure to drugs such as cyclophosphamide and benzene and radiation. Because this patient has several risk factors, cystoscopy is indicated to exclude a malignancy.

Hematuria may develop in patients taking NSAIDs or anticoagulants but should not automatically be attributed to these agents; appropriate evaluation for glomerular or nonglomerular disorders should still be performed in this setting. In addition, although this patient's INR is above the target of 2.0 to 3.0 for patients with deep venous thrombosis, discontinuation of warfarin may place him at risk for further thromboembolic disorders; a reduction in his warfarin dosage, however, may be warranted.

This patient's slightly increased serum creatinine level is suggestive of glomerular disease, which often manifests as a decrease in kidney function. However, glomerular hematuria is commonly associated with dysmorphic erythrocytes and erythrocyte casts. Glomerular disease also is unlikely in the absence of protein on urinalysis. Therefore, kidney biopsy, which is often used to evaluate patients with glomerular disease, would not be appropriate for this patient.

The nonobstructing stone in the right kidney revealed on kidney ultrasound may be causing his hematuria. Metabolic stone evaluation is indicated to assess the stone promoters and inhibitors in patients with active nephrolithiasis, but cystoscopy is a more appropriate next step in a patient with a high risk for genitourinary tract malignancy.

- In patients with nonglomerular hematuria, kidney ultrasonography and cystoscopy are indicated to exclude a genitourinary tract malignancy in individuals with risk factors for this condition.

Bibliography

Cohen R, Brown S. Microscopic hematuria. N Engl J Med. 2003; 348(23):2330-2338. [PMID: 12788998]

Item 39 Answer: A

Educational Objective: Diagnose amyloidosis.

This patient most likely has AL (light-chain) amyloidosis, and the most appropriate next step is an abdominal fat pad biopsy. This condition commonly manifests as fatigue, weight loss, an enlarged tongue, and easy bruising and may lead to progressive organ dysfunction. Kidney involvement includes the nephrotic syndrome with large amounts of non–light-chain proteinuria, and azotemia develops late in the disease course. Cardiac involvement manifests as thickening of the septum resulting in heart failure and arrhythmias. Patients with peripheral nerve involvement have sensorimotor neuropathy. A bleeding diathesis also may be present.

Detection of monoclonal immunoglobulin in serum, blood, or tissues differentiates AL amyloidosis from other forms of amyloidosis. This distinction is critical because the course of this disease can be halted with anti–plasma-cell therapy. The presence of a serum or urine monoclonal protein and amyloid deposition seen on a tissue biopsy specimen is diagnostic of AL amyloidosis.

Any organ that appears to be affected by amyloidosis is an acceptable target for biopsy. However, the least invasive procedure should be selected, particularly because some patients may have a bleeding diathesis that can complicate biopsy of internal organs where local control of hemostasis cannot be achieved. Abdominal fat pad biopsy is the least invasive method of obtaining tissue in this patient.

- Diagnosis of AL amyloidosis is established by the presence of a serum or urine monoclonal protein and amyloid deposition seen on a tissue biopsy specimen.

Bibliography

Nishi S, Alchi B, Imai N, Gejyo F. New advances in renal amyloidosis. Clin Exp Nephrol. 2008;12(2):93-101. [PMID: 18175051]

Item 40 Answer: C

Educational Objective: Manage chronic kidney disease.

The most appropriate study for this patient is a spot urine albumin-creatinine ratio. This patient has risk factors for chronic kidney disease (CKD), including coronary artery disease, hyperlipidemia, and hypertension. The National Kidney Foundation's Kidney Disease Outcomes Quality Initiative (NKF K/DOQI) clinical practice guidelines recommend that patients at risk for CKD undergo screening with urinalysis, serum creatinine measurement, and estimation of the glomerular filtration rate (GFR) using the Modification of Diet in Renal Disease (MDRD) study equation in order to classify the stage of CKD. This equation is most accurate for estimating the GFR in patients with an estimated GFR below 60 mL/min/1.73 m². Measurement of the albumin- or protein-creatinine ratio using a first morning void urine sample would help to determine the protein- or albumin-creatinine ratio, which would be sufficient to document proteinuria.

Although rarely clinically indicated, a 24-hour urine collection for creatinine clearance is recommended to estimate the GFR in patients with a normal or near-normal GFR. However, mathematical equations to estimate the GFR generally are preferred over 24-hour urine collection, which is cumbersome and often inaccurate.

Kidney ultrasonography is recommended in patients with CKD to evaluate for structural abnormalities. However, performing this study would be premature until a diagnosis of CKD is established.

- Patients with risk factors for chronic kidney disease should undergo screening with urinalysis, serum creatinine measurement, first morning void random urine protein- or albumin-creatinine ratio, and estimation of the glomerular filtration rate (GFR) using the Modification of Diet in Renal Disease (MDRD) study equation when the estimated GFR is below 60 mL/min/1.73 m².

Bibliography

Jaar BG, Khatib R, Plantinga L, Boulware LE, Powe NR. Principles of screening for chronic kidney disease. Clin J Am Soc Nephrol. 2008;3(2):601-609. [PMID: 18032791]

Item 41 Answer: B

Educational Objective: Manage atherosclerotic renovascular disease.

In patients with chronic kidney disease (CKD), primary care physicians should establish a partnership with a nephrologist who can recommend care and strategies to slow kidney disease progression and to reduce cardiovascular risk. Nephrologists should assume more responsibility as patients develop systemic complications secondary to CKD, which usually manifest in stage 4 disease when the glomerular filtration rate decreases to below 30 mL/min/1.73 m². Patients with CKD should be referred to a nephrologist before the glomerular filtration rate decreases to 30 mL/min/1.73 m².

The most appropriate management of atherosclerotic renovascular disease remains controversial. Patients with atherosclerotic renal artery stenosis may have coexistent essential hypertension, which confounds the diagnosis as well as the treatment of this condition. Clinical trials suggest that medical therapy rather than angioplasty or revascularization can effectively manage renovascular hypertension secondary to atherosclerosis and may be the best option for patients with well-controlled blood pressure on medical therapy alone.

Revascularization of a slowly progressive lesion may not result in improved kidney function. Revascularization also has been associated with significant morbidity due to complications of angioplasty or surgery and should not be performed unless definitively needed. This intervention should be considered only when blood pressure cannot be adequately controlled.

KEY POINT

- Medical management is appropriate in patients with renovascular hypertension secondary to atherosclerosis whose blood pressure is well controlled.

Bibliography

Losito A, Errico R, Santirosi P, Lupattell T, Scalera GB, Lupattelli L. Long-term follow-up of atherosclerotic renovascular disease. Beneficial effect of ACE inhibition. Nephrol Dial Transplant. 2005;20(8):1604–1609. [PMID: 15870215]

Item 42   Answer: B

Educational Objective: Diagnose pentamidine-induced hyperkalemia.

The most likely cause of this patient's hyperkalemia is impaired kidney potassium excretion, which commonly develops in patients treated with pentamidine. This agent inhibits sodium reabsorption in the distal nephron, which leads to a decrease in luminal electronegativity and subsequent inhibition of potassium secretion. Amiloride, triamterene, and trimethoprim have similar effects on potassium secretion. Pentamidine-induced hyperkalemia usually resolves within several days once this agent is discontinued.

Rhabdomyolysis may be associated with hyperkalemia and is a potential complication of highly active antiretroviral therapy (HAART) as well as HIV infection and AIDS, but this patient has no additional signs or symptoms of rhabdomyolysis such as an elevated serum creatinine level or blood on dipstick urinalysis.

HAART may cause lactic acidosis as a result of mitochondrial toxicity, but lactic acidosis in this setting is not typically accompanied by hyperkalemia. Although lactic acidosis due to hypotension or hypoxia can be accompanied by hyperkalemia as a result of cell death or ischemia, this patient has no history or clinical findings suggestive of tissue ischemia. Furthermore, lactic acidosis is associated with

an elevated anion gap metabolic acidosis, whereas this patient has a normal anion gap metabolic acidosis.

Proximal renal tubular acidosis (RTA) can cause a normal anion gap metabolic acidosis as seen in this patient, and proximal RTA may occur in patients undergoing HAART. However, proximal RTA causes hypokalemia, not hyperkalemia. Proximal RTA also is usually associated with evidence of proximal tubular dysfunction, such as hypophosphatemia, glycosuria, hypouricemia, or aminoaciduria and is unlikely in a patient with a normal urinalysis.

Adrenal insufficiency can be caused by various factors in patients with HIV infection, including infection with pathogens such as cytomegalovirus, but hyperkalemia due to adrenal insufficiency is usually slowly progressive and would not develop within 1 week. Furthermore, hyperkalemia in this setting would be accompanied by evidence of kidney salt wasting, including hyponatremia and hypovolemia, which are absent in this patient.

KEY POINT

- Hyperkalemia due to impaired kidney potassium excretion commonly develops in patients treated with pentamidine, amiloride, triamterene, and trimethoprim.

Bibliography

Gabriels G, Stockem E, Greven J. Potassium-sparing renal effects of trimethoprim and structural analogues. Nephron. 2000;86(1):70-78. [PMID: 10971156]

Item 43   Answer: B

Educational Objective: Manage anemia associated with chronic kidney disease.

The most appropriate next step in this patient's management is iron therapy. Patients with stages 3 and 4 chronic kidney disease (CKD) may have anemia that is primarily caused by reduced production of erythropoietin and often have concurrent iron deficiency.

A transferrin saturation below 20% and a serum ferritin level below 100 ng/mL (100 µg/L) are diagnostic of iron deficiency in predialysis patients with CKD. In this population, iron deficiency should be corrected before initiation of an erythropoiesis-stimulating agent (ESA), because adequate iron stores are necessary for these agents to be effective. Furthermore, a significant percentage of these patients respond to iron therapy and do not require an ESA. Epoetin alfa is indicated for patients with CKD who have hemoglobin levels less than 10 g/dL (100 g/L) in whom other causes of anemia have been excluded. Serum erythropoietin measurement would not help to diagnose anemia or guide therapy in patients with CKD, who invariably have low erythropoietin levels.

A bone marrow aspirate and biopsy are indicated when isolated anemia is associated with a low absolute reticulocyte count in the absence of iron deficiency or an elevated serum creatinine level; when there is pancytopenia, a leukoerythroblastic reaction, lymphadenopathy, or spleno-megaly; or when multiple myeloma is a consideration. Bone marrow examination therefore would not be warranted in a patient with a well-established diagnosis of CKD, nor-mocytic anemia, and a normal leukocyte count.

> **KEY POINT**
> - In patients with chronic kidney disease, iron deficiency anemia should be corrected before initiation of an erythropoiesis-stimulating agent.

Bibliography

Fishbane S. Iron management in nondialysis-dependent CKD. Am J Kidney Dis. 2007;49(6):736-43. [PMID: 17533016]

Item 44   Answer: C

Educational Objective: Manage a patient with myeloma cast nephropathy.

This patient has multiple myeloma, which is characterized by kidney failure, anemia, proteinuria, and a monoclonal protein in the plasma and urine. This patient's bilaterally enlarged kidneys also are consistent with multiple myeloma. The most appropriate next step is hemodialysis, plasma-pheresis, and chemotherapy.

The most common cause of kidney failure in multiple myeloma is myeloma kidney, which manifests as chronic kid-ney failure that results from tubular injury and intratubular cast formation and obstruction. This patient's light chain excretion is characteristic of myeloma cast nephropathy. Ini-tial management in patients with myeloma cast nephropathy should include volume expansion, alkalinization of the urine, discontinuation of nephrotoxic agents, and avoidance of radiocontrast agents. In this patient with evidence of fluid overload and no hypercalcemia, volume expansion is not necessary and may be hazardous.

The goal of therapy for patients with myeloma kidney is to remove the light chains as quickly as possible by decreasing their production with chemotherapy and enhancing their removal with plasmapheresis. Dialysis also is appropriate for patients with symptomatic uremia. The 2-month mortality rate of patients with multiple myeloma who undergo dialysis is 30%, but those who survive have a median life expectancy of 2 years. Hemodialysis or peri-toneal dialysis can be performed, but the same catheter used for plasmapheresis can be used for hemodialysis.

Finally, approximately 10% of patients with myeloma kidney who undergo plasmapheresis recover kidney func-tion and do not require chronic dialysis. Furthermore, this intervention is associated with minimal side effects.

> **KEY POINT**
> - Chemotherapy and plasmapheresis are indi-cated for patients with myeloma kidney and may be accompanied by dialysis in those with symptomatic uremia.

Bibliography

Bladé J, Rosiñol L. Complications of multiple myeloma. Hematol-ogy/Oncology Clinics of North America. 2007;21(6):1231-1246. [PMID: 17996596]

Item 45   Answer: C

Educational Objective: Treat chronic essential hypertension during pregnancy.

The most appropriate treatment for this patient is labetalol, which is a pregnancy risk category C drug. Women with preexisting hypertension are at increased risk of adverse pregnancy outcomes, but treatment of chronic hyperten-sion during pregnancy is controversial. Maternal and fetal benefits are difficult to demonstrate and may partially depend on the severity of hypertension, presence of end-organ disease, and other comorbidities. This patient has rel-atively high blood pressure, and most experts would rec-ommend treatment.

Labetalol is used extensively in pregnancy because of its combined α- and β-blocking properties. Methyldopa also is used extensively in pregnancy and is one of the only agents in which long-term follow-up of infants exposed in utero has proved to be safe. Furthermore, methyldopa is the only agent classified as a pregnancy risk category B drug. However, controlling blood pressure with single-agent methyldopa is often difficult, and many women are bothered by its sedating properties.

Compared with labetalol, use of pure β-blockers such as atenolol in pregnant patients has been associated with lower birthweights. However, conditions previously associ-ated with β-blocker use in pregnant patients such as neona-tal hypoglycemia and bradycardia have not been clearly linked to exposure to these agents and may be attributed to underlying maternal hypertensive disease.

Angiotensin-converting enzyme inhibitors and angiotensin receptor blockers are contraindicated in preg-nancy (pregnancy risk category X drugs) because of adverse effects on fetal kidney function and abnormalities in fetal limb length, particularly after second- and third-trimester exposure. However, avoidance of these drugs is indicated during all trimesters of pregnancy because of the risk for negative fetal outcomes.

Diuretic agents may interfere with the normal physio-logic volume expansion associated with pregnancy. There-fore, initiation of diuretic therapy during pregnancy usually is not recommended in the absence of kidney insufficiency. However, if needed, patients with hypertension treated with chronic diuretic therapy before conception may con-tinue treatment with these agents at lower doses.

> **KEY POINT**
> - Methyldopa and labetalol are safe for treatment of hypertension during pregnancy.

Bibliography

Frishman WH, Veresh M, Schlocker SJ, Tejani N. Pathophysiology and medical management of systemic hypertension and pre-eclampsia in pregnancy. Minerva Med. 2006;97(4):347-364. [PMID: 17008838]

Item 46   Answer: D

Educational Objective: **Evaluate options for kidney replacement therapy in a patient with chronic kidney disease.**

This patient has stage 4 chronic kidney disease due to IgA nephropathy and will need kidney replacement therapy. She prefers kidney transplantation but may need to undergo dialysis before an appropriate donor kidney is available. Although she can be referred to a transplant center, she cannot accumulate time on the deceased donor transplant waiting list until her glomerular filtration rate is 20 mL/min/1.73 m² or less. The most appropriate next step in management is therefore placement of an arteriovenous fistula and training for home hemodialysis.

Compared with peritoneal dialysis, daily home hemodialysis is associated with better control of hyperphosphatemia, blood pressure, and volume overload in patients with chronic kidney disease. Furthermore, peritoneal dialysis requires an intact peritoneum and is unlikely to succeed in a patient with a history of fistulous Crohn disease and multiple abdominal surgeries whose peritoneum is unlikely to be intact.

Evaluation of this patient's parents as potential kidney donors would not be appropriate. This patient and her parents are not ABO compatible, and kidney transplantation would most likely cause an early and immediate allograft rejection. Furthermore, most transplant programs do not perform ABO-incompatible transplants. Preemptive kidney transplantation is associated with better patient and allograft survival but often is not possible in the absence of a suitable living donor because of the long wait for a deceased donor kidney transplant.

> **KEY POINT**
>
> - **Compared with peritoneal dialysis, daily home hemodialysis is associated with better control of hyperphosphatemia, blood pressure, and volume overload in patients with chronic kidney disease.**

Bibliography

Dombros N, Dratwa M, Feriani M, et al; EBPG Expert Group on Peritoneal Dialysis. European best practice guidelines for peritoneal dialysis. 2 The initiation of dialysis. Nephrol Dial Transplant. 2008;20(Suppl 9):ix3-ix7. [PMID: 16263750]

Item 47   Answer: C

Educational Objective: **Diagnose multiple myeloma.**

This patient most likely has multiple myeloma, and the most appropriate diagnostic study is urine immunoelectrophoresis.

This patient has anemia, an elevated total protein level, hypercalcemia, and kidney insufficiency. Multiple myeloma is the most common cause of hypercalcemia in patients who have decreased kidney function and anemia. Myeloma-induced osteolytic lesions would explain this patient's back pain, and his hypophosphatemia, low serum bicarbonate level, and glycosuria raise suspicion for Fanconi syndrome.

This patient's glycosuria also is suggestive of diabetes mellitus, which would warrant glucose tolerance testing. However, the normal plasma fasting glucose level argues against diabetes and instead suggests proximal renal tubule dysfunction. Diabetes also would not explain this patient's anemia, hypercalcemia, and low serum bicarbonate and phosphorus levels.

Primary hyperparathyroidism could account for this patient's hypercalcemia, hypophosphatemia, weakness, and nausea; a normal or elevated parathyroid hormone level would support this diagnosis. However, primary hyperparathyroidism would not explain this patient's proximal (type 2) renal tubular acidosis or anemia.

Distal (type 1) renal tubular acidosis is characterized by a urine pH consistently above 5.5, which reflects the inability of the distal tubule to acidify the urine. In proximal renal tubular acidosis, the urine pH varies and may be low in patients with low serum bicarbonate levels. In this patient, urine pH testing would be unnecessary because distal renal tubular acidosis does not manifest as glycosuria or hypercalcemia and is an unlikely diagnosis.

> **KEY POINT**
>
> - **Multiple myeloma may manifest as hypercalcemia, anemia, kidney insufficiency, and proximal (type 2) renal tubular acidosis.**

Bibliography

Blade J, Rosinol L. Complications of multiple myeloma. Hematol Oncol Clin North Am. 2007;21(6):1231-1246. [PMID: 17996596]

Item 48   Answer: B

Educational Objective: **Diagnose sarcoidosis-associated interstitial nephritis.**

This patient most likely has sarcoidosis. This multisystem, granulomatous, inflammatory disease of unknown cause most commonly affects young and middle-aged adults, and black Americans appear to have the highest prevalence rates. Common initial manifestations include involvement of the lymph nodes, lungs, eyes, and skin. More than 90% of patients with sarcoidosis have lung involvement, and approximately 33% have constitutional symptoms.

The incidence of kidney involvement in sarcoidosis is not well established. Kidney manifestations of this condition include interstitial nephritis with granuloma formation; hypercalciuria; nephrocalcinosis; and, more rarely, various glomerular diseases. This patient's sterile pyuria, leukocyte casts on urinalysis, and mild proteinuria are suggestive of interstitial nephritis, which also may cause kidney enlargement.

Sarcoidosis may cause hypercalcemia with elevations in 1,25-dihydroxyvitamin D, which is associated with an increased risk for hypercalciuria, nephrolithiasis, nephrocalcinosis, polyuria, and chronic kidney disease. The differential diagnosis of sarcoidosis includes lymphoma and granulomatous infections such as tuberculosis.

Amyloidosis can cause enlarged kidneys and the nephrotic syndrome but is unlikely in the absence of nephrotic-range proteinuria. Amyloidosis also would not explain this patient's hilar lymphadenopathy and urine sediment findings.

Sjögren syndrome may manifest as interstitial nephritis associated with an elevated serum creatinine level, sterile pyuria, and tubular function abnormalities. The patient's extrarenal manifestations are not consistent with Sjögren syndrome, which is characterized by keratoconjunctivitis sicca, xerostomia, and the presence of multiple autoantibodies.

Systemic lupus erythematosus can cause acute interstitial nephritis that is usually associated with glomerular disease. Lupus nephritis typically manifests as glomerular hematuria and erythrocyte casts and/or proteinuria (often in the nephrotic range) and may cause kidney insufficiency. Lupus is an unlikely cause of hilar lymphadenopathy, hepatomegaly, or hypercalcemia.

KEY POINT

- **Kidney manifestations of sarcoidosis include interstitial nephritis with granuloma formation, hypercalciuria, nephrocalcinosis, and various glomerular diseases.**

Bibliography

Joss N, Morris S, Young B, Geddes C. Granulomatous interstitial nephritis. Clin J Am Soc Nephrol. 2007;2(2):222-230. [PMID: 17699417]

Item 49   Answer: D

Educational Objective: Treat pheochromocytoma.

This patient has pheochromocytoma, and right adrenalectomy is the most appropriate management. This patient's elevated plasma metanephrine levels and MRI findings confirm this diagnosis. The treatment of choice for pheochromocytoma is surgical resection. Pheochromocytomas are relatively rare, occurring in 0.01% to 0.1% of patients with hypertension. Nearly 90% of tumors develop within the adrenal glands, whereas 10% are extra-adrenal (paragangliomas), 10% are familial, 10% are malignant, and 10% are clinically asymptomatic (called "the rule of 10s"). Up to 25% of asymptomatic pheochromocytomas contain the *RET* proto-oncogene mutations responsible for the multiple endocrine neoplasia (MEN) syndrome type 2A or 2B. Although this patient does not have severe hypertension or any symptoms, pheochromocytoma is

associated with excess morbidity, and adrenalectomy is therefore recommended.

Cardiovascular manifestations of pheochromocytoma include arrhythmias and catecholamine-induced congestive cardiomyopathy. Atrial and ventricular fibrillation may result from precipitous release of catecholamines during surgery or after therapy with tricyclic antidepressants, phenothiazines, metoclopramide, or naloxone. Although cardiogenic pulmonary edema may result from cardiomyopathy, noncardiogenic pulmonary edema also may occur as a result of transient pulmonary vasoconstriction and increased capillary permeability. Finally, seizures, altered mental status, and cerebral infarction may occur as a result of intracerebral hemorrhage or embolization. Before surgery, all patients must receive appropriate α-blockade, typically with phenoxybenzamine, followed by β-blockade, if needed.

Some patients with pheochromocytoma remain hypertensive after surgery and require long-term antihypertensive treatment; however, the initial step in the management of pheochromocytoma is removal of the tumor, if possible. Successful surgical treatment can reduce the morbidity and mortality associated with pheochromocytoma and may be the only way to discover if the lesion is malignant.

KEY POINT

- **The treatment of choice for pheochromocytoma is surgical resection.**

Bibliography

WM Manger. Diagnosis and management of pheochromocytoma–recent advances and current concepts. Kidney Int. 2006;70 (Suppl 1):S30–S35.

Item 50   Answer: C

Educational Objective: Diagnose prerenal azotemia in a patient with chronic kidney disease.

Nausea, vomiting, and anorexia accompanied by relatively low blood pressure in the absence of edema or urine sediment abnormalities strongly suggest prerenal azotemia. Prerenal disease is usually associated with oliguria and a fractional excretion of sodium (FE_{NA}) below 1%, but patients with chronic kidney disease have a decreased capacity for tubular sodium reabsorption and therefore may have a higher FE_{NA} in the setting of prerenal disease. This finding therefore may suggest other causes of acute kidney injury such as acute tubular necrosis, which is the most common cause of acute kidney injury in hospitalized patients. However, the urine sediment in acute tubular necrosis usually shows muddy brown casts or tubular epithelial cell casts, which this patient does not have.

Acute interstitial nephritis may be caused by use of certain drugs, including antibiotics and NSAIDs, and classically manifests as pyuria, leukocyte casts, or eosinophils on urinalysis. Fever, rash, and blood eosinophilia also may be present.

Renal vein thrombosis is an uncommon cause of acute kidney injury associated with hematuria and nephrotic-range proteinuria. This condition is most often associated with membranous nephropathy, malignancy, trauma, or hypercoagulable states. This patient's normal urinalysis and lack of risk factors make this diagnosis unlikely.

> **KEY POINT**
>
> - Prerenal disease is usually associated with a fractional excretion of sodium of less than 1%, but this value is usually higher in patients with chronic kidney disease.

Bibliography

Nguyen MT, Maynard SE, Kimmel PL. Misapplications of commonly used kidney equations: renal physiology in practice. Clin J Am Soc Nephrol. 2009;4(3):528-534. [PMID: 19261813]

Item 51   Answer: D

Educational Objective: Manage urinary tract obstruction associated with acute kidney injury.

This patient most likely has urinary tract obstruction, and the most appropriate next step is nephrostomy tube placement. Partial urinary tract obstruction may initially manifest as polyuria due to loss of tubular function or excretion of excess retained solute. Most patients also have hydronephrosis visible on kidney ultrasound. Nephrostomy tube placement is indicated for initial management of urinary tract obstruction associated with acute kidney injury when the obstruction is not relieved with bladder catheter placement.

Furosemide therapy is unlikely to improve this patient's oliguria without definitive correction of the obstruction.

In this patient, dialysis is not warranted in the absence of immediate life-threatening complications of acute kidney injury. Dialysis should be considered only if kidney function does not improve after nephrostomy tube placement.

The cause of this patient's suspected urinary tract obstruction should be further evaluated. However, use of radiocontrast or gadolinium-enhanced magnetic resonance imaging would place this patient at risk for contrast-induced nephropathy and gadolinium-associated nephrogenic systemic fibrosis, respectively.

Observation after bladder catheterization would be warranted in a patient with bladder neck obstruction, but this condition is unlikely in the absence of distention observed on physical examination. In addition, relief of bladder neck obstruction after catheterization would usually be associated with a higher urine output in the absence of concurrent severe volume depletion. Bladder catheterization would not adequately manage a patient with a possible obstruction in the distal ureter.

> **KEY POINT**
>
> - Nephrostomy tube placement is indicated to manage urinary tract obstruction associated with acute kidney injury when the obstruction is not relieved with bladder catheter placement.

Bibliography

Hausegger KA, Portugaller HR. Percutaneous nephrostomy and antegrade ureteral stenting: technique-indications-complications. Eur Radiol. 2006;16(9):2016-2030. [PMID: 16547709]

Item 52   Answer: A

Educational Objective: Treat severe, acute exercise-induced hyponatremia.

This patient has exercise-induced hyponatremia, and the most appropriate next step is an infusion of 3% saline, 100 mL over 10 minutes. Intense exercise, particularly during an endurance event such as a marathon, predisposes patients to hyponatremia.

An increase in fluid consumption is the primary risk factor for exercise-induced hyponatremia, and patients with this condition typically either have no weight loss or experience a weight gain despite excessive exercise. In this setting, delayed absorption of ingested water may lead to a further decrease in the patient's serum sodium concentration. Additional risk factors for exercise-induced hyponatremia include female sex, a low BMI, and lack of athletic training.

Most hyponatremic athletes are asymptomatic or have mild symptoms including nausea, dizziness, weakness, and headache. More severe manifestations may include confusion, seizures, coma, and collapse. This patient's disorientation and seizure are consistent with acute, severe hyponatremia.

When treating a patient with hyponatremia, the serum sodium concentration should be increased at the same rate at which it decreased. Therefore, treatment with a bolus of hypertonic saline is indicated for a patient with acute, severe hyponatremia. Rapid correction of hyponatremia may potentially cause osmotic demyelination in chronic hyponatremic states, but this condition is unlikely to occur in the setting of hyperacute hyponatremia.

Because this patient's plasma glucose level is 120 mg/dL (6.66 mmol/L), intravenous glucose would not help to resolve her neurologic symptoms or her severe hyponatremia.

This patient has no evidence of volume overload; therefore, furosemide would not help to treat her life-threatening acute hyponatremia.

Administration of hypotonic or isotonic fluids should be avoided in patients with acute exercise-induced hyponatremia, because these fluids can exacerbate the hyponatremia. Isotonic saline may be helpful in patients with mild hyponatremia and evidence of volume depletion but would not help a patient with significant hyponatremia without evidence of hypovolemia.

- **Treatment with a bolus of hypertonic saline is indicated for patients with acute, severe exercise-induced hyponatremia.**

Bibliography

Hew-Butler T, Almond CS, Ayus JC, et al; Exercise-Associated Hyponatremia (EAH) Consensus Panel. Consensus statement of the 1st international exercise-associated hyponatremia consensus development conference, Cape Town, South Africa 2005. Clin J Sport Med. 2005;15(4):208-213. [PMID: 16003032]

Item 53   Answer: B

Educational Objective: Manage hypertension in a patient more than 80 years of age.

The most appropriate next step in this patient's management is low-dose hydrochlorothiazide and follow-up in 1 week. Antihypertensive therapy has been shown to benefit patients between 60 and 80 years of age. Furthermore, a trial published in 2008 demonstrated that antihypertensive therapy in patients over 80 years of age is associated with a decrease in stroke and cardiovascular mortality. Most guidelines recommend lowering systolic blood pressure in patients older than 60 years of age to less than 160 mm Hg and, if possible, to 140 mm Hg or lower if tolerated.

Diuretics enhance the antihypertensive efficacy of multidrug regimens and are inexpensive. According to the Seventh Report of the Joint National Committee on Prevention, Detection, Evaluation, and Treatment of High Blood Pressure (JNC 7), thiazide diuretics should be used as initial therapy for most patients with hypertension, either alone or in combination with one of the other classes of antihypertensive agents. JNC 7 also recommends that older individuals with hypertension should follow the same principles outlined for the general care of hypertension as younger patients. Because older patients with hypertension are more likely to be salt sensitive and responsive to a diuretic, low-dose hydrochlorothiazide would be appropriate for this patient. Follow-up evaluation in 1 week also is indicated to assess for electrolyte abnormalities or azotemia.

Follow-up in 3 to 6 months without further treatment would not be appropriate. Patients with stage 2 hypertension (systolic blood pressure ≥160 mm Hg or diastolic pressure ≥100 mm Hg) usually require treatment with multiple drugs to achieve target blood pressure levels.

Adding an angiotensin-converting enzyme inhibitor or an angiotensin receptor blocker would be less likely to benefit an elderly patient than a diuretic.

- **Low-dose diuretic therapy is appropriate in older patients with hypertension, because these patients are more likely to be salt sensitive.**

Bibliography

Beckett NS, Peters R, Fletcher AE, et al; HYVET Study Group. Treatment of hypertension in patients 80 years of age or older. New Engl J Med. 2008;358(18):1887-1898. [PMID: 18378519]

Item 54   Answer: D

Educational Objective: Diagnose bone disease due to secondary hyperparathyroidism in a patient with end-stage kidney disease.

Chronic kidney disease (CKD) is associated with progressive alterations in mineral and bone metabolism that can cause bone disease. In patients with end-stage kidney disease (ESKD), the kidney's inability to excrete phosphorus leads to hyperphosphatemia. Loss of kidney function also is associated with 1,25-dihydroxyvitamin D deficiency. Hyperphosphatemia along with decreased 1,25 dihydroxyvitamin D levels result in hypocalcemia, which leads to direct stimulation of parathyroid hormone secretion. Furthermore, decreased 1,25 dihydroxyvitamin D levels cause increased production of parathyroid hormone. Therefore, bone disease due to secondary hyperparathyroidism, the most common bone pathologic finding seen in patients with ESKD, develops. This patient's hyperphosphatemia, hypocalcemia, and elevated serum parathyroid hormone and alkaline phosphatase levels are consistent with secondary hyperparathyroidism.

Adynamic bone disease commonly occurs in patients with ESKD and may cause fractures. However, unlike bone disease associated with secondary hyperparathyroidism, adynamic bone disease is often associated with hypoparathyroidism caused by excess vitamin D intake and/or calcium loading. This condition usually manifests as bone pain accompanied by a serum parathyroid hormone level below 100 pg/mL (100 ng/L) and a normal alkaline phosphatase level.

Osteoporosis is defined by low bone mass, which is associated with reduced bone strength and an increased risk of fractures. Osteoporosis occurs most commonly in postmenopausal women but may develop secondary to drugs such as corticosteroids and anticonvulsants. Osteoporosis does not affect the concentrations of serum calcium, phosphorus, or alkaline phosphatase.

Avascular necrosis is caused by transient or permanent lack of blood supply to bone, which causes death of bone and bone marrow infarction that results in mechanical failure. Patients typically present with chronic bone pain and not fracture.

- **Bone disease due to secondary hyperparathyroidism commonly occurs in patients with end-stage kidney disease and may be associated with elevated serum parathyroid hormone and alkaline phosphatase levels, hyperphosphatemia, and hypocalcemia.**

Bibliography

Fukagawa M, Nakanishi S, Fujii H, Hamada Y, Abe T. Regulation of parathyroid function in chronic kidney disease (CKD). Clin Exp Nephrol. 2006;10(3):175-179. [PMID: 17009074]

Item 55   Answer: B

Educational Objective: Diagnose acute tubular necrosis–associated acute kidney injury.

This patient's elevated serum creatinine level, minimal proteinuria, and muddy brown casts on urinalysis are most consistent with acute tubular necrosis. This condition usually develops after a sustained period of ischemia or exposure to nephrotoxic agents such as cisplatin, intravenous aminoglycosides, or radiocontrast.

Acute interstitial nephritis most commonly develops after exposure to certain medications, including trimethoprim. Manifestations of this condition may include rash, pruritus, eosinophilia, and fever. Urine sediment findings include pyuria, leukocyte casts, microscopic hematuria, and tubular-range proteinuria. These features are absent in this patient.

Cyclosporine and tacrolimus, even when present in the serum at nontoxic levels, can cause kidney injury. Chronic calcineurin inhibitor nephrotoxicity is characterized by an elevated serum creatinine level, hyperkalemia, hyperuricemia and gout, and a normal anion gap metabolic acidosis. High-dose calcineurin inhibitor therapy may cause acute nephrotoxicity associated with urine sediment findings similar to those of acute tubular necrosis. However, this patient previously had stable kidney function on a stable dose of tacrolimus, which decreases the likelihood of acute calcineurin inhibitor toxicity. Furthermore, the onset of this patient's acute kidney injury is closely related to her exposure to tobramycin. Calcineurin inhibitors also can induce a thrombotic microangiopathy with associated acute kidney injury, but this condition is unlikely in the absence of anemia and thrombocytopenia.

Trimethoprim can decrease renal tubular creatinine secretion but would only cause a self-limited increase in the serum creatinine level of 0.5 mg/dL (44.2 µmol/L) or less.

> **KEY POINT**
>
> - Acute tubular necrosis usually develops after a sustained period of ischemia or exposure to nephrotoxic agents such as cisplatin, intravenous aminoglycosides, or radiocontrast and is associated with muddy brown casts on urinalysis.

Bibliography

Choudhury D, Ahmed Z. Drug-associated renal dysfunction and injury. Nat Clin Pract Nephrol. 2006;2(2):80-91. [PMID: 16932399]

Item 56   Answer: A

Educational Objective: Manage acute hyponatremia induced by 3,4-methylenedioxymethamphetamine (ecstasy).

This patient has acute hyponatremia induced by use of the illicit drug 3,4-methylenedioxymethamphetamine (ecstasy), which is associated with an increased risk for developing potentially fatal hyponatremia. The most appropriate next step in her management is administration of hypertonic saline.

3,4-Methylenedioxymethamphetamine stimulates thirst and induces antidiuretic hormone secretion. Furthermore, this drug may decrease gastrointestinal motility, which can lead to retention of several liters of water in the lumen of the stomach and small intestine. This water can be absorbed abruptly once intestinal motility is restored, which causes sudden-onset severe hyponatremia that can be fatal. This condition may cause seizures and cerebral and neurogenic pulmonary edema. Rapid normalization of the extracellular fluid osmolality with hypertonic saline is indicated in patients with hyperacute symptomatic forms of hyponatremia to reduce brain edema and prevent cerebral herniation and death.

Conivaptan blocks vasopressin receptors and is approved for the management of chronic euvolemic hyponatremia and hypervolemic hyponatremia. However, the efficacy of this agent in the treatment of acute hyponatremia has not yet been established, although it is believed that combination therapy with a vasopressor receptor antagonist plus hypertonic saline may be the most appropriate treatment for this condition.

When overcorrection of the sodium concentration has occurred or is likely to occur in patients with hyponatremia who are treated with hypertonic saline, desmopressin administered with or without hypotonic fluids may be warranted to slow the rate of correction. However, this agent concentrates the urine, functions as an antidiuretic, and is likely to worsen hyponatremia and is therefore not indicated for a patient with acute hyponatremia.

Furosemide alone would increase this patient's serum sodium level, but the rate of correction would be much slower than with hypertonic saline.

> **KEY POINT**
>
> - In patients with symptomatic, acute hyponatremia, rapid normalization of the extracellular fluid osmolality with hypertonic saline is indicated.

Bibliography

Rosenson J, Smollin C, Sporer KA, Blanc P, Olson KR. Patterns of ecstasy-associated hyponatremia in California. Ann Emerg Med. 2007;49(2):164-171. [PMID: 17084942]

Item 57   Answer: C

Educational Objective: Manage a female patient at risk for calcium oxalate stone formation.

An estimated 33% of patients with kidney stones have a family history of stone formation, and most of these stones are caused by hypercalciuria. This patient is therefore at increased risk for stone formation, and the most appropriate next step in management is an increase in her dietary calcium intake. Calcium oxalate stones can develop when calcium binds to oxalate in the urine. Adherence to a high-calcium diet (generally defined as 1 to 4 g/d of calcium) has been shown to decrease the risk of calcium oxalate stone formation by binding calcium to oxalate in the gut and preventing oxalate absorption and its filtration into the urine.

Calcium supplementation in addition to or in place of increased dietary calcium intake has not been shown to decrease the risk of kidney stone formation. Furthermore, calcium carbonate supplementation with meals may be associated with slightly increased rates of stone formation.

Animal protein intake contributes to increased purine metabolism and uric acid production and has been associated with uric acid stone formation. Animal protein ingestion also leads to decreases in urine citrate and increases in urine calcium. In a randomized, controlled trial to prevent stone formation, a diet with increased calcium content and reduced animal protein and salt was shown to effectively decrease stone recurrence in men with hypercalciuria compared with a reduced-calcium diet; however, this intervention has not been shown to prevent the incidence of calcium stones in women, and a low-protein diet alone has not been shown to reduce calcium stone formation in either men or women.

Increased dietary intake of sucrose appears to increase urine calcium excretion independent of calcium intake and has been shown to increase the risk of incident kidney stones in women. This intervention would not be recommended for a patient at risk for stone formation.

KEY POINT

- Adherence to a high-calcium diet (generally defined as 1 to 4 g/d of calcium) has been shown to decrease the risk of incident and recurrent calcium oxalate stone formation.

Bibliography

In the clinic. Nephrolithiasis. Ann Intern Med. 2009;151:ITC2. [PMID: 19652185]

Item 58   Answer: D

Educational Objective: Manage hypertension in a young patient.

Lifestyle modifications are recommended for all patients with hypertension, including prehypertension. The Dietary Approaches to Stop Hypertension (DASH) study showed that 8 weeks of a diet of fruits, vegetables, low-fat dairy products, whole grains, poultry, fish, and nuts, along with a reduction in fats, red meat, and sweets, caused an 11.4-mm Hg decrease in systolic pressure and a 5.5-mm Hg decrease in diastolic pressure. In addition, patients using the DASH diet who consumed less than 100 mmol/d of sodium had a systolic pressure 3 mm Hg and a diastolic pressure 1.6 mm Hg less than those who consumed high amounts of sodium.

Weight reduction in a patient whose weight is 10% above ideal body weight lowers blood pressure by an average of 5 to 7 mm Hg. Alcohol consumption should be limited to two drinks daily for men and one for women, because excess amounts of alcohol may contribute to hypertension and resistance to antihypertensive medications. Regular aerobic exercise also modestly decreases blood pressure. In addition, this patient should be counseled about smoking cessation.

In patients with stage 1 hypertension, lifestyle modifications should be tried before antihypertensive medication is initiated. In patients with stage 1 hypertension who do not have evidence of cardiovascular disease or target organ damage, therapeutic lifestyle changes can be tried for 6 to 12 months before initiating drug therapy. In addition, β-blockers and diuretics may exacerbate insulin resistance and should be used carefully in patients at risk for type 2 diabetes mellitus.

KEY POINT

- In young patients with stage 1 hypertension, lifestyle modifications should be tried before antihypertensive medication is initiated.

Bibliography

Elmer PJ, Obarzanek E, Vollmer WM, et al; PREMIER Collaborative Research Group. Effects of comprehensive lifestyle modification on diet, weight, physical fitness, and blood pressure control: 18-month results of a randomized trial. Ann Intern Med. 2006; 144(7):485-495. [PMID: 16585662]

Item 59   Answer: A

Educational Objective: Diagnose acute phosphate nephropathy.

This patient most likely has acute phosphate nephropathy. This condition typically develops within a few days of exposure to an oral sodium phosphate bowel preparation but often remains unrecognized until laboratory studies are performed at a later time. Manifestations of acute phosphate nephropathy may include hyperphosphatemia out of proportion to the degree of kidney failure and minimal abnormalities on urinalysis.

Because phosphate nephropathy may develop even in patients with normal kidney function, safer bowel-cleansing agents such as polyethylene glycol should be used instead of oral sodium phosphate.

Acute urate nephropathy is usually a component of the tumor lysis syndrome, which also may manifest as hypocalcemia and hyperphosphatemia. However, tumor lysis syndrome usually occurs in the presence of a tumor with a high cell-turnover rate, which is not suggested by this patient's clinical presentation.

Hemolytic uremic syndrome (HUS) may develop after enteric infection with verotoxin-producing strains of *Escherichia coli* (VTEC), but only 6% to 12% of cases occur in adults. Within 1 to 2 days of toxin exposure, abdominal pain and watery diarrhea with subsequent bloody diarrhea develop. In addition to acute kidney injury, patients with HUS have thrombocytopenia and microangiopathic hemolytic anemia, which are absent in this patient. Furthermore, this patient's pattern of decreased vascularity seen on colonoscopy is more consistent with ischemic colitis than with infectious colitis.

This patient's absence of postural hypotension, tachycardia, and progressive azotemia despite ongoing hydration with normal saline argues against prerenal azotemia. This condition also is rarely associated with a serum phosphorus level above 13 mg/dL (4.2 mmol/L).

KEY POINT

- **The cathartic agent sodium phosphate may cause acute phosphate nephropathy resulting in acute kidney injury and hyperphosphatemia out of proportion to the degree of kidney failure.**

Bibliography

Rocuts AK, Waikar SS, Alexander MP, Rennke HG, Singh AK. Acute phosphate nephropathy. Kidney Int. 2009;75(9):987-991. [PMID: 18580858]

Item 60   Answer: B

Educational Objective: Evaluate a patient with suspected nephrotic syndrome and diabetes mellitus.

The most appropriate management for this patient is kidney biopsy. This patient's edema, hyperlipidemia, nephrotic-range proteinuria, and lipiduria (oval fat bodies seen on urinalysis) strongly suggest the nephrotic syndrome. She also has an elevated hemoglobin A_{1c} and a history of type 1 diabetes mellitus. Because this patient has only a 3-year history of diabetes and no evidence of diabetic retinopathy, diabetic nephropathy is excluded.

Until kidney biopsy is performed, the cause of this patient's clinical presentation cannot be confirmed and appropriate medication cannot be initiated. In patients with the nephrotic syndrome, biopsy frequently is needed to determine the diagnosis, indicate the cause, predict the natural history and prognosis of the glomerular injury, and direct treatment. Kidney biopsy is a commonly performed diagnostic study in adults with the nephrotic syndrome or glomerulonephritis with no obvious cause of postinfectious glomerular disease and all patients with acute kidney injury of unclear cause.

An immunosuppressive agent such as cyclosporine would benefit patients with severe membranous glomerular disease but would not be first-line therapy in this setting. In addition, cyclosporine should not be used unless a diagnosis is established.

Empiric treatment with prednisone may be helpful in patients with minimal change disease, which commonly causes the nephrotic syndrome in younger patients. However, a kidney biopsy specimen is needed to establish a definitive diagnosis of this condition before treatment is begun. Furthermore, corticosteroids will exacerbate this patient's diabetes mellitus and would not be recommended unless a diagnosis is established.

Waiting 3 months to perform a repeat urinalysis would not be appropriate. This patient's proteinuria may decrease within 3 months with the addition of an angiotensin-converting enzyme inhibitor, but this intervention would not stop the progression of the underlying disease or help to determine the prognosis or whether additional therapy is indicated.

KEY POINT

- **In patients with the nephrotic syndrome, kidney biopsy is indicated to evaluate the cause of this condition and guide appropriate treatment.**

Bibliography

Molitch ME, DeFronzo RA, Franz MJ, Keane WF, Mogensen CE, Parving HH; American Diabetes Association. American Diabetes Association. Diabetic nephropathy. Diabetes Care. 2003;26(Suppl 1):S94-S98. [PMID: 12502629]

Item 61   Answer: D

Educational Objective: Diagnose obstructive nephropathy.

This patient most likely has obstructive nephropathy, which causes chronic tubulointerstitial disease and often manifests as hyperkalemic renal tubular acidosis. Cervical cancer is one of the most common causes of obstructive nephropathy in women. Kidney damage is typically irreversible if an obstruction is present for longer than 8 to 12 weeks; therefore, to ensure a prompt diagnosis, obstructive nephropathy must always be included in the differential diagnosis of a patient with acute kidney injury.

The presence of hydronephrosis and/or renal pelvis dilatation visible on kidney ultrasonography or noniodinated contrast CT is diagnostic of obstructive nephropathy. Relief of obstruction may lead to the reversal of acute kidney injury.

Cisplatin nephrotoxicity typically occurs within the first 2 weeks after drug administration and manifests as a Fanconi-like syndrome of glycosuria, phosphaturia, aminoaciduria, and renal wasting of magnesium and hypomagnesemia. Furthermore, cisplatin nephrotoxicity that develops weeks or months after beginning treatment is more commonly associated with thrombotic microan-giopathy. These findings are absent in this patient.

Membranous nephropathy is associated with malignancies and may manifest as proteinuria. However, this condition is unlikely to develop after the malignancy has been treated and is usually associated with nephrotic-range proteinuria and a more slowly progressive decline in kidney function.

Hypovolemia is one of the most common causes of acute kidney injury in patients admitted to the hospital, and this patient's vomiting and decreased oral intake are suggestive of volume depletion. However, hypovolemia usually is associated with orthostasis. In addition, this patient's lack of response to saline infusion argues against this diagnosis.

KEY POINT

- Obstructive nephropathy must always be included in the differential diagnosis of a patient with acute kidney injury to ensure prompt diagnosis and reversal of kidney injury.

Bibliography

O'Reilly P, Philippou M. Urinary tract obstruction. Medicine. 2007;35(8):420-422.

Item 62   Answer: C

Educational Objective: Manage a patient with hypertension and type 2 diabetes mellitus.

The maximum target blood pressure for this patient is less than 130/80 mm Hg. The Seventh Report of the Joint National Committee on Prevention, Detection, Evaluation, and Treatment of High Blood Pressure (JNC 7) defines normal blood pressure as less than 120/80 mm Hg. Cardiovascular risk correlates directly with blood pressure stage beginning at 115/75 mm Hg and doubles with each 20/10 mm Hg increment. In persons older than 50 years, systolic blood pressure is a much more important cardiovascular risk factor than diastolic blood pressure.

Initial drug therapy is determined by the degree of hypertension, specific patient factors, and the presence of other compelling indications. The development of hypertension in a patient between 18 and 54 years of age who has a family history of this condition is suggestive of essential hypertension. The goal of antihypertensive treatment in patients with essential hypertension is to reduce blood pressure to less than 140/90 mm Hg. However, patients with diabetes mellitus have an increased risk for cardiovascular morbidity and mortality. Therefore, the target blood pressure goal for these patients is less than 130/80 mm Hg, which is associated with a lower rate of cardiovascular outcomes.

A similar blood pressure target is appropriate for patients with chronic nondiabetic kidney disease not associated with significant proteinuria. A target blood pressure of less than 125/75 mm Hg is recommended for patients

with kidney disease accompanied by a urine protein-creatinine ratio above 1 mg/mg. However, this level of blood pressure control is not indicated in this patient, because he does not meet the proteinuria criteria based on his urine albumin-creatinine ratio.

KEY POINT

- The target blood pressure in patients with type 2 diabetes mellitus and nondiabetic chronic kidney disease in the absence of proteinuria is less than 130/80 mm Hg.

Bibliography

Kidney Disease Outcomes Quality Initiative (K/DOQI). K/DOQI Clinical Practice Guidelines on Hypertension and antihypertensive agents in chronic kidney disease. Am J Kidney Dis. 2004;43(5 Suppl 1):S1-S290. [PMID: 15114537]

Item 63   Answer: C

Educational Objective: Diagnose drug-induced acute kidney injury in a kidney transplant recipient.

Both erythromycin and tacrolimus are metabolized by cytochrome P450 3A4. Because these agents compete for this enzyme, adding erythromycin to this patient's drug regimen would decrease tacrolimus metabolism. Serum tacrolimus levels would then increase, resulting in tacrolimus toxicity. Tacrolimus causes afferent arteriolar constriction and consequently can lead to prerenal acute kidney injury.

Azithromycin does not inhibit cytochrome P450 enzymes to the same degree as erythromycin and is unlikely to cause clinically significant drug-drug interactions; therefore, this agent is a reasonable alternative macrolide antibiotic to erythromycin in patients using tacrolimus.

The dosages of cephalexin and ciprofloxacin may need to be adjusted in patients with impaired kidney function. Trimethoprim may block the collecting tubule sodium channel, resulting in hyperkalemia. However, none of these agents would affect this patient's serum tacrolimus level and are acceptable for this patient.

KEY POINT

- Use of tacrolimus and another cytochrome P450 3A4 inhibitor can cause tacrolimus toxicity, which may lead to acute kidney dysfunction.

Bibliography

Bowman LJ, Brennan DC. The role of tacrolimus in renal transplantation. Expert Opin Pharmacother. 2008;9(4):635-643. [PMID: 18312164]

Item 64   Answer: C

Educational Objective: Manage a patient with a complex kidney cyst.

Surgical resection would be appropriate for this patient. Kidney cysts are common, particularly in older patients and those with hypertension and chronic kidney disease. The risk of malignancy determines whether further evaluation of a cyst is warranted. Complex cystic structures or mass lesions, especially those greater than 4 cm, should raise suspicion for malignancy.

Bosniak category III cysts are characterized by irregularly shaped walls with septal calcification. These cysts enhance after the administration of iodinated contrast agents. Approximately 50% of Bosniak category III cysts are malignant; therefore, surgical resection is indicated for patients with these cysts.

Kidney biopsy in patients with cystic or mass lesions is associated with a risk for bleeding and may be associated with metastatic spread via the biopsy tract. In addition, this study may not be diagnostic because of sampling errors and failure to obtain an abnormal specimen.

A repeat abdominal CT performed in 6 to 12 months would be indicated for patients with Bosniak II to IIF kidney cysts. These cysts are characterized by a few thin septa with thicker walls, may have calcification, do not enhance on administration of contrast agents, and are associated with a low risk of malignancy.

> **KEY POINT**
>
> - Surgical resection is indicated for patients with Bosniak category III and IV kidney cysts.

Bibliography

Israel G, Bosniak M. An update of the Bosniak renal cyst classification system. Urology. 2005;66(3):484-488. [PMID: 16140062]

Item 65   Answer: D

Educational Objective: Treat resistant hypertension.

This patient has resistant hypertension, and the most appropriate management is spironolactone. Resistant hypertension is defined as blood pressure that remains above goal despite treatment with the optimal dosage of three antihypertensive agents, including a diuretic. Patient characteristics more likely to be associated with resistant hypertension include older age, BMI above 30, higher baseline blood pressure, diabetes mellitus, and black race. Excessive consumption of dietary salt and alcohol contributes to resistant hypertension. Many patients with resistant hypertension have secondary hypertension caused by primary aldosteronism or renovascular hypertension, and these conditions should be excluded.

Treatment of resistant hypertension should include appropriate lifestyle modifications, discontinuation of agents that may increase blood pressure such as NSAIDs, and correction of secondary causes of hypertension. Mineralocorticoid receptor antagonists are particularly effective in treating resistant hypertension even in the absence of hyperaldosteronism. The Anglo-Scandinavian Cardiac Outcomes Trial evaluated the efficacy of spironolactone among 1411 participants with an average age of 63 years who received this medication mainly as a fourth-line antihypertensive agent for uncontrolled blood pressure. After 1 year of treatment, blood pressure in these patients decreased by approximately 21.9/9.5 mm Hg.

The benefit of β-blockers in older patients remains uncertain. Older patients also are more likely to respond to calcium channel blockers or diuretics. Furthermore, combination therapy with an angiotensin-converting enzyme inhibitor and a β-blocker may not have an additive antihypertensive effect.

Clonidine may help to lower blood pressure but is associated with significant side effects such as fatigue, drowsiness, and dry mouth. This agent has not been evaluated as rigorously as spironolactone in patients with resistant hypertension.

Doxazosin has not been shown to be as effective as other drugs in reducing cardiovascular endpoints. In the Antihypertensive and Lipid-Lowering Treatment to Prevent Heart Attack Trial (ALLHAT) study, the doxazosin arm was prematurely terminated because of an increased risk of heart failure compared with chlorthalidone noted during an interim analysis.

> **KEY POINT**
>
> - Mineralocorticoid receptor antagonists are particularly effective in treating resistant hypertension.

Bibliography

Chapman N, Dobson J, Wilson S, et al; Anglo-Scandinavian Cardiac Outcomes Trial Investigators. Effect of spironolactone on blood pressure in subjects with resistant hypertension. Hypertension. 2007;49(4):839-845. [PMID: 17309946]

Item 66   Answer: B

Educational Objective: Diagnose polyarteritis nodosa as a cause of kidney failure.

This patient most likely has polyarteritis nodosa, which is characterized by a necrotizing inflammation of the medium-sized or small arteries without glomerulonephritis or vasculitis of the arterioles, capillaries, or venules. Clinical manifestations of this condition include fever; musculoskeletal symptoms; and vasculitis involving the nervous system, gastrointestinal tract, heart, and nonglomerular renal vessels that is associated with hypertension, kidney insufficiency, proteinuria, and hematuria.

Polyarteritis nodosa most commonly affects the kidneys and may cause significant hypertension, kidney insufficiency, and renal vasculitis associated with proteinuria and hematuria. Prompt immunosuppressive therapy is critical to reduce the risk of irreversible kidney failure, but a definitive diagnosis must be established before beginning this treatment.

Sural nerve biopsy may establish the diagnosis of polyarteritis nodosa, and kidney angiography can support this diagnosis. After exclusion of other causes of medium- or small-vessel vasculitis, angiography of the renal arteries is often performed when there is no appropriate tissue to biopsy. Specific angiographic findings in patients with polyarteritis nodosa include microaneurysms or a beaded pattern with areas of arterial narrowing and dilation.

Abdominal fat pad aspiration may help to diagnose AL amyloidosis, but this condition is unlikely in a patient with normal results on serum and urine immunoelectrophoreses.

Kidney biopsy may yield a false-negative result for polyarteritis nodosa and is associated with an increased risk for bleeding secondary to transection of an intrarenal aneurysm. Biopsy of normal skin has a low diagnostic yield for polyarteritis nodosa because of the minimal histologic abnormalities associated with this condition.

KEY POINT

- **Polyarteritis nodosa most commonly affects the kidneys and may cause significant hypertension, kidney insufficiency, and renal vasculitis with classic angiographic findings.**

Bibliography
Schmidt WA. Use of imaging studies in the diagnosis of vasculitis. Curr Rheumatol Rep. 2004;6(3):203-11. [PMID: 15134599]

Item 67   Answer: C
Educational Objective: Manage staghorn calculi.

This patient has a 4-cm staghorn calculus, and the most appropriate next step in management is percutaneous nephrolithotomy. Most patients with a staghorn calculus present with a urinary tract infection, hematuria, urine pH persistently above 7.0, possible mild flank pain, and a complex kidney calculus seen on abdominal imaging.

In patients with staghorn calculi, stone removal is indicated to prevent obstructive nephropathy, loss of kidney function, or pyelonephritis and sepsis. Percutaneous nephrolithotomy is the initial treatment of choice for staghorn calculi, particularly those that are larger than 4 cm in diameter. This intervention allows for direct visualization of the kidney and verification of stone removal via nephroscopy and is associated with an estimated initial cure rate of 80%.

Some experts recommend use of extracorporeal shockwave lithotripsy (ESWL) in the treatment of staghorn calculi, but this intervention is associated with a high risk for residual stone fragmentation that may cause future infection and stone growth. Therefore, ESWL is recommended only for patients with stones smaller than 4 cm in diameter and is often combined with percutaneous nephrolithotomy to allow for direct visualization of stone removal.

Because infection in patients with staghorn calculi originates within the stone, antibiotic therapy alone would not sufficiently treat this condition or prevent recurrent infection. Patients with staghorn calculi often have chronically infected urine, and intravenous antibiotics would be indicated for those with sepsis, pyelonephritis, and/or urinary tract obstruction associated with infection. However, this patient's normal leukocyte count and absence of fever and constitutional symptoms argue against pyelonephritis or sepsis.

Potassium citrate is indicated as prophylactic treatment for recurrent kidney stone disease. Alkalinization of the urine in uric acid stone formers and patients with hypocitraturia increases the solubility of uric acid. However, the addition of potassium citrate to a patient with staghorn calculus kidney disease who already has alkaline urine would not reduce the stone formation rate or decrease the stone size.

KEY POINT

- **Percutaneous nephrolithotomy is the treatment of choice in patients with staghorn calculi.**

Bibliography
Goldfarb DS. In the clinic. Nephrolithiasis. Ann Intern Med. 2009;151:ITC2. [PMID: 19652185]

Item 68   Answer: C
Educational Objective: Diagnose ethylene glycol poisoning.

This patient has ethylene glycol poisoning, which may manifest as acute kidney injury associated with an increased anion gap metabolic acidosis and an increased osmolal gap. The osmolal gap is the difference between the calculated plasma osmolality and measured plasma osmolality. In this patient, the osmolality is calculated using the following formula:

$$2 \times [\text{Sodium}] + [\text{Glucose}]/18 + [\text{Blood Urea Nitrogen}]/2.8 = 296 \text{ mosm/kg } H_2O$$

The difference between the measured and calculated osmolality is 20 mosm/kg H_2O (20 mmol/kg H_2O). The normal osmolal gap is approximately 10 mosm/kg H_2O (10 mmol/kg H_2O). An elevated osmolal gap suggests the presence of an unmeasured osmole that is most commonly ethanol but can be ethylene glycol or methanol. However, only ethylene glycol is associated with kidney injury and calcium oxalate crystals in the urine.

Although alcoholic and diabetic ketoacidosis and lactic acidosis can cause an anion gap metabolic acidosis, none of these conditions is associated with an osmolal gap.

KEY POINT

- **Ethylene glycol poisoning is associated with an anion gap metabolic acidosis, an increased osmolal gap, kidney injury, and calcium oxalate crystals in the urine.**

Bibliography
Megarbane B, Borron SW, Baud FJ. Current recommendations for treatment of severe toxic alcohol poisonings. Intensive Care Med. 2005;31(2):189-195. [PMID: 15627163]

Item 69   Answer: B

Educational Objective: Treat a patient with hypertension who is contemplating pregnancy.

The most appropriate next step in this patient's management is to discontinue lisinopril. Exposure to angiotensin-converting enzyme inhibitors during the first trimester has been associated with fetal cardiac abnormalities, and exposure during the second and third trimesters has been associated with neonatal kidney failure and death. Angiotensin receptor antagonists such as losartan have been associated with similar fetal toxicity as angiotensin-converting enzyme inhibitors, most likely because of the dependence of the fetal kidney on the renin-angiotensin system. Therefore, both of these agents are considered category X agents in pregnancy and are contraindicated in pregnant women.

Diuretics such as hydrochlorothiazide may be continued during pregnancy, particularly in women with sodium-sensitive hypertension or edema and when these agents have been used before conception. In addition to hydrochlorothiazide, the only pregnancy risk category B drugs are methyldopa and pindolol. Calcium channel blockers, β-blockers other than pindolol, α-blockers, clonidine, and hydralazine are pregnancy risk category C drugs.

KEY POINT

- Angiotensin receptor antagonists and angiotensin-converting enzyme inhibitors are contraindicated during pregnancy.

Bibliography

Cooper WO, Hernandez-Diaz S, Arbogast PG, et al. Major congenital malformations after first-trimester exposure to ACE inhibitors. N Eng J Med. 2006;354(23):2443-2451. [PMID: 16760444]

Item 70   Answer: D

Educational Objective: Diagnose hypophosphatemia in a patient with chronic alcoholism.

Severe hypophosphatemia rarely manifests as physiologic disturbances and most often develops in patients with chronic alcoholism who have poor oral intake, decreased intestinal absorption due to frequent vomiting and diarrhea, and increased kidney excretion due to the direct effect of ethanol on the tubule. Despite total body phosphorus depletion, these patients may have normal serum phosphorus levels on admission to the hospital.

Severe hypophosphatemia often develops over the first 12 to 24 hours after admission, usually because of intravenous glucose administration. This agent helps to release insulin and rapidly reverses alcoholic ketoacidosis, which causes phosphate to shift into cells.

The sudden development of hypophosphatemia may cause confusion, rhabdomyolysis, hemolytic anemia, and severe muscle weakness that can lead to respiratory failure. Treatment involves preventing the serum phosphorus level from decreasing below 1 mg/dL (0.32 mmol/L). Oral phosphate is the preferred treatment in this setting, but intravenous administration may be needed if oral therapy cannot be tolerated.

Hypercalcemia may manifest as decreased neuromuscular excitability that causes decreased muscular tone. Hypercalcemia is most commonly caused by alterations in calcium absorption from the gut and bone resorption due to primary hyperparathyroidism, malignancy, and granulomatous diseases. Primary hyperparathyroidism and thiazide diuretic use also may cause this condition. The development of hypercalcemia in this patient is unlikely.

Hypokalemia can cause diffuse muscle weakness, gastrointestinal tract atony, respiratory failure, and cardiac arrhythmias. In chronic hypokalemia, muscle weakness is unusual in patients with a serum potassium level above 2.5 meq/L (2.5 mmol/L) but may be precipitated by a sudden decrease in potassium. However, the risk of profound hypokalemia is low in a patient receiving potassium supplementation. Furthermore, hypokalemia would not explain this patient's mental status changes.

Early signs of hyponatremia typically include nausea, vomiting, and headaches; progressive manifestations include impaired mental status and seizures. These symptoms are not compatible with this patient's presentation.

KEY POINT

- In the hospital setting, patients with chronic alcoholism may have normal serum phosphorus levels on admission to the hospital but often develop severe hypophosphatemia over the first 12 to 24 hours.

Bibliography

Moe S. Disorders involving calcium, phosphorus, and magnesium. Prim Care. 2008;35(2):215-237. [PMID: 18486714]

Item 71   Answer: D

Educational Objective: Diagnose focal segmental glomerulosclerosis in a kidney transplant recipient.

This patient most likely has recurrent focal segmental glomerulosclerosis (FSGS). This patient's microscopic hematuria, hypertension, edema, proteinuria, and elevated serum creatinine level are consistent with this condition. FSGS is the most common cause of primary nephrotic syndrome in the United States, especially in black individuals.

This patient has a history of FSGS causing end-stage kidney disease involving his native kidneys. This condition can recur soon after kidney transplantation, sometimes within minutes or hours of this procedure.

Diabetic, IgA, and membranous nephropathy may present with nephrotic-range proteinuria. However, this patient's original diagnosis was FSGS. These conditions therefore could only develop if this patient received a kidney from a person affected with one of these conditions, which is unlikely because living donors undergo screening for proteinuria.

Furthermore, diabetic, IgA, and membranous nephropathy are unlikely to have developed de novo in this patient within 2 weeks. This patient's nonfasting plasma glucose level also is not diagnostic of diabetes, and diabetic nephropathy is unlikely in a patient with a normal funduscopic examination.

> **KEY POINT**
> - Focal segmental glomerulosclerosis can recur soon after kidney transplantation, sometimes within minutes or hours of this procedure.

Bibliography

Ijpelaar DH, Farris AB, Goemaere N, et al. Fidelity and evolution of recurrent FSGS in renal allografts. J Am Soc Nephrol. 2008;19(11):2219-2224. [PMID: 18579640]

Item 72   Answer: A

Educational Objective: Manage persistent proteinuria and hypertension in a patient with chronic kidney disease.

Control of hypertension is the single most important intervention to delay progression of chronic kidney disease (CKD). Extracellular fluid volume expansion is one of the most important factors leading to persistent hypertension in patients with CKD. Older individuals and black patients are more likely to be salt-sensitive and exhibit an antihypertensive response to sodium restriction or diuretic therapy.

If hypertension and proteinuria persist despite sodium restriction, the addition of a diuretic may be beneficial. Thiazide diuretics, if not used as a first-choice antihypertensive drug, are almost always indicated as an additional drug in patients with incompletely controlled hypertension, because these agents augment most other agents used as monotherapy.

Combination therapy with an angiotensin-converting enzyme (ACE) inhibitor and either an angiotensin receptor blocker (ARB) or a nondihydropyridine calcium channel blocker can have an added antiproteinuric effect in patients with CKD but should only be considered if the urine protein level remains above 500 mg/24 h (500 mg/d) after controlling the hypertension. While the combination of an ACE inhibitor and an ARB has a synergistic effect on lowering protein excretion in patients with CKD, long-term outcomes have not been studied in patients with nondiabetic nephropathy. In patients with diabetic nephropathy, the combination of an ACE inhibitor and an ARB was associated with an increased incidence of adverse outcomes, including the possibility of increased mortality.

Adding metoprolol to an ACE inhibitor would be less effective than adding a diuretic, because diuretics may help to reduce intravascular volume.

> **KEY POINT**
> - In patients with chronic kidney disease who have persistent hypertension and proteinuria, a diuretic should be added if an angiotensin-converting enzyme inhibitor or angiotensin receptor blocker and restriction of dietary sodium are not helpful.

Bibliography

Palmer BF. Improving BP control with combined renin-angiotensin system blockade and thiazide diuretics in hypertensive patients with diabetes mellitus or kidney disease. Am J Cardiovasc Drugs. 2008;8(1):9-14. [PMID: 18303933]

Index